QUEER RELAJO

TRIANGULATIONS
Lesbian/Gay/Queer ▲ Theater/Drama/Performance

Series Editors
Ramón H. Rivera-Servera, University of Texas Austin
Sara Warner, Cornell University

Founding Editors
Jill Dolan, Princeton University
David Román, University of Southern California

RECENT TITLES IN THE SERIES:

Queer Relajo: Feeling the Nightscapes of Mexicanidad
    by David Tenorio

The Taylor Mac Book: Ritual, Realness and Radical Performance
    edited by David Román and Sean F. Edgecomb

Queer Nightlife   edited by Kemi Adeyemi, Kareem Khubchandani,
    and Ramón H. Rivera-Servera

Translocas: The Politics of Puerto Rican Drag and Trans Performance
    by Lawrence La Fountain-Stokes

*Prismatic Performances: Queer South Africa and the Fragmentation
    of the Rainbow Nation*   by April Sizemore-Barber

Ishtyle: Accenting Gay Indian Nightlife   by Kareem Khubchandani

The Bodies of Others: Drag Dances and Their Afterlives
    by Selby Wynn Schwartz

*Charles Ludlam Lives! Charles Busch, Bradford Louryk, Taylor Mac,
    and the Queer Legacy of the Ridiculous Theatrical Company*
    by Sean F. Edgecomb

Memories of the Revolution: The First Ten Years of the WOW Café Theater
    edited by Holly Hughes, Carmelita Tropicana, and Jill Dolan

Murder Most Queer: The Homicidal Homosexual in the American Theater
    by Jordan Schildcrout

Butch Queens Up in Pumps: Gender, Performance, and Ballroom Culture in Detroit
    by Marlon M. Bailey

Acts of Gaiety: LGBT Performance and the Politics of Pleasure   by Sara Warner

Performing Queer Latinidad: Dance, Sexuality, Politics
    by Ramón H. Rivera-Servera

A Menopausal Gentleman: The Solo Performances of Peggy Shaw
    edited by Jill Dolan

QUEER RELAJO

Feeling the Nightscapes of Mexicanidad

David Tenorio

UNIVERSITY OF MICHIGAN PRESS

Ann Arbor

Published in the United States of America by the
University of Michigan Press
First published August 2025

A CIP catalog record for this book is available from the British Library.

Library of Congress Cataloging-in-Publication data has been applied for.

ISBN 978-0-472-07760-1 (hardcover : alk. paper)
ISBN 978-0-472-05760-3 (paper : alk. paper)
ISBN 978-0-472-90518-8 (open access ebook)

DOI: https://doi.org/10.3998/mpub.12700279

The open-access publication of this book was supported by University of Pittsburgh,
Dietrich School of Arts and Sciences, Edwards Publication Fund.

The University of Michigan Press's open access publishing program is made possible
thanks to additional funding from the University of Michigan Office of the Provost and the
generous support of contributing libraries.

Authorized Representative: Easy Access System Europe, Mustamäe tee 50, 10621 Tallinn,
Estonia. gpsr.requests@easproject.com

Cover art image by Fabián Cháirez. Digital image of "Amanecer," oil on canvas,

"Y miré a la noche,
Ya no era oscura,
Era de lentejuelas"
(And I looked at the night,
It was no longer dark,
It was sequined)
—Gloria Trevi, "Todos Me Miran," Queer Mexican Anthem

Contents

List of Illustrations   ix

Acknowledgments   xi

Introduction. Reflections of A Mirrorball   1

PART I: DRAGGING MEXICANIDAD

1. The Chromatic Axis of Piña Colada   27

2. The Broken Records of Drag Performance   66

PART II: FUMBLING TOWARD URBAN NIGHTSCAPES

3. Play, Sex, and Dance in the Queer Underground   99

4. Reflections of a City's Nightscapes   130

PART III: THE SHADE AND SHADOW OF TRAVESTI NIGHTLIFE

5. The Shadowy Frames of Travesti Nightlife   165

6. The Kaleidoscope of Travesti Nightlife in Casa Roshell   188

Coda: Glows of Jotería   229

Notes   253

Works Cited   271

Index   283

Digital materials related to this title can be found on the Fulcrum platform via the following citable URL: https://doi.org/10.3998/mpub.12700279

List of Illustrations

1. Piña Colada poses, wearing a colorful crown — 30
2. Piña Colada stands at a private function — 40
3. Author as a child dressed in a pageboy suit, carrying Aunt Wendy's crown — 43
4. Aunt Wendy poses as Queen of Actopan — 45
5. Piña Colada lip-syncs at Pittsburgh's Blue Moon — 48
6. Author as a dancer in elementary school festivals — 54
7. Piña Colada looks at the mirrorball at Casa Roshell — 62
8. Wigs, books, and sequin dresses — 79
9. Roberto Cabral performs as Roberta in *Roberta y las otras chicas del montón* — 82
10. Lia García (La Novia Sirena) with her MC and court of *chambelanes* inside a subway platform — 102
11. A gay couple kisses inside a subway car — 109
12. Eriko Stark holds a young lover in front of the camera — 119
13. Gerardo waits for Bruno outside a subway station — 146
14. Coral and her mother have lunch in their apartment — 156
15. Raquel and Carmen laugh by a fountain at La Plaza de la Soledad — 162
16. A passionate kiss between Pancho and La Manuela — 174
17. Film poster of *El Baile de los 41* — 185
18. Film poster of *Casa Roshell* — 202
19. "Tú Estás Siempre En Mi Mente" — 240
20. "Noa Noa Instituto de Investigaciones" — 242
21. Film poster of *Wildness* — 244

Acknowledgments

What started as a comparative study about contemporary LGBTQ+ cultures in Cuba and Mexico turned into a fascinating odyssey that has led me to bask in underground night spaces typically associated with vice, risk, and unproductivity. Behind my seemingly wasteful ways of "studying," I have had the fortune to learn from queer friends, mentors, and lovers how to carve other times and spaces that refuse disheartened 24/7 utilitarianism. I have been carried, accompanied, loved, kissed, and literally dragged out of long nights by many loved ones that have always ensured my safety in physical, intellectual, and psychic ways. It has been in the nightly practice of queer intimacies that I have found respite, refuge, and a vital site for queer hemispheric liberation despite the ongoing cruelties of our world. As I attempt to list those who have sustained me, in one or many ways, throughout the completion of this project, I extend to them all my deepest gratitude.

This book first emerged as a thought experiment within a cocoon of unending love, careful guidance, and cunning advice offered by my longtime mentors Emilio Bejel, Robert M. Irwin, Sergio de la Mora, Laura Gutiérrez, Antonio Marquet, Desirée Martín, Amina Mama, Maxine Craig, and Beth Freeman†. Without them, I would not have been exposed to the various queer ways of surviving and existing in academia with ethical integrity, radical situatedness, intellectual generosity, and promiscuous curiosity. My intellectual trajectory, nonetheless, has been marked by the existing legacy of fellow scholars who have paved different pathways of dis/entangling the role of performance, sexuality, capital, technology, and affect across the Americas. Engaging with Diana Taylor, José Esteban Muñoz, Juana María Rodríguez, Martin F. Manalansan, Iván Ramos, Kareem Khubchandani, Jennifer Tyburczy, Doris Sommer, Larry La Fountain-Stokes, Arnaldo Cruz-Malavé, Alejandro Madrid, Marcia

Ochoa, Macarena Gómez-Barris, Jossianna Arroyo, Martha Toriz, Paola S. Hernández, Gastón A. Alzate, Verónica Gago, Lucí Cavallero, Sayak Valencia, Irmgard Emmelhainz, Arjun Appadurai, Sara Ahmed, Erin Manning, Brian Massumi, and George Yúdice among many others, has taught me that intellectual complicities beyond academic conventions are possible. Being part of McKenzie Wark's seminar at The New School's Institute for Critical Social Inquiry hosted by Ann Laura Stoler in the summer of 2023, helped me reimagine ways of brewing a radically committed scholarship rooted in fun, love, and pleasure.

I would also like to stress the importance of engaging in a hemispheric politics of travesti liberation through our very own practices of knowledge production, like the writing of this book. A good portion of it not only deals with the ways in which travesti and trans folk find pleasure at night in Mexico, and across the Americas, but also with how travesti forms of fun can help us recognize and experience first-hand the atrocities facing femme-presenting bodies in public spaces. My infinite love and gratitude go to Cole Rizki and Marlene Wayar. Cole's invitation to present my work as part of a graduate seminar on travesti politics in the Americas was fundamental to rearranging chapter 6. Cole has continually shared his brilliance, eloquence, and care; Marlene is a goddess whose radiance lights up the darkest of rooms. I am appreciative of the work of Eric A. Stanley, Jack Halberstam, Grace Lavery, Jules Gill-Peterson, Sara Wagner York, Siobhan Guerrero, McKenzie Wark, Eva Hayward, Cael M. Keegan, Francisco J. Galarte, Alan Pelaez Lopez, and Marquis Bey, for flipping conventions and for inspiring conversations about trans studies from transdisciplinary perspectives and locations.

Building knowledge from a queer hemispheric lens has showed me to appreciate a transnational network of intellectuals whose work pushes against set categories of cultural analysis, as in the work of Cinthya Ammerman, Camilo Lund, Justin Pérez, Giancarlo Cornejo, Ever Osorio Ruiz, Alfonso Fierro, Jorge Sánchez Cruz, Paul Michael Leonardo Atienza, Liliana Gil, Xiomara Cervantes, Fernanda Díaz-Basteris, Perla Guerrero, Manuel Cuéllar, or Raúl Romo, to name but a few. In this spirit, my queer network of conspirators, allies, and interlocutors reaches far and wide across continents, time zones, and places. In Mexico, Oswaldo Calderón† (aka La Súper Perra), Daniel Vives (aka La Súper Mana), Rodrigo Laguarda, Benjamín Martínez, Tadeo Cervantes, Mirna Roldán, Liz Misterio, Alex X.A.B., Mipanocha Rurru, Marisa Ruiz Trejo, Rodrigo Parrini, Lia García (La Novia Sirena), Jessica Marjane, Viviana Rocco†, Fabián

Cháirez, Xabier Lizárraga†, Salvador Irys Gómez, Fernando Osorno, Octavio Peña, Arturo Castelán†, Roberto Cabral, Coral Bonelli†, Eriko Stark, Fershow Escarcega, Franka Polari†, Vicky Letal, Roshell Terranova, Liliana Alba†, Gloria Davenport, Rafael Mondragón, Roberto Fiesco, and Julián Hernández, have always welcomed me with open arms every time I return to Mexico City. I remain indebted to Caro Novella, director at Onco Grrrls, for guiding me into the magical nightscapes of Mexico City, as well as grateful to Fabián Cháirez, Lia García (La Novia Sirena), Eriko Stark, Roberto Cabral, Alex X.A.B., Liz Misterio, and Julio Salgado for sharing their artwork with us all.

In Cuba, Norge Espinosa, Alberto Abreu, Roberto Zurbano, Pedry Roxana Rojo, Nelda Castillo, Mariela Brito, Ramón Silverio Gómez, Ulises Quintana de Armas, Nomi Ramírez, Alexis Álvarez, Eduardo Hernández Santos, Rocío García, René Peña, José Ángel Pérez, Pedro de Jesús López Acosta, Ernesto Pérez Chang, Elaine Saralegui, Lidia Romero, Mel Herrera, Yadiel Cepero, Yoelkis Torres, Juana Mora, Julio Pagés, Anna Lidia Vega Serova, Jimmy Roque Martínez, Ulises Padrón, Yasmín Silvia Portales, Lázaro J. González González, and the Red TransCuba, have so kindly showed me how to exist in the heartbreak of revolutionary utopias and embrace each other in the here and now as a form of resistance. In Canada, I thank Pepa Novell, Miquel Bota, Ana Belén Martín Sevillano, Alejandro Zamora, Margarita Feliciano, Jerzy Kowal, Esther Raventós-Pons, Sophie Pires, Stephanie Graham, Carlos Martínez, Mina Yoon, Mihaela Andrei, Wendy Rohkin, Fabiola Flores, Greg Brown, Antonio Benito, Denis Rochon, and Tara Downs Rocchetti, for their love, guidance, and advice.

In the US, the list grows exponentially, as does the loving support I have received along the years, even before this book came into fruition. Much of my fascination with affect studies is thanks to my intellectual power group, Escritoras Superpoderosas, that started as an intimate writing space with Julia Morales Fontanilla, Diana Pardo Pedraza, and Manuel R. Cuéllar amid the covid shutdown. The deep and generous conversation, attentive reading, and illuminating feedback from them have served me as inspiration to enact a sensuous vitality through my writing. Since then, our writing group has expanded and provided shelter to many women, femme presenting, and queer of color scholars navigating the troubled waters of academia. I am glad to be part of this community and remain forever thankful to them for being present in my life despite the many distances we are forced, at times, to inhabit.

I have been graced with the radical generosities, intellectual joys, and close friendships of Carmen Valdivia, Fernanda Díaz-Basteris, Alejandra Torres (Perikita Jackson), Cinthya Ammerman, Tania Lizarazo, Ana María Emma Escandón, Tomasito López, Emily Frankel, Barbara Gunn, Lia Locquiao, Paloma Duong, María de los Ángeles Gutiérrez Bascón, Adriana Sánchez-Solis, Daniel Minkel (Scarlet Fairweather), Kenya Dworkin, Yairamarén Román Maldonado, Perla Guerrero, Sharada Balachandran, Mireya Loza, Caitlin Bruce, Imani Owens, Paul Johnson, Liz Rodriguez Fielder, Peter Campbell, Jules Gill-Peterson, Salvador Vidal-Ortiz, and Juan Llamas-Rodriguez. My playful escapades with #QueerswithAura, alongside Liz Reich, Mary Zaborskis, and Patrick McKelvey, gave me the necessary glitter, banter, and drive to survive the Pennsylvanian winter months leading up to the pandemic.

Approaching Julio Salgado and Xandra Ibarra have been rewarding, exhilarating and challenging, as their continued presence stands in contrast to the very notions of Mexicanidad so ingrained in cultural nationalism, and so familiar to my own attachments to Mexico. Their work truly unsettles assumptions about what home feels like. I'd like to thank them for their openness in discussing and sharing their work with me. Mil gracias, queridos! In a genuine gesture of queer solidarity and commingling—with no questions asked—Brian Rogers at Chocolate Factory Theater gave me access to the collab performance "This Bridge Called My Ass" by Miguel Gutierrez. I have also benefitted from the deep engagement, dialogue, and insight from colleagues such as Ellen Gerdes, Olivia Sabee, and Bethany Formica Bender at Swarthmore College; Sheena Malhotra, Pavithra Prasad, Liliana Gonzalez, Bobbie Emetu, and Marie Cartier at Cal State University Northridge; Laura Anh Williams, M. Catherine Jonet, and Cynthia Bejarano at New Mexico State University; and Paloma Martinez-Cruz, Laura Podalsky, Eugenia Romero, Guisela Latorre, Javier Jasso, and Carlos Rivas at The Ohio State University.

As with any academic publication, this one would not have been possible without the generous support of various funding programs at the University of California, Davis, and the University of Pittsburgh. At UC-Davis, I would like to particularly thank all the encouragement and support I received from the Humanities Institute, the Hemispheric Institute on the Americas, and UC MEXUS. Against all odds, the University of Pittsburgh and its various funding research initiatives have been instrumental in my conducting field work and regularly staying in Mexico, Cuba, and California, including the Edwards Publication Fund. Of note stands the Center for Latin American Studies, particularly Keila Grinberg, Luz Amanda Hank, Manuel Román-Lacayo, and Luis G. Van Fossen Bravo, as well as Victor Figuereo, Israel Herndon, and Zuly Inirio at the Center for Ethnic Studies Research, for their unending support, encouragement, and guidance. They have all welcomed and supported my unorthodox ways and ideas, as well as ensured my sustenance abroad.

My colleagues Caitlin Bruce—who warmly connected me to Sara Cohen at University of Michigan Press—, Todd Reeser, Dolores Lima, Marcela González Rivas, Ana Paula Carvalho, Nancy Glazener, Áurea María Sotomayor, Gonzalo Lamana, Daniel Balderston, and Christopher Bonneau alongside esteemed colleagues in the Department of Spanish and Portuguese, and across the Dietrich School of Arts and Sciences at the University of Pittsburgh, provided me with the necessary resources to work, research, and collaborate inside and beyond university spaces. In the spirit of queer kinship, I am particularly thankful to Alex Crawley and Karen McEwen for helping me reshape this book's structure, and for believing in my ability to finish it. Daniel Kaple's dexterity in digital images proves how necessary it is to have digital humanities specialists at college libraries. To my editors at University of Michigan Press, my utmost respect, admiration, and affection. Thank you LeAnn Fields and Sara Cohen for believing in my project since the beginning, and for facilitating a smooth transit across the gates of production. With their support, two attentive anonymous readers provided wonderful reports that helped this book project mature. To them all, thank you for sprinkling your intellectual magic over my life!

My enchantment with popular nightlife probably occurred in my early years as a skimpy kid growing up in Mexico City, where I would look in awe at the bright-lit marquees scattered around downtown streets. It was also in the complicities and complications of family dramas that I remember nightlife being a site where all the worries of the present would disappear—even if momentarily, where we would laugh at the absurdity of life in the most precarious of situations. Although I left my home country at nineteen for various reasons, including an urgent need to protect my own queerness from violence, machismo and misogyny, there is always a part of me that stays in Mexico City and that allows me to navigate the long nights as if I hadn't left my first home.

From the bottom of my heart, I thank my immediate family for allowing me to flourish and for showing me that life beyond heterosexual conventions is possible. To David Raúl, Benjamín, and Verito goes my most heartfelt appreciation, for sharing with me their time amid the chaos of city life. My tías and primas have been pivotal in my understanding of feminism, one that takes place in the backdoors of kitchens, in the terse whispers of gossip after a meal, in the comfort of improvised bedframes and in the hardship of mourning and heartbreak. To Carolina, Wendy, Anani, Elia, Camelia, the two Gracielas, Denny, Valeria, Crystal, Tía Patty, Rachel, Yaarah, Margarita, and Claudia, thank you for understanding the importance of queer relajo and for making my world shine with endless fantasies. And just like the night's glow slowly fades away with the first rays of sunrise, so have my lovers, date mates, and partners like Scott Hall, Monte Labash, Bruno Moura Nunes, Silvio Balladares, and Clemente Barraza. Through countless encounters, romantic and otherwise, they have left an enduring trace on me and reminded me of emotional intensity, mutual care, radical joy and possibility.

As a far-right, fascist, and authoritarian presence in the US continues to grow, let's take a moment to reflect on all those queer moments of collective struggle through which we have found a force of renewal and liberation. Let us be reminded of the queer power of fun, laughter, and pleasure in dislodging a culture of compulsory heterosexuality, toxic masculinity, excessive productivity, inhumane exploitation, and economic indenture. Our possibilities for joy can potentially spark various ways of existing and having fun beyond precarity. Let this book be an offering to our queer altar of pleasures, as its charms can, and indeed, shape our most radical fantasies amid impossibility. Thank you to all who have touched me along this journey, and let's give it up to all those queer and trans folk we've lost along the way, so we may find their kindred afterglow guiding us through the mystery of nightscapes.

Introduction

Reflections of A Mirrorball

On a crisp summer night in 2023, I walk into the iconic Casa Club Roshell to do a lip-sync performance as drag queen Piña Colada. Alongside outside scenes of violence, infrastructural collapse, and a water crisis in one of Mexico City's working-class neighborhoods, the stage inside looks like a jewel whose shine cuts through a sea of darkness. I find myself surrounded by the embrace of nightcrawlers like travesti women, trans chasers, fellow drag queens, and many others who have also walked through a hefty security system upon entry. Once inside, we are all waiting for the performance to start. I stumble to make my way onto the glistening stage while wearing a fitted animal-print dress in twelve-inch red stilettos. As I stand in front of a velvety curtain of glittery bangles, the stage light coming from above hits my eyes way too hard, making it almost impossible to fully appreciate the faces sitting in the audience.

Under the stage lights, I see everyone turn into a giant aura of blinding resplendence that hides all textures, and crevices, all imperfections, and dirty secrets. I raise my arms up in the air, evoking the gestures of Spanish song divas, and I wait for the first beat to play. As the soundwaves of a distinct ballad fill the stage, the room turns pitch black, while the mirrorball's reflections of colorful spots make me wonder about the miniscule, almost invisible, synoptic connections of feeling and sensation that, taking place across queer and trans nightclubs, dance floors, performance stages, and other nighttime-like scenes like this one, bind us all together.

To the voyeuristic eye our hanging out might look like an everynight affair that casually brings out travesti, trans, and queer women, men, and everyone in between, on a Friday night. But the complex realities affecting queer and trans lives in 21st century Mexico, and specifically Mexico City, are no laughing matter, considering that the country ranks high as one of the deadliest countries in the Americas for women—cis, trans, and otherwise—as well as for LGBTQ+ people, despite existing legislation allowing name and gender changes on official documents, same-sex marriage, and adoption of children for same-sex couples.[1]

Aside from constantly zigzagging the nightly and daily dangers of gender- and sexual-based violence, queer and trans folk in Mexico also face an increasing privatization of public life introduced by state neoliberal policies since the 1980s. In 1979, queer Mexican writer José Joaquín Blanco precisely critiqued the socioeconomic privilege of white gay mestizos, that is, a gay male position drawing advantage from the postcolonial, patriarchal, heterosexual, and whitened structures of the nation-state. Alongside the socioeconomic transformations undergoing the Mexican middle-class, the implementation of neoliberal policies, for the queer writer, would also bring Mexican sexual dissident cultures in contact with global networks of sexual consumption, replacing a radical politics of queer sex and intimacy for inclusive and tolerant markets where the circulation of identity-based products would characterize the emergence of a "democratic" capitalist society (185). Simply put, Blanco began to grapple with the transnational manifestations of queer neoliberalism, as apolitical forms of sexual dissidence would otherwise marginalize queer and trans folk already living on the edge of precarity, forecasting the rampant privatization, commodification, and extraction of sexual and gender nonconforming practices.

Like a mirrorball reflecting across time and space, Blanco's prognostic writing shed light on the current queer configurations in urban Mexico. Unintentionally, his warning signs would materialize almost four decades later when then-mayor Miguel Ángel Mancera[2] officially declared Mexico City as "gay friendly" in 2015.[3] After this coming out statement, the Office of LGBTQ+ Tourism reopened and published in 2019 its first queer tourist guide as part of a state-driven campaign marketing the city's queer nightlife scene. In bold green font, the guide's title "Capital LGBTTTI," (Secretaría de Turismo, n.d.) contrasts with an amber-pink cover page showing a rainbow flag. Hyping a queer cosmopolitan avant garde befitting the 21st century, the guide seeks to entice potential consumers with a full range of options, including museums, restaurants, nightclubs, cabarets, and theaters, making explicit the city government's plan to benefit from the economic conversion of sexual desire. Spotlighting venues in the predominantly posh queer districts of Zona Rosa, Polanco, and Chapultepec, the guide highlights specific urban socioeconomic zones that resemble other global queer meccas like San Francisco, Berlin, Rio de Janeiro, Madrid, or New York, while excluding from the list other popular and working-class nightlife venues like Casa Club Roshell, or La Cañita, one of the very few locales for lesbian, queer and trans nightlife that existed in the city from 2017 to 2022.[4] Although popular night clubs along Mexico City's downtown queer corridor República de Cuba like La Purísima or Marrakech Salón are included, I read the absence of local and underground queer and trans nighteries in the city's queer tourist guide less as a concern with bringing visibility to local scenes of queer sociality than an attempt to craft a neoliberal vision of queer urban space; a vision needing further probing.

More than providing a list of public programs ensuring the well-being of LGBTQ+ people, like health care community clinics, food banks, or affordable housing options, the city's queer guide offers a business catalog of joyful possibilities available for purchase, exposing the stratification of queer citizenship. This stratification occurs alongside other socioeconomic reforms that have yielded privatized monopolies of public services, foreign-controlled industries, and overall social inequality since Mexico embraced neoliberalism in the late 1980s with the signing of the Brady Plan to partially reduce its debt with the US (Harvey 2005, 103). Moreover, it raises important considerations as to what becomes worthy of showcasing, and who might benefit from an advertising campaign that ends up modifying access to urban space. Whether peripheral, queer/trans nightlife holds no immunity to neoliberal conversion, which can transform nightlife's seeming marginality into corrugated sites of consumption, extraction, and commodification. An example can be found in the transformation of República de Cuba. Known for housing historically gritty and shabby underground cabarets, bars, and nightclubs, the new corridor features fancy neon-lit sex shops and queer bars that aesthetically incentivize a market for pinkwashed consumerism. The replacement of queer shabby exteriors highlights a trend following Mexico City's downtown gentrification since 2010s, cautiously prescribed by Blanco's chronicle.

The economic drive guiding Mexico City's public investment on developing a market infrastructure around "LGBTTTI capital" furthermore reveals the complex mutations of a neoliberal relationality driving the commodification of queer identity, and the financialization of queer space in the twenty-first century. The neoliberal commodification of queer/trans nightlife in Mexico City, and largely of cities across the Americas, materializes in designs that profit from the value of queer play, fun, and pleasure, while drawing up new zones for the extraction of sexual capital despite their constant surveillance and marginalization. Not only does neoliberal commodification predicate on the capture of public space to produce extractable value, but also restricts passage of those unable to pay the costs to move across privatized spatial designs. As such, the neoliberalization of Mexico "also needs to be understood . . . not as a machine that produces inequality, but as a process of the regulatory restructuring of various spatial scales" (Emmelhainz 2021, 79). In this sense, neoliberalism encompasses more than just a set of economic policies but asserts forms of administering and experiencing life under economic terms. As Wendy Brown argues, "neoliberalism . . . is at once a global phenomenon, yet inconsistent, differentiated, unsystematic, impure" (2017, 20) in creating uneven zones where extraction exists alongside wealth, where depletion takes place amid redistribution, and life and death hang in the balance.

Alongside neoliberal transformation, a critical reflection on Mexico City's contested affair with queer night scenes reveals a repeating history of violence, criminalization, policing, drug trafficking, and exploitation affecting queer/trans belonging, intimacy, and relationality. Broadly discussed and historized in literary scholarship, the infamous Dance of the 41,[5] a secret drag ball raided by police in 1901, emerges as one of the early seizures of queer and trans nightlife in the city. More than a hundred years later, the attacks on queer/trans night-making—that is, attacks on the social, affective, performative, economic, and material interrelations that produce queer/trans nightlife—have persisted not only in the capital city but across the country. In 2004, for instance, Tito Vasconcelo's Cabaretito bars were shut down when the renowned queer cabaret performer openly criticized then-city mayor Manuel López Obrador for mishandling resources destined to help people living with HIV/AIDS, while the once exhilarating queer nightclub Lipstick Lounge Bar, sitting on the corner of Calle Ámberes and Paseo de la Reforma in Zona Rosa, was charged with multiple fines by city officials in 2008 leading to its permanent closure shortly after.

In 2017, Mexico City's Secretariat of Public Security carried out Operation Cyclone, a raid that involved the deployment of more than five hundred police units to bust the nightly operations of twenty-one bars, including the downtown queer clubs Antro Oasis, Bar Viena, El Wawis, Bar Secret, and Bar 69. Most recently, the Zona Rosa's Rico Club and Cabaretito were closed following various reports on violent assaults inside and in the nearby vicinity in 2023, and 2022, respectively. In recent years, similar queer bar closures have been reported in other Mexican states such as Aguascalientes, Puebla, San Luis Potosí, and the State of Mexico. More than isolated events, these incidents are symptomatic of a complex reality in which homophobia, transphobia, and misogyny are not only co-constitutive to Mexican national cultures, but also to transnational cultures of heteronormativity disrupting and advancing a neoliberal agenda that holds a vexed relationship to sexual and gender nonconforming practices.

In the context of Mexico City, old cultural sentiments that remain alive, like the hygienist politics of 1950s and 60s that posit the idea that nightlife is a site of immorality (Pulido Llano 2018, 3–5), intersect with a radical politics of queer liberation that, in turn, has shifted through global market forces that respond to the complex flows of queer neoliberalism. It is easy to be misled by appearances, as by the misconception that sexual cultures in these coordinates of the global south are essentially premodern, meaning that they are nonexistent, or are repressed by moral conservatism. Rather, they are coproduced by various local, regional, and global forces that further complicate the social choreographies of queer and trans nightlife. In other words, they coexist alongside the socioeconomics of violence in a country that has experienced a reorganization of life under neoliberal reform, permanent state corruption, rapid militarization, and the implacable strength of a narcostate.

Against this backdrop, *Queer Relajo: Feeling the Nightscapes of Mexicanidad* examines how queer and trans performances of *queer relajo*, or what I call situated and economically racialized queer renditions of play or relajo, like flirting, dancing, cruising, or longing, reshape queer spaces of consumption to assemble underground ambiances, or *nightscapes*, for queer and trans worldmaking during nighttime and beyond. As a way of building an archive of broken, dark, and loose affects negotiating queer neoliberalism, I examine a vast range of queer cultural performances, films, documentaries, TV shows, visual art, amateur pornography, autoethnographic vignettes, and more, spanning from the last quarter of the twentieth century to the second decade of the twenty-first. In this sense, *Queer Relajo* considers how affective networks transform queer/trans modes of perception, affection, and consumption in racialized "gay-friendly" urban spaces in a globally neoliberal Mexico City. Considering the material and political implications of what takes place when queer/trans folk occupy the night, I argue that these playful modes of feeling and sensing disorient neoliberal commodification and capitalist extraction.

By highlighting a sense of letting go, the nightscapes ensembled by queer relajo reconfigure urban space from below. With below, I refer to underground spaces, as well as to a series of embodied working-class queer tactics that reshape public space, and through such reshaping, mediate displacement, privatization, and commodification. I thus fathom the popular not only as a socioeconomic location, but also as a racialized way of navigating an increasingly privatized nighttime. While positioning myself in queer/trans working-class, popular formations, my focus highlights ways in which queer/trans actors negotiate multifaceted forms of violence underpinning the neoliberal operations connecting whiteness to socioeconomic value. Although ephemeral, these playful tactics expose the queer strategies that collectives from below enact to regain their agency amid an uneven neoliberal reordering of things, a complex process driven by a national impetus for securing future progress.[6] In this sense, the playful embodiments of queer relajo rehearse social choreographies that deviate from the transnational trajectories of neoliberalism, while politicizing access to queer forms of joy, fun, and pleasure to saturate national circuits of heterosexuality.[7]

Amid the encompassing effects of neoliberal transformation, what impels us to keep coming out at night? As I stand atop a stage in front of a vast group of travesti, trans, and queer folk who have traveled far and wide to get here tonight, I couldn't help but notice the loud sounds of laughter, the clinking of cocktail glasses, the whispers of gossip, the secret rush of confession, or the echoes of heels tapping against the dance floor when musical group Los Ángeles Azules's cumbia plays in the distance. I suddenly realize that my senses are overtaken by the nightly ambiance orchestrated in the company of queer/trans kin. A mirrorball reflection then makes me appreciate that queer nightlife emerges as a precious lifeline for many of us, as vital as is legal recognition to the sustenance of queer/trans ways of life in a global city. Being immersed in the queer ecologies of nightlife forces me to encounter and come to terms with an exhilarating strangeness. Queer relajo thus prompts me to foreground my place in the night and make sense of the many textures, modulations, and dimensions composing a queer politics of space under capitalist logics. At the club, I reflect on the importance of being present, as well as of reclaiming the urban terrains of the night, pondering on how queer nightlife might mobilize us politically in the face of economic precarity, rampant violence, and social uncertainty.

Gliding over the condensation of sweat, tears, and saliva, the deceiving stasis of a mirrorball hangs above the club crowd as if overseeing all the drama, listening into the intrigue, and joining in the fun that we come seeking. That is why whenever I am on stage, I often look for the shimmering reflections of a mirrorball to connect with a different set of colorful rays, directing my attention to the conflicting yet sensuous possibilities inside the nightclub and beyond. Like a spinning mirrorball, *Queer Relajo* mimics the motions of a glittery apparatus to focus on three distinct axes of reflection spanning across three sections with two chapters each, Part I: Dragging Mexicanidad, Part II: Fumbling Toward Urban Nightscapes, and Part III: The Shade and Shadow of Travesti Nightlife. As small, mirrored facets, each part reflects on the everlasting affect of queer relajo, or playfulness, running through Mexico City's queer nightlife circuits. Tracking spatial and affective transactions, *Queer Relajo* thus examines instances of queer/trans relajo found in the nighteries of urban Mexicanidad. These queer modes of play function as space-making tactics in places that complicate the transit of queer and trans desires. In other words, queer relajo is queer worldmaking. By highlighting the embedded looseness of queer relajo, I situate queer/trans acts and out-of-worldly performances that reshape urban landscapes by choreographing ambiances in which the abundance, flow, attunement, and modulation of queer affects offer tactics to fend off a logic that equates zones of sexual tolerance with zones of socioeconomic trade and extraction in "a gay friendly" Mexico City. Shining through the book's contents, these queer diffractions allow me to perceive queer/trans nightlife as an underground geography of queer Mexicanidad.

Mimicking the circular gestures from twisting my wrists when Piña Colada begins to lip-sync, my intention in this introduction is threefold. I first perform a queer reading of relajo, or *queer relajo*, as a way of highlighting a queer sense of looseness contesting the neoliberal expansion of the masculinist Mexican nation. My deployment of a term so embedded in Spanish names a queer Brown refusal against a (white) neoliberal order of things. Second, by indexing a mode of queer playfulness in my critique of Mexican heteronormativity, I adapt queer relajo as an analytic rooted in play, fun, and joy to reclaim a transfeminist praxis of pleasure against queer/trans necropolitics not only in Mexico, but across the Americas. And third, by engaging a playful method of queer cultural analysis, I situate a hemispheric transfeminist praxis embodied through popular, working-class, and ordinary forms of queer/trans relationality, assembling ambiances, or what I refer to as *queer nightscapes*, to sense nightlife otherwise amid the global flows of capital in Mexico City. Collected across six chapters, which will be unpacked in what follows, the affective fluctuations of nightscapes subvert, minimize, and negotiate neoliberal violence affecting queer/trans folk in urban Mexico.

Getting Loose: Toward A Queer Sense of Relajo

Queer Relajo loosely plays and replays with instances of letting oneself go to forge queer communion and trans connection in the dark. Located within a complex social matrix, the cultural artifacts comprising this book move beyond the realm of signification to appreciate the rich textures of queer/trans night sociality. Although not all of them take place at night, or are specifically about the night, the night and its enveloping darkness emerge as gestures and traces of a queer sociality, and as such, they are read as instances in which queer relajo signals nightly modes of interaction, connection, and engagement that scatter, expand, and redraw the very spatial and temporal limits of nighttime. Not strictly confined by hours of darkness, acts of queer relajo question the conventional times and spaces where queer and trans folk can have fun, accenting varying ambiances of action and feeling to shape the nightscapes of queer playfulness. Out of nighteries, or urban sites of queer nightlife, looseness describes a sense of disarray and disorganization affixed to sexual locations holding little to no value in neoliberal economies of heteronormative re/production and extraction. A sense of letting loose allows us to turn to joy and pleasure as embodiments of queer refusal and trans refutation that denounce the everyday violence, policing, and scrutiny affecting minoritarian ways of life. Letting oneself loose not only refers to a quality of detached unsettledness, but also to queer motions and trans movements across time and space, gesturing toward a queer opening into the world, a queer chance for turning things upside down and tossing them out of bounds during and after nighttime. Looseness extends into an embodied territory of queer affects that map out instances of wildness or failure (Halberstam 2020, 2011), odd tempos (Freeman 2010; Keeling 2019; Puar 2007), queer locations and disorientations (Ahmed 2006). Looseness thus sparks a sexual possibility of playfulness marking zones of queer contact. As such, this book tunes into a queer sense of looseness, or what I refer to as queer relajo, shaping embodiments of queer Mexicanidad—social, cultural, and affective attachments questioning conventional and heterosexual renditions of Mexican identification.

As a way of describing how queer relajo engages this book's gestures, methods, themes, and contents, I first situate relajo as a concept stemming from a strand of critical thought looking to find the essence of Mexican identity, or "lo mexicano." Drawing from Grupo Hiperión's obsession with defining a sense of Mexicanidad,[8] Jorge Portilla's *Phenomenology of Relajo* (1984) outlines a tantalizing connection between the demand of a particular value and its socioeconomic and moral reaffirmation.[9] While ambivalent when outlining what a value is, or entails, the philosopher interprets relajo as a spontaneous "loud collective mockery" (123) emerging from everyday life, while recognizing value as vital to a shifting field of moral, cultural, and socioeconomic relations involved in the making of Mexican sociality. As such, Portilla's phenomenology theorizes a postcolonial condition and establishes what is seen at the time as a necessary dialogue with continental philosophy's appeal to abstract universality. Looking for a sense of Mexicanidad, the thinker finds in relajo "a system of relationships" that, binding the universal, historical, and contextual, develops into a "form of consciousness so incidental and transitory to understanding essential characteristics of the human condition" (124). If, for Portilla, seriousness marks one's willingness to accept a value, the lack thereof would lead to questioning the established order, resulting in a desire to disobey that tragically turns into self-destruction and chaos. Contrastingly, upholding a value would lead to a sense of freedom, and subsequently develop into an individual form of consciousness, or "agential liberation" (Garcia Torres 2023, 12). Giving into the alluring universality of western thought signals a form of intellectual whitening that, notwithstanding its connection to popular, working-class collectives, embodies an irresolute contradiction at the base of national belonging, magnifying a pull toward modernity, as well as a push against orthodoxy.

Aside from its puzzling universalist claims, Portilla's study of relajo spots the embodied gestures of looseness that allow the outright rejection of any value, including the negation of freedom, something the author sees as "the negative side of a 'freedom to,' or the given of responsibility" (187). Although not explicitly stated by the Mexican thinker, relajo, or "a suspension of seriousness" (Sánchez 2012, 38), refers to a premodern condition immanent to the national character, or a loose and backward character defining Mexicans. Warning against relajo's "self-destructive," or "irrational" drive, Portilla locates an affect in negating value itself, through which the "relajiento," or someone acting out relajo, "is literally an individual without a future" (147), someone who refuses to take anything serious at face value, and therefore is pushed out of the national scripts of history.

I read Portilla's contradictory position toward relajo as an unyielding adherence to teleologies of progress, as well as a form of agency that places pleasure over duty. Considering play as a subversive performance against national development, Portilla states that "the behaviors [. . .] mean that the actions of the individual that performs them are predictable and outline a comprehensible future based on the realization of a value-filled self" (Sánchez 2012, 147). In other words, someone's affirmation to normative values moves them toward a "straight" trajectory of progress and becoming, but under the current sociopolitical conditions, a future tense thrives on neoliberal modes of relation, interaction, and consumption. Given the author's preoccupation with forging a modern Mexican character, Portilla not only fathoms relajo as intrinsically dangerous to national development but finds in collective playfulness a host of dissenting practices for place-making that, in turn, move things, bodies, and affects away from a national futurist ontology. By rejecting normative values, relajo thus embodies forms of "digression," marking a "deviation from something," specifically a straight orientation, or a teleological line of time and action, manifesting instead surreptitious paths moving toward reflection, bewilderment, and wonder beyond the fatherland.[10] Rather than reducing the relation between relajo and value to a mere concept, its interplay offers situated embodiments of the amplifying excess of relajo that counteract a drive for neoliberal progress within a matrix of violence in Mexico—a violence manifested in the killings of non-binary electoral magistrate Jesús Ociel Baena in 2023, and of trans activist Samantha Gómez Fonseca in 2024, as well as the assault of media influencer Paola Suárez in 2024.

In this context, national striving for futurity exposes a contradictory oscillation between stagnation and renovation, or a cultural logic of "regression" (Yépez 2010, 193), that advances a patriarchal and increasingly masculinist project of the nation in globalized times. Not to mention that the Mexican political project of the nation has been extremely androcentric from the outset, fostering a homonational cult of toxic hypermasculinity that has shifted from the revolutionary caudillo in 1920s, passing through the untouchable father-like presidential figure of the 1940s and onward, to the violently benevolent drug lord of the mid-2000s. More than revealing a complicated logic of underdevelopment, Mexico's homonationalist participation in global circuits of capital with China, Europe, and the rest of the Americas, further shows the country's complicit engagement with "predatory logics that—along with *spectralization* and *speculation* in financial markets—foment and implement radically violent practices" (Valencia 2018, 22–23). In this sense, Mexico's aspirational model of the future is not only violently modern, in that it mimics the straight trajectories of whitened modernity, but also foundationally exclusionary to other constituents and existing forms of sovereignty, like those linked to Indigenous cosmologies in Chiapas, Oaxaca, and the Yucatán, or to contradictory, diasporic, and opposing articulations of Mexicanidad.

Drawing from its potentiality for refusal and deviation, I queer the concept of relajo to interrogate an inherently masculinist political project thriving on neoliberal transformation. In other words, relajo needs queerness to expose the heteronormative set of values driving national belonging, as well as to question the seeming universality of national identity. In doing so, queerness reclaims an apparent "premodern backwardness" framed less as a subaltern position than as a complicated field of action from below. By turn, queerness needs relajo to expand and recognize the ways in which popular, and working-class queer/trans folk engage fun, joy, and play as political affects through acts of, but not limited to, dancing, kissing, cruising, longing, crying, chasing, and touching, etc. Put differently, queerness repositions ordinary acts of queer/trans intimacy as playful operations within a wide range of political possibilities moving across the privatization of pleasure.

Queer relajo thus finely attunes our understanding of what joy and pleasure allow us to do politically, as it reconsiders what is up for play, but also what is at risk of being lost to the dangers of playing. In this sense, queer relajo orchestrates strategies to laugh back at power, "empowering the one who dared to laugh it off" (Pérez 2012),[11] while reshaping the affective economies producing spaces for pleasure to "help play take place within bounded space while still remaining open to the creative, appropriative capacities of [queer] activity" (Sicart 2014, 55). Because queer nightlife usually allows public expressions of queer intimacy without much rebuke, acts of queer relajo stretch the spatial and affective boundaries of the night, calling on a queer sense of looseness beyond nighttime. As a queer way of letting loose, queer relajo thus fosters a sense of urban space amid heteronormative enclosure, and neoliberal privacy.[12]

An example of how queer nightlife can ooze out of nightclubs through queer relajo can be found in a digital incident that prompted queer users to respond online to Mexico City's catholic authorities in 2016. In "The (Fa-bo-lous) Gay Empire," an op-ed for news magazine *Proceso*, feminist writer Sabina Berman traces the hashtag phenomenon #ImperioGay (i.e., #GayEmpire), that erupted after Hugo Valdemar, Mexico City's catholic church spokesperson, warned against "a dictatorship of homosexuals" taking over the country.[13] As if responding to a hot party call, queer users rushed to social media outlets to invoke queer pop music idols like Gloria Trevi, Juan Gabriel, Freddie Mercury, or Lady Gaga, to laugh at the possibility of crafting the new culture under a looming "gay empire." Queer social media users deployed memes, music soundtracks, and performances as playful strategies to mock the absurdity of the church's claims.

Although trivial, the media posts embodied a sort of "party [that] was unstoppable and amidst the confetti rain, LGBTQ+ supporters had regained their best tactics against intolerance: humor, fantasy and laxness" (Berman 2016). Elements of queer nightlife such as music anthems, festive dance moves, or a pair of red stilettos were invoked to enact queer night-making in the digital sphere. It is precisely the ordinariness of queer relajo that, inspiring social media content, made cyberspace turn into a confetti party to counteract a dogmatic conservatism through play, fantasy, and fun. Under a queer lens, relajo thus contributes to a more generative and nuanced understanding on the political tactics, acts, and performances of refusal queer/trans folk engage in, extending lifelines to survive and thrive amid the transregional manifestations of violence. As such, queer relajo manifests a sense of racialized looseness that indexes playful forms of queer troublemaking and disruption against the heterosexual nation-state.

By departing from a cishet neoliberal system of values, acts of queer relajo invest in a reconfiguration of space, redrawing the distance between what an object or person holds in terms of their actual worth. Given its insistence on distance and expansion, queer relajo plays with the relational spaces between things, bodies, and feelings. By moving away from teleological trajectories of progress, queer relajo deviates from well-trodden paths of neoliberal becoming, marking a spatial refusal, while remapping a spatial relation to value itself. In an act of queer relajo, the connection to a normative value is not only disrupted, but also spatially reconfigured. The further away one stands to value, the better one can reattune the senses to feel the world beyond extraction. These queer acts relocate and reshape worth, tracing other coordinates that demand revalorization, not in terms of economic capital, but in terms of our capacity to affect and be affected by the many worlds around us.

Questioning (neo)liberal value systems based on the accumulation of property, the exercise of individual agency, the privatization of public space, and the gendered division of re/productive labor, a queer bend on relajo offers an embodied practice that veers away from heteronormative futurity, as well as from various forms of violence. As a situated affect, and embodied performance, queer relajo circumvents the paralyzing effects of neoliberalism, sending out a shocking vibration from the popular to shake up neoliberal sociality. I am not suggesting that queer relajo offers a redemptive capacity, or even a utopian impetus, but rather allows for a different fluctuation of values, and by doing so, rehearses social mappings that move beyond capitalistic gain. In other words, queer relajo situates practices of refusal against extraction, dispossession, and feminized labor, opening circuits of care and joy that exist alongside perverse modes of neoliberal relationality.

With one playful touch, as in Piña Colada's performance, the heteronormative world unravels, and, through its unraveling, we retreat into the crevices of queer/trans nighteries. As a mirrorball's colorful diffraction, "Part I: Dragging Mexicanidad" turns to a juncture of national belonging, temporality, and queer nightlife. Across two chapters, the first axis reflects on the possibilities of drag performance, as extensions of queer relajo, to destabilize static notions of Mexican belonging and identity in the now. In chapter 1, "The Chromatic Axis of Piña Colada," my personal story of drag becoming as Piña Colada allows me to trace transnational circuits connecting queer relajo with the X in Latinx and drag culture through performance, autoethnographic vignettes, and personal photos. From childhood experiences of Mexican culture to the pedragogy experienced in a diasporic movement between Pittsburgh and Mexico City—a term I borrow from Mexico City-based drag performer and theorist Benjamín Martínez/Walpurgis Gara to refer to various ways of learning and living through drag—Piña Colada reveals the productive tension that destabilizes and subverts white modernity and neoliberal capitalism through processes of queer homemaking, worldmaking, and belonging that are continually recreated and reconfigured spatially amid imperfection, dislocation, and uncertainty.

Engaging with my own practice as a drag queen, I incorporate autoethnography to give voice to Piña Colada, as my performances critique the racialized, gendered, and classed structures of Mexicanidad, as well as those of US academia. Thinking and feeling with Piña Colada makes evident the queer practices of relajo shaping material encounters between bodies, objects, and feelings. These encounters point to a body of knowledge on how to navigate space through queer play.

While tracking the emergence of my drag persona Piña Colada in the previous chapter, in chapter 2, "The Broken Records of Drag Performance," I contrast the literary representation of drag queens in the Americas, to trace the emergence of an *ecology of drag*, a material network connecting performance, objects, spaces, and moving bodies. Following how these networks manifest in the cabaret performance of Mexico City-based drag queen Roberto Cabral, my discussion exposes how the politics of sexuality and race expand on a critique of national history in neoliberal times. In this transversal approach to queer literature, and drag performance, including Piña Colada's interactions with second-hand sequin dresses, jewelry, and luscious wigs, I argue that drag culture mixes queer playfulness as a way of critiquing history through the notion of *broken record*, an affective drive that connects queer memory with the sensorial experiences of queer and trans folk living on the fringe.

Queer Relajo as Method

Queer Relajo presents instances to learn about ways of feeling the world as a "place of ecstasy," where pleasure and danger dance together (hooks 1994, 3). While thinking with queer formations and methods in the US, I insist on a queer hemispheric framework that recognizes race, gender, citizenship, and space as intrinsic elements of cultural analysis, paying particular attention to the socioeconomic networks of queer/trans nightlife in a globalized Mexico. While the US scholarly debate around queerness in Mexican culture has remained an almost exclusively literary affair, my book's transdisciplinary approach flips such analytical conventions to attend to the transformations of a queer/trans cultural field from the first three decades of the twenty-first century.

In the spirit of refusal, queer relajo emerges as a playful analytic for queer cultural inquiry that allows me to draw from and move through a transversal methodology that includes close reading, media analysis, performance, and autoethnography. Not only anchored in performance and affect studies, but also relying on other modes of queer fugitivity inaccurately seen as wasteful, excessive, and valueless by the rational lenses of (white) academia, queer relajo as method joins and borrows from a long genealogy of insurgent practices of knowledge production that break away from abstraction and high theory, and push "into a more chaotic realm of knowing and unknowing" (Halberstam 2011, 2), by mixing feminist media studies, critical infrastructure studies, night studies, queer/trans of color critique, and global south epistemologies across the gleaming edges of this book.

While reckoning with "low theory," queer relajo throws out of bound the geopolitical configurations of sexuality studies, ethnic studies, and area studies. By broadening the scope of nation-bound cultural studies, in this case Mexican and Latin American studies, a method of queer relajo disarrays conventional modes of reading set cultural archives, as well as of disciplinary studies in/from/about Mexico, situating instead a hemispheric lens of queer analysis. As a way of complicating existing heritages of modernity, imperialism, and neoliberalism, shaping the geopolitics of sexual knowledge in the Americas, queer relajo shines critical light on lowly, popular, and ordinary queer/trans practices that, taking place during nighttime, grapple with the complex and contradictory flows of neoliberal value in Mexico City after dark.

Building on performance studies' transdisciplinary understanding of knowledge and power as a process of embodied mediation, this book reconceptualizes cultural production as a site of queer nightlife, that is, we feel the night when its echoes affect us by listening to the music waves of a song or staring at the revolving disco lights of a movie scene, or feeling the rush of a recorded performance. As method, queer relajo attunes our ability to sense queer nightlife as an intricate network of sociality constituted by the interactions among sentient actors, both human and non-human.[14] In other words, we inhabit queer nightlife when feeling, and sensing its contours in the cultural artifacts that, more than constituting technologies of capture, let the night loose through the glistening pages of this book.

By unsettling the very boundaries of cultural form, genre, and analysis, I loosen dominant tenets of cultural analysis anchored in representation to argue that nightlife is a contested transregional space built through queer and trans practices of negotiation with the labored commodification of affects like joy, fun, and pleasure. A form of sensorial engagement with cultural artifacts, or sensorial reading, becomes possible in the active participation of creating queer knowledges about the night through the transversal method of queer relajo. At the same time, it allows me to disorient and undo myself from the perverse rigidity of disciplinary constraints legitimizing practices of queer cultural analysis and knowledge production. Moving beyond dichotomous frameworks, like word/image, thinking/feeling, mind/body, fantasy/history, etc., a queer method of play recognizes our co-inhabited vulnerability in building queer/trans knowledges that resist and call out the violence of extraction, exploitation, and subordination.

I thus highlight how nighttime practices rehearse sensorial choreographies, as well as build affective ambiances, or what I call nightscapes, that make possible the transference of queer/trans knowledge through playfulness, pleasure, and excitement. Feeling with and sensing cultural artifacts as vital records of queer/trans sociality awakens the "repertoire of embodied knowledge and practice," that is, "all those acts usually thought of as ephemeral, nonreproducible knowledge," that "[keep and transform] choreographies of meaning" (Taylor 2003, 19–20). Although the repertoire is intricately embedded in economies of production, distribution, and consumption, this book highlights how queer knowledge is also transmitted through moods, senses, and feelings evoked in queer cultural artifacts. Also sensorial, the repertoire enacts queer modalities of producing, transmitting, and storing knowledge through feeling beyond established systems of meaning and value.

Tuning into the polyphony, multiversity, and texture of queer relajo helps me interrupt the dehumanizing and commodifying lenses of scholarship, as it pushes me out of a passive place of observation and extraction, into collaborative processes of playful action and participation, like those discussed in "Part II, Fumbling Toward Urban Nightscapes." In chapter 3, "Play, Sex, and Dance in the Queer Underground," I consider how queer dance, erotic play, and m4m sex reshape Mexico City's underground subway infrastructures through the urban manifestations of queer relajo like jostle and friction. By tracing queer and trans playful interactions inside subway lines in Lia García's performance *Próxima Estación: Mis XXy años*, and in amateur porn videos of subway m4m sex, I argue that dancing and cruising assemble *choreographies of touch*, making bodies, feelings, and places stick together to circumvent a neoliberal logic of efficient re/production, as well as Euro-American sexual paradigms of queer- and transness. By later comparing the photography of David Graham's *The Last Car: Cruising in Mexico City* (2017) and Mexico City-based artist Eriko Stark's *Furias Nocturnas* (2022), I expose the exploitation of narratives about a pre-modern and backward sexuality found in the global south. Reflecting on my own memories of cruising and playing in the subway, the concept of *queer underground* emerges to name alternative circuits of queer connection beyond neoliberal capture.

Those partaking in queer relajo resist the commodification of urban space by holding on to old tapes, scripts, and pictures. By expressly refusing to accept a privatized version of queer life, they insist on a politics of presence extending beyond nighttime. Like Piña Colada's shuffling of family photos in Part I, I am interested in tracing how the sensations and feelings evoked when interacting with the lively records of queer/trans nightlife carry residues, traces, sparks, and specks—like a sequin piece, a lipstick mark, a wig, a tune, a phone number, a dance move, a hangover, a crush, a tear, or a bruise—leave their marks on Part II's second half. In chapter 4, "Reflections of a City's Nightscapes," I tease out how Mexico City's queer nightscapes produce an *afterglow*—a residual force lingering after dark—that challenges the neoliberal futures imagined in mainstream Mexican media. Attending to the spores of queer/trans urban encounters, afterglow sheds light on a politics of queer and trans presence, revealing how rhythms of pleasure can resist capitalist extraction while sparking a sense of hope for queer and trans intimacy in broad daylight. I begin by showing how a Televisa's *Solidaridad* video transmits a vision of an ostensibly unified future that reproduces white mestizaje's neoliberal nationalism.

I then turn to three narrative and documentary films that center Mexico City's poor and working-class queer nightlife to show how they follow an afterglow that unsettles a white neoliberal nationalist sentiment in the *Solidaridad* video. First, Julián Hernández's *Mil nubes de paz* (2003) reveals how the afterglow of Brown working-class queer nighttime encounters makes white queer neoliberalism sweat with anxiety by locating belonging in the continual presence and repeated impossibility of longing, waiting, and cruising. I then show how in Roberto Fiesco's *Quebranto (2013)*, the protagonist Coral's refusal to dispose of (and indeed her cherishing of) objects from her travesti nights challenges the temporality of neoliberal nationalism: her inventory of objects embodies a travesti praxis of survival that brings back what seems to be lost and insists on a politics of presence amid urban displacement and gentrification. Finally, I track how Maya Goded's *Plaza de la Soledad* (2016) centers Mexico City's shadow economies to highlight how the people within them repurpose urban infrastructures to refuse gentrification and commodification, making possible queer worlds from below. Together, these films insist on a queer presence that exists out of touch with neoliberal logics of hetero- and homonormativity.

More than inert objects of cultural representation, these lively artifacts enact ways of toying, playing, and replaying, to sense out a strand of queer/

trans worldmaking, complicating affective economies of white modernity in postcolonial contexts. *Queer Relajo* thus tunes into the vitality of queer and trans cultural artifacts by expanding on their animacy, as these carry a life of their own. They are not only full of stories, but also of enactments, affects, and dispositions that invite us to feel the night otherwise in its rawness, enwrapped in all fantasies and dangers.

A method of queer relajo flirts with our intellectual curiosity by questioning conventional and utilitarian boundaries shaping the production of space, as well as the space of production, while laughing at the absurdities of rigidity.[15] As blissful lessons in queer pedagogy, sensorial readings nonetheless foster a place for intimacy, feeling, and belonging amid violence. At the transdisciplinary intersection of fields, queer relajo allows us to reconsider what constitutes knowledge, how knowledge is produced through play, feeling, and sensing, and how queer play can take hold of space—academic or otherwise. Because of its reconsideration of place and value, queer relajo emerges as a method for queer cultural analysis that embraces a hemispheric, diasporic, and reterritorialized sensorium harkening to feelings, affects, smells, sounds, textures, visions, and intuitions attached to the racialized and gendered inhabitations of sexual dissidence. Queer relajo as method breaks the illusion of containment, manifesting a disruptive form of intimacy when interacting with these artifacts. For instance, we make kin with a group of elderly sex workers that sing along with La Sonora Santanera's "Amor de cabaret," through a film screened inside a university classroom. Queer relajo thus makes us come into real contact with economies of production, as well as with obstacles that limit and hinder underground circuits of queer knowledge production in the Americas.

Into Queer Nightscapes

While shunning an optic obsession with corruption, death, and violence, as signs of underdevelopment in Mexico, a method inspired in the performances of queer relajo allows me to let loose queer nightlife ambiances, or *queer nightscapes*, across time and place. Amid Mexico City's complex state-driven commodification and privatization of queer urban life, the term queer nightscapes names underground, fleeting fields of action and feeling moving across space like the revolving diffractions of a mirrorball. Nightscapes describe intimate flows of affect emerging from queer nightlife circuits, as they jump from bodies into objects, from rhythms into embraces moving across enclosed, commodified, and privatized spaces, to open them up, blurring the lines between capitalist privacy and consumerist commons.

Tracing the intensities and modulations mediating encounters across dance floors, cruising grounds, or nightclub stages, and their labored conversion into cultural artifacts like film, digital media, visual art, cultural performance, and performance art, to mention a few, queer nightscapes refer to a shifting queer infrastructure of sociality. Queer nightscapes trace how instances of queer relajo, like longing, waiting, touching, cruising, singing, and dancing, or "the situated moments wherein infrastructures impinge on social relations, and the unsettling, affective and 'marvelous' dimensions of these relationships" (Harvey and Knox 2012, 525), reattune our senses to feel and move through space otherwise, prompting a different urban consciousness (Monsiváis 2010, 266). In doing so, nightscapes enact queer modes of fugitivity, informality, illicitness, and unintelligibility to reconsider how the various fields, scales, and textures of queer/trans play grapple with the manifestations of neoliberal violence. Unlike queer impressions of utopia, queer nightscapes emerge as fleeting landscapes of sensation that, taking over subway corridors, downtown streets, open plazas, or rural town fairs, reminds us that playfulness and joy can and does happen even in the darkest of times.

While corporations gentrifying Mexico City's downtown core rely on a discourse of danger and chaos to disenfranchise working-class economic practices of survival to protect their interests in revitalizing and maintaining downtown's cultural heritage (Moctezuma Mendoza, 2021), queer nightscapes illuminate a politics of urban space by highlighting alternative circuits of consumption that rely on popular, working-class dynamics shaping queer economics of exchange, recycle, and reciprocity. That is to say that alternative queer spaces for economically-marginalized queer and trans folks rest on shadow economies—informal, underground networks of consumption—that function through small-scale affective and economic transactions beyond neoliberal terms. Exposing how urban displacement is multimodal and affectively gradient in these scenarios, queer nightscapes activate reparative circuits of joyful care and playful healing for queer and trans folk alongside systems of debt, oppression, and feminized labor.

For working-class people living in downtown Mexico City, displacement not only translates into experiencing spatial loss, but also into feeling the "evanescing presence of unbelonging and deterritorialization" (Moct-ezuma Mendoza, 2021). In this sense, the feeling of displacement makes it seem like urban queer space is an exclusive zone available to those with adequate socioeconomic resources, whereby mostly white gay male mes-tizos can afford access to queer pleasure. Erupting as joyful happenstances across urban space, queer nightscapes affectively restructure and alter access to existing zones of queer contact under neoliberal reform, reshap-ing utilitarian understandings of what nightlife can allow us to do, while unsettling how spatial designs are reinhabited and refashioned. As such, queer nightscapes unsettle set perceptions of public space, broadening the very limits of queer/trans nightlife. While shaped by play and pleasure, queer nightscapes not only "engage complex combinations of objects, spaces, persons and practices," but also assemble provisional platforms "providing for and reproducing" queer/trans life in the city (Simone 2004, 407–8). Queer nightscapes thus bring into focus the affective mediation with the infrastructures and ambiances where the excess of queer feelings move through the erotic economies, cultural artifacts, and social geogra-phies of nightlife in Mexico.

I am by no means suggesting that all urban space restricts the free tran-sit of queer/trans folk, or that alternative sites for queer/trans intimacy are nonexistent or inherently reparative. Rather, I highlight how nightscapes rely on contingent and improvised practices of queer relajo to block eco-nomic capture and extraction, while saturating the neoliberal mechanisms commodifying queerness as palatable. In doing so, queer nightscapes foreground the affective operations that "contest and sometimes even sub-vert the imagined worlds of the official mind and of the entrepreneurial mentality that surround them" (Appadurai 1996, 33).[16] Choreographing a working-class queer underground in Mexico City, like the one emerg-ing from playful acts of subway cruising, touching, and dancing discussed in Part II, queer nightscapes negotiate privatization and commodification through intensities, modulations, attunements, and attachments under neoliberal capitalism.

In neoliberal economies of late capitalism, a safe queer/trans future in nationalistic terms is not only affectively impossible but financially unten-able, as it remains contingent on the ability to accumulate capital, a para-doxical task for those who already perform feminized, precarious forms of labor in postcolonial contexts. By connecting how the feminization of labor driving neoliberal relationality affects queer/trans vitality, "the femi-nist movement has demonstrated how the precarity caused by neoliberal policies constitutes a specific economy of violence in which feminicide and travesticides are its culminating scene" (Cavallero and Gago 2021) not just in Mexico but across the Americas. Extraction, dispossession, and feminized labor not only conform to an arsenal of capitalist operations but define some tenets of a neoliberal relationality affecting queer and trans ways of life.

In this book, I borrow from fugitive modes of betrayal, disloyalty, and disavowal in resonance with a praxis of transfeminism, "to thus inhabit the fugitive spirit of this un/gendering is to incite a radically different way of living. It is a secretive and shadowy force that presents the conditions of possibility for possibility" (Bey 2022, 81). Alongside the liminality of transness, queer nightscapes fold in hemispheric gestures of queerness and travestismo to an "already (and always) . . . transgressive motion" (85) across fields of feeling. As "Part III. The Shade and Shadow of Travesti Nightlife" shows, queer nightscapes manifest the chimerical repertoires that bring colloquial understandings of travesti and trans becoming into action as life and death is negotiated on screens, out in the streets, and on the bodies of the night.

In chapter 5, "The Shadowy Frames of Travesti Nightlife," I argue that the re/presentation of travesti vitality, or ways of being and becoming travesti, in Mexico's queer culture has been eclipsed and overshadowed by the emergence of a neoliberal homonational subject. Although visually apparent, this shadowing effect can be traced in the film *El lugar sin límites* (1978), the web series *La Casa de las Flores* (2018), and the film *El Baile de los 41* (2020). By drawing on the mediatic on-screen presentation of travesti becoming, I aim at locating a visuality relying on their necropolitical conversion extending off-screen, casting a *fatal frame* that places the emergence of a proto-travesti identity in the shadows. This visual code helps maintain a tension between homosexuality and machismo, that is, a homosocial temperament that, despite its disdain for homoeroticism, defines the interrelation of gender, sexuality, race, and class within a heteronormative neoliberal social grid.

In this sense, queer nightscapes make evident the modulations of travesti identity, as their embodiments move through a gradient tonality between light and shadow. Modulating between shade and shine, or moving through hypervisibility, and invisibility, defines the cultural representation of travesti embodiments, further situating fugitive modes of trans relationality to negotiate capitalist capture. In chapter 6, "The Kaleidoscope of Travesti Nightlife in Casa Roshell," I perform a playful reading of Camila José Donoso's docufictional film *Casa Roshell* (2017) to tap into travesti women's worldmaking capacities at a working-class nightclub and cabaret. While the defining underground character of the cabaret later becomes entangled in and commodified by the media economies of television and online streaming in the early twenty-first century, as discussed in Part III, the queerness of the cabaret, or the places and feelings of queer nightlife, remain a source of transformational potential to challenge the violent hypersexualization of femme bodies, the abuses of political power, and the cruel nightmares of neoliberal nationalism.[17] While not all my analysis is about the cabaret per se, queer nightscapes carry a "feeling of kitsch" (Monsiváis 2006, 7) through which we wander around all night long, yearning to touch, seeking respite at the dance floor, and suddenly find joyful excitement to resist the productive use of time inside the worn-down walls of a hidden queer bar like Casa Roshell.

Chapter 6 further considers the practices of performance taking place in a Mexico City travesti cabaret/nightclub, to examine how Casa Roshell's collective grapples with the powerful forces of dance and movement, to embody tactics of survival that help undo and cope with the trans necropolitics of urban nightlife. Namely, I argue that Donoso's docufiction tracks sounds, whispers, lights, conversations, and changes of everynight interactions, mimicking a galactic feeling, an outer worldliness reflected onto the screen. Such affective interrelations flee the eye of hetero-cis neoliberal rationality while collaborating in a shared night space for travesti worldmaking through its evanescing splendor. Borrowing from Piña Colada's intimate encounters at Casa Roshell, specifically discussed in Part I, this chapter closes with a *Nightlife Travesti-festo* guiding clubgoers, both from in and out of the film, to engage with the nightly modulations of travesti becoming.

While moving across Casa Roshell's stage, Piña Colada struggles to find a balance so that I don't trip and fall during our performance. The 14-inch red stilettos I wear were purchased in the US, and while feeling the paralyzing pain in my feet, I turn again to the mirrorball. In this instance, I think of how difficult it might be for travesti and trans women to walk Mexico City's patchy streets in this type of shoes. Most importantly, wearing these shoes makes me reflect on the difficulties travesti and trans feminists in the global south must face when trying to walk in the stilted shoes of white feminism, performing a doubly feminized form of labor by trying to be legible to the liberal agenda of whiteness, while engaging in feminist work beyond the whitened walls of academia.

By focusing on queer affective economies in the global south, I decenter a US-based queer optic located within the geopolitical configurations of white feminism in the Americas. I thus propose a transfeminist praxis through which value is remade, juggling with commodification, and extraction, while accounting for the multiple and contested unfolding of neoliberal capitalism, as its redistributions adapt to transregional specificities and locations (Bohrer 2020, 537).[18] In this sense, *Queer Relajo* repositions queer nightlife as a transfeminist issue, centering on an anticapitalist transfeminist praxis "against a profound internalized colonization" evident in the very naming of queer Mexicanidad (Moraga 2011, 149). By a popular transfeminist praxis, I refer to mundane, ordinary acts and nightly negotiations occurring within and alongside working-class, migrant, gendered, and racialized spheres sustaining the infrastructures of whiteness under neoliberal capitalism in Mexico.[19]

Drawing from feminist understandings of capitalist gain and resource extraction (Arruzza, Bhattacharya, and Fraser 2019; Brown 2019; Hartman 2008; Gago 2020; Galindo 2021; Mohanty 2003; Segato 2022; Valencia 2018; Wark 2019), my hemispheric lens of transfeminism fathoms queer nightlife as a produced space that intersects various social, economic, political, and affective spheres, not only pushing against the labored division of private/public, of feeling/thinking, but also recognizing the political struggles centering the right to fun, pleasure, and leisure for already exploited and economically precarious subject positions like migrants, sex workers, trans/queer folk, Indigenous, Black, Brown, and other racialized minorities. Under a transfeminist lens, play and pleasure are not perceived as individually private endeavors, but rather focus on collective and mutual forms of caring and healing. Demanding a right to public space, as well as recognizing a sensual engagement with the world—through its aromas, textures, attunements, modulations, and structures—are central to a feminist rush for nightlife. Queer nightscapes make evident a queer politics of intimacy to feel what is missing and try to make up for what has been taken away by the violence of heteropatriarchal neoliberalism.

I thus consider queer tactics that play affectively and materially to minimize the "ways [in which] neoliberal sexuality and the sexual capital . . . contribute to reproducing capitalism" (Kaplan and Illouz 2022, 18). A popular transfeminist praxis calls attention to how queer relajo enacts ordinary negotiations with the precarity of life under neoliberal capitalism, which "has as much to do with Walmart, *maquiladoras*, and microcredit as with Silicon Valley and Google. And its indispensable workers are disproportionately women, not only young single women, but also married women with children; not only racialized women, but women of virtually all nationalities and ethnicities" (Fraser 2013, 220). If "a new mode of domination" (Fraser 2013, 225) benefits from feminized positions of labor, a hemispheric transfeminist praxis highlights how situated forms of queer agency can get around neoliberal forms of oppression and indeed alter the "processes of production and reproduction of life" across "the differential[s] of exploitation" (Cavallero and Gago 2021). Embedded in a playful method of queer analysis, a transfeminist praxis recognizes the interrelations between sexual capital, racial formations, and glocal histories of neoliberal expansion, configuring a diasporic "framework that produces new models of cross-cultural understanding about queer sexuality" (Lim 2005, 387).[20] *Queer Relajo* thus reconsiders the grades of agency in recognizing how play and pleasure are intrinsic to a transfeminist praxis.

When the arrival of a better future fades away, a transfeminist praxis might disrupt cishet systems of value, twisting around a neoliberal relationality to give back stolen queer/trans vitality, and ultimately fend off forms of economic violence. By refusing heteronormative and neoliberal values of the future, *Queer Relajo* highlights the electric charges of sensation and feeling that take place during nightlife. In doing so, this book insists less on a liberal sense of agency tethered to capital, property, and individual rights, than on an erotic sovereignty resisting exclusionary visions of time and space, through which the abuse, misuse, and overuse of power has historically inflicted irreparable wounds. Ultimately, *Queer Relajo* recognizes the existence of multiple worlds interacting all at once, gesturing toward other terms of engagement and practices of consent, that do not prey on the exoticization of minoritarian becoming, but find a restorative potential in their fondling with night-making.

As Piña Colada ends her performance with arms up in the air, the mirrorball stops spinning around. Leaving us in the shadows. Piña Colada grabs the microphone. Her echoes sound across this book. Extending you the warmest of welcomes, Piña Colada and I look right into your eyes, and shout in unison,

Damas y caballeros, jotas, jotitas y jototas,
vestidas, inventadas, panzonas, lenchas, chacalonas y chingonas,
¡Buenas noches! Good evening!
Unbuckle and let loose in the mist of queer nightscapes.

PART I

Dragging Mexicanidad

ONE

The Chromatic Axis of Piña Colada

This chapter delves into the complications of piecing this book as an itinerant jota moving across queer hemispheric diasporas in the US. Composed of fragments, impressions, and traces on the page, this chapter is thus a queer incursion into the modalities of drag performance through my drag persona, *Piña Colada,* who emerges at a critical juncture of displacement, queer femininity, and academia. From childhood encounters with Mexican culture to the pedragogy—an explanation of the use of this concept is coming up in a few pages—experienced in a diasporic movement between Pittsburgh and Mexico City, Piña Colada reveals the productive tension that destabilizes and subverts white modernity and neoliberal capitalism through processes of queer homemaking, worldmaking, and belonging continually recreated and reconfigured amid imperfection and uncertainty. Piña Colada's story thus traces queer relajo through the X in Latinx and drag culture, mapping how drag performance condenses a similar destabilizing force to the X in Latinx, that is, drag not only evokes a constant state of reconfiguration, situated materially in crowns, dresses, and makeup, but situates queer modes of relation and connection across different nightlife spaces.

Through feminist storytelling, autoethnographic vignettes, and community multimedia archiving, namely family stories, pictures, and experimental drag performance and visual records, drag emerges as a reconfiguration of a fleeting subject assembled in the dispersed geographies of the Mexican diaspora in the US. Drag performance, I contend, extends a transfeminist recalibration of the world through a distinct fondling with bodies, objects, and feelings. As such, my drag performance crisscrosses borders, nightlife geographies, and audiences, not only to localize a dark, Brown affect, but also to center practices that shape and give meaning to diasporic queer subjects. Singing along, rubbing, touching, and standing in at the club, rehearse ephemeral practices that sustain drag performance, which in turn, give life to a feeling that helps wipe off the white (tone-deaf) affect of neoliberal capitalism.

The X on My Ass

Piña Colada:

Yet another polyp cock-blocking my ass; its fleshy disruption makes me, somehow, appear more appealing to those masc guys looking for a "virginal" hole to fuck. It's funny to think about what people assume an ass to be. Some see in it a place of death and excretion, where all unwanted excess is disposed. Others define it as a dead end, particularly for the macho imagination, in which a penetrated ass deflates the masculine embodiment of Mexicanidad. But my ass is a sacred place, not a grave, not a dead end, but a riveting Brown asterisk full of possibilities, textures, and sensations. It is a dark site of connection where the carnal enveloping of others refuses an act of possession, but fosters a cumming together, a liquid binding in the flesh.

"Latinx is not for everyone," argues Alan Pelaez Lopez to confront the multiple Latin American diasporas in the US with the indelible marks of the racism and classicism at the heart of national attachment and belonging. This confrontation, however, has sparked a serious debate within the trans and queer ranks of the diasporas around "the practical use" of the term Latinx. Inspired by the dialogue held with Nigerian storyteller, Kemi Bello, Pelaez Lopez regards "the X as a scar that exposes four wounds," namely "settlement, anti-Blackness, feminicides, and inarticulation" (2018). In other words, the X marks post/colonial and neoliberal forms of violence, erasure, indenture, and capture.

It would be nice to think that such wounds are now part of the past, that our liberal democracies have eradicated the root of all evil, brought to justice those who have consistently abused power, and that by now, have restored, repaired, and restituted ordinarily sacred ways of being and living across the Americas. But the many realities around us have proven and continue to prove otherwise. In the US, the X awakens huge contradictions, heated debates, and civil derision as part of a political strategy within twenty-first century culture wars. At their core lies the multiple diasporas, including the Mexican one, living, breathing, and working in the US. Drawing a fine line, each intersecting axis forming an X holds the tension between identity and belonging, where affective strands of national belonging clash and run through the paralyzing violence of whitened nationalist projects. The "anti-Blackness" mentioned in Alan Pelaez Lopez's writing is real, as is the violence against minoritarian Brown subjects. In other words, the X not only poses an uncomfortable question as to what the US social fabric is, but also prompts a huge enigma as to what place does the X occupy in relation to Mexico, and by extension Latin America and the Caribbean.

Latinxs carry within themselves the very contradictions of failed nation-building projects of (white) modernity, as each romantic evocation of the motherland in the present, through the vast diasporic cultural practices, reinscribes the social circuits of violence sustaining the fantasy of the nation. This romantic hologram also operates transnationally, reproducing at times, similar racial, gender, and class dynamics inherent to the (white) nation. The case of the Mexican diaspora, however, is not unique, as we continue to see how those who hold a proximity to whiteness also carry a privilege that translates into easier passage through and across geopolitical borders.

In my current location, as a diasporic queer of color, working in US academia, the X offers a productive tension in a new configuration between American Ethnic Studies and Mexican Studies, a new formation where X is an inherent site of LatinXamerica. At a time when Departments of Spanish and Portuguese, which stand in the US academy as intellectual sites in charge of studying and producing knowledge about Mexican, Latin American, and Caribbean cultural realities, as well as their diasporas in the US, continue to operate through and within a colonial "white settler" framework, an epistemological move and shift is far from urgent but vitally necessary, to imagine a critical dance across disciplines as well as a choreography of methods that respond to the pressing sociocultural contradictions in the intermingling of ethnicity, race, gender, sexuality, citizenship, immigration status, labor, capital, and the nation-state across the Americas.

What can queer nightlife and queer/trans jotas across the Mexican diaspora offer to this intermingling dance? For starters, our presence in the conventional echelons of the lettered city and its post-structuralist school of thought along its textual tyranny, must continue to cause discomfort and disruption. Our bodies serve as living proof of the resistance

Fig. 1. Piña Colada poses, wearing a colorful crown. Photo by Adriana Sánchez-Solis, 2023.

against structural surveillance, exploitation, and death, which many of us endure to exist in a place that we very well know only tolerates difference but exploits and commodifies it in the name of diversity, inclusion, progress, and (white) democracy. Conventional ways of approaching Mexican Studies from a humanistic stance continue to flatten existing sociocultural complexities to issues of literary representation, reducing g-local agencies, or attempts to collaborate with collectives doing so, to traditional forms, genres, and contents, furthering an epistemological violence that turns the vitality of cultural practices into mere objects of study for western eyes. The reality is that many US-based scholars talking, writing, and making a living about the complex cultural realities happening across the many Mexicos, from a humanistic and cultural lens, not only lack a research ethic, but also live and are far removed from every day and ordinary manifestations in which cultural practice is not an object of study to be dissected but a way of negotiating life and death.

Already occupying a marginal space within the cishet structures of academia, queer and trans nightlife practices offer a reformulation of the ways, methods, and approaches to a new meXican studies, where the X holds the place of contradiction, a contradiction that both eliminates yet enriches simple conclusions and deductions about the Mexican diasporic condition, which is after all at the very core necessary to complicate the Mexican condition. Indeed, X points to multiple deaths and erasures; it brings to life the continual absences in the naming of a political project resting on the whitening technology of mestizaje, the fatal armory of macho patriarchy, and the gender- and racial-based violence in Mexico. The riveting axis of an X thus dislodges a rationalizing logic seeking to give unity to a sociocultural and political site that currently sits in shambles, holding political in-fighting for power.

Piña Colada:

X in sex is about intersection, about the possibilities my shiny ass holds at night. Sex is like crossing a bridge into the unknown. You don't know what patiently throbs inside those clothes. X awakens a queer sense of wonder, as I cross into a new body, territory, or flesh. In that crossing I am no longer what I have been envisioning of myself. I am rendered void, but not because I hold no value or meaning, but because I let go and merge into the folds of ecstasy and unwavering touch. X is a reminder that sensing can only be transformative when bodies lay

*against each other, crossing into fantasies, where they melt into one
another, and the boundaries of oneself are blurred, if only for a night.*

*It is 3:00 a.m. An overflowing stream of eclectic sounds wave into
Calle Amberes in Zona Rosa, one of many queer night ecologies within
Mexico City, the one known to open the gates of queer excess. A street
stand selling candies, cigarettes, and if you are lucky, even condoms,
is a point of queer communion, while the music of Ana Gabriel plays
in the background alongside Britney Spear's voice chanting "hit me
baby." One more time, all vanishes with the smoke of cigarettes. A rat
crossing the street, neon lights lighting up a sex shop billboard . . . The
night dims the blinding reflector of everyday life, to cast in all beautiful
imperfections. The night drips down its gown. On its glittery tail lives an
expansive ecology, a breathing territory of feeling that excites the senses:
vibrations, rhythms, whispers, silences, touches, and vapors hover over
the dance floor. Outside the smell of fried food, of quesadillas, of tacos,
of fritanga, awaits overexcited clubgoers. The night opens a darkroom
of possibilities. A cramped room where interactions and encounters
between matters, objects, shades, and spectra, take place. In the distance, the jingle of two earrings clapping against each other mark the
tempo of a travesti's walk. Shiny objects leave a long-lasting print on a
drag queen's stitched night dress. Their glow leaves behind a specter hard
to grasp, but affectively, intimately, I know I carry it within me. Later,
that same glow lights up a queer sense of meaning while I stand in a
corner, searching for a soft caress, cruising for fugitive SEXXX.*

The playful arrangement of meXican is joined at the center by a large
X, forming a sort of bridge connecting two seemingly distant cultural territories: meX and Xican. The former might condense a coded genealogy
mapping conquest, contact, and contention; the latter might stand for
continuity, connection, and renewal. Mexican and Xicanx/a/o are joined
by the hip by an X, sutured by the unspeakable violence of border crossings. Beyond neoliberal scriptures of citizenship and surveillance, there
is great commonality. We both cry, we both suffer, but we also know how
to party, how to escape through the playfulness of the night. It is a way of
resisting the inclemency of tomorrow's daylight. The X embodies a sign of
pause, a sign waiting to be sung and played with. Once spinning, it cannot be stopped, but becomes contagious with mobility, with crossing, with
movement.

A festive disposition in the arrangement of an X echoes what Anita

Tijerina Revilla and José Manuel Santillana call "Jotería identity and consciousness," a multidimensional commitment to social justice and activism "rooted in fun, laughter, and radical queer love" (2014, 174). By outlining some queer characteristics of a Latinx and Chicanx jotería consciousness, Tijerina Revilla and Santillana bridge their personal stories as queer Latinx and Chicanx with their scholar-activist practice to claim queer of color (dark, Black, Brown, and Indigenous) immigrant and working-class lives and experiences as alternative sources of knowledge and empowerment. Rejecting the violent logics of academic extraction and epistemic violence in the twenty-first century, Xamuel Bañales signals that "Jotería as a political project values and creates new forms of knowledge, particularly coming from below and from ourselves, our various families, communities, ancestors, and histories" (2014, 160). Mobilizing nightlife practices across regions, jotería shapes a way of being in the world for diasporic queers and trans folk across Mexico and the US. Jotería evokes dissonance and consonance, dispersing fantasies that are felt through night practices assembling a fleeting queer underground. Performing jotería thus reveals the affective economies attached to bridging queer forms of (un)belonging and intimacy across time, space, and region, suspending and underwriting dominant regimes of sensation dispersed across homonationalism, heterosexuality, patriarchy, and capitalism.

Piña Colada:

After dancing exhaustively, I suddenly realized that my purse was sacked, and my cellphone stolen. I stand disoriented outside Candy Bar. I feel anxious. My need for control, which deep inside, lies as an irresolute fear of life, of remaining open and flexible to the unexpected eventualities of every night life, kicks in. No phone, no self. What seems to hold value suddenly stops to matter. What's the purpose of holding a smartphone at the club? No connectivity to check for potential hookups through cruising apps? What stops us from learning how to follow gestures and become versed in the choreographies of flirtation? There are certainly other forms of sustenance, of finding connection. What if my ass was that big X of connectivity? What if what we understood as value was something else? Not in a utilitarian or an economic sense, but something different that sustains life, like a name that spells our yearning for connection. Would it be "value" as we know it? How about naming it after a vital force that makes things matter?

I feel my body pulsating. I sense a river running through my veins, reaching out to the farthest confines of my soul, traveling across, from head to toe, from mind to heart, throbbing in my ass.

What would writing, academic writing be like, if we were to turn our attention to basic vital forces that drive our yearning to touch, our longing for connection and knowing? Would that type of writing be seen and perceived under a different lens of value? Would our sustained emotions and sensations be considered "rational" enough to be worthy of our "scholarly" attention?

If queer nightlife shows us how little things come to matter and how big stuff does not hold as much value as we'd like it to hold, writing about queer nightlife would smear in the specks, stains, and smudges of the night. How can we thus subvert, challenge, and avoid that type of academic writing that seems to hold the most value? If queerness is a messy contingence, a playful making and a lustful unmaking; ephemera, horizons, senses, as José Esteban Muñoz would call it, how would queer writing, or rather writing about queer stuff, unmake or lessen what holds academic value? In other words, what kind of academic value do I let go of when engaging in queer nightlife, and when I let a feeling in from my ass? I stand in disorientation; my compass is a fleshy ass-terisk, an embodied artifact that guides me through nightly unknowns, gravitating toward a vulgar phenomenology of dallying experiences, sparking a night sensorium only accessible through queer disorientation.

Dissonance sounds through and through Miguel Gutierrez's collab performance *This Bridge Called My Ass* (2018), which features broken clichéd Spanish songs, synth sounds, cables, and blankets, that roll in a felt sameness. Alongside five Latinx performers, including John Gutierrez, Xandra Ibarra, nibia pastrana santiago, and Evelyn Sanchez Narvaez, Gutierrez's experimental performance plays on Cherríe Moraga and Gloria Anzaldúa's seminal 1981 anthology of feminist writings *This Bridge Called My Back*. Rather than standing in opposition to Moraga's and Anzaldúa's queer intersectionality, Gutierrez expands on "the limitations of discourse to imagine new ways of being together," moving from an identity-based politics to a queer sensorial re-attunement, as tongue twisters reveal that objects, music, and bodies appear as extensions of one another. Although critical of Moraga's utopian identity politics, the performance bears naked a need for connection, for a carnal enrapture echoing Cherríe Moraga's queer Brown politics, a "[Queer] "Aztlán" as our imagined homeland . . . a nation strong enough to embrace a full range of racial diversities, human sexualities, and expressions of gender" (2004, 235). As such, the collab stirs up a radical politics rooted in minoritarian sexual cultures, while inviting the audience to embrace a hemispheric sexual critique that finds queer resistance in disarticulation, dissonance, and unbelonging.

This Bridge Called My Ass focuses on the laboring body, and particularly on the role of sensation, located in the metaphor of the ass, to highlight how the body is but a powerful energetic device in charge of establishing connection. If queer worldmaking is about affective connections with others—human or otherwise—the sensorial is thus also political. While six naked performers crouch on all fours, forming a distinct doggy style, their butts raise high up like an antenna, embodying a connection that renders the ass a receptor of the world. Under Gutierrez's *ass*ertion, the X, as point of contact, is less a marker of identity than a synthesizer of sensation. Performing a bold gesture against a politics of colonial assimilation like Gutierrez, Mexican writer Alfonso Reyes found in the "x" an itinerant crossroads, a dark spot through which a new contradictory yet converging path can indeed begin. Entitled "X on the Forehead" (1952), Reyes's collection of essays expounds and defends the use of the "x" over the "j", to spell out Mexican identity. In this sense, it is my ass that both, signifies, and embodies, a path for connection, but one that leads to the unknown, to the risks that must be welcomed to receive the night with a sense of queer wonder. That is why I prance with the X on my ass.

"LatinX is tinged with doubt," Latinx Studies scholar Claudia Milian reminds us. The instability of "X," Milian argues, "generates a continuous rethinking of networks and relations. X assemblages reconstitute themselves. X is a possibility for exploring the unknown and the peculiar and for thinking through new political moments, geographies outside the Americas, and subject formations" (2019, 6). "The x" also "turns away from the dichotomous, toward a void, an unknown, a wrestling with plurality, vectors of multi-intentionality, and the transitional meanings of what has yet to be seen" (Gómez-Barris and Fiol-Matta, 504, in Milian 2019, 19). Doubt, pain, joy, and hope can condense some of the feelings evoked by the revolving axis of an everchanging X still in formation. Despite the unrelenting speed characterizing life under neoliberal capitalism, the quality of fast transformation and renewal seems only open to certain subjects, particularly to the amorphous subjects of whiteness, while racialized minoritarian transformation sparks a generalized anxiety evident, for instance, in Arkansas Governor Sarah Huckabee Sanders's abrupt banning of "Latinx" in 2023. Even more, the quality of such rapid (white) transformation is usually indexed to qualifiers of "innovation," "value," or "development," complicating the materialization of any future incessantly striving for "life, liberty, and the pursuit of happiness." X marks multiple intersections and constant reconfigurations, as well as an interrogation of Latinidad, as two powerful axes riveting to create a sort of queer mechanics impel unfathomable change.

The anxiety provoked by the possibilities of X presupposes that Latinx is a destabilizing minoritarian force, gesturing toward a transfiguration of life as we know it. Milian further expands on such transubstantiation, "different self-imaginings dissolve and are put together again in this mixxxxx-and-match (or, mixxxxx-and-patch). Ways of living and being alive are invigorated: Xs are activated through sensorial experiences, chaotic sounds, wandering melodies, and visuals" (2019, 22). X realizes an unknown possibility that for many queer and trans Latinxs in the US is reminiscent of a radical project of liberation. But queer/trans futurity does not have a place in the grand narratives of (new) nationalist or imperialist becoming, or in the safeguards of marriage equality, or in the transactional operations of identity, but rather in the everyday interactions with sentient beings around us, as well as in the daily operations that require us to engage with the world and implicate ourselves in full body, heart, and spirit. The legacy of queer/trans theorizing around futurity precisely insists on the very questioning of linear, or straight, trajectories of progress and development (Halberstam 2005; Edelman 2004; Freeman 2010; Muñoz 2009; Puar 2007; Ahmed 2010), as well as the heterosexuality embedded in the very visions of imagining an apparently radical futurity.

X reminds us that queer/trans liberation can only occur in crime with other minoritarian intersections, experiences, and formations that have also endured the violence of erasure. But X also inaugurates a huge conundrum for the vitality of queer/trans Latinxs. Amid the ongoing extermination of queer/trans Brown and Black life, how does X allow us to mobilize in action and seek alternatives for relational vibrance and sensual connection while dodging the circuits of necrocapital? This question prompts me to tap into a pool of queer resilience found in my memories of queer femininity.

Piña Colada: Pineapple, Coconut, Glitter, and Rum

My cousin Tomasito persuades me into climbing the stairs of Club 69, a second-floor queer club near Eje Central and Bellas Artes. After some drinks and a couple of turned-down dance invitations, I begin to feel the humidity steaming from the dance floor. On a regular night, the DJ plays a mix of quebradita, salsa, bachata, pop, and ranchera, urging clubgoers to dance the night away. Skilled dancers usually begin swinging around, pulling shy on-watchers into the open dance floor. You can feel that peculiar Mexico City vibe swaying bodies into musical action. No one really knows how the dancing happens, but people seem to naturally follow the rhythm of the songs. Scattered tables and random people start conversing, a room full of strangers suddenly turns into a large family living room, where people banter, laugh, and cheer as acts of connection through song and music. A bucket of beers is dropped atop our table. Like the flow of music, beer also runs through my system. Tomasito pulls out a cigarette. While lighting it up, he pokes fun by asking me to say, again and again, what I had in mind. His face turns red when I pull him out of the table and take him into the dressing room where tonight's drag performers are getting ready.

At the club everything can fade away into the night, or anything can happen. It is a gentle reminder of the night's shimmering possibilities. More than a platonic relationship, Tomasito and I share a maternal love. We usually refer to each other using feminine pronouns, to allow for a charged affectivity to not interfere with a subdued masculinity. For some Mexican men, expressing emotion is a matter of faggots, and not of real, real men. But the love we both share transcends any categories and manifests into signs of care and tenderness. His 6-foot figure often offers me unwavering protection when walking at night like across the streets of Colonia Doctores or Plaza Garibaldi. Few really know how to walk Mexico City, as the megapolis can throw its incantations and distractions as a sort of self-defense mechanism, to fend off any attempt to really get to its core. The city offers many traps where many get lost in its deadly sins, from gluttony to lust, from pride to sloth and greed. To be simply honest, I often feel enwrapped by the urge to eat and fuck while I am there. But tonight, Tomasito and I give into other excesses and dance away with fellow clubgoers. Kissing, hugging, drinking seems to be an improvised code of queer nightlife. Once the multiple buckets of beer are absorbed, I turn to the dangerous practice of cocktail mixing. At around midnight, the waves of piña coladas start pouring onto our table.

A warm heat offers some comfort from the coolness of the night. We are all brewing inside but rest glad in the agitation of the nightclub. Dancing, drinking, smoking. Tomasito talks to me about his latest love affair. I call him, "madre." He calls me "hija." We fondly remember the occasions when I used to laugh aloud as a kid, usually making fun of family drama. In the roar of the night, Tomasito brings in a sense of calmness, as every time I see him, I can feel the soft hands of his mother, Tía Patty, combing my hair. Tomasito brings me closer to home, as he reminds me of an impossible future and of a forbidden past, of an uncertain instability that marks my displaced queer body. I left my home country at 19; I was running from my own queerness and the dangers that might have unleashed upon me by my kin. More than a decade later, I am now sitting at Club 69 with Tomasito by my side, hoping to come to terms with a side of me that stayed behind, and that lives on as the memory for those who, like me, have moved on. In a way, queer Latinx diasporic lives like mine carry the instability and uncertainty of queer nightlife. But the not knowing what the night holds for us doesn't stop us from finding a brief resolution when our bodies come together through dance and banter. In queer nightlife, we also find ways of continual renewal and reconfiguration. As I secretly whisper into Tomasito's ear, I confess that drag offers me a chance to sparkly inhabit and move across displacement and uncertainty.

Big glasses of piña colada keep on filling our table. I lose count, but I can only taste that smooth creaminess, a tropical shock to my system that keeps on feeding my endless cravings for something sweet. Rumor has it that, in the late nineteenth century, Puerto Rican pirate Roberto Cofresí would give his crew a concoction made with pineapple, coconut, and white rum to boost up morale. The recipe for piña colada was accredited to Spanish bartender Ramón Portas Mingot while working in the iconic Barrachina restaurant in San Juan, Puerto Rico. Regardless of its point of origin, piña colada is the quintessential Caribbean drink, made with the juice of strained pineapples, coconut cream, and rum. Far from being a symbol of Caribbean unity or pride, the making of piña colada also follows the intersecting histories of colonization, slavery, commodification, exploitation, and exoticization, a common story in the making of the American hemisphere.

Like the contradictions of Latinx, Piña Colada carries a story about colonial trade and the making of a modern world that continues to rely on old-world wrecking and destruction. Tonight, I keep on drinking that contested history of contradiction, of indenture and trade, of capture and death, of displacement and punishment, but also of recreation, renewal, and liberation that gesture toward the X in Latinx. The endless pouring of piña coladas catches the attention of performing drag queens and travesti women at Club 69. Closer to the end of the night, they join our table, seduced by Tomasito's distinct flirtatiousness; he offers them some beer, and asks them if they have any advice for a young drag queen. One of them mentions the importance of having a memorable name, a name that would make them want you, she says. The drag queen impersonating Paquita la del Barrio talks about having a glitzy wardrobe, while Bibi commands great makeup skills. Drag queens can be cruel with each other, demanding their sisters to embody and defend a super glittery femininity. Sometimes I wonder who is really in charge of defining what a queer femme is supposed to act and look like. But we all give into the bantering of the night, throwing shade at each other, and flirting with clubgoers. Tomasito cracks up in laughter. Without telling me just yet, he has figured out my drag name, as he keeps on flirting with one of the gurls. You haven't seen how this one has been chucking piña coladas all night, he says while trying not to laugh. Bibi quickly swings back, of course. They both look at me with a distinct hazy gaze and scream aloud, Piña Colada. You are looking at the one and only, Piña Colada! They say you are what you eat, and in this case, I certainly become what I drink.

Piña Colada wears for a crown a wild mane from New Orleans; its golden complexion carries the shiny sands of Cuba and Puerto Rico. Her sensuality borrows from the genealogy of vedette women, from Wanda Seux to Olga Breeskin, from Gina Montes and Lyn May to Francis. Piña Colada carries the musical repertoire of Spanish romantic ballads, her gestures hypnotize those in her path. She won't turn you into stone but might as well bite you off. She is no chaser. You either bask in the glow of her presence or wish you hadn't spent time with her. Piña Colada knows no borders, knows no authority, and bows to no one, except her sisters, drag mom, and the brightness of the stage light. She knows how to play the system, but make sure she does not rip you off. Her prosthetic beauty is disarming, as she carries the eyelid features of her mother Scarlet Fairweather, and sister Calypso. She was trained with chimeras and dragons. She was an intimate friend of late drag icon Súper Perra, and distant apprentice of Walpurgis Gara. Although close to her families, she dwells in no house. She brews with the spirits of Selena, Rocío Jurado, Isabel Pantoja, Rocío Dúrcal, and María Félix. While basking in the excess of the night, she is cosmopolitan but carries her humble beginnings from a small town in Central Mexico. She is elusive, but firm; loving, but protective; loyal, but spiteful; giving and generous, but demands reciprocity. She only prefers shiny and glitzy things; glitter is her crib. She is made of the

Fig. 2. Piña Colada stands at a private function. Photo by Cinthya Ammerman, 2016.

stardust that was left when the Aztec pyramids were destroyed. Growing up as a scrappy kid in Mexico City's downtown, she knows how to speak with tongues of fire and dress enveloped in a serpent's feathers.

For Piña Colada, drag is an orientation in material, physical, and affective terms. It does not expect mastery, but constant change and flexibility like the instability of X in Latinx. As such, Piña Colada is a faithful practitioner of pedragogy, as drag is not only a way of learning about sexually dissident artistry, but also a way of sensing and feeling the world. "PeDRAGogy" is a term coined and deployed by Benjamín Martínez, aka Walpurgis Gara, to describe and "talk about the interrelations between travestismo and pedagogy from the viewpoint of visual culture, artistic training, and emotional education" (2020, 30). Walpurgis formulates a drag practice that undoes conventional spaces where "teacher/student" relations are debunked and deconstructed. She takes good care of each drag daughter by guiding them over the threshold of magical spells and bodily incantations. Her proposal rehearses an underground queer politics by *contaminating and occupying* the rationality-protected walls of (white) academia with glitter, crashing down the "teacher's closet" to destigmatize creative processes that focus on everyday queer experiences. Through her own drag practice, Walpurgis exposes a "transversal travesti pedagogy," to unmake socially imposed limits separating formal education and sexual dissidence, devising "course curricula, workshops, and contents from a queer feminist and LGBTQ+ perspective," while embodying a critically situated praxis that combines cultural critique, artistic practice, and queer sexualities—the echoes of our queer ancestor bell hooks sound through Walpurgis teaching for sexual transgression.

One of the first lessons of drag is about adaptation. To be flexible is both a tactic of survival and a skill for thriving. Piña Colada understands the power of being chameleonic, to blend in against a background that, despite all odds, offers little protection, and just like the tigress ready to attack, falls back and waits for the right time to throw a bomb of glowing disruption. A typical classroom thus turns into a night stage, where thinking discursively offers real limitations, and instead the stage requires summoning deeper intuitions, ways of feeling that are also ways of learning in full heart, body, and mind. Those willing to embrace their inner drive can attune themselves to other frequencies and motions, to be able to sense what is unfathomable, but sensibly real. It is a task only accomplished by the determination to unlearn what we have assumed as truly setting the world; a task that does not happen in isolation, but through the ongoing mediation and interaction with others. Drag situates a mode of learning beyond apprehension and capture but centers on liberation, potentiality, and renewal. Pedragogy is, for Piña Colada, a way of finding liberation through play and dress-up in a world that is so obsessed with the perfection of repetition, of doing and redoing the same thing over and over again, of holding onto a meaningless script for the sake of keeping appearances. Drag is about shattering those meaningless appearances, to bask in and delve into practices that matter and guide us through dark times. Drag is about relation, of finding a way in the dissonance of the world, but it is in disarray where we can and do find purpose. Pedragogy is going about life with your chin up, ready to play and hoping to fuck up.

Queer Relajo & The Axial Crown of Piña Colada

The first time I stood in close range of a beauty queen crown was when I was around 5 years old. All dressed as a pageboy for my aunt Wendy's coronation, wearing a velvet burgundy cape with matching short pants, white stockings, and a pageboy hat with a white feather, while carrying a red velvet cushion in my arms. Its golden shine and aquamarine rhinestones gave it an otherworldliness quality not easily describable for a young kid. The glitzy crown and scepter mesmerized everyone in the audience. Its structures resemble an intersection of metallic gold vectors embellished with tiny beads of amber and zirconia. The head piece displayed a regal luxury that veiled the classed and rural workings of a coronation hall. The crown was made of intersecting metal axes, giving the shape of an asterisk in suspension. The golden scepter featured three large crystals attached to a stem that bifurcated into several strands of shimmering crystals. No one paid attention to the improvised main stage, nor were they looking at the wooden sets of stairs shaking as I was walking up to face the crowd. I somehow made it onto the stage, carrying a beauty queen's crown, which looked like an ornate relic taken from a Spanish baroque church. The audience only looked at the stage, adorned with large flower arrangements of red, white, and yellow gladiolus. My aunt Wendy was seated on a large chair covered with a velvet turquoise fabric. It was supposed to be her throne for a warm night in July. A sort of innocent bliss shines through her eyes, as she holds her head straight waiting for the town's mayor to bestow her crown and name her queen of a rural town in central Mexico.

Piña Colada's first crown appears as a radiantly golden helix. Resting on a red velvet cushion, the shimmering object looks like a mythical phoenix with its wings held wide open, as if ready to take off and carry this kid into a queer fantasyland where Ana Martín's 1982 song "Dulce amor" would welcome the young visitor. Dulce amor's music video shows Ana Martín dressed in a quinceañera-styled pink dress, strolling through a secret garden and sitting on a swing, as she carries a white baby bunny and sings into a birdcage. The bucolic ambiance of romanticism paves the way for a queer landscape filled with an excessive sentimentality of love-searching, as the young Martín sings, "El amor me llegará/ Algún día en cualquier lugar" ("Love will come to me/ Someday, anywhere"). One of the last surviving stars from the Golden Age of Mexican cinema, Ana Martín won Miss Mexico in 1963 to later compete in Miss World in London that same year, where she was disqualified for being underage. "Dulce amor" played as the soundtrack in the 1982 Mexican soap opera *Gabriel y Gabriela*, starring Martín as a young woman trying to pass as a man, that is, a woman in drag. The song was later reused in the opening scene of Mexico's first LGBTQ+ late-night TV variety show, *Desde Gayola*

Fig. 3. Author as a child dressed in a pageboy suit, carrying Aunt Wendy's golden crown. Photo courtesy of Wendy González.

(2001–2006; 2008–2013), created by Horacio Villalobos. Following a similar format to Saturday Night Live, the show featured a series of parodies about Mexican sexuality, culture and politics usually performed by several transgender actors, that is, *puro relajo*.

The song is a chant of queer longing, or the wishing of an impossible aspiration that nonetheless moves us into action. "Sweet love," carols the young singer, as queer imaginings found in a subtle ocean breeze, or a blooming flower bed, open spaces for queer breathing and vibrance. *Desde Gayola* not only adopts Ana Martín's Dulce amor's queer visions but also rewires modes of queer feeling and sensing through the appropriation of mainstream pop media culture. The traces of "Dulce amor" appear in the feminine configurations indexed in the photographic archive of my aunt Wendy's coronation, pointing to a strong affective link between social formations and cultural imaginings. In other words, modes of queer feeling and sensing attached to a sense of Mexicanidad do not occur in a void, but are intricately connected to popular performances of femininity, romance, and spectacularism. *Desde Gayola*'s reuse of "Dulce amor" rehearse a queer coding of femininity, that is, appropriating pop femininity as an expression of queer worldmaking.

My deployment of drag is less interested in what those pop cultural imaginings might mean than in what they might inspire us to do. In other words, how their residual force, or afterglow, sustain queer/trans worldmaking, while exposing how the affective economies impelling their making participate in their displacement, situating them away from the very confines of Mexican identity. Piña Colada, in this sense, embodies a queer sense of Mexicanidad through dislodgment, fragmentation, but follows as a reconfiguration of queer of color nightlife through material bits. My deployment of drag thus plays with the residues of queer Mexican pop culture to trace how excessive modes of queer feeling and sensation guide the emergence of nightlife infrastructures where the material, the spatial, and the affective, assemble a queer/trans politics of presence through each nightly occupation. As in the case of *Desde Gayola*'s appropriation of Ana Martín's song "Dulce amor," Piña Colada enacts a drag ecology that locates yet critiques and disrupts a sense of Mexicanidad, as it displaces racialized affects across the queer geographies of neoliberalism. Piña Colada is thus a pastiche, a tapestry of queer impressions, sensations, and feelings summoned during queer nightlife, but that travels across time and place to render relation and connection amid "dispossession, debt, dislocation, and violence" (Halberstam 2005, 5). Piña Colada embodies the displace-

Fig. 4. Aunt Wendy poses as Queen of Actopan. Photo courtesy of Wendy González.

ment of a queer Mexicanidad whose tectonics strongly vibrate at the dance floor where queer and gay vaqueros convene for dancing quebradita and banda music, or within the Latin bar whose stage features a drag queen lip-syncing to Selena's "Como la flor," or Rocío Dúrcal's "Costumbres." Drag becoming as transfeminist recalibration interrupts the logics of capitalism by making kin with the useless, broken, residual, and opaque.

Once in a Blue Moon

Wednesdays offer a night of enchantment at the Blue Moon. The iconic Pittsburgh bar has been the drag nest of superstars Sharon Needles and Alaska Thunderfuck. Although buried under a rusty past of failed economic development, corruption, rampant racism, and urban gentrification, Pittsburgh remains one of the few cities where you don't have to starve to be a drag performer—unless you are attracted to bootlegged diamonds and fake rhinestones, like me. A few days before that last Wednesday in June, I dmed my drag mother, more like an auntie, since I am older by a century. Scarlet carries the love of a thousand care bears with her embrace. She will say yes when it comes to help a sister—almost every time. People tend to associate drag queens with drama, shallowness, and narcissism in a similar fashion that rural beauty pageant contests might seem to be about one thing on the surface. There is a bit of everything in the mix, a whole world of relations that, underneath all the supposed superfluousness, let us carry a magical touch for love and care. I often feel out of place in Pittsburgh; it is not just the abounding whiteness and lack of Brown disruption. Combined with a toxic workplace, it's an eerie feeling resonating. It's like sensing bad juju, like sensing a dark energy that lingers in the air, and turns things into tragedy—toxic derailments, low air quality, water contamination, nuclear waste, etc.—and death will sadly linger until all debts are paid back, and real reparations begin to take place. Amid the man-provoked toxicity of the Pittsburgh region, Blue Moon has been a queer shelter against storms of ice and heartbreak, against the common unwelcoming racism extended by the city. Against all odds, Blue Moon does justice to its name, as the ambiance of the bar extends a warmth of feeling at home. I want to thank all those queer and trans folk that show up every Wednesday night not only to showcase their talents, but also that come in to foster communion and bask in a subtle strangeness only felt in the company of queer and trans kin.

On this Wednesday night, Scarlet welcomes me into her drag den. Two clothing racks filled with unimaginable creations, from clown suits to sequin dresses, from large wigs to tiny ones, serve as space heaters inside a cool basement. All colors, all smells, all specks of glitter carry the lingering spirit of queer nightlife. As I sat down in her changing mirror, I notice the frowning lines in my forehead. "Nothing the magic of makeup can't hide," says Scarlet in a display of infinite wisdom. She carefully shows me the tricks of drawing two imperfect eyebrows. "They are not twins; they are sisters, so they are never going to be the same," Scarlet strikes again. This makeup mantra tells a lot about how drag orientates us toward the world: there is always imperfection; whatever appears to be symmetrical is only an illusion accomplished through rehearsed precision. The careful application of makeup, of drawing a brown shadow, slowly starts to make my face look like a blank canvas. Glue stick, eyebrow combing, setting powder, glue stick again, setting powder, and a first layer of foundation. Scarlet says my color palate is too pale, as she blends in a darker tone to give dimension. No highlighter for tonight; only the existing paleness of my complexion. Pink and blue will be the tones for my eyeshadow, a complement to the navy-blue rhinestone studded bodycon dress I will be wearing tonight. Strokes of pink and blue leave their powdery feel on my chest. It's like being dusted by an angel, as the blush applied gives a glowing finish. Undergarments, insert hips, and a girdle make Piña Colada stand tall in an inner shell. After putting on a pair of black stockings, Scarlet helps me with my wild wig. While putting on the finishing touches, she shows me her outfit for a Nancy Reagan parody. If she only knew what kind of legacy she left behind, she would have probably joined the ranks of queers and trans for Trump long ago. Nancy Reagan is the sort of camp conservativism America craves for: resoluteness, firmness, and passive-aggressiveness with a touch of peach pink blush and two lines of Mexican coke. Some gurls prefer getting all ready at the club. I, on the other hand, like driving with my mane on. I have always dreamed of driving while wearing heels. It doesn't matter whether I can see through the rear mirror, or whether fellow drivers wonder, if they ever wonder, who or what's driving my car. It offers me relief from thinking of time passing by. Wearing heels makes me not think about time according to the number of words typed onto an empty page. The night gives me solace, a sort of feeling that helps erase the mundane structures of a workday. After getting Scarlet's blessing for the night, I take my time driving across the highway on my way out to the Blue Moon.

Tonight, two of my best friends and boyfriend will be joining the club

Fig. 5. Piña Colada lip-syncs at Pittsburgh's Blue Moon bar. Photo by Adriana Sánchez-Solis.

crowd. I appear as a radiant beauty standing at almost 6 feet tall. As I walk from the parking lot into the bar, the guys outside the next-door bar, Remedy, greet me gingerly. Upon arrival, Adriana helps me put on my flashy nails. I ain't drinking tonight because I gotta keep my head straight and my mane on. Tonight's talent show will feature at least 10 performers including a trumpeter, an s/m Lady Gaga, an a cappella duet, and a Barbie doll queen. Before the start of the show, Cindy Crotchford takes us all back into the dressing room and breaks it down for us. She basically spells out the rules of the game: be nice and show support for each other. I had originally planned to lip-sync to Isabel Pantoja's, "Así fue," a love song for queer nostalgia. I had rehearsed a simple choreography of slow swaying, of spinning slowly, and extending my arms as a way of flirting with the audience. But right when it was the time to go on stage, I changed the song last minute to Daniela Romo's "Yo No Te Pido La Luna." The decision came after sensing the affect left from the previous performances. Many carried a feeling of nostalgia and even sadness. Isabel Pantoja's song would have just made everyone cry even if they didn't understand the lyrics. Music traverses all barriers through its resounding frequencies and so strange people from all walks of life can find a binding force while being together for a night. Once on stage, I raise both of my arms, and let the music find steps of improvisation. "Yo No Te Pido La Luna" is a chant of queer presence. Daniela Romo's song is about simplicity and contentment in enjoying someone's love and affection. It's a song about being content for what we have. The song invites us into embracing a lover's touch, taste, and sexual connection, while letting go of silly expectations and unrealizable dreams, "kiss me and in my lips, you will find warmth." The song's actual title gestures toward that present state by simply stating, "I am not asking for the moon, I am only asking for this moment." It was in such queer spirit of presence that I let myself go into the music. My heels were not a great prop; I almost tripped on my dress, but the feeling was felt far and wide, to the point where a queer kid screamed something like "te quiero" in Spanish. The song's upbeat rhythm awakened a collective desire to be present at Pittsburgh's Blue Moon.

Looping back to the picture of Aunt Wendy's crown, its metallic structures form an intersecting asterisk that mirrors the instability of the very "x," constituting the multiple vectors of Latinxness. Its material assemblage, that is, the sheets of brass plied into shimmering rows of rhinestones, also expose different workings, and reveal multiple forms of labor. Piña Colada's axial crown not only underscores the material and political

economies of minoritarian queer/trans worldmaking, but also unpacks
the affective resonances that spark queer/trans nightlife. Under the shining rays of a drag queen's crown, queer/trans nightlife does not respond
to a static place, set in a particular time and space, but rather, echoes what
queer Mexican performance artist and intellectual, Tadeo Cervantes, has
called, "a cuir territoriality" where "there are mixtures, interconnections,
flows, contaminations, tension between [ways] of inhabiting space,"

> Cuir territoriality is the meeting places of fags, those places that are
> not necessarily limited to monetary logics. Places that exist in a cer-
> tain liminality, that cohabit in an odd margin of legality, that squat
> space in a different way. They make the public space weird. They
> are not circumscribed to the good gay citizen. They are the cruising
> spots. They are, for example, the last car in the Mexico City subway.
> It is the graffiti that claims a space. That tags it. (2020)

Queer/trans nightlife as a *cuir* territory first enacts a form of betrayal
and disloyalty to whitened modes of liberal civility, queer identity, and sexual capital. Following the work of borderlands transfeminist Sayak Valencia, "cuir" enacts a minoritarian and hemispheric queer/trans sensibility
that flourishes in the undergrounds of failed heteropatriarchal projects of
nationalist development (2010, 190). The spaces of queer/trans nightlife
resist necropolitical commodification, especially, they extend lifelines of
sustenance and protection amid capitalist extraction and dispossession.
Practices of cruising, longing, dancing, or touching, map out a fluctuating territory, a changing topography of affects whose intensities, textures,
and modulations enact the co-existence of diametrically opposed bodies
of matter. That is to say that that queer matter, normatively perceived as
excessive, wasteful, dirty, or disposable, reconfigures space itself, morphing into sites of play, joy, and pleasure amid the attending presence of
death and violence. Such a fluctuating territory relies on a set of affective
infrastructures, expressly, fleeting queer social compositions rehearsed
through night practices, that play and replay with linear understandings
of time and space. For instance, the wearing of a golden crown might
acquire a different dimension whether it is used as part of a coronation
ceremony, or as part of its parody. But a zirconia-studded crown carries
the impressions of a residual force that inspires queer/trans worldmaking
to remain alive, adding a material dimension to queer practices of relation

and connection. Within this affective assemblage of matters and bodies, Piña Colada can be situated as a glittery infrastructure that participates in the displacement of queer Mexican identity inasmuch as her drag performance prompts a reconsideration of how queer modes of feeling and sensing traverse spatial displacement and material reconfiguration. So, to understand the axial crown of Piña Colada first requires one to critically trace her queer mappings, then to later situate how her drag performance enacts a spatial reconfiguration of queer Mexicanidad.

It's 1989. The sound of spectacular explosions sparks up a clear summer night. People's chattering become muffled by the clinking of party glassware. An accordion pleat mixes with the tropical beats of bongos, and marimbas, as the large crowd in attendance turns increasingly animated by a music vibe that combines the Portuguese words, "chorando se foi." Grupo Latino's interpretation of the song "Lambada," originally performed by French-Brazilian pop band Kaoma, plays in the background of Actopan's queen coronation dance. Located north of Mexico City, about 75 miles away, Actopan is a city in the state of Hidalgo, within the geographical region known as Mezquital Valley. Once a settlement of Indigenous Otomí people that succumbed to the Mexica conquest of 1427, Actopan's name comes from the Nahuatl *atoctli*, which means "thick, humid, or fertile land," and *pan*, meaning "in" or "on." In other words, Actopan would roughly translate as "on thick, humid and fertile land." Known as a rich land of harvest, the city is widely known for its gastronomy, especially for ximbo and barbacoa, traditional pit-barbecued meat dishes, as well as for masa dough specialties like gorditas and chalupas. After the Conquest of Mexico in 1521, an encomienda, a Spanish slave system, was established in Actopan. The small town was founded on July 16, 1546, and elevated to the category of village in 1575. But the anniversary of its founding is commemorated on July 8. Every year, the municipality celebrates the city's founding with the Actopan Fair, or la feria de Actopan, an annual regional event featuring concerts, open markets, bullfighting, amusement rides, fireworks, and sociocultural activities, including a beauty pageant that crowns the city's queen. In the 1970s, Actopan could have been described as a rural small town whose local economy mainly relied on small-scaled agriculture, specifically on the harvesting of corn, tomatoes, and alfalfa. Actopan's social arrangements followed a common characteristic to most towns in central Mexico, namely a heavy catholic church presence, a strict social hierarchy based on socioeconomic location, respectability politics entangled with factors of race, and ethnicity, as well as conventional forms of heterosexuality, including an oft-marginalized space for women and, more incisively for poor Brown, Indigenous women.

Although the Mexican Revolution sought to bring democracy as a model of government, it failed to renew and detach its previous sociopolitical structures from a process of modernization, inheriting and reenforcing colonial habits, including its rigid caste system whereby fair-skin color is associated with high socioeconomic status. The aftermath of the Mexican Revolution brought into power a single party rule defined by fraud, authoritarianism, and corruption (Yépez 2010, 195), leading to what is currently called a "narcostate." Mexican anthropologist Federico Navarrete examines the logics of Mexican racism whose racial formations not only carry the specters of a colonial caste system but continue to carry the ghosts of mestizaje (2017). The myth of mestizaje, or the intermixing of European and Indigenous blood, lies at the very core of Mexican identity, both at home and across the diaspora. The aftermath of mestizaje continues to steep deeply into every social interaction, and Actopan's social assemblages are no exception. The myth of mestizaje, I argue, must be framed within a larger genealogy of whiteness, not as a biological and essentialist marker of skin, but both, as an ideology and a way of interacting with the world, as a postcolonial mood that has affected sexual and gender formations across the hemisphere.

A product of postcolonial interrelations, namely of the mix between Indigenous Otomí people and fair-skinned mestizos, my mom's family occupied a fortunate space within the social mappings of a small town's working-class population, whose social status mostly stem from my grandfather Chon's family-operated harvesting farm. Composed of seven sisters and a brother, my mom's family followed a traditional dynamic, whereby women would perform domestic chores and, shortly after reaching young adulthood, be expected to get married, while men would be expected to participate in farming activities. At the age of eighteen, my aunt Wendy, the youngest of all seven sisters, was volunteered by her parents to enter the competition of the 1989 Miss Actopan pageant. More than a celebration of young female empowerment, the contest was a display of economic resources and town connections, as each contestant rushed to fundraise money for donations to the town's fair organizing committee. The candidate with the most money would be crowned Actopan's queen. My drag becoming intersects the respectability politics of heterosexuality in a rural town in central Mexico, as the beauty pageant is not simply about a sort of feminine beauty, but also about socioeconomic relations and resources connected to national belonging and local pride like those shaping the socioeconomic relations of drag performance despite contextual differences.

My story about beauty queens reveals my own affective attachments to gown and glitter, as well as to drag and dress-up, as these interconnections also tell complex stories about the politics of sexuality and the circuits of labor that inform sexual and gender makings. From a young age, I was exposed inadvertently to playful forms of drag in the Mexican education system. A typical school is plagued with civic holidays and celebrations consistently commemorated with festivals and sociocultural activities, such as Mother's Day, Spring Fling Day, Flag Day, or Father's Day. Each holiday gives teachers and parents the opportunity to showcase students' talents. Whether singing a song, staging a Mexican folkloric dance, or a theater play, school kids are dressed in many ways, shapes, and forms, to fit the occasion. For instance, I once dressed as a panda for the Spring Fling Festival, or *Día de la Primavera*, as a polka dancer, and as a twist dancer for another festival.

Without a doubt, indoctrination informs the development of school curricula, which is performed and staged as a form of bodily discipline for citizens to learn acceptable forms of social attachment and national belonging (Cuellar 2022; Reynoso 2023). What is perceived as acceptable, however, carries the immanence of an ideology of whiteness. As one of the founders of the Mexican education system during the early twentieth century, during the postrevolutionary era, the then Secretary of Education José Vasconcelos implemented and developed educational policies to teach modes of Mexican identity, infusing school curricula with a civilizing mood attached to social progress, development, and refinement. In other words, as the crafter of the ideology of mestizaje, Vasconcelos thought of and conceived an educational system that would not only enshrine and exalt the wonders of mestizaje, but also ensure the incorporation of such values into the physical and affective bodies of students.

A case in point directs our attention to the nationalistic allegiance performed at Mexican schools. As early as seven in the morning, young kids are lined up in the school's main yard to sing the national anthem and pay tribute to the flag, usually carried by a squadron of young kids mimicking a military march. The allegiance pledged to icons of Mexican nationalism every Monday morning serves as a sort of needle that stitches together young bodies and ideologies of the national. That is, forms of belonging are

Fig. 6. Author as a child dancer in elementary school festivals. Photo courtesy of Verónica González.

not only fostered from a young age but are also intimately performed and attached to young bodies and minds, promoting the formation of an affect tethered to national belonging. It is thus in the public stages of school that mestizaje, that is, a mood toward whiteness, is presented at an early age as a way of becoming Mexican. With such notions of the national, a plethora of masculine icons would also be seared into young minds. Ranging from the virile revolutionary fighter to the lettered politician, a sense of becoming Mexican, or performing Mexicanidad, would also carry a gendered and sexualized attachment (Gutiérrez 2010; Cuellar 2022). In the national scripts of Mexicanidad, whiteness thus is associated with racial progress and development, as well as gendered ideas about the future of the nation, crafting an ideal Mexican citizen, that would embody a series of desirable attributes, such as heterosexual, fair-skinned, male, and urban, and that would ensure national progress.

The scripts of masculinity and femininity in the Mexican context are far less strict than malleable, as a different disposition located in drag and travestismo can also serve as a device for unlearning civilizing ideologies of whiteness embedded in the project of mestizaje; a device that is also present in the very space fostering nationalist ideals. At a young age, I was taught how to playfully deploy masks, to conceal, hide, and obscure the whitening pulsion of education. I soon learned about the powerful magic of drag performance and its liberatory potential through playfulness and physical modulation. Through the various school acts I performed, I tapped into my own unnamed queerness to find in playfulness queer modes of protection. Octavio Paz, a Mexican writer, once insisted that the Mexican character tended toward enclosure and preservation, and that regardless of their social location, Mexicans resorted to masking as a way of life. From *El laberinto de la soledad*, Paz describes a characteristic of Mexicanidad as a sign of hermeticism, as well as an impasse to social and cultural development. I would argue, however, that in the case of queer Mexicans the deployment of masks not only points to a tactic of survival and resilience, but also highlights a playful disposition toward experiencing crisscrossing and displacement. Playing with various masks was thus central to my queer and drag becoming, which interestingly, was shaped within the affective infrastructures of a white mestizo nationalism at school.

Each school performance also reveals how queer play shapes our understanding of space in a heteropatriarchal world, as well as how queer play can enact the creation of different spaces for relation and belonging amid violence, like in dancing to a "son jarocho," or in posing as prince charming for an adapted scene of "Cinderella" for Mother's Day. Each performance, moreover, requires that we find ways to negotiate contradictions through situated embodiments. Similarly, queer space opens possibilities of resistance that perhaps unfollow and divert from the neoliberal paths of activism and political struggle. In this sense, I would like to entertain the possibility of interacting with and situating queer/trans nightlife as a political site that departs from the individualization of activism, pleasure, and space.

What I am gesturing toward is a liminal infrastructure not only composed of bodies in motion and minoritarian subjects but also of matter, objects, and sites, usually rendered valueless in the political economies of global capitalism. What I am arguing for is not a place that holds exceptional value, but rather one that comingles with the dark and dirty contours of queer/trans worldmaking; an affective infrastructure that dwells on opacity and unintelligibility, yet does not foreclose any desire for experimentation, but rather, insists on playfulness as a code and practice for queer sociality. Such a dark queer space exists and thrives less on opposition than on a fluctuating capacity to morph, recycle, and coexist amid vigilance, extraction, and commodification. Under the metallic axis of a queen's crown, within the revolving helices of instability, drag formations emerge as method and practice participating in the choreographic assemblage of queer affective infrastructures. The malleable instability of drag, as a form of performance, sexual formation, and material ecology, depends on finding intention in what has been deemed excessive, useless, and broken, while rehearsing a poetics of play, joy, and pleasure, mere gestures of lush.

My point of departure, or rather contested arrival at a social orchestration of spectacular femininity, evident in the exaltation of feminine play, commodification, and dress-up, is inevitably entangled with my own displacements as an academic, as well as trajectories of migration within the queer Mexican diaspora. In other words, my intimate stories with spectacular femininity—like the 1989 Actopan coronation—are entangled with sociopolitical flows that have not only shaped my own migration experiences but have also reworked my understanding of the sociocultural fabric of two bordering territories, namely Mexico and the US. Despite a rich history of border crossings, anti-immigration and anti-Mexican sentiments inform a nativist rhetoric fueling hatred and violence across social fantasies, political mappings, and lived realities of the US today.

Queer playfulness, or queer relajo, marks a racialized disposition and a particular orientation toward enjoyment and pleasure, enacting festive modes of queer/trans being that celebrate life amid impending threats—be it death, be it physical violence, or interruption. A queer sense of the festive layers a refusal to participate in the political economies of heteropatriarchy and neoliberal capitalism. By this latter, I follow the feminist reading of debt and economic precarity presented by Lucí Cavallero and Verónica Gago.[1] In a similar way, circuits of queer nightlife have also turned into "dynamic territories" for capital and new valorization, relying on the feminized labor of those involved in night economies. Seen as disruptive, shadow economies of queer play offer a way out of a culture of compulsory heterosexual capitalism, by means of valueless pleasures and desires.

As a shadow economy, a town's fair offers a powerful instance of queer relajo at play, particularly as such a festival relies on communal forms of economic sustenance centered on raffles, food vending, or community-based fundraising. Most of these practices of economic exchange are led, organized, and managed by women who build strong networks of support and alliances to raise enough money to position their favorite candidate as a top contestant, complicating their own positionality within socioeconomic structures of ethnicity and class privilege. In this sense, queer relajo houses alternative modes of economic relation that do not predate on extraction, or exploitation, but reaffirm communal belonging and protection. Going against capitalist understandings of debt, which Cavallero and Gago see as "function[ing] and spill[ing] over into territories as a compulsory mechanism for subjugation to precarization (in the conditions, times, and violence of work), morally reinforced as an economy of obedience" (9), town fairs, and by extension the local beauty pageantry held within them, depart from "an economy of obedience," as its modes of interaction promote mutual gain, experimentation, and disruptiveness. The local orchestration of beauty pageantry circumvents the dynamics of debt in that their socioeconomic formation advances community relations that disarticulate modes for commercial unification and consumption, positioning local women as agents arranging economic ventures that favor local networks.

In this sense, local economies of queer relajo, like those rehearsed through local town fairs, disrupt the gendered division of labor, that is, the exploitation of feminized labor, to expand on alternative modes of consumption that do not prey on extraction, but rehearse mutuality, commonality, and equal transaction to navigate complex cultural and socioeconomic entanglements with late-capitalist neoliberalism. However, shadow economies of queer relajo do not represent a constant or sustained drive, but rather fade, fail, and disappear. Their short liveliness and latent potency offer examples of a queer modulation that flows, stops, and recharges, highlighting embodied tempos that unfollow the hectic rhythms of capitalist production and individual extraction, but open queer times for feeling pleasure. Such cycles are affectively embodied, for instance, in the coexistence of drag practices and civic nationalism at Mexican grade schools. The multiple instances of dressing up responding to civic festivities celebrate the enactment and performance of seemingly disparate forms of belonging and becoming, such as drag and dress-up.

Like the multiple forms of drag enacted at school, my aunt Wendy's involvement in local beauty pageantry not only exposes a mode of social relationality based on festivity—one that is usually exoticized as exceptionally Mexican—but nonetheless reveals the workings of a queer sense of relajo, or playfulness. My encounter with forms of drag and dress-up from an early age point to the pliability and malleability of social formations; that is, how social valves of eruption and leaking are inherent to queer/trans worldmaking, especially in a patriarchally nationalist culture. With a luscious display of glow and glitter, the crowning ceremony, as part of a town fair, presents an example of shadow economies of queer relajo that might facilitate other forms of relation and connection that divert from capitalist extraction and heterosexual commodification despite its obsessive display of femme embodiment.

The town fair serves as an interruption of everyday life's cycles of re/production, while rehearsing a social choreography of queer relajo, in which forms of drag and dress-up guide the conventional arrangements of the social, cultural, and economic, without it being recognized as disruptive or transgressive. Incorporating a fantasy rhinestone crown, a reused party dress, and mimicking aunt Wendy's queen poses, Piña Colada's reinvention of the town's beauty queen not only performs a parody that can help trace the entanglements of femininity and queerness in a rural Mexican context, but also draws from the amateur aesthetics of local beauty pageants. Restyling a beauty queen's poses, gestures, and look engages a sensorial methodology of queer relajo in that queer memories are not only playfully reshuffled but embodied to displace a rural queer sensibility that breaks away with the (white) staging and production of the femme and the queer transnationally.

This drag playfulness asks that we stop for a minute and smell the roses of a queer garden, like the one in Ana Martín's "Dulce Amor" video. The flower's terse textures might make our embodied imagination jump into other instances of queer daydreaming, through which the remnants of queer nightlife, as in my memories of a night coronation, scrumptiously ponder on the possibilities of queer action. My own rearrangement of memories condensed in the pictures, videos, and things from the past, serve as the plateau from which Piña Colada emerges as a fleeting embodiment that disarray scripts of time and space. The potency of queer relajo is evident in transforming a storage space into a coronation stage, creating the illusion of pomp and circumstance in the rural town of Actopan, Hidalgo, Mexico. Such an operation is what I call *queer infrastructures*, material and affective assemblages that sustain acts of play, joy, and pleasure even amid the grimmest of possibilities. Given their short-liveness, queer infrastructures leave their impressions around our bodies, like in the beats of Kaoma's "Lambada," echoing across my aunt's memories. As the Afro-Caribbean rhythms of axé swirl, the actual song speaks to a queer afterglow, to a reminiscent force that inscribes a past feeling into sensing the present,

> Chorando estará ao lembrar de um amor
> Que um dia não soube cuidar
> Canção riso e dor, melodia de amor
> Um momento que fica no ar
> (Crying will be when remembering a love
> That one day I didn't know how to care for
> Song of laughter and pain, melody of love
> A moment that hangs in the air)

In this sense, drag performance emerges as a tactic of queer relajo to mediate social choreographies of Mexicanidad, as well as to challenge the whiteness tainting situated social arrangements. In doing so, it activates a displaced form of queer resilience amid violence, border crossing, and patrolling. The axial crown of Piña Colada not only exposes the material economies necessary for queer nightlife, but also embodies queer relajo as a way of worldmaking.

Glowing Exposures

Punto de Partida

Located in Colonia Alamos, Club Roshell is known for its Friday night talent shows. The invitation is open and often advertised throughout the club's social media accounts. Mostly catering to a unique clientele of travesti and trans women, including admirers, and chasers, Club Roshell stands as a stronghold for travesti intimacy like no other nightclub in the city. More than just a bar, it is a community hub for trans and travesti folk, a real shelter where you can truly express who you want to be at night. It is a haven for anyone wishing to perform and start their practice of travestismo. The minute I walk in, I can immediately breathe in a soft calmness, rare for Mexico City's night scene. I soon realized why Club Roshell prides itself for being a private, even hermetic space where anonymity and confidentiality are not only valued, but highly protected. As we make our way inside, I am taken to the dressing rooms. I see house rules posted on the walls: no picture- or video-taking is allowed without previous consent.

Tonight, I am accompanied by my best friend Perikita Jackson, a short-lived Twitter influencer who was known for being critical about the "left-wing" government in Mexico City. I feel under the weather, as Mexico City greeted me with its Montezuma's revenge, a short-lived stomachache that is only a sign of adaptation. It is a reminder that the more I travel to my hometown, the more I become an itinerant visitor. Although my family roots are in this beautiful city, every time I travel back, I feel somehow distant. It feels like the sudden moment when two ex-lovers run into each other after years of breakup. Their faces remain familiar and indelible to their heart, but deep inside, they both know things have changed. They have changed. If diaspora is about the discomforting irresoluteness of never finding home. Dwelling in a queer diaspora is about feeling astray constantly, of running along displacement, and somehow, finding multiple homes. It is only a different way of feeling at home, of making kin with estrangement. In such a spirit, I decide to wear the animal print dress with red stiletto pumps for tonight. Those fuckers kill my feet, standing at 15 inches high, but make me look like a statue, like Lady Liberty gone rogue; Lady Xochimilco, the place I call home when I am in Mexico City, famous for its water canals and its bucolic imagery. The 1943 movie *María Candelaria*, starring super movie star Dolores del Río, was partly filmed in Xochimilco, and the main female protagonist was punished for allegedly being a duping sex worker going against good morals. Piña Colada can be Lady Xochimilco, but unlike Dolores del Río, she doesn't really care for good morals.

Pau is helping me with makeup; she has decided to use copper and golden tones for my eyeshadow, to go with the animal-print dress. Her advice to redraw my lips is to start from the top. Begin by drawing a heart following the natural line of your upper lip, she suggests. The night is still young, and putting on makeup here does not, should not, take too much time. Only the right amount, as we want to get to the tones of a natural beauty. While getting ready at the dressing room, I ask Roshell if I can lip-sync tonight. It's going to be a talent show, she replies. We want to look fabulous but effortlessly. Time must be spent socializing with other girls, and perhaps, strike conversation with some of the men that frequent the place. Once I am ready, I join Perikita and other girls by the outside patio. The night sits quietly. The disco ball reflects its shine on the dance floor; a star machine projects tiny speckles of green light. Sitting around a circular garden table, we start sharing our experiences of dressing up out in public. For some, dressing up is only a luxury they can afford when they enter Club Roshell; for others, tonight is business as usual. Lilly tells Perikita that it is hard to get here. She needs to travel across the entire city to join people at the club; her family doesn't know about her, and she usually spends the night elsewhere.

The women surrounding us come from many walks of life and from many parts of the city; one girl comes from Querétaro, a large city about 150 miles northwest of Mexico City. Conservatism is contextual, they say. We talk about the difficulty of teaching people every day about trans and travesti experiences. Some people genuinely want to know about our lives. Some of the women here are not afraid to speak up and demand respect; our ancestors have already paid the price. Perikita, a cis Brown woman, identifies with the many issues being talked about. It is a form of transfeminist knowledge weaving through *chisme*, gossip. To talk about how you feel, how you overcome challenges, and most importantly, to share what you thought of at the time violence chased you. A trans couple makes fun of each other, and while discussing very sensitive topics, we manage to laugh at misfortune and thank life for what we have tonight. Trans intimacy is about enjoying this very moment, of being in the here and now because, as Roshell reminds us, we might not even be here tomorrow. While chatting, a photographer comes around asking for our permission to take a picture. One girl says no. If they find out, I'll get in real trouble, she shouts in a jokingly fashion. When we come into the club, we have no idea about what kind of challenges each is facing, or even what kind of obstacles we face to come here tonight. For a moment, we forget whatever happened in the outside world, and join in the banter and conversation. The photographer takes a picture of Perikita and I seating down. My friend is wearing a lavish pink dress. It's Barbie Night tonight, I soon

Fig. 7. Piña Colada looks at the mirrorball at Casa Roshell. Photo by Alejandra Torres, 2023.

realize. Most girls are wearing pink, but Piña Colada wants to stand out with an animal-print fitted dress, long red stilettos, and a stomachache that throws silent bombs.

My stomach is killing me, so I excuse myself and retreat into the main hall. I seat in a comfortable booth near the stage. I take a short nap; the girl in front of me watches over me like a guardian angel. There is a guy in the distance; he looks interested. He will eventually ask someone, anyone, for something. When I wake up from my nap, Perikita is next to me. The pain keeps getting worse and feel like I am going to faint. She asks me to stop my drama and focus on the moment. The show is about to start around 11 p.m. The main hostess begins with a beautiful dance about Barbie dolls and asks us to sing along Club Roshell's own melody to start tonight's show. The song is like a blessing for the night. My stomachache suddenly goes away after the soothing melody of the opening act. Once the cabaret stage is opened, the requests for lip-syncing and talents come in shy. After a couple of performances, Perikita throws herself into the stage to sing a cappella Rocío Dúrcal's iconic "La Gata Bajo La Lluvia," a sad love song about breakup. Notice how many of the love songs we claim our own are about breakup, unrequited love, and disappointment. It is probably the reason why these songs are absorbed into the affective fabric of queerness and transness in the Americas. They teach us how to face a world that does not respect, or even tolerate, other forms of being intimate, or being loved. These are queer chants of survivance, hymns to thrive amid every-day violence. That is why we probably know them too damn well and by heart. After her masterful execution, Perikita receives a standing ovation. Her singing is like a mermaid's voice luring those who hear it and leaving her audience screaming "encore." She will perform again later tonight. As I manage to get up to head over to the powder room to get ready, I am intercepted by a handsome man. He wants me to join him in the dark-room by the back. Under different circumstances, I would have dropped my act, but not tonight. The stage is calling me, baby, maybe another time, I firmly reply.

Lines of glitter and sequins hang from the back curtain. The main reflec-tor makes me wonder about the mesmerizing incandescence of shine. No matter the mood, no matter the space, no matter the crowd, shine, glitter, and glitz are always present, illuminating our way onto the dance floor, into the darkroom, or onto the stage. Shine, glitter, and glitz are more than just material manifestations of a queer glow, a queer feeling that runs through the night; they are also our companions, our complements, they are material manifestations of queer worldmaking. Yes, they also carry their own political and material trajectories. Yes, they might contribute to pollution and consumption, but they are never-ending reminders of queer glow. It's what becomes available to us at any given time.

My time is up. I decide to lip-sync to Rocío Jurado's "Punto de Partida." Produced by Juan Pardo and released in 1989, right before the coronation of Tía Wendy, Jurado's song is a queer tour de force. The song is a hymn to moving on, to turning the page on a next chapter that will not bring us closure. The song's rhythm blends in the Spanish romantic ballad, mixing in flamenco and copla beats that complement a feeling of longing. "Punto de Partida" is not only about longing but embodies an open wound of healing. As I rehearse "Yo te busco," I am reminded of all those lovers who decided, at one point or another, not to stay over, not to try being together. It is the night that gives me solace. The night is where I come to face my own wounds and weaknesses. It is a time when I find the resolution to move on, to not crave in others for what I have not craved for myself. As the stage light follows me, I swerve my body following the beats of the song, making some flamenco hand moves. All that matters at that point is to keep looking at the light. I notice the audience moving in front of me, distant faces that offer their awe or salutation, but I focus on letting my body get enveloped by the music. The song's slow tempo makes me move my body and play with gentle gestures. To embody means to stop being for a moment and become one with the feelings of the music. The song's ending chorus stresses on the importance of moving on, of getting to that turning point of healing, of letting go of those who no longer wish to stick around. That was probably the resounding message I got from Jurado's song, to know when it's time to walk away because, maybe, that bed was only meant for me to lay down briefly. The music stops playing and the reflector comes off.

The show ends with a beautiful competition. Perikita scores first place and receives a luscious pink wig for a prize. I came in second. My reward is fusing with the music, along with a pair of flashy loop earrings. As the show nears its end, Liliana Alba, Roshell's partner, closes with more jokes and begins to sing Juan Gabriel's "El Noa Noa," a song about a queer magical night land, an epic place where everything is different, where everything and everyone is oddly queer. Closing the show with this song reminds me of the powerful magic of queer nightlife, of a different time and place away from the disappointments of everyday life. It is not that the night doesn't bring its fair share of disillusion, but those hiccups are reworked in the spirit of queer relajo, of playful bantering that somehow makes them more bearable, even pleasurable. We are at a place where we feel special, where we are treated like queens, like real royalty. We are certainly at a spot evoked in Juan Gabriel's "El Noa Noa," a place for dancing, playing, and laughing, a place for queer glowing, a different place where night-dreaming chases us into an ever after.

TWO

The Broken Records of Drag Performance

Yo te ayudo a olvidar el pasado
No te aferres
Y ya no te aferres
A un imposible . . .
 —Juan Gabriel, Mexican queer diva

Drag queens are fantastical creatures fleeting apprehension. In this chapter, I borrow from the playful nightscapes of drag, as their materiality extends rays of shine to examine the ways in which drag queens are accounted for in the literature of authors in the Americas, such as Carlos Monsiváis and Severo Sarduy. I contrast these representations with my interactions as Piña Colada with social economies of used objects to build on what I call an *ecology of drag*, a material network connecting performance, objects, sites, and moving bodies—human and otherwise. These networks function by ways of feeling and sensing through saturation, disassociation, and fragmentation, while helping queer nightscapes resonate across the moving bodies of nightlife space. I situate these modes of sensing in the cabaret performance of a drag queen from Mexico City, Roberto Cabral, whose cabaret performances expose how the politics of sexuality and race critique national history by gestures of parody.

Through this playful approach to queer nightlife, combining literature, performance, and personal memories, I propose that drag culture expands on the affect of queer relajo to twist a cishet vision of historical becoming, while fostering queer belonging in nightlife venues. In doing so, ecologies of drag instantiate performances of shine, that is, everynight gestures, poses, and feelings that, drawing from Piña Colada's second-hand sequin dresses, jewelry, and glittery wigs, reflect on a queer politics of presence amid neoliberal transformation in the Americas. The embodiment of shiny fragments referring to drag culture, as in the case of Piña Colada, can be better understood by the notion I call *broken record*, an affective drive that connects queer memory with the sensorial experiences of queer and trans folks living on the fringe. Broken records combine a mix tape, or musical repertoire compiled by Spanish-language musical waves, that help modulate the charges of queer/trans feeling across and beyond nightlife. By establishing an affective link with the popular, I associate drag performance with practices of queer relajo, establishing contact with the "shadow economies" (Kendall 2020, 146) that sustain queer nightlife amid economic precarity.

Broken records complicate the linearity of time condensed in a nostalgic nationalism, intermixing temporality, experience, and queer cultural practices in the era of neoliberalism, one that is also challenged as the practices of consumption turn sexual dissidence into cultural and sexual capital with which queer and trans collectives negotiate everynight life in Mexico City. This sense of brokenness of records metaphorically illustrates historical silences, erasures, violent acts, and misrepresentations sexual dissident cultures endure for worldmaking, but nonetheless highlight queer forms of fugitivity and escape from extraction. In this sense, drag performance is a cultural form that alters practices of consumption by generating queer and trans belonging mediated by a sonic affectivity within global circuits of queer culture, satirizing a national nostalgia embedded in the heroic masculinization of historical figures, while ruffling set definitions of Mexicanidad—embodied attachments to a transregional sense of Mexican culture.

Literary, Drag!

From very diverse styles of writing, a plethora of literature[1] in the Americas has traced the figure of the drag queen—their shapes and contours, their twists and turns, their cultural aesthetics, social imaginaries, and political provocations—as a form of travestismo.[2] The works of Pedro Lemebel, Néstor Perlongher, Reinaldo Arenas, Severo Sarduy, Carlos Monsiváis, Manuel Puig, Mayra Santos-Febres, John Rechy, and more recently, Juan Carlos Bautista, Mario Bellatín, Joseph Cassara, Camila Sosa Villada, or Alexandra Rodríguez de Ruíz engage with drag themes, symbols and metaphors of excess, disease, marginality, fragmentation, emptiness, and oversaturation. As such, literary representations of drag queen culture typically draw from a baroque aesthetics of excess as a way of complicating the embedded cishet white normativity of literary canons, as well as of connecting queer forms of relation, connection, and meaning beyond textual space.[3]

In this strand of literature, the drag queen is further situated at the intersection of cultural consumerism, sexual agency, and material excess. Carlos Monsiváis describes the drag queen's (i.e., travesti) unwavering success in the underworld of entertainment as follows,

> Si algo manejan con destreza los travestis es su versión de una veta esencial de las mujeres: el triunfo en el espectáculo. La meta, se dice, ya no es el ejercicio del dolor y la ternura, o la maternidad ilimitada. No, la mujer más mujer es la que atrae más reflectores, la que no tiene tiempo de estar en la cocina porque ocupa el pro-scenio. En contra de las suposiciones habituales, los travestis no imitan a la Mujer [. . .] sino a la Mujer de Éxito, categoría distinta, sujeta a las más encomiásticas parodias, creaciones y recreaciones. (2010a, 280)

Monsiváis links performance and spectacle to the gestures and attires of drag queens, making a distinction between the category of "woman" and "successful woman," as the latter appears to be contingent on stag-ing satire and parody. By intertwining performance, economy, and con-sumption, the queer chronicler alludes to Severo Sarduy's seminal essay *La simulación* (1982), in what seems a revisitation of the latter's treaty on neobaroque aesthetics, which finds in drag queen gowns, posture, and makeup a powerful epitome,

> El travestí no copia; simula, pues no hay norma que invite y mag-netice la transformación, que decida la metáfora: es más bien la in-existencia del ser mimado lo que constituye el espacio, la región o el soporte de esa simulación, de esa impostura concertada: aparecer que regula una pulsación goyesca: entre la risa y la muerte. (1982, 13)

In imagining drag practices in the age of late capitalism, Monsiváis's invocation of Sarduy maps a queer cultural geography: drag performance appears as a site where transformation not only appears in contention with bodies and stages but also as an affective force binding the sociopo-litical infrastructures of queer belonging in urban Mexico.

As a cultural performance, drag queens embody forms of transgression by playing with gender variance to destabilize the essentialist logics of heteronormativity. While Judith Butler's notion of gender performativity finds in drag culture a case in point, cultural critic Antonio Marquet believes that drag queens embody an art of the ephemeral while seeking to attract the gaze of the other (2010, 398). Marquet asserts that the terms travesti and drag queen are interchangeable and intertwined within the underworld of queer performance in Mexico, and further argues that drag queens and travestis occupy a double void in psychoanalytic terms. Like many other drag writers, practitioners, organizers, and allies, Marquet joins in on lively political forms of "theatrical gender-bending" through which "drag performers construct, reproduce, bend, and challenge identity" to expand on other-than-English "drag discourses" (Heller 2020, 3) across the Americas.[4]

At its very onset, drag performance emerges from within the bleeps and blurs of queer collectives, of bars, dance floors and cabarets, improvising queer nightscapes of feeling through music, parody, and pleasure. These nighttime spaces for queer sociality also draw liminal zones of "*incongruity, theatricality,* and *humor*" (Newton 1979, 106) and, as Carlos Monsiváis and Antonio Marquet have argued, it is in these hybrid spaces that violent attacks against queers are reappropriated, resignified and challenged with satire, banter, and laughter. Both Monsiváis and Marquet envision drag as a cultural practice of resistance against stigma and marginalization. Similarly, the material composition of drag queens, that is, their art form and content, playfully engages a neobaroque aesthetics of saturation, making us feel "the drag of queer life" when "pasts are likewise always present" (McGlotten 2019, 33), or a queer sense of time. Feeling the rich textures of drag queens reminds us that our queer existence thrives on repetition, accident, and happenstance, un/folding multiple layers, accessories, and threads alongside poses, gestures, and moves that contrast with linear trajectories of subjective and historical becoming.

Like other places in the global south undergoing neoliberal reform, the case of Mexico points to the transregional trajectories of modernization. Entangled in the afterlives of coloniality, developmentalism, nationalism, and globalization, neoliberal modes of consumption are not straightforward, but very much like the policies they enact, are complex, vectorial, and polymorphous in their advances, and disruptions. In these contexts, the concept of "neoliberalism from below" helps situate glocal complexities in what Verónica Gago[5] describes as "a set of conditions that . . .

beyond the will of a government . . . turn into . . . the motor of a powerful popular economy that combines community skills of self-management
and intimate know-how as a technology of mass self-entrepreneurship in
the crisis" (2017, 6).

In their interaction with queer practices, the emergence of a pink market might contribute to an increasing privatization of sexual citizenship
by giving the illusion that the advances of homonormativity—that is,
rights to same-sex marriage, adoption, or even name-changing, tethered
to a set notion of the citizen—signal an overall improvement of the living
conditions for minoritarian queer/trans lives. In Mexico's neoliberal consumerist economies, queer cultural practices, like drag, point to complex
vectors of consumption and commodification, leading to a politicized
mutation of LGBTQ+ dissident practices. In this sense, the circulation of
pink commodities also drags out strategies to playfully negotiate, contest,
and, at times, neutralize economic neoliberal policies reshaping sexual
citizenship.

Recognizing a politics of genderbending and its challenges to essentialist gender binaries, my engagement with drag queens situates a cultural contingency in which the sensorial, material, spatial, temporal, and
economic overlap to animate other practices of queer and trans night-
making alongside their commodification. In this sense, I track the "drag
labor," that is, the work drag queens perform on- and off-stage, during
and beyond nightlife, to orient "identities, histories, and geographies not
immediately apparent" (Khubchandani 2020, XV). Here, I fathom drag as
a cultural practice that, sparking out of the night, questions the politics of
authenticity, value, and representation within and across queer Mexican
cultural production.

Curling up lines of progressive development, drag cultures bask in the
excess of reused, recycled materials to expose the contradictions of impossible consumption in postcolonial contexts under neoliberal reform. Drag
practices embrace a recycled neo-baroque aesthetic of wasteful consumption, a saturation not only of meaning but also of materials crafting subjectivities, centered on material repurposing and recycling. In other words,
looking for dresses, accessories, and other paraphernalia in thrift stores,
flea-markets, swap meets, *paca* shops, or *tianguis*—the shadow economies
of drag repurposing—enacts other terms for consumption, while highlighting a situated praxis for queer/trans care, an embodied "know-how"
lying within queer undergrounds.

Animating ways of experiencing time and space otherwise, alternative practices of consumption underpinning drag shadow economies contrast with the official scripts of economic development by garnering old artifacts, discarded objects, and worn-out materials perceived to be valueless and out-of-time. Reigniting queer political imaginings, drag assembles queer ecologies challenging neoliberal extraction. As such, drag ecologies name a contingent materiality that interrupts the accumulation of property in neoliberal terms by engaging second-hand material economies. The drag queen finds it difficult to identify along the neoliberal spectrum of sexual subjectivity, and instead shatters the possibilities of neoliberal identification by activating a "practice of historical memory" (188) through which drag slows down progress and makes sense of time "on our own terms" (Rivera-Servera 2017, 193). Drag queens thus deploy a temporal and spatial dissidentification[6] against historical becoming in Mexico by fondling with the *out-dated-ness* of recycled materials, while carving a counterpublics in underground spaces to outshine temporalities of progress.

By focusing on the cultural and socioeconomic contingencies of drag queens, like Piña Colada or Roberto Cabral, I complicate the literary representation of drag queen culture to animate a queer nightscape through cultural criticism. That is, I expand on the material nature of drag through my playful searching for and interacting with sequin and glitter, to move beyond literary abstraction. A queer materialist praxis that David William Foster describes as a coming out from the tyranny of the text,

> Salir de la cárcel del lenguaje, hacia una utopía *gay* de nuevos sistemas significantes, sistemas tensados en signos resistentes al sistema-retórica vs. gramática, expresión vs. represión-donde existe un constante proceso de desplazamiento como estrategia para evadir el sistema cerrado del patriarcado. (2000, 53)

Intimately felt through a lens of queer relajo, drag queens radiate a peculiar immanence and magnetism: the strokes of shimmer, shine and shadow not only rely on a practice of genderfucking but also speak of an intimate convergence between human and non-human agents beyond discourse. Queens cast a queer spell, transposing memories, emotions, sensations, and dreams into an open dance stage, where queers sway to the rhythms of Kylie Minogue, Cher, or Flans. Under a mirrorball, drag performance combines affective charges, material objects, and bodily gestures to reimagine nightlife as a queer way of taking back stolen time and space. Or, as iconic drag queen Sasha Velour glamorously puts it, "drag is a queer and feminist project because" it questions the power matrixes of oppression, while reinventing the world through art (2023, 7). Drag thus plays with bottled up, fueled, or used up mixed feelings to unbind the imposed cishet constraints against the free movement and expression of queer/trans folk.

Drag queens are shiny rays of liberation that shed a different light on the worn-out-ness of undesired objects. Stirring a queer politics of time, that is, a critical examination of the social rearrangements under neoliberal capitalism, queens absorb old heels, wigs, attires, shiny makeup, sequin garments, or music records, forging a residual materiality under the nightlights of bars, cabarets, dance clubs, and other queer undergrounds. Dealing with questions of identity, consumption and belonging, I ground my drag within an affective tectonic, a traveling queer nightscape, that fluctuates between spaces and feelings, prompting queer folk to remain fierce during and after dark. I therefore tease out the dissident theatricality, both in performative and material terms, that guide drag queens to cast ephemeral aesthetics of waste, as recycled forms of performance intrinsic to queer nightlife. From these locations, multiple shadow economies, including flea markets, improvised concession stands, quesadilla and taco street booths, street vending, or panhandling, surface heteronormative space, and just like wig extensions, improvise queer networks of consumption under neoliberal capitalism.

Toward an Ecology of Drag

In speaking about queerness in modern Mexico, José Joaquín Blanco notes:

> Sin embargo, la homosexualidad–como cualquier otra conducta sexual–no tiene esencia, sino historia. Y lo que se ve ahora de *diferente* en los homosexuales no es algo esencial de personas que eligen amar y coger con gente de su mismo sexo, sino propio de personas que escogen y/o son obligadas a inventarse una vida–pensamientos, emociones, sexualidad, gustos, costumbres, humos, ambiciones, compromisos–independiente, en la periferia o en los sótanos clandestinos de la vida social. (1981, 183–84)

Blanco points to the capacity of queer collectives to craft their own stories that, like mine, resists the erasure of official accounts of sociality through storytelling. If understood as queer agency, these stories not only carry political potentialities in their echoes but serve as proof for modes of queer becoming that make sense of the world through sensorial engagements. That is, by noticing how our queerness comes to be alongside other bodies, aromas, materials, textures, objects, feelings, and spaces around us, a queer sensibility arises and sets us apart from the conventions of heterosexuality in neoliberal postcolonial contexts.[7]

Referencing a phenomenology of queerness, in other words, a way of making sense of marginalization through experiencing our sexuality, Blanco ruminates on the idea that a queer way of life has no essence. Rather, it comes into being by a series of practices, of thoughts and feelings, of tastes and commitments orienting our bodies. In this way, Blanco evokes a queer sense of time and space. By temporal, I am referring to "historia" (i.e., history) as a do-it-yourself queer way of life; by spatial, to the locations queer and trans folk occupy to try to make sense of it all. Queer culture thus comes together as an accumulation of experiences and practices, of fucking, loving, and becoming. In this sense, queer storytelling is also about our material engagement with the world.

In what I imagine as a conversation with Blanco's understanding of a queer phenomenology, Sara Ahmed notes that "this way of encountering objects involves disorientation: the touch of the thing that transmits some thing . . . by bringing objects to life in their "loss" of place, in the failure of gathering to keep things in their place" (2006, 165). This "loss of place" mobilized in Ahmed's argument is what characterizes the queer search for life, that is, a life out of cishet time and place. As noted by Ahmed and Blanco, queers willingly forge, or are forced to embrace other forms of belonging, of inhabiting time to find their place in the world. While scrapping the essence of sexual difference, both queer writers insist on the historical and spatial contingencies that fashion a queer way of life, webbing other fantasies, fears, dreams, dares, and aspirations.

Like queer culture, drag interlayers temporal and spatial positions to polish a movement of agents establishing contact—human and nonhuman, objects, species, etc. If a queer way of life means reinventing one's life, reimagining a personal story, and recasting history, drag performance's fragmentary aesthetics piece collective histories through a glittery style absorbing figments and fragments seen as valueless. Perceiving the world through a fragmentary lens also embodies a playful stance against the neoliberal sensibilities of efficiency, reproductivity, and extraction. In this sense, if the drag queen is rendered an outsider of official heterosexual history[8] and instead curates a fragmented story,[9] a collage of odds and ends, of bits and pieces, drag performance then offers a contingent force for historical reinvention and political revival through and across the night, while extending sensorial ways of responding to neoliberal accumulation by excess, pleasure, and exhaustion. Gleaning from the fragmentary events of queer life, drag queen culture thus glistens as broken records of a heteropatriarchal straightness, challenging the teleological verticality of heterosexual nationalism, and supreme heterocracy in/across/beyond Mexico.

In what I read as a critique of consumerist societies, Mexican queer writer Salvador Novo discusses the implications of mechanical reproduction as an economic strategy for consumption and commercial democratization in *En defensa de lo usado y otros ensayos* (1938): "La producción en serie nos arrebata bruscamente un afecto que comienza a fructificar en el ajuste tibio de nuestra persona, nos quita de las manos el juguete y nos deja ante el enigma de uno nuevo, frío [. . .] para que unos meses después el fenómeno se repita" (8–9). Despite the seeming historical distance that separates Novo's impressions from the present moment, what remains latent is a recognition that objects, in this case, old and antiquated ones, carry a particular affectivity in assembling a fantasy of queer belonging.

For Novo, maintaining close contact with objects generates an affective attachment to them, a form of happiness in the space of the workshop, where the crafter spends time confectioning their work: "[. . .] el privilegio de su tallercito privado, en el que hacía a mano las cosas, las hacía bonitas y buenas, lograba desarrollar un valioso amor por su oficio [. . .]" (1938, 7). In this tactile practice of fondling with things and matters, an affective resonance stems from the material interaction between human touch and touched objects. Novo precisely reflects on the affect of objects that emanates from every touch. In other words, the object triggers an affective memory that is later embodied.

Objects affect the construction of sociocultural meaning and belonging. The common characteristic that links second-hand buyers and antique collectors, for instance, Novo asserts, is the trace of human touch in the object, and the memory of the object in the human. Accordingly, objects carry a "haunted livingness" (McGlotten 2019, 33) that allows a queer restructuring of the senses:

Los liga sin embargo con él, sin que los perciban unos ni otros, un hecho inherente a todos los objetos de segunda mano, ya sean útiles como un incunable o un Goya, o serviciales como un Chevrolet 1934 o unos Florsheim adquiridos en la Lagunilla: el calor humano de los anteriores propietarios, manifiesto en las huellas digitales que ostentan sus hojas, en el cómodo hundimiento de los cojines anteriores, en lo amoldado que está el calzado o el traje a las peculiaridades de una anatomía de pobre a quien cualquiera le sienta bien. Sin saberlo, sin advertirlo, anticuarios y compradores de objetos de segunda mano se la estrechan en la búsqueda de una huella humana que está ausente de los productos mecánicos nuevos, pero presente ya, tibia, familiar y satisfactoria, en los usados. (1938, 11–12)

In touch with Salvador Novo's understanding of materiality and affect, drag cultural practices make use of recycled materials to light on a different shine that saturates the fields of straight vision with every performance. This shininess also reflects on the neoliberal accumulation of property and capital, embodying a different relation to belonging in consumer neoliberal capitalism. Under this light, drag culture thrives on a recycled materiality that stirs the temporality of objects in the shadow economies of bars, crisping the folds of consumerist practices in a pink market. Drag recycling thus appears as a mode of breaking the linearity of heterosexual time, as well as a playful form of agency amid overconsumption.

A sense of excitement comes when browsing the racks of used clothes at thrift stores and swap meets. Overtaken by the euphoria of RuPaul's "Sissy That Walk," a music hit from Drag Race's Season 6, I sissy my walk into a local Goodwill shop in Davis, California in 2015. From the stacks of oversized shirts, stained fabrics, and chipped glassware, I stumble upon one of my most precious second-hand acquisitions, a fabulous night dress. Featuring green and blue sequins carefully stitched across long sleeves, the dress is short and sexy, with a back opening and triangular cleavage in front. The black fabric wrapping my body contrasts with the shiny rows of sequin that flash a peacock-feather-like fluorescence when I stretch my arms. I ignore who might have held this beautiful dress in the past, but when holding it, I feel a transference of shine running through my body, as if I were feeling the waves of the dress's past fabulousness when maybe worn at a fancy 80s cocktail party or hanging quietly in someone's closet. Drag dresses also tell stories. Feeling the shiny sequin patterns throws me into flights of whimsical speculation to connect my story of drag becoming with that of a flashy dress found buried amid a wasteful surplus of clothing.

An account of the materiality and temporal fragmentation of drag cultures appears in the first pages of queer Cuban writer Severo Sarduy's *La simulación*. Proposing a complex treaty, the Cuban exile fathoms drag queens, or travestis, as avatars of a neo-baroque material ecology: "La erección cosmética del travestí, la agresión esplendente de sus párpados temblorosos y metalizados como alas de insectos voraces, su voz desplazada, como si perteneciera a otro personaje, en *off*, la boca dibujada sobre su boca, su propio sexo, más presente cuando ese ícono, aunque falaz omnipresente: [. . .]" (1982, 13). Through colorful similes, Sarduy reflects on the juxtapositions of objects and bodies that build a form of communication through drag. Describing the shine of queens, Sarduy folds in provoking words such as, "agresión esplendente," "insectos voraces," or "temblorosos," to signal the mimetic gestures of a transfemininity. In particular, the writer alludes to makeup as a raw material for building an architectural glitz, a mimesis to the metallic shades of butterflies. And, through this description, the author spots the affective charges flowing through the shiny architecture of drag queens, whose eyelashes capture their audience's attention, as voracious insects mesmerize their mates. In doing so, Sarduy accounts for the fragmentary neo-baroque-ness rupturing the linearity of time and subjectivity.

The performance of drag un/becoming is thus a site to reflect on the latent affect that resides in their assembling materials: the plastered-on makeup, star-reaching eyelashes, and sky-reaching high wigs of drag queens, capture a queer imagination as these blinding strokes of glitter suspend the laws of cishet relationality. Eye shadow, eye blush, eyelashes, shine and glitter creatively chisel an ecology of drag. This ecology of objects also maps "the particulars a diva conducts to chart a method of moving the body through the world, a style that . . . particularly queens, have found essential. It is a camp style of resistance and self-protection, a way of identifying with other queer people across invisibility and disgrace" (Koestenbaum 1993, 85). Glitter as political defiance; radiance as self-protection; shine as queer disruption. Sparkles are everywhere. Sequined gowns with glitzy rings and earrings illuminate the dark nightlife of Mexico City.

Like an amulet of protection, my blue and green sequin dress has traveled far and wide with me, from northern California to New York City and across to Mexico City, and now Pittsburgh. It is precisely a sense of belonging felt through the sequin dress that, whenever I fondle with it, brings me back to childhood memories of my mom and aunties venturing into the Tepito neighborhood for dress shopping. Known to be one of the toughest neighborhoods in Mexico City, Tepito holds a huge open-air market where you can find a vast assortment of legit and bootlegged goods for cheap since before the 1980s. It was also abuela Carmen, my mom's mom, that began shopping there for cheap bargains on luxurious dresses and garments in 1981. And for several years, my grandma, aunts and mom relied on these popular market bargains to support their family income by reselling brand new and new-like outfits to friends and neighbors in the late 1990s—amid one of Mexico's deepest economic devaluations. Staring at my dress's shiny sequins throws me back to playing hide and seek inside the Tepito clothing shops. "We are taught to believe glitter, like drag, is artificial," but "there's nothing more real" than "sparkles flying" (Maxx Goodman 2023, 16). Like my looking for radiant night dresses inside thrift stores and local second-hand markets, the modulations of shine remind me of the unassuming feminist economic resilience that can happen when basking in the excessive materiality of usedness.

The hypnotic state provoked by admiring drag architectural performance also speaks to a type of affect that cracks open the cishet erections of time. In the January 2015 issue of the online art journal *e-flux*, entitled "Politics of Shine," the editorial team reflects on the "cross-sections of power and aesthetics in the material and immaterial discourses of shine—past, present, and future" (Holert et al. 2015, n.p). This conceptualization of shine proposes a critique of neoliberal temporality: the structures that allow social actors to position themselves as active narrators in the annals of history and, as such, as agential actors in the teleologies of progress. Embodying shine responds to a sparkly aesthetics that amass cultural capital and affective value from material objects. In shine, the authors also find a "paradox," where "surface effects, of glamour and spectacle, of bling-bling contingency" make modern regimes of visuality hiding from plain sight, as "bodily shine helped to increase slaves' worth, to heighten their assimilation and visual verisimilitude to the world of objects" (Thompson 2015, 233). As in the case of enslaved persons of African descent, the glaring reflection of Brown and Black bodies participates in the production of commodity value in late capitalism.[10] Under the playful light of queer relajo, entertaining shine as a concept for queer cultural analysis in Mexico, and largely in the Americas, brings to the fore the luminosity of sexual dissidence to highlight a flaming drag aesthetics of fragmentary saturation as a way of mediating capitalist extraction.

At the intersection of sexuality, new materialism, and performance, I evoke Xavier Villaurrutia's poem *Nocturno de Los Ángeles* (1938), whose metaphor situates "una enorme cicatriz luminosa" (an enormous, luminous scar, 44) on the yearning bodies of sexual dissidents. I am therefore interested in the diverse ways through which this "luminous scar," or what I refer to as shine, is embodied, engendering a *performance of shine* manifested in drag performance. Shine also sparks multiple possibilities of establishing practices intertwining desire and consumption within queer enclaves in the Americas today.[11] And while these might animate an ephemeral sense of bliss, such practices reflect on a contested form of sex and capital. In their potentiality for temporal and spatial digression, however, I fathom drag performances as *broken records* of a cultural historicity that remains gendered, stratified, racialized, and neocolonial, but whose inherent starburst kindles different approaches to consumptive transgression in a neoliberal aftermath.

If consumption of luxurious accessories and garments, such as jewelry, clothing, and other expensive goods marks an existing social divide that restricts an equal distribution of wealth, resources, and access to basic needs globally, the glitz inherent in drag culture diffracts practices of capture and extraction by basking in the shadowy shines coming from recycled dresses, wigs, accessories, ornaments, shoes, and eye lashes, piecing an excessive aesthetics of fragmentation. A performance of shine, therefore, activates a poetics of hope by queerly playing with old and valueless things. Through the acts of queer relajo with objects, drag becoming ruptures the temporal projects of modernity, and neoliberal transformation from queer undergrounds, while questioning racialized notions of civility and citizenship reproducing tolerable forms of sexual and gender subjectivity.

I seek to find hope in shine, as does the editorial of *e-flux* when concluding on the potentialities of an alternative ray of light amid cultural contradictions and socioeconomic precarity across the Americas: "a different discourse of light and exuberance, a counter radiance that outshines the sun that shines on the privileged, an insurgent technology of brilliance in the service of those who are doomed to do the rubbing." Those lashes of radiance coming from the architectural glitz of drag queens unequivocally remit to a potentiality in the horizon, to a flirting with the unknown. That materiality of shininess sheds light upon queer underground practices reilluminating history through queer incandescence.

Like Villaurrutia's body of luminosity, I have found mine resonating in the colorful rays of used sequin dresses. Their radiancy orients me

Fig. 8. Wigs, books, and sequin dresses.

to find a place of comfort in the world, surrounded by other drag gar-ments that go with my green and blue sequin dress. While searching for the textures of dresses, accessories, wigs, and shoes, I was mesmerized by a similar bodycon black sequin dress I saw lying in a second-hand bazaar at Pittsburgh's Glittersty in 2022.[12] Though this time the gleaming second-hand dress had stitched gold sequins around its padded shoul-ders. Its glittery materiality immediately transported me into past nights of play, dance, and pleasure when Piña Colada would sissy walk in a peacock-feather-like dress. The vibrations of shine connected me with other times and places spliced through the bliss of the night. The gold sequin dress found at Glittersty evokes the everlasting force of shine that, like the peacock reflection of the Goodwill dress, cuts through the neoliberal economies of dispossession, to renew and be reborn from the ashes of disposability as a queer phoenix.

Shine emanates then from a displaced Mexican context into a larger hemisphere as a concept to trace the invisible marks of those embodied desires occluded by official history. And, following Novo's articulation of a material symbiosis, shine embodies a way of relating to the social. In the case of drag culture, material shininess is characteristic of their performance, one that appears as a mechanism of perception ingrained in queer and trans night-making. To find the forces of queer longing in glitter points to the non-human agents that incite desires to tease out a different experience of time, of being otherwise. The glitter of drag queens activates modes of perception found in diversion, fascination, and fixation as disruptive forms of consumption. In the queer nightlife of bars and performance stages, drag culture symbolizes broken records that trace geographies of erasure and saturation, performative assemblages of bodies and objects, and ecologies of sex, capital, and desire.

Dragging National Scripts: The Temporal Fissures of Drag Cabaret Performance

With over 20 years of experience as a drag queen performer, Roberto Cabral first debuted as a performer in the comedy troupe *La Chinga* alongside Jesusa Rodríguez, Tito Vasconcelos, and Diego Luna. A year after auditioning, Cabral began studying at the National School for Theater Arts in Mexico City, but it was Jesusa who taught the seasoned drag queen the transgressive power of political cabaret, "[she] taught me that if you have a mic in hand, you are like a surgeon, what you say can hurt or transform the life of others."[13] Directed by cabaret performer and activist Ana Francis Mor, *Roberta y las otras chicas del montón*[14] (2015) is a drag cabaret show featuring Roberto Cabral, whose stage performances follow a line of Mexican political cabaret, foregrounded in the work of Jesusa Rodríguez, Tito Vasconcelos, Liliana Felipe, Regina Orozco, Las Reinas Chulas, and Astrid Hadad. Opening this piece, a video performance by film director Ximena Cuevas shows a playful remixing of a televised speech by former president Enrique Peña Nieto, making a direct allusion to the single-party rule that came into power after the post-revolutionary period of the 1920s with the consolidation of the PRI, *Partido Revolucionario Institucional.*

Roberta y las otras chicas del montón tells the story of three women, Alicia, Roberta, and Susie Pussy, whose dreams of finding everlasting love are frustrated by a cruel reality that shatters their romantic fantasy. Divided into three main acts, and through the lives of these drag protagonists, the show stages a satirical revision of Mexico's history condensed in three episodes (i.e., the colony, the revolution, and neoliberalism). Affect, intimacy, and national history are intermeshed in this performance, providing the basis for a careful examination of the national symbols exposed in this piece. The first scene opens with a short clip of the 1951 animated movie *Alice in Wonderland*, which I read as a fable of innocence, fantasy, and adventure.

A romantic pathos evinced in Disney's fairy tales serves as a point of departure from which Alicia, the first drag character in this performance, confronts the audience with the everlasting presence of romantic love an expected affective attachment to heterosexuality.[15] Cabral's dragging of the fairytale character of Alicia draws on the naïveté, candor, innocence, and, at times, obliviousness characteristic of a heteronormative stereotype of femininity. By staging an absurd gullibleness, Alicia exposes the affective mechanism through which the technics of fairy tales produce a whitened notion of love masked as an idealized affair with dominant forms of mestizo masculinity. But her failure in finding prince charming, who is supposed to bring about sheer happiness, economic stability, and everlasting security, brings out the contradictions of waiting for white heterosexual love, questioning the values of self-sacrifice and self-constraint upon which a better tomorrow is usually imagined.

Playing with the structures of a traditional love story, the second drag character, Roberta, appears dressed as a *china poblana*, a folkloric women's dress from the Mexican southeast. The nationalist emblems of her attire bring forward a shiny code of arms embroidered on her skirt, showing an eagle eating a snake. This second part of the performance inserts colonial violence, sexual rape, and indigeneity as a critique to the idealization of romantic (white mestizo) heterosexuality. Roberta, who is read as an Indigenous woman from rural Mexico that migrated to the capital city in search of social mobility, narrates her journey as a domestic worker who has been a target of sexual violence, mistreatment, and silence upon arriving in the big city. Humor and irony serve as theatrical strategies to decry the injustices of displacement, discrimination, and violent erasure Indigenous populations and, in this case, Indigenous women, have endured in Mexico. The displacement of Indigenous populations is indirectly addressed in Octavio Paz's notion of "los hijos de la Chingada," treated and elaborated in the 1950 publication *El laberinto de la soledad*. But if for Paz "La Chingada" is that violated mother who engenders a sense of Mexicanness, Roberto Cabral's performance is less concerned with defining a national ethos than with showing the contradictions of believing in universalizing fairy tales of national developmentalism. Roberta's story

Fig. 9. Roberto Cabral performs in *Roberta y las otras chicas del montón*. Photo courtesy of Eriko Stark.

depicts a blunt racist nationalist ideology embedded in the treatment of Indigenous people.

Cabral's treatment of the relationship between domestic labor and indigeneity reveals the degree in which *mestizaje*, as an erasure of ethnicity and race, abjectly permeates humor and satire. Moreover, representing domestic labor proves problematic as it assumes that Indigenous women embody a certain economic domesticity when entering the racialized and classed urban space. When talking about finding everlasting love, she alludes to her experience of rape by her boss, looping back to the image of "La Chingada." As what is performed to be a domestic worker, Roberta is seen as a disposable body that gets paid to be at the service of her boss's sexual requests.

After being pulled and pushed in a frantic dance, Roberta exits the stage for the audience to watch another video montage featuring political discourses by former presidents Vicente Fox, Felipe Calderón, and Enrique Peña Nieto. Their remarks point to government reforms characterizing a neoliberal turn in Mexican socioeconomic and political infrastructures. Roberta now returns to the stage showing the signs of pregnancy and lamenting that her dream of finding prince charming has been shattered. She now faces the challenge of embracing single motherhood in a social milieu that doubly restricts her mobility not only for appearing to embody indigeneity but also for being a woman.[16] Her bearing of a fatherless child pinpoints to an unresolved colonial legacy that has had not only sociopolitical implications but also affective consequences in the Mexican pathos.

Trauma emerges as a colonial legacy that stems from the logics of dispossession. This wound associated with the violence of imperialism indicates that different temporalities of emotion are layered within sociality. If every episode of Roberta's performance animates a particular set of affects and emotions, a lacking disposition by political institutions to deal with those emotions only serves to condense the bottled-up feelings that are inevitably intermixed in the performance. In reference to the condensation of affect, I am not referring here to a psychoanalytic process of condensation and transference but to a multilayered complexity where contingently marginal sociohistorical experiences coexist. Staging an emotional release, *Roberta y las otras chicas del montón* begins to crack the linear model of nationalist development, showing how the queer laughter, as a cathartic manifestation of queer relajo, unleashes a form of critique through which (neo)colonial trauma is satirized and brought to the surface as a reparative gesture of a queer hermeneutics (Muñoz 2009, 28).

Despite the satirical portrayal of the birth scene, a confused Roberta ponders the emotional consequences of raising single-handedly a child in a country where inheritance, belonging, and kinship heavily influence the status of subject positions within complex assemblages of class, ethnicity, sociality, and citizenship. The outcry of Roberta's grim expression when holding her newly born child, who was delivered in an abrupt, violent birth, suggests that the trauma of the fatherless child will not only affect generations to come, but will also question the romantic stories of nationalism, further fissuring the affective strands of Mexican history. By dragging a historical conflict embedded in the arbitrary periodization of national history, condensed in three acts (i.e., fight for Independence, the armed Revolution, and the advent of Modernity in Mexico), the performance poignantly decrypts a foundational violence through parodical acts of queer relajo. While exposing the charges of violence running through the scripts of the nation, the drag show suggests that carnage and violence in Mexico have continually produced the otherness of bodies as a biopolitical tactic making modern time since colonization.

Making a swift transition into the age of globalization, the third drag character "Susie Pussy" suddenly appears on stage. With fluffy blond pig-tails and whitened skin, this drag queen aspires to embody the "American Dream," as she practices her English with a humorous Spanish accent. By signaling the Americanization of Mexican sociality, as well as the waves of labor migration to the United States—hoping to find better opportunities for social mobility and economic stability, her story alludes to a neoliberal alignment of Mexico, markedly by signing the 1994 NAFTA agreement after which the country evidently embraced trading policies favoring foreign investment and macroeconomic policies that significantly dam-aged local economies (Dussel Peters 2004, 64–65). As in the case of the previous drag character, Susie's exposed femme sexuality—say her name again—gestures toward an exposed body that further feels the violent con-sequences of opening to neoliberal trade, while pointing to the economic policies altering the national scripts of modern development.

The migrant body embedded in Susie's drag unveils the contested politics of migration circulating in public culture. As a fugitive body unsettling the imagined boundaries of the nation-sate, Cabral's drag persona teases out the borders of citizenship, gender, class, and sexu-ality, reflecting on the potency of drag performance as an embodied critique of progressive becoming in a post-national era. More than recurring to a flawed, dystopian, or even "backwards" reinterpreta-tion of history, the character of Susie fuses the social contradictions of embracing neoliberalism as a way of life vis-à-vis Mexican nation-alism: learning English, mimicking Anglo-American whiteness, and embracing mainstream US culture.

Drag, in this context, embodies the contested politics of citizenship. Susie's wardrobe choice resembles an exaggerated style of kitschy Amer-icana that brings out the contradictions of "dressing up" as a tactic for socioeconomic camouflage, evident in her over-ornamentation of cloth-ing when attending her visa appointment at the US embassy. This drag-ging of social class signals a performative potency that alters social catego-ries through costume while reading social class as a structure that relies on an on-going simulation. Cabral indirectly reflects on the flux of migra-tion into the US. But Susie's performance highlights a motive seared in dominant national culture: the migrant represents a displaced body that abandons the nation, and through such geographical distancing, critiques the shortcomings and structural failures impinging on job mobility, eco-nomic retribution, and social security. In this sense, the migrant body puts pressure on the nation-state's embracing of progress while leaving behind the imagined national space to enter the violently ambiguous zone of the US-Mexico border.

Making a direct reference to a complex relationship between history and violence shaping Mexican sociality, Cabral's performance exposes the trauma glossing over conjunctural conflicts emerging from the legacies of colonization, modernization, and globalization, as well as from an everlasting history of violence. Through queer forms of satire, drag political cabaret performance challenges a monolithic nationalism, while grappling with its sociocultural residues exposing the disposability of Indigenous bodies, the institutionalization of misogyny, and a well-structured class system tinted with colonial overtones. Cabral's drag performance further complicates an anxiety resting at the core of national history and identity through a drag aesthetics of saturation, fragmentation, and shine. From a drag reenactment of Mexican history, another way of sensing historical becoming emerges through the body of the performer. Throughout the three drag queen performances, the constant re-inscription of exploitation, marginalization and violence of the Indigenous body not only highlights the twist and turns of temporal dispossession, or a feeling out of time marking racial and sexual difference, but also troubles the audience with confronting their own complicity in the commodity consumption of violence.

A critique of history performed by the drag queen allows the audience to redirect the screened images of temporal dispossession, gender and racial violence as difficult images carefully examined through the medium of performance. In *Teatro de cabaret*, Gastón A. Alzate provides a concise analysis of the aesthetics shaping political cabaret as a form of cultural critique that goes beyond textual analysis and interpretation, but that tunes into social worlds to feel political pressure points for releasing satirical humor (2002, 33). Borrowing from the tradition of tent theaters, or *teatros de carpa*, traveling performing troupes that brought popular entertainment to the urban working-class, political cabaret uses humor, satire, and improvisation to reimagine and recreate "an inclusive form of theater," connecting performance "and the exercise of critical citizenship vis-à-vis Mexican neoliberalism" (Alzate 2002, 62). As Laura G. Gutiérrez notes about the role of cabaret in questioning social norms, "the artists who work within political cabaret [also] interrogate those fixed notions of gender and sexuality that permeate and are continuously and adamantly perpetuated throughout Mexican society and culture" (2010, 102). The long-standing presence of drag performance in political cabaret makes their alignment resonate with an impetus not only to foster a critical political consciousness across publics, that is a deep critique of the status quo and its real-life consequences, but also to reposition working-class experiences as valid knowledges emerging from stage interactions between publics and practitioners to challenge the assumed normalcy of conventional sexual and gender formations.

To position drag performance within genealogies of political cabaret in Mexico further situates peculiar forms of drag that, through playful gestures and maneuvers, exposes a long-contested history of censorship and dirty war tactics deployed by official institutions to keep an illusion of national progress in Mexico. In this sense, drag performance expands the repertoires and sites of feminist critique, as they can take the stage inside a black box theater or remain in the improvised podiums of queer nightlife, while reconfiguring urban space with camp and neo-baroque aesthetics characterizing queer/trans lives. Whether at the nightclub or in the small theater, drag cabaret thus exposes the contradictions of aspiring to an irresolute fantasy of progress, a utopia that vanishes at the sight of the economic inequalities and ongoing violence, putting pressure on the seemingly redemptive models of neoliberal transformation.

If drag queens are socially read as ungovernable sexual anomalies that threaten gender uniformity and the sanity of the cishet nation, the genre of political cabaret, along with its punches of satire, mediate the representation of marginal positions. Marginalization thus becomes a part of drag satire, which is inevitably linked to a travesti subject position. Carlos Monsiváis describes this drag-travesti satire (i.e., "sarcastic representation") as a playful strategy to respond to discrimination and gender violence:

> Son, sí, los que peor la han pasado y la pasan, y para llegar a la mínima aceptación debieron renunciar a cualquier identidad personal. Son la apropiación constante de lo que no son, son la actuación incesante, el interpretar lo femenino con ironía reverente o respeto sarcástico, el estudio científico del maquillaje, la supremacía en el bordado, el depositar las revelaciones del sueño en los vestidos, los zapatos de tacón alto, los postizos, la observación a la vez exacta y satírica de voces y andares y miradas [. . .] Y detrás de cada escenificación, del fasto y el delirio en las noches de las discos, están las historias personales, marcadas por las humillaciones y golpes y vergüenzas familiares y acentuación de la diferencia por la marginalidad de toda índole. El travesti se arriesga en demasía, son legión los asesinados y torturados y golpeados. A ellos se les dedica el tor-

rente de burlas y menosprecio, y para sobrevivir deben asumir a fondo la visión degradada que se les impone (2010a, 281).

Following his description, the drag queen, or travesti, renounces to any signs of identity. The drag performer signals the void of national identity. In feeling Cabral's performance, drag queens and travesti women embody a rupture of the patriarchal structures that permeate Mexican sociality. By grappling with the temporal condensation of Mexican history, Cabral's drag political cabaret deeply performs a fissuring of the historical scripts of the nation. As a transgressor of any "essential" space, the drag queen performs temporal dispossession and sheds light on the erasures and silences of official history by filling them in with the Brown excess of indigeneity evident in a material pastiche of wigs, gowns, and glitter. What Cabral's performance brings to the fore is the playful embodiments of queer relajo by highlighting the displacement, erasure, and dispossession of Indigenous women. By exposing that the official periodization of Mexican history (i.e., the colony, the revolution, and the era of globalization) impedes the Indigenous body from accessing historical becoming, and therefore their human condition is unrecognized, the drag cabaret performance grapples with legacies of trauma and violence, while recasting the presence of Indigenous and mestiza women from the blind spots of national culture. By staging the search of everlasting love, the performance reveals how the logics of heterosexuality have advanced modern forms of intimacy as foundational to the love of nation. In this sense, the virile white mestizo nation satisfies the affective needs of the abused Indigenous body through her own erasure. But as the drag characters suggest, giving into loving the nation can and indeed turns into a site of violence.

By breaking open the white affect of national belonging, the performance welcomes a critical vision of time, allowing the audience to disidentify from progressive becoming. The performing drag queen, that is, a moving body drenched in a glitzy neo-baroque aesthetic, exposes the contradictions of any sort of development—national, sexual, or otherwise—as queens, by the excess of their own assemblage, embody the bits and pieces of a shattered way of life. The historical fragmentation performed by drag performance gestures toward forms of queer relajo that propose a poignant critique of national identity, but must importantly, make evident the playful strategies queer/trans folk resort to in order to move through the structures of trauma and violence in Mexico. In displaying visual violence, engaging semantic maleficence, and fracturing a linear temporality, *Roberta y las otras chicas del montón* invests in a renewal of sociality by confronting the cruelty of neoliberal modernity, while bringing into question the neo-developmental paradigms fossilized as the bedrocks of Mexican belonging, which tend to graft individuals against exclusionary forms of citizenship.

In recognizing the cruelty of modern utopias, the cabaret performance seeks to evoke the audience's empathy through the painful misfortunes of three drag characters. By fathoming pain as critical affect for feminist action, cultural critic Sayak Valencia asserts that pain and suffering need to become political strategies to reflect on a carnal politics of unbelonging—or what it feels to not belong according to cishet narratives.[17] Néstor García Canclini further argues that temporality in the Americas can be understood as a multilayered assemblage of historical periods that coexist in contention with multiple signs and cultural practices across social spheres (2005, chap. 7). Canclini's argument resonates with Diana Taylor's assertion that, "in Mexico we have always been queer" (2016, 210). By contrast, the three views sustain an inherent *queerness* in the temporal formations of Mexican sociality, that is, a convoluted assemblage of time carrying the painful hauntings of coloniality, modernity, and neoliberal progress.

Against this backdrop, Cabral's drag cabaret playfully interacts with queer shadow economies, as well as with the markets of queer gentrification. In this sense, queer relajo is not automatically liberatory, but rather names the adaptable capacities urban working-class queer/trans folk draw to actively negotiate with the logics of neoliberal consumption and neocolonial extraction. By transporting the affect of queer nightlife, however, queer relajo detonates possibilities of disrupting the economic transactions of queer neoliberalism after dark with playful interactions. Although affective, acts of queer relajo also depend on the contingencies of state regulation, commodification, and consumption.

In tracing the distinct wavelengths modulating the interactions between visual art practitioners, institutions, and market forces in urban Mexico, Caitlin Frances Bruce calls "attunement" a complex process by which contending interests of counterpublics find harmony through "frequencies of recognition, shared vibrations, audibility," as well as "noise, static, or interference . . . and energizing expulsion at worst" (2024, 4). Along this vein, the queer relajo of drag cabaret performance spots embodied strategies that sexually dissident bodies devise to move across and apart, flow through and in, and circumvent neoliberal consumerism across urban spaces under state regulation and surveillance. More than drawing a line separating overlapping spheres, acts of queer relajo—like the laughing and humor of drag cabaret performance—map the shifting positions of queer folk when making sense of market consumerism, state interventionism, and queer commodification, while banking on a different sort of queer capital, one that is not strictly economic, but affectively embodied. In doing so, drag cabaret performance gestures toward relational fields of queer agential action, or queer nightscapes, that attend to the socioeconomic and cultural geographies of queer nightlife. As such, a drag cabaret critique that relies on affective capital can and indeed should produce disruption through queer play in the face of global dispossession, while disarticulating the paradigms of modernity, neo-developmentalism, and neo-interventionism.

Drag cabaret thus challenges the nationalist scripts of progress by questioning neoliberal aspirations of sexual citizenship. To this effect, Cabral's drag cabaret performance makes apparent the fissures of a national subject by exposing the temporal cracks at the core of Mexican belonging, including ethnic dispossession, forced displacement, and racial assimilation. Dragging post-national scripts on the cabaret stage cuts through the smoke curtain of national unity—a political project originally curated by an elite lettered culture. Inspired by playful acts of queer disturbance, Cabral's drag critique joins a larger hemispheric transfeminist praxis of queer cultural analysis, in which performance, cultural practice, and embodied criticism converge to inspire collective ways of knowledge formation that respond to the contextual contingencies sustaining queer and trans nightlife transregionally.

As with any form of political cabaret, Cabral's drag critique involves the active participation of audience members. In the last act, a person from the audience joins the drag queen on stage to aid her in changing her outfit. The cabaret stage is then turned into a queer collective workshop where a short-lived sense of bliss is felt. As manifestations of queer relajo, satire, humor, and laughter serve as the binding glue for a queer sense of intimacy in a small black box theater. But the ambiance created by the different stage elements, like the neon lights, smoke curtains, and fast-paced music, are reminiscent of a queer nightlife ambiance surrounding the stage where Cabral's drag cabaret performance first debuted during the May–July 2015 season at the city-sponsored black box theater *Foro A Poco No*, along the street República de Cuba, steps away from one of Mexico City's queer nightlife enclaves. With the rapid commodification of queer culture in the capital city, *Roberta y las otras chicas del montón* also played in December 2022 at Teatro-Bar El Vicio, in collaboration with the producers of the BearMex festival, and in April 2022 at Zona Rosa's independent queer bookstore and cultural center Somos Voces. The multiple presentations of Cabral's drag cabaret performance shows the shifting hybridity and blurriness of queer and trans nightlife, as it runs through a large circuit of venues that make evident the morphing textures of the urban spaces that sustain queer and trans night cultures amid their commodification. These shadow economic circuits of queer/trans capital extend ways of participating in the creation of counterpublics through queer acts of playfulness, joy, and pleasure, prompting, nonetheless, a critical reflection on state neoliberalization, urban displacement, and queer consumption.[18]

As playful strategies of queer relajo, drag cabaret performance builds on the political force of collective emotion. When commemorating the 60th anniversary of Teatro La Capilla, a theater venue founded in 1953 by queer poet and playwright Salvador Novo (1904–1974) who also made a home out of this space, Jesusa Rodríguez, prominent political cabaret performer, playwright, and now senator, noted "[e]s inconcebible imaginar este lugar sin el amor; esto sólo se sostiene por amor, si no tienes un cómplice amoroso que te acompañe, está del carajo."[19] During the 1980s Teatro La Capilla and its adjacent performance stage El Hábito were combined to house a larger cultural complex for cabaret performance and theater. Mainly integrated by three stages (i.e., Teatro-Bar El Vicio, Sala Novo, and Teatro La Capilla), this performance venue in Mexico City's south-end neighborhood of Coyoacán celebrated its sixty-sixth anniversary in 2019.[20]

Similarly, El Foro A Poco No, Teatro Cabaret, where Cabral performed this cabaret piece, has become a performance venue that not only houses alternative, emerging plays that intertwine cabaret and experimental performance, but has become an intrinsic space of queer nightlife along the downtown strip of República de Cuba. Partially funded by Mexico City's Department of Culture, El Foro A Poco No, Teatro Cabaret is strategically located steps away from queer nightclubs such as El Tahúr, El Marrakech, La Purísima, La Sacristía, El Oasis, and a couple of blocks away from the iconic Cabaret La Perla.[21] This nocturnal circuit of bars, cabaret stages, and shabby downtown streets points to the emergence of complex and contested affective infrastructures of queer nightlife, where queer relajo rehearses other possibilities of negotiating night-making alongside its commodification.

Carlos Monsiváis describes how urban queer space is built by the modulating sensibilities of queer relajo in Mexico City:

> El gay que se urbaniza atraviesa el espacio secreto y público a la vez donde "la raza maldita" se reconoce gracias a la mirada posesiva y la mirada braguetera, y a partir de allí, se palpa febrilmente, sitúa su identidad con el apoyo inevitable de la burla y el choteo, se asegura de su lugar en la sociedad atendiendo a los atropellos policiacos, usa el melodrama como intermediación literaria y si no va hasta el límite es porque, en los convenios de su cultura formativa, el límite ha sido su punto de partida. (2010a, 136)

It is from within urban queer nightscapes, that *Roberta y las otras chicas del montón* debunks official accounts of history, mediating through queer play the distance separating a nostalgic nationalism and an irresolute future in neoliberal terms. But more than harping on the neo-developmentalist strategies toward futurity, Cabral's embodied dissonance activates other playful practices of queer relationality. Moving beyond neoliberal scripts of sexual citizenship, their rehearsal of a queer melodrama retouches trauma, to create bonds of intimacy through political cabaret. Here is where drag performance offers a shiny potentiality by fostering queer night belonging through the laughter of queer humor, while outshining the pain and violence from the dark episodes of history.

Broken Records: The Resonance of Queer Memory

Queer nightscapes erupt from the playful negotiations between the multiple actors involved in queer practices of night-making. At their core, drag queens assembled an ecology of social, material, transactional, sonic, and affective economies that bring out lesbian butches, femme queens, *jotitos*, *travestis*, *transmarilenchas*, and other transfeminine dissident bodies, to play at night. Immanent to ecologies of drag, the notion of *broken record* becomes more pertinent to my discussion of the resonance of queer nightlife. As a figure of speech in English, this cliché is frequently used to express annoyance at someone's endlessly repeating opinion or statement. In Spanish, a similar slang term is used to convey a similar exasperation: *disco rayado*. Both idioms nonetheless carry a material, sonic, and musical relation given that to break a record can also refer to perform better than anyone else, or to the physical destruction of a music disc. With the notion of broken record, the lip-syncing of drag queens sheds a different light on the affective replays of nightlife.

On the binding power of queer music, drag queens play a pivotal role in producing sonic ambiances vital to queer and trans nightlife. Across queer bars, dance floors, social media apps, block parties, *sonideros*, kara-okes, or drag queen lip-syncing performances, the sounds of a queer pop mix, ranging from the euphoria of Kylie Minogue's "Come Into My World," Ariana Grande's "Break Free," Cristina La Veneno's "Veneno Pa' Tu Piel," or Daniela Romo's "Yo No Te Pido La Luna," to the gloom of Rocío Jurado's "Punto de Partida," Cher's "Believe," Celine Dion's "All Coming Back To Me," Amanda Miguel's "Castillos," or Ana Gabriel and Vikki Carr's "Cosas del Amor," bind us together and make us feel at home. Tareke Ortiz and Nayar Rivera maintain that music plays a vital role in the formation of queer collectives, as behind every song and tune lies not only a sense of freedom, but also a way of making sense of our queerness (2010, 188). In this sense, the power of queer music travels across time and place to boost the affective ambiance of queer nightscapes, as well as the transfer of knowledge about our racialized queer condition through sonic sensa-tion, lyrical attunement, bodily rhythm, and sentimental sound.

Harking back to a style of excess and saturation, the broken records of drag performance bind together bits and pieces that otherwise would hold no meaningful value in the neoliberal economies of intimacy. By carrying an excess of second-hand materiality, drag queens attune our senses to feeling the textures of time, to notice the convergence of differ-ent stories, like the sparkly blue chaquira ring a close friend gifted to me, or the pair of earrings I found abandoned after a drag show in Mexico City. Ortiz and Rivera further draw on drag queen and travesti matters, noting that, despite mimicking a male-imposed femininity, as "voices of feeling," queens combine makeup, wigs, implants, foam padding, lipstick, and shiny dresses to cast "jewels of our heritage in terms of emotional intelligence" (2010, 192). Expanding on the liberating echoes of queer music, drag queens are carriers of an intimate queer knowledge, a history of queer feeling that, resonating through song, voice, and sound, carry us through the night to otherwise grapple with disillusion, happiness, sad-ness, or hope, not as failed positions of social straightness, but as ways of fostering kinship and belonging away from compulsory heterosexuality. Radiating queer memory, drag queens once more repurpose the repertoires of popular Spanish music resonating across queer nightscapes. Lip-syncing to a well-awaited playback song, drag queens bring us closer to heal together, and find strength and resilience wrapped in sound.

I stand in front of my bathroom mirror and, in the absence of a hanging mirrorball, direct my attention to the gold sequin rows around my shoulders. Wearing velvet platform shoes, I also found at a thrift store, I prance around my floor and rehearse the slow moves of my Wednesday performance at the Blue Moon. The life of an aspiring drag queen in academia is not easy, as I must choose between writing or performing. Big Daddy gets jealous and only wants me to spend my days and nights fantasizing about the next administrative move that will land me a steady role in serving the self-interests of the academic institution I work for. But tonight is different. I have let Piña Colada take over my schedule, as she will be performing in front of a crowd who probably hasn't listened yet to the slow tempos of bolero and Latin ballad.

Call me oversentimental, but ballads sound out a groove indescribable in words. They are charged with an inner knowledge, or with an intuition that reminds us that what we hope for is, at times, unattainable—something that resonates somewhat with Lauren Berlant's "cruel optimism." The worst is that what we have felt for a long time transforms into knowing that what we have hoped for has been impossible from the get-go. That is why Latin ballads remind me of a queer feeling of impossibility, of knowing that sometimes queer love is an impossible deed. And not because I think that queer people cannot love each other, but that queer love can be impossible because of the toxic masculinity and fatal heterosexuality around us. At times, that toxic presence does well what it's supposed to do: fill our spirit with hate, fear, and doubt toward what we've known all along, that our way out is to embrace that queer sense of impossibility. It's what keeps us going.

With a broken heart, makeup done, wig fastened and secured, and shiny second-hand gold dress, I let my body follow the sweet notes of Isabel Pantoja's "Así Fue," a song written[22] and produced by the one and only Mexican queer diva Juan Gabriel—of course, there is Selena, but that's another story.[23] Featured in Pantoja's 1988 album *Desde Andalucía*,[24] "Así Fue" deals with the singer telling her ex-lover she has moved on and found a new love partner in the aftermath of their abrupt vanishment. The popular interpretation of the song, however, boils its charged sentimentality down to a mere "I've moved on, and you should too" kind of heterosexual attitude. But the queer undertones make me suspect that such a reading is the reason why many Latinx queers across the Americas, have adopted this song as an anthem of queer impossibility. For my rehearsal, I pick this song not only because I am going through a breakup, but because its wavelengths speak to the queer impossibility of holding on, to a queer refusal of letting go.

By tuning into its slow tempo, the music moves my arms up in the air. Gesturing flamenco-like floreo, or arm positions simulating a flower, I channel a messy mix of pain and sorrow. And with every slow hand gesture, I tacitly access "the archives of Latina/o memory queerly," while tapping into "the youth knowledges about the ways we live, love, and struggle as queers and Latinas/os" (Rivera-Servera 2017, 190). Going against the imperatives of conventional intimacy, Juan Gabriel's song stirs up the straightness of time by invoking the presence of the past when a long-awaited lover comes back unexpectedly.

Moving away from the Spanish copla style, Isabel Pantoja's high notes powerfully evoke an everlasting heartache. While "pasado," "nada," or "imposible" are choices indexing a long-gone past, "olvidar," "culpa," or "perdonar" reinscribe the pain of losing a loved one into the present. In referencing the past with "así fue," the singer dwells in a mixed time where an impossible love comes back to life, enticing the singer into escaping from the heteronormative logics of possession and reproduction. By playing with the queerness of the past, the song rehearses a queer time amid the impossibilities of the lived present. As the song continues to play in my change room, I mix in a slow two-step sway, letting the music channel my own sadness to embody sharp poses that reflect a dramatic feeling of loss.

"Así fue" further invokes the past by bringing back scenes of a once-exhilarating love affair that make the singer crack open in confusion. By looping back into a sudden romantic breakup, love and pain intermingle in the present, as the singer struggles to contain the over-excitement of seeing again the departed lover, "¿cómo decirle que te amo?" The unexpected return of the ex-lover inspires the writing of the song, as the singer not only asks the ex-lover to stop holding on to the impossibility of being back together, "ya no te aferres," but also considers becoming a friend to help them heal by forgetting the past, "si tú quieres seremos amigos/ yo te ayudo a olvidar el pasado." While I try to remember the moves I make for tomorrow night's show, replaying the song in my mind brings back memories of my own breakups, but much like the singer, of also looking for new beginnings that nonetheless resonate in the past.

According to Juan Gabriel, Isabel Pantoja sought him in Ciudad Juárez, where they recorded the song together. The release of Pantoja's single further marked Juan Gabriel's distancing with his former Spanish muse, Rocío Dúrcal, who collaborated with the Mexican composer in eight record-setting albums from the early 1970s to the mid-1980s. Rumor has it that Juan Gabriel secretly slept with Dúrcal's partner and career manager Antonio Morales Barretto, known professionally as Júnior, and upon finding out, the Spanish singer and actress distanced herself from her long-time friend and musical producer. Despite the rumors, Juan Gabriel's emotional charges of "Así Fue" make us feel the queer possibility of the past disrupting the here and now. The song, in this sense, echoes a temporal dissonance indexing the impossibility of queer intimacy, while extending an ode to queer longing that resonates as part of a queer musical repertoire chanted across queer bars, dance floors, and nightclubs.

Resonating as a lyrical queer memory, the song's queer refusal of letting go is queerly felt when attending a drag queen's lip-sync performance through which we improvise an emotional response to facing disillusion, absence, or heartbreak, while fostering queer forms of care and bonding at the club. Within the very confines of queer nightlife, drag queen performance animates invisible spaces intimately stitched with song, feeling, and touch. Representative of a towering queer repertoire of broken records, "Así fue" unbinds the queer affect of the past, whose excessive resonance remains unreadable and undetectable to the re/productive logics of neoliberalism. In doing so, the song and its subsequent lip-sync performances mix fantasies of a queer time.

Attending to the resonance of queer memory, I am therefore eschewing the negative connotation attributed to the term broken record to infuse it with the echoes of queer impossibility. In doing so, I am devising a materialist tool to debunk traditional methodologies of historiography that fail to account for the emergence of nightlife practices pushed to the margins of progress and history-making. Broken records are thus material, sonic, and performative archives that make possible the impossibility of queer and trans night-making. Invested in a popular musical repertoire, broken records transmit affects, sensibilities, and knowledges that highlight the vibrancy of sexually dissident cultures. In displaying a material shininess, drag queens are at the core of these agential modulations in which glitter, music, and affect animate a sense of bliss to imagine a time away from the heteronormative logics of development, reproduction, and consumption. They presently animate an out-of-place-ness that is felt in the carnal intimacy of others. They exert their ownership by playing with nighttime.

Drag queens embody a material fissure in the straightness of time. Their playful rupturing cracks a critique that moves across ecologies of sociality, mining hierarchies of knowledge production and blurring the lines of a nationalist nostalgia in Mexico and across its diaspora. Lip-syncing is at the core of drag performance, as it involves the multilayering of dissonant sounds, experiences, and objects. By intercalating music tracks, affects, and queer knowledge, a drag queen's lip-sync performance curates more than a rhythmic medley, a mixtape for queer survival. Drag performance thus plays with the power dynamics of historical coherence, to cast away the cishet delusion of historical rape. In the gritty materiality of drag queens, I feel a broken record not only as a patchy ornament whose vibrations play out loud, but also as a concept to materialize the epistemologies of drag culture, assembled by broken pieces, unwanted objects, residues, and marginalia, whose resonance layers, ruptures, and obliterates straight time. As a broken record, Mexican drag performance deploys a playful potpourri of fantasies that, like Roberto Cabral in *Roberta y las otras chicas del montón*, and Piña Colada's memories and rehearsals, dance away with the night, sparkling a queer affectivity from an ocean of junk that resists and challenges the cruel visions of neoliberal transformation in the Americas.

PART II

Fumbling Toward Urban Nightscapes

THREE

Play, Sex, and Dance in the Queer Underground

Cumbia tunes sound across the subway car, as commuters' eyes blink in the luminescence of neon wavelengths disappearing with the speed of light. Everyone onboard avoids the discomfort of making direct eye contact. As my heart's palpitations intensify, a young kid selling boot-legged cumbia CDs, carrying a heavy sound speaker on their back, juggles through a shifting floor and grabs on metallic rail handles. The loud music sends out vibrations felt through flesh and matter. As the train pulls into the station, the doors unleash a forceful crowd, and the young CD vendor runs to quickly hop onto the next car. On the platform, two men leaning against a mounted bright billboard sensuously embrace each other. Their hands move swiftly as if looking for something to be unveiled, but the shimmering intrusion of bright station lights has already exposed what others would prefer to keep in the darkness of public life.

My broken memories of what takes place in Mexico City's dark underground bring about a queer way of feeling space that repositions our senses to appreciate the world otherwise.[1] In perceiving subway tunnels differently, queer intimacy sustains a space that makes visible the tentacle-like movement of arms roping moving bodies, as in my memory of two queer guys making out. Their intimate contact merges with other sounds, rhythms, fragments, and bodies, like a youngster selling bootlegged CDs for a living, piecing together a queer underground alongside subway structures.

Attending to a condensation of queer relajo from the jostle and friction flowing through the subway system, this chapter considers the shifts and moves of queer dance, erotic play, and m4m sex in one of Mexico City's most essential infrastructures. In here my argument is three-fold. By trac-ing how queer and trans folk playfully interact inside subway lines, I first argue that dancing and cruising assemble *choreographies of touch*, mak-ing bodies, feelings, and places stick together to circumvent a neoliberal logic of efficient re/production, as well as a Euro-American sexual paradigm of queer- and transness. To this end, I interact with trans activist and performer Lia García's "Mis XXy años," a public performance I attended inside Mexico City's Metro Pino Suárez in 2015. I then look at short DIY-porn videos from porn websites that record practices of m4m cruising inside a rear-end subway car known in popular queer parlance as *la cajita feliz*, or "The Happy Meal," in reference to fast-food global corporation McDonald's kid food box.

While underground circuits of queer and trans touch enact forms of resistance against a neoliberal relationality, these scenes of dancing and cruising can and indeed turn into commodifiable goods of a queer global economy, prompting me to consider in my second point that such an underground zone of queer contact exists alongside the contradictorily uneven flows of queer capital. By comparing the photography of David Graham's *The Last Car: Cruising in Mexico City* (2017) and Mexico City-based artist Eriko Stark's *Furias Nocturnas* (2022), I situate in the former a neoliberal queer gaze that, commodifying queer undergrounds, expose the exploitation of narratives about a pre-modern and backward sexuality found in the global south. By making evident the interaction between the stickiness of queer nightscapes, and everyday subway infrastructures, my last contention is that a queer underground emerges, emplacing racialized, poor, and working-class queer/trans modes of care to mediate neoliberal extraction. Such an intimate engagement thus invites us not only to reposition our modes of interacting with the dirty contours of sexuality in the global south, but also to position ourselves alongside the contradictions of a queer underground to sense invisible choreographies of dancing and cruising. Recalibrating our understanding on the spaces where care can enliven queer and trans intimacy, this chapter ultimately grapples with how queer relajo disrupt the everyday cycles of heteronormative re/production, reminding commuters that nightscapes also abound in public daylight.

Quinceañera in Transit: Dancing Across The Queer Underground

For over ten years, transfeminist performer, and educator Lia García (La Novia Sirena) has interacted with popular and working-class spaces to connect her trans body with that of others in what the artist calls, *affective encounters*. As a radical pedagogy of touch, an affective encounter allows the artist to unbind enclosed museum spaces to take up streets, schools, markets, hospitals, and prisons, while bringing awareness about trans women's experiences with everyday violence and marginalization in Mexico, and across the Americas. By tapping into the potential of tender loving care through physical touch, the performer's method asks participants to find in their own lived experience a connection to unfixed gender embodiments, and create a short-lived sense of kinship through shared vulnerability.[2] Interacting with working-class urban passersby, Lia García (La Novia Sirena) restages a quinceañera party in *Próxima Estación: Mis XXy años* (*Next Station: My XXy years*) at the busy Pino Suárez subway station[3] in 2015, further building on her pedagogy to celebrate trans becoming.[4]

A quinceañera waltz exposes a complex social choreography whereby material economies, social locations, such as socioeconomic status, class, race, citizenship, ethnicity, etc., cultural capital, and popular practices converge while staging a scene of feminine becoming. Typically held at privately rented dance halls, or under a big tarp out in the streets at night, a quinceañera party confirms the arrival of femininity, that is, it serves to openly acknowledge a young girl's passage from child- into adulthood, celebrated in the close company of relatives, friends, and loved ones. Parties held out in the streets mark the working-class condition of nightlife manifesting in public, as those unable to rent a party hall usually occupy streets, cut off traffic, and disrupt transit in the face of economic precarity and marginalization. To affirm her social status as a full-grown woman— who can marry, work at home, and bear children—each family member dances a short piece with the birthday girl. In this sense, quinceañera parties can function as display windows showcasing the available resources granting social status to working- and middle-class families inasmuch as they cast forms of Latinized femininity not only in Mexico but across the Americas (Cantú 1999; González 2019; Rodríguez 2013). By setting up a quinceañera party inside the subway, Lia thus highlights how dance and celebration serve to negotiate socioeconomic and material conditions in the making of femininity but shifts its focus from gender affirmation to gender reconfiguration.

A picture taken as a party memento shows Lia smiling on a platform along the pink line, as the performer looks right at the camera. Wearing a black suit, her MC and court of seven *chambelanes*, or escorts, surround her. A bright, orange-colored subway car appears suspended in the background, while the blue fabric of ties and lapel flowers stands out for its iri-

Fig. 10. Lia García (La Novia Sirena) stands with her MC and court of *chambelanes* by the subway platform. Courtesy of Lia García (La Novia Sirena).

descent shine. After a short walk, Lia arrives at the station in the company of her trans entourage. With a silver headpiece, she flounces in a bright metallic blue dress toward a long tunnel where the frantic transit of daily commuters forms a crowd awaiting her regal entrance. Because the station crisscrosses the pink and blue lines, Lia follows this color code to dance in a space that not only alludes to the colors of the trans flag, but also hints at a symbolic site of gender un/becoming across subway routes, mobilizing trans as a suffix to embody disruption, and transformation. Commuters who join in form a circle around the performance and wait attentively while popular music plays aloud. As I stand in the audience encircling the improvised performance stage, I notice how commuters take a closer look at Lia. Their eyes reveal an unstoppable curiosity; they look perplexed and wonder why a quinceañera is in transit, as a drag king MC announces the name of the performer in the middle of the station's busy corridor.

In its very title, *Próxima Estación* (*Next Station*) gestures less to fixed embodiments than to transient states of gender, sexuality, and productivity, pondering about what will come next. The performance starts with a waltz between the quinceañera and her chambelanes, who dance to Puerto

Rican singer Chayanne's song "Tiempo de vals" (1990), carrying the audience into a queer fairyland of piano and trumpets.[5] As I feel the vibrations of a hefty speaker system sounding across the halls, subway commuters around me recognize the song and begin to sway to its rhythm, as others watch closely a two-step waltz. Following the conventions of a quinceañera party, Lia invites members into the stage, altering the boundaries of trans intimacy and urban movement. After swirling with her for a couple of minutes, each dancer pays a tribute to the performer by bowing with their head. While some improvise moves, others smile, clap, or dance in their spots to the song's fast tempo, transforming an adjacent tunnel near the Aztec ruins into a party stage.

In *Próxima Estación*, the song's queer theatricality transports scenes of nightlife, such as dark rooms, colorful lights, or sparkly outfits, into an underground corridor filled with street vendors, hectic commuters, and fast trains. García's dress's metallic blue chiffon, for instance, broaches the luminescent bangles of stage curtains, or the eyeshadows of drag queens, invoking a feeling of being at the queer nightclub, further heightened by shiny party signs, bright balloons, and musical notes, to recreate a predominantly working-class night ambiance across subway tunnels. Assembling yet dissolving nightlife's affective registers, Lia's dance awakens the residual potentiality of queer ephemera by including festive queer artifacts, such as romantic pop songs, blingy tiaras, and flashy attires. Bearing the sensorial capacities of queer nightlife, the party attunes the audience into understanding how queer and trans folk experience the world through dancing, playing, and touching. The performance thus plays with spatiotemporal limits by transporting the material ornaments of queer nightlife into an everyday working-class commute, making a festive night scene, or a queer nightscape, stick to subway lines. It is through touch that a queer nightscape emerges from the underground, exposing how the vulnerability of the trans body and its material affectivity remake the very constructs of space. By drawing from Chayanne's "Tiempo de vals" queer temporality, Lia's dance emerges as a silver-lining amid the turbulence of commuting, activating a space-making practice that moves through the resplendence of trans touch, blurring the divides of public/private, of day/night, of masculine/feminine.

We are unaware of the subway stations that commuters-turned-into-audience have traveled to get here, but through Lia's trans touch, we are confronted with the strangeness of each other's moving state, finding comfort in the instability of being together momentarily, while retouching a feminine archetype into a *transceañera*, or a quinceañera in transit. By engaging with the pulses of queer relajo, passersby recognize both, the staging of a social choreography of femininity, as well as the performer's intention to ephemerally recreate nighttime in the middle of a transfer station. If tenderness describes a feminine quality of being soft to cut or chew, while innocence marks a state of purity, virginity, and conceitedness, Lia's quinceañera saturates the affective economies of femininity by intimately making palpable the unstable contours of the trans body. In doing so, a swirling quinceañera unframes the socially-choreographed passage into femininity, as well as reclaims an underground urban infrastructure to remap queer zones of trans contact across the city.

Echoing the words of Jennifer Tyburczy, *Próxima Estación* stages "a love letter," a collective embodiment of trans joy, pleasure, and ultimately love where touch fosters affective encounters and material frictions, suspending, even if momentarily, the hectic rhythms of urban productivity. When the rushing stops, a sense of wonder sparks a need for connection that remixes public space. The performer touches their face, at times staring into their eyes, as if looking into their soul, trying to find a connection. In this sense, Lia's playful touch alters neoliberal rhythms by basking in the surplus of a queer time, swirling away from efficiency. As it draws from a sense of being in transit, her touch activates an affective transportation that unfolds when a queer dance floor emerges from a subway corridor. Jamming a logic of extraction with every touch, Lia conflates her own transness with passersby's own state of transit, suggesting that trans becoming, and city commuting are not as different a position as one might think, but rather embody too similar states of instability. The performance thus ponders on the contagiousness of trans touch in what Sayak Valencia calls, "queer multitudes, who through the performative materialization of their bodies are able to develop different kinds of g-local agency" amid violence (2018, 263). The performance's invitation to inhabit *tiempo de vals* sparks other temporal strands that insist on a shared sense of transientness beyond a neoliberal paradigm of sexuality-as-complete-and-stable.

On the capaciousness of trans touch, Lia herself reflects on a transfeminist praxis,

> I am never alone in photos of my performances: there are always other people with me, who are also displaying their transition. In this way, I am going through a collective transition. This doesn't mean I'm homogenizing the term trans so that everyone can

now identify as trans. In the end, the transition and trans identities should be contagious. They should be able to expand to other terms, because a cis-hetero man who starts seeing me will also confront a series of social prejudices. This implies a total oppression. Although a certain branch of feminism may object to putting men in a position of victimhood, this is a reality. I reiterate, transitioning is not just about me, since there is a whole social structure that also transitions and comes out of the closet. (2019)

For the performer, transness refers to an ability to move from one place to another by means of sticky contact. Relying on the contagiousness of touch, such a transfeminist praxis enacts an expansive field in which transness travels to alter the socio-spatial structures that constrain passage of gender nonconforming bodies, taking them "out of the closet." Waves of trans touch unfollow teleological trajectories of neoliberal development and subjectivity. Rather, trans touch takes us into unexpected places of wonder "to see the world as something that does not have to be, and as something that came to be, over time, with work" (Ahmed 2014, 180). A wild sense of wonder also "opens up the possibility of unmaking and unbuilding worlds" (Halberstam 2020, 3–4), as it playfully disrupts the everyday mechanics of labor ever so present in the making of the working-class, the invisible urban poor, and the economically marginal. As such, trans touch makes contagious the possibilities of becoming otherwise, away from hardened ontologies, away from the sexual arrangements of neoliberal capitalism, and away from a system normalizing patriarchal exhaustion and depletion of othered life. In other words, "a haptic tactic" that "reveals the materiality of the trans-ness of touch and its inherently migratory state" to contend with the preemptive logics of state law, violence, and heterosexuality (Delgado Huitrón 2019, 167).

Lia's dance not only intensifies the sentient capacities of impressing and being impressed by bodies and objects in movement, but also reconfigures space for transness to erupt, moving nightlife into the ordinariness of the underground subway.[6] Trans touch rebuilds an interdependent infrastructure of affects in which commuters and trans/queer folk find nightly respite amid the hectic rhythms of urban life. In this sense, *Próxima Estación* shapes a collective trans body that, bridging urban infrastructure, queer nightlife, and working-class commuting, improvises a choreography of touch, shifting architectural surroundings through a dance of intimacy, "not only because the surrounds are generative in and of themselves but because bodying begins to take shape differently, identitarian and volitional presuppositions at the heart of agency dancing to another logic" (Manning 2020, 207). In other words, transient touch reminds us of the urban infrastructures of intimacy, as subway cars carry the stains of cum, the smudges of saliva, a dried teardrop left after leaving the club, an embrace leaving behind a shirt crumbled.

There are certainly many risks priming nightlife in Mexico City. According to Transgender Europe's monitoring, Mexico occupies the second most dangerous place for trans people in the Americas after Brazil, with 772 reported feminicides from 2008 to 2024 without accounting for unreported cases.[7] Gender-based violence, transphobia, and homophobia sadly appear as typical consequences for those who transgress the publicness of gender and sexual life in Mexico, an alarming phenomenon having strong precedent since 1901.[8] The statistics I refer to here, however, are indicative of a larger problem beyond making a personal decision to put one's life in danger. Dangerous positions not only mark queer and trans life in Mexico City, but also leave indelible marks on queer, trans, and femme activist and cultural collectives. As such, the intense flows of violence in Mexico should be understood within a larger framework of hemispheric differentials Sayak Valencia calls *gore capitalism*, which interlocks neoliberal capitalism, violent heteronormativity, government corruption, and the dynamics of a narcostate.

Insisting on how queer nightlife is a process of un/becoming through material practices and political economies, the transceañera party drills through the necropolitical dimension of trans life, pointing us to issues of public space, accessibility, and trans vitality, while questioning neoliberal notions of sexual freedom when the moving of trans bodies is not only constrained by everyday violence, but also by the social arrangements of time and space. Jean-Ulrick Désert contends that "queer space crosses, engages, and transgresses social, spiritual, and aesthetic locations, all of which is articulated in the realm of the public/private, the built/unbuilt environments . . ." (1997, 20).[9] Yet the necropolitical realities of trans life expose the differing levels of violence that structure neoliberal spaces for queer consumption, like exclusive gay bars, elite shows, and costly nighttime paraphernalia. If trans and travesti people are often objectified and reduced to the stage of gay nightclubs (Namaste 2000, 11–12), García's performance upends the repetitive necropolitical conversion of trans life by setting a dance stage for trans intimacy away from the neoliberal economies of gay consumerist culture, echoing what thomas f. defrantz notes about the distorting capabilities of queer dance, in the revelation of this crucial relationship of object/viewed to viewer/interpreter, we confirm that queer is a collaborative assemblage; queer dance is a distortion, hopefully in useful way, toward something unanticipated and awe-ful (awful) that exists *now, here,* and *for this gathered community.* dance enhances queer visibility, queer dance emerges from being and doing, perhaps, but its contents are brought into focus by the making of its various audiences who can narrate the queerness at hand. (178)

In finding a space for trans touch, city commuters come into close contact with transness, undoing the necropolitical violence marking trans lives in Mexico. As Lia takes off her tiara and holds it against the face of a woman, these touching gestures, of holding objects against the surface of skin, confront a trans necropolitics by establishing a tender link with the audience. The performance's force is not only enabling trans touch, but also suspending the plasticity of neoliberal violence affecting trans lives, as well as economically marginalized, working-class sectors. As people in attendance continue to dance, the feeling of interdependent togetherness questions the utilitarianism of the daily commute, disrupting the order of bodies, places, and things. Building a sensorial infrastructure for trans worldmaking, she reconfigures feminine archetypes to recast the vulnerability of the trans body. That is, instead of engaging images of trans violence, the performer resorts to dancing and touching as trans gestures to reshape people's relationship to transness.[10]

While moving through queer space, Lia García's performance distill a state of being in transit, of hopping from one station to another, eluding a final (gendered) destination, connecting city commuting with a touch of transness. In this sense, *Próxima Estación* celebrates a femininity in transit, in a state of un/becoming and possibility. This unstable femininity also connects with the audience's unfinished commute, while dancing highlights the interdependency of trans-worlding, that is, of a transient state of un/becoming, and through such un/doing, the possibility of worlds emerging and converging at the collapse of bodily and material boundaries. Lia's transceañera thus uplifts transness not as a private affair discussed at a medical facility, but as a public affair requiring the bodily and affective involvement of those who are passing by.

Bridging trans and queer epistemologies through performance, *Próxima Estación* repositions the place trans studies occupies in relation to queer studies by challenging the categories that have reduced transness to a mere object of queer analysis. As the transceañera prompts commuters to stop their transit and assume an active role in the performance, they too arrange their bodies spatially in a fashion that mimics the revolving force of an asterisk, slowing down the cardiac rhythms of urban labor to make the performance's epicenter swell. If seen up from above, blue swirls would index the very wildness of a trans asterisk, exposing the conflicted dance between transness and queerness, but more importantly, situating a necessary alliance between subject formations, political imaginings, and hyper/in/visibility attending to the disruptions of neoliberal practices of queer consumption.

Through her performance, Lia García (La Novia Sirena) establishes contact with her audience by activating a shared sense of queer relajo, rearranging the utilitarian routines of subway infrastructure. Making commuters follow trans touch, *Próxima Estación* remaps a queer night-scape in broad daylight, making kin with working-class Brown, mixed, and Indigenous folk amid everyday violence. Trans dance and touch shift the margins of the underground subway system, improvising choreographies that move bodies to engage with a playful sense of transientness. At the end, interrupting everyday commute through a quinceañera party challenges the repetitive cycles of queer nightlife, while activating a spatio-temporal dissonance for bodies in trans*it.

Tiempo de vals, tiempo para abrazar
La pasión que prefieres y hacerla girar
Y elevarse violenta como un huracán
Es tiempo en espiral

Cruising the Line: Public Sex in the Queer Underground

In a video posted to X, formerly Twitter, by user @Monitoreo103 (Monitoreo de Redes Sociales) in February 2019, two men have anal sex onboard a subway in broad daylight. Tagging the accounts of Mexico City's government (@GobCDMX), then-city mayor Claudia Sheinbaum (@Claudiashein), police forces (@SSP_CDMX), and official account of Mexico City's subway transit authority (@MetroCDMX), the post includes several hashtags like #SiLoReconocesDenuncialo, #HijosDeLaChingada, #Sexo, #Hombre, #mamada, #Homosexual, or #gay. [11] Taken in a slanted angle, the video begins by showing two men seated next to each other inside a subway car. A fellow commuter sneaks to record the brief sexual encoun-

Fig. 11. Eriko Stark, "El último vagón del metro" from the series *El Octavo Pasajero*, 2015. Courtesy of photographer.

ter in an over-a-minute clip using a phone camera. As the subway moves, the two men exchange no words; they are directed in action by their careful gesturing, gazing, rubbing, and showing. As one man partially removes his underwear, the other watches closely to give back a quick caress before unbuttoning his pants to have sex. The camera tracks the exact moment at which one seats on top of the other.

Aware of the surroundings, they cruise with caution, embodying a silent choreography, that is, an invisible score that guides a dance between the movement of bodies and the tempo of a subway car coming down in speed. As the two men put their pants back on and return to their seats, the videographer moves away toward the exit. Although there is no actual law punishing public sex in Mexico City,[12] the Secretaría de Transporte Colectivo, the local government office in charge of managing subway service and infrastructure activated at least five Monitoring Security Centers across stations in 2020.[13] With CCTV in place, more than five-thousand security cameras constantly monitor transit and watch for unlawful activities across the subway system.[14] Although @ Monitoreo103's post functions as a social form of surveillance by shaming public sex acts before authorities, men cruising the underground deploy a heightened sensitivity not only to evade non-cruising commuters, but also to protect their anonymity.

With 115 underground stations, Mexico City's Metro provides a perfect setting to feel forms of queer relajo, like sexual contact and cruising, shaping a queer nightscape in motion. With the increasing gentrification of the city's nightlife scene, the subway constitutes an underground infrastructure sheltering sexual subcultures amid violence, marginalization, and policing. In reference to McDonald's happy meal, or "la cajita feliz" as it's better known in Mexican Spanish, the last subway car is a shifting site known to house anonymous sex between men, a sort of boxed happy meal in its own terms. In queer popular parlance, cruising men are known as "metreros," or "subway cruisers." Departing from a privatized way of having gay sex, like going to a hotel room, a bathhouse, or inside a car, "metreo" thus names a queer practice inspiring a vast cultural production, from documentary photography and academic literature to amateur porn videos and social (panic) media posts (Galindo and Torres 2018, 320–22). Like Lia García's playful dance in *Próxima Estación*, metreo unfolds as a rapidly improvised choreography of touch in which no set order of steps guides a willingness to move across the subway.

In this section, I feel the silent gestures in eight amateur videos downloaded from the porn site XVideos,[15] to later in the chapter, turn to ethnographic and visual accounts of m4m cruising in Mexico City's subway. By examining digital, ethnographic, and visual records of metreo, I entertain how embodiments of queer relajo not only transform affectively the space of commuting into one of careful watching and playful touching, but also enact alternative forms of bodily consumption beyond neoliberal capture. Doing away with mainstream modes of cruising through social media apps like Grindr or Scruff, these acts of queer relajo ooze out a sense of looseness to reclaim a public infrastructure via touch, play, and sex, making a queer nightscape stick to the material economies of city commuting. While centering on how metreo queerly redefines the limits of public space, I consider the ethical and sociopolitical implications guiding the production, distribution, consumption, and accessibility of queer digital archives like these. I thus engage with amateur porn video clips less as filmed objects of desire than as digital traces of working-class men's playful agency to negotiate queer intimacy in public.

Found across the web, amateur porn clips of metreo include scenes of jerking off, sucking, rubbing, fucking, and touching recorded with phone cameras by cruisers themselves. Tracing moves and gestures, the videos focus on the size of cruisers' penises, the technique of their stroke, the silence of their gaze, or the awe of their witnessing. For instance, "Metrô Cidade do México," a 42-min video posing as a documentary subtitled in Portuguese, stages a long journey of metreo, from 10:00 am to almost midnight of the following day. The video interweaves different clips of men walking and cruising with a soundtrack by Panic Girl. One clip shows two men seating and jerking each other off until a guy squirts on a dirty blue floor. A voice-off announcing the arrival into a station, "próximo arribo a la estación Agrícola Oriental" (i.e., *Arriving Soon at Agrícola Oriental Station*), cuts off the scene building up suspense.

Far from reducing public sex to objects of ocular consumption, these digital records decenter a straight focality, that is, videographers not only partake in sexual acts, but physically jerk the camera around, making the engaged viewer feel the textured infrastructures facilitating queer encounters. Featuring mostly working-class Brown men, videos portray sex acts in subway cars, corridors, platforms, stairways, and escalators, making palpable how gestures of queer relajo happen at different times and places. While some men only hold a phone for recording, others engage in both, the filming, and the touching. Even some look directly into the camera, as they focus on spotting the perfect time to touch in public, embodying swift, decisive, and silent moves. More than just looking for an orgasm, cruisers find pleasure in a queer touch otherwise stigmatized under public light. For a regular commuter, these men appear meandering and loitering, but their careful waiting and watching is only a façade to the untrained eye that sees them wear jeans, shirts, running shoes, and carry backpacks to cover body parts.

The assemblages of public sex, subway infrastructures, and playfulness spark a gravitational field of affect, that is, a queer nightscape converging in the liminal space of underground stations where the material, the carnal, and the affective stick together through touch. Portraying the interior of a station, a 4-min video entitled "Salida," or "Exit," brings in and out of focus a ceiling with bright halogen lights, floor tiles, wall panels, exit signs, metal doors, and a subway platform with an orange train moving in the background along the red subway line in the city's northern region (Línea 6: El Rosario-Martín Carrera). Because it is recorded by a metrero, or subway cruiser, the camera jerks, filming a partially naked threesome gathering at the bottom of a stairway. In this sense, the video mobilizes a sort of voyeuristic gaze that, nonetheless, becomes undone when lenses stop recording men in action, tracking instead pants, shirts, shoes, floors, or signs.

As a form of queer relajo, metreo establishes a different intimacy with the material economies of city commuting, for these men take unexpected steps, turn back and forward, lean against walls, or stop whenever their moves pose the risk of being seen by outsiders. Back to "Salida," the three-some's make-out session is again interrupted by another passerby, as the audio picks up the sound of shoes clacking in the distance. The video exposes various embodied trajectories that move men toward or against an engagement with touch. In other words, the camera traces how their bodies enact possibilities of touching other male bodies, or on the contrary, of distancing from them, making us notice the hidden steps directing how and where their movement interplays in the subway. As if bound by a queer nightscape, their hands passionately touch their bodies, face, lips, ears, and buttocks interrupting their daily commute. With these gestures, subway cruisers mimic the exchanges of fluids, kisses, and caresses that characterize nightlife, exposing a desire to establish queer intimacy with other men in transit.

Quickly dispersing, the trio walks away from each other and leans against a cream-colored wall facing the opposite direction until a passerby leaves the stairs. Only two guys, in this video, touch again, as one kneels to give a blowjob. After sucking, they jerk off and kiss each other against a platform wall. These spontaneous moments of encounter mark a relation of proximity, or as Keguro Macharia calls "frottage," an interplay between "the aesthetic" and "the libidinal" that "so gestures to the creative ways the sexual can be used to imagine and create worlds" (2019, 4). Drawing from Macharia's idea, I invoke the viscosity of a queer nightscape that, in its thick and sticky consistency, emerges from the friction between sexual acts and dirty underground infrastructures underscoring erotic economies in Mexico City. By making a queer nightscape stick, these men worry the binaries of public and private, queering subway infrastructures, while redrawing routes built to sustain heteronormative flows of re/productive labor.[16]

A queer nightscape's viscosity names the affective links binding together queer bodies in motion as in cruising, dancing, or touching beyond nighttime locales. Their coming together leaves an invisible trace that feeds a desire for reenactment, materializing a cumming back, even if its realization is often impossible. Cruising the underground thus enacts queer moves that bind the physical, the bodily, and the material through a sensuous consistency shifting between solid infrastructures and fluid exchanges. As such, the choreographies of touch subway cruisers rehearse inspire ways of connecting through friction, like the jostling taking place inside queer nightclubs when, for instance, you stumble upon someone on your way to the bathroom, or when you "accidentally" spill a drink on someone's shirt.

The stickiness of queer nightscapes echoes what José Esteban Muñoz calls, "an other-worldly glow," in describing the queer ghosts of public sex haunting the work of Tony Just and John Giorgo.[17] Videos of metreo do not directly address a politics of AIDS remembrance; however, they deploy a similar magnetic force that leaves its binding specks impressed across the bodies of cruisers: the smell of dried saliva, the greasiness of lubricant, the tingling sensation of a freshly left kiss, the evanescing warmth of an embrace, the swiftness of jerking off, the flakiness of dried cum. Amid the ravaging effects of the COVID pandemic, public sex also troubles the politics of touch inasmuch as it challenges state hygienic measures that administer life and death to minoritarian queer subjects. The social panics around the stickiness of queer touch weave in forms of violence prompting the regulation, containment, and marginalization of queer excess in the ongoing aftermath of the AIDS and COVID pandemics.

Watching these scenes points to the multiple diversions urban commuters take, as m4m cruising reframes our senses to see beyond the evident. Trying not to be pulled apart, the two men having sex stand next to a train's doors in "Sexo en el vagón." Slightly bent forward, one guy exposes his butt, while the other, holding onto the handrails, fucks him from behind. Seen under a bright light, this sex scene makes a noticeable contrast with dark tunnels as cables, signs, and wires flash through the door's crystal panels. The couple sways together to remain in sync with each other inside the train they travel in. No speech mediates their interaction, nor their eyes establish direct contact, but by concealing speech and interpreting bodily gestures, their sex act requires a re-attunement of the senses. By having sex, the friction between strangers not only embodies the "worldmaking properties of queerness" (Muñoz 2016b, 371), but also highlights the ways through which queerness reframes a sensing of the world.

Brewing a multisensorial and multisensual kind of embodied knowledge, queer touch names a capacity to playfully move through a labyrinth-like public infrastructure otherwise unable to care for queer sex. Through silences and shift moves, a young guy standing in front of the access doors, strokes the dicks of what I perceive to be two construction workers in the video "Vagón parados." As one unties the button of his pants and gently takes out his penis, the other reaches out to grab the young stroker's butt.

Their touch aligns their bodies to feel the space around them, embodying an invisible dance score to move with no explicit instruction. After briefly stroking their shafts, the young guy disengages, exits the car into a station's platform, and moves on with his commute. As such, queer touch helps them navigate their desire to carve, as Gerko Egert reminds us, "a space for multiple relations, haptic and affective touches," (2020, 13). Metreo thus points toward the overflowing of the private into the public, erotically embodied in scenes of playful touch inside trains in motion, untying the potentiality of friction and rubbing from a linear sex paradigm of seeking orgasm, that is, whether their encounter ends in ejaculation, it is the actual looking for and engaging with touch that unfolds the risks of queer relajo.

To better situate a sensorial re-attunement enacted by the moves and gestures of metreo, I turn to the contingent dance between the material structures of subway cars and the men cruising for sex inside them, as seating arrangements provide a level of protection from outside bystanders. Individual seats are located next to automated doors, while pairs of two seats are grouped together. The inside structural design is arranged in a way that hold bars protect a stand-alone single seat on different corners of a car, facilitating easy exit and cover. In some videos, single seats are usually taken by solo men jerking off, while hold bars inside sustain the movement of cruisers, particularly when trains are fully packed. When no empty seats are available, men stand next to each other, camouflaging their desire to make physical contact, as in "Albañil nalgón." Unlike other ones, this video only shows two men kissing framing a tall, bearded jock wearing a tight outfit from behind. Holding another guy by the waist facing the door, the standing tall guy gently caresses and kisses his cruising partner's ear inside a crowded train. Their kissing, and licking make them stick together, inciting a sensorial knowledge that balances the movement of bodies inside a moving car. As touching intensifies, the video's short length leaves us wondering what will come next since the videographer suddenly stops recording to avoid getting caught.

Metreo thus pushes the boundaries of what it means to care and of where care is possible. Where to walk, when to look, how to feel, when to remove their clothing while a car is in motion, conjures a praxis of care invested in playful touch. A two-part video, "Metro gimiendo" portrays a young man kneeling to give oral sex next to an entrance door. Carrying a backpack, he holds the handrails inside a moving car. In its very title, "Metro gimiendo" hints at the ways subway cruisers tease pleasure out of architectural designs, figuratively making the subway moan. The second part of the video features the young sucker and his cruising partner seating down a long seat. They remain locked, exchanging passionate kisses.

As the train enters the station, both men stop touching, and one decides to cover his dick under his pants from incoming commuters. Cruising as caring demands inhabiting a space of vulnerability, physically and affectively, amid a punishing hypervisibility. Once back in motion, they continue with the oral task, paying close attention to their surroundings, as one guy covers the other one's face with his arm. As maps to feel out space, subway designs aid cruisers by facilitating and protecting their encounters against shame, or public denunciation. Cruising subway lines thus exposes a vast knowledge around decoding gestures, navigating urban spaces, and equally important, around playfully looking for pleasure in unexpected places despite the risk and violence of exposure.

The playful risks these men take, nonetheless, remain embedded in their digital records. The way in which these videos exist out in the web prompt me not only to consider how, as engaged viewers and consumers of DIY porn, we become entangled in such risks, but also how our sensorial engagement with these digital records also participates in the global commodification of gay cruising. More than looking for an answer, I would like to cruise contradictions by presenting an example of how queer *relajo* can provide a research method demanding that we inhabit such risks as an ethics of queer intimacy, expressly of building other relations when cruising queer digital archives. While issues of production, distribution, and storage certainly impact the emergence of a queer digital repository, like a porn website, I am thus interested in teasing out the ethical implications of watching and interacting with the traces of cruising men's agencies, or rather in teasing out how the practices of *metreo* asks viewers to make kin with a queer underground by playing with risks.

When finding these videos on the web, their specificities are flattened by porn websites' search categories. On XVideos, tags like "Latino," and "public sex," serve as indexers to cruise a larger digital catalog. What is characterizing about DIY porn videos of *metreo* is that their editing and compiling is mostly done by amateur users. For instance, "Metrô Cidade do México," was posted to XVideos by user "sexogostosorio.com," an amateur 48-year-old Brazilian exhibitionist and edited by another amateur porn user, Victor Rios. I previously mentioned that this video stands as an invented documentary, as a legend in Portuguese, "documentário," flashes in the first minutes, while mixing in various clips, perhaps downloaded from other websites, to give the impression that the camera holder spent more than a day filming different sexual encounters across the subway. By recording and posting cruising videos, nonetheless, these sexual acts are turned into commodities freely circulating the web, enriching the capital of transnational porn companies through the increasingly common practice of amateur porn production. I am tempted to even consider that the posted video might have also surfaced other porn websites like PornHub, or XNXX, facilitating the global distribution and consumption of metreo.

The open access offered through free porn video streaming platforms, like XVideos,[18] poses questions about who might benefit from the commodification of public queer intimacy in the global south, as well as about the place these men's agency occupies in relation to the open access of queer digital archives. As Zeb Tortorici notes about flea markets as popular archives of erotica in Mexico City, the afterlives of archived materials "tell us about how popular modes of pornographic conception intersect with the producers and distributions of erotica, always mediated by social class and access to capital" (2020, 1349). In other words, I ponder about the ethical considerations of feeling modes of queer relajo given that queer commodification and consumption rely on making underground sites hypervisible, following a similar logic of exposure present in gestures that seek to shame these practices, like in @Monitoreo103's post. If cruising men understand the importance of caring by remaining anonymous, how is a queer practice of care present, or absent, in our interactions with porn digital repositories?

Alongside visual and digital commodification, video recordings of public sex pose important considerations as to how underground queer practices participate in building, producing, conserving, and accessing archives that, otherwise, appear to be wasteful and useless for academic practices that privilege textual hardcopy evidence. For Achille Mbembe, "the status and the power of the archive derive from [an] entanglement of building and documents. The archive has neither status nor power without an architectural dimension . . ." (2002, 19). Because metreo ties in together a virtual catalog indexing the material infrastructures of the subway, Mbembe's comments ask to reconfigure our relation to queer archives. Here, I am not referring to the obvious digital catalog of porn videos in the XVideos website, but rather, to the place and function queer nightscapes play in producing queer archives.

If, for Mbembe, an archive is traditionally constituted by a multiple materiality and by the confines of such a physical structure, what are the textures, dimension, and densities of queer archives, and where are those located. Can the conventional role of the archive also apply to understand practices of accessing perverse sexual pleasure? In other words, what then happens when archives are embodied?[19] José Esteban Muñoz's conceptualization of "ephemera" helps further my own line of questioning, particularly as the video recordings I have accessed show no evidence of readable speech acts, but rather present us with bits and pieces of urban sounds, of trains rushing into the station, of beeps and train tracks screeching, of clothing rubbing against fingers and body parts. These recordings move beyond the grammars of speech, meaning, and signification, and bask in the depths of playful silence as a lively language. For Muñoz, "the notion of ephemera as evidence" calls on a "modality of anti-rigor and anti-evidence that . . . reformulates and expands our understanding of materiality" (1996a, 10). It invokes a relationship between memory, embodiment, and performance. "Following traces, glimmers, residues, and specks of things," ephemera not only opposes dominant systems of cataloguing, ordering, and classification, but also is "firmly anchored *within* the social." Instead of focusing on the potential meaning queer acts might hold, the Performance Studies scholar invites us to play in "open new ground by focusing on what acts and objects do in a social matrix" (12).

The archived videos I engage in this part of the chapter track the affective residuality of queer contact, as they haptically repurpose the function of public infrastructures. To tap into the residues of metreo, I resort to a critical method of engagement located in queer relajo. Visual records of public sex thus point us to follow the gestures, affects, materials, and interactions, as forms of queer texture, dimension, and density present in the making of queer undergrounds. To decipher the silence contained within these recordings, as many who hold the camera also interact sexually out in public, does not point however to filling in a gap in meaning or signification, but approaching playfulness as a conscious act of queer refusal, of embodying unintelligibility as a queer praxis of play. The defining silent play of metreo, in this case, performs a refusal against identificatory practices within liberal understandings of sexual deviance and perversity. But the choreographies of touch they rehearse, inspire ways of connection and friction through a queer sense of relajo, guiding a dis/position to play with hypervisibility.

The navigation of porn sites can also provide playful ways of mediating our interaction with queer archives, as well as of unleashing the affective capacities of queer nightscapes. Like men's playful touching, queer relajo as method balances out the risks of being exposed and denounced as anti-rigorous and finding vitally pleasurable knowledges to thrive out in public. In this sense, cruising embodies a queer playfulness that, by "diversion, irregular connections, and disorderly encounters," informs carnal ways of producing, transferring, and storing knowledge; that is, queer relajo takes us on a detour to finding knowledge, making us rest unsure as to what we are looking for, "or if you will come across something you never knew you wanted, or even existed" (Ofield 2005, 357). As such, playful touching emerges as a mode of sensing that connects us to both, the erotics of queer underground cruising, and a mode of approaching, deciphering, and feeling queer archives that would, otherwise, disappear as these practices are regarded as holding no value to conventional academic practices. Nonetheless, critical practices of queer relajo are about finding pleasure in the material and affective entanglements of public sex amid everyday violence.

In watching videos of m4m cruising in Mexico City's subway, I resist to give into an ocular-centric mode of analysis, as these men's movements and gestures reveal more than just a queer way of building knowledge. They reveal the potency of sensorial and embodied forms of interaction, alongside a resistance against neoliberal (academic) paradigms of sexuality, as their sexual identity is never disclosed. Those engaging in underground cruising repurpose Mexico City's subway infrastructure as a safe space for anonymous sex and intimacy, rare in the cruising scene built around social media apps with tracking capabilities like Grindr, Sniffies, or Scruff. Instead, they focus on looking, gesturing, and stroking as embodiments of queer relajo, to erotically play with each other along with the infrastructures around them. In their nightly, or daily, commute across the underground, these men learn how to care for one another, while cruising subway lines.

Touching Underground

David Graham's *The Last Car: Cruising in Mexico City* (2017) offers a visual itinerary of Mexico City's queer nightlife scene, portraying Calle Ámberes, Zona Rosa, República de Cuba, Glorieta Insurgentes, as well as various subway stations and train cars. Incorporating a shadowy lens, Graham's multiple angles and shots zoom into the textures, depths, and densities of an everchanging nightscape, materially assembled by bright neon-lit signs hanging in queer bars, phone booths and street planters

Fig. 12. Eriko Stark, "Young Americans" from the series *El Octavo Pasajero*, 2018.

serving as standing support for queer kissing, smoke screens, mirror balls, sweaty windows, alcohol-filled bars, tall buildings, or cracked-pavement streets used as runways for trans women walking in high stilettos. Arranged against pitch dark backgrounds, each photograph contrasts with bright colors, overextending images as if trying to get out of the page. Although referencing exclusively "the happy meal" in its title, the collection features over a hundred photographs of subway stations, queer bars, hotel rooms, city streets, buildings, and queer locales crowded with partygoers, strippers, dancers, and nightcrawlers, taken during eight visits over a two-year period.

As a local queer artist, Stark's *Furias Nocturnas (2022)*, I argue, offers a different glance into queer relajo by journaling contemplative gestures of care, as well as by becoming intimately entangled with the metreros photographed. A queer transfeminist ethics find a referent in Stark's mode of becoming affected by a sense of queer relajo. In contrast to Graham's visual commodification, Stark's photojournalism inhabits the risks of public exposure alongside subway cruisers, inviting us to go down with them into a queer underground to sense the weary, valueless, dirty, and dark, contours of queer nightscapes. In doing so, Stark expands a visual engagement to enact forms of queer care through playful touch, activating a sensorial knowledge about how sexuality morphs across space. Embodying queer care, these records of queer relajo play with neoliberal definitions of gender, sexuality, consumption, and citizenship by highlighting how gender and sexual embodiments become impressed by material surroundings.

In its introduction, Graham reminisces about a lost queer underground in his native New York City as if looking for clues to find a new one, "[old]-school street cruising seems a primal relic of the past in our modern mega cities with their endless interconnectivity . . . Now historically, gay cruising locales peppered western cities from darkened parks to quiet streets and vacant bus station bathrooms . . . Now, viral connections lead to meetings in safety behind closed doors in apartment or hotel rooms in a gay version of eBay."

Despite Graham's exoticizing gaze, a sense of queer playfulness floats and flows through his collection, as the album portrays Mexico City's subway as a site of queer intimacy, where a young hunk, looking right into the camera, fiddles with a cellphone inside a moving subway car. The picture features the densities of a queer nightscape, the set wall concrete structures inside a subway station, the metal sewer cover, the marble walls show many drawings and inscriptions as public sex becomes an intrinsic dimension of an underground infrastructure.

More than constituting a means of transportation, the subway also functions and mediates queer intimacy, echoing what Aaron Betsky says about the relationship between public space and sexual pleasure, "[t]hese queer spaces infected and inflected our built environment, pointing the way toward an opening, a liberating possibility" (5). The immense brutalist aesthetic of subway infrastructure wears out to give into a different texture produced through the friction of queer sex. While David Graham offers a rich visuality of Mexico City's queer nightscapes, a politics of looking, and cruising are inevitably tied to a queer ethics of desire when "[t]aking photographs in a subway after dark is a difficult and potentially dangerous position . . . As a foreigner, it's impossible to be anonymous, particularly with a camera dangling around my neck."

Although subway cruising carries its own risks, differing subject positions across class, ethnicity, race, gender, and socioeconomic location, etc., mediate and negotiate such risks in the case of Mexico City's underground. According to Norman Monroy's own situated knowledge, their rural, working-class queer Brown experience offers a poignant counterpoint to Graham's invocation of a "dangerous position." Dangling a camera around might definitely make Graham stand out as a foreigner from a subway cruising scene, but it is precisely that exception to remaining anonymous that speaks to a privileging whiteness that primes the photographer's intention to capture "a past" and expose the underlying process of the commodification and consumption of a queer underground in the global south by an outsider's gaze. A sense of whiteness nonetheless also runs through his opening remarks, particularly as his nostalgia for lost cruising sites in his home New York forgoes a historical contextualization of the gentrification of New York's Time Square, so eloquently problematized in Samuel Delany's *Times Square Red, Times Square Blue* (1999). Conversely, the loss of queer space must be framed within a larger history of material dispossession priming capitalist neoliberal conversion.

It is a similar extractivist practice that guides Graham's photographic work in Mexico City. From his introduction, it remains unknown whether the photographer decided to let go, or even question, a consuming gaze, looking for "a primal relic of the past in our modern mega cities with their endless connectivity." Although he acknowledges his hosts and friends in Mexico City, it is unclear as to whether any of the people portrayed were aware of their representation, or whether he became intimate with any of them. The shots of young men lying on a bed, or resting inside a hotel room, would implicitly suggest that perhaps, Graham also established sexual intimacy, further banking on a white foreign privilege. As he closes his introduction, a sense of wonder emerges when noting, "however, the pleasant surprise of realizing men and women could hold hands, embrace, and kiss—not only in the depths of the last car at night, but openly and comfortably in most streets of this giant metropolis—became an unexpected angle for this project." His remarks reveal the operating logics of queer neoliberalism, and the ways through which whiteness, as a structure of feeling, bring about images of postcolonial spaces seen as backward, progress-lacking, dirty, or disordered. As Graham further expands, "Mexico City was not the place I was expecting to see as a progressive den of modern ideas and liberalism."

Considering that the photographer is nowhere to be seen in any of the pictures taken, I further question: is he also participating in queer commodification by remaining distant to the bodies portrayed? How can his distanced lens relate to an economy of care that forgoes material accumulation and bodily extraction? Is such exposure further reproducing a global commodification of jotería, or queer Mexicanidad, as a rare find that now seems to come as a substitute for extinct "gay cruising locales" that once "peppered western cities"? According to Graham's introductory remarks, what a "global political climate [shifting] to the right" seems to be doing in terms of queer neoliberalism, is exporting white queer idealism to other locales of the American hemisphere, activating a global circuit of queer consumption that positions white foreign queer travelers as explorers of unexpected lands. An operating logic that has long guided US neoliberal expansionism through military, cultural and socioeconomic interventions across the hemisphere.

Similarly, by romanticizing the loss of cruising sites in western megapolis, a white tone of queer loss overtakes the exotic racialization of foreign locales. Of course, as Graham points out, Mexico City is no "gay nirvana," but who gains pleasure and who turns into an object of desire carries serious implications as to what, how, and who can be perceived to hold value within global erotic economies. In other words, *The Last Car*'s visual capture of a queer underground is co-constitutive to US neoliberal expansionism and to the making of an economy that reduces LGBTQ+ identities to sexual commodities.

Although an important record of queer nightlife, *The Last Train* prompts questions about who consumes, profits, and benefits from the extractive exposure of its "explorations" just like in my discussion on m4m amateur porn. Graham's cruising the unexpected leaves ground to further question what the photographer hoped to find in a place like Mexico City: what kind of queer relics was he looking for to begin with? Describing Mexico City as a "den of modern ideas and liberalism," contradictorily erases a history of material, economic, and affective transformations leading to the country's neoliberal conversion. The so-called neoliberalization of Mexico City has occurred through violent practices of gentrification, displacement, and overdemand, causing rising prices of living and furthering a socioeconomic restructuring of the city that pushes out locals into the city outskirts where the reach of neoliberal development falls short. The many forms of hetero-capitalist violence and the transregional effects of queer neoliberalism are evident in the continued production of nonnormative genders, sexualities, and bodies as eccentric commodities available for gay (white) global consumption.

Contrastingly, Mexico City-based Eriko Stark's *Furias Nocturnas*, a solo exhibit that commemorates the seventy-first anniversary of state-run Galería José María Velasco in 2022, a fine arts gallery designed to showcase emerging artists. Featured as one of three series within *Furias Nocturnas*, "El octavo pasajero: un catálogo de la sexualidad clandestina gay" ("The Eighth Passenger: A Catalog of Underground Gay Sexuality," 2014–2018), envisions an in-depth autoethnographic work of photojournalism. Inspired by Stark's own encounters with subway cruising, "The Eighth Passenger," borrows its title from Ridley Scott's 1979 film *Alien*, whose translation in Spanish was completely changed. According to his blog post, the "eighth passenger" refers to both, an older man cruising, and a young man sniffing paint thinner, respectively.[20] The direct reference to Scott's sci-fi movie gestures toward the undesirability, discomfort, and unpleasantness subway sex generates in public. "The Eighth Passenger" revisions an undesired subway user stalking the good rhythms of city transit and commuting; an unwanted presence that can only be cast away through shame and violence.

Reworking the negative affects formative to queerness, and specifically to the galvanizing moral panic that renders public sex a wasteful and dirty marginal practice, Stark's frontal portrayals of proud, decisive men challenges conventional definitions of pleasure. In many of the series photographs, men stand right across the camera, achieving a balanced position in each portrait. In a picture, a senior man's gaze pointing to the back of the train, as if searching for someplace or someone, reveals the underground choreographies of touch. The eighth passenger is, nonetheless, seeking new forms and shapes of experience, new connections and events that can rekindle an indelible mark, a luminous wonder. What would the older man say if allowed to speak in a space that communicates through gestures, signals, gazes, and silence? His waiting time remains unknown. I can only venture into a critical mode of speculation to track the tonalities and intensities of queer relajo. He is seeking, perhaps, the warm embrace of a young man's hand, as he appears to be looking to reconnect with someone known. This sense of familiarity activates the affective fibers of touch, materializing into a form of embodied knowledge growing out of an expected anticipation that, in this case, guides the older man's desire to look for an embrace, as can be seen in the many detours men take when wanting to engage in subway cruising. His awaiting fuses the urges of anticipation prompting queer contact. Speculating about Stark's comments on the alienation of the eighth passenger, brings out a queer sense of discomfort, risk, and danger, as an older man cruising the queer underground highlights a free degree of circulation.

More than focusing on explicit sexual acts, Stark enacts a gentle touch through his camera, respecting the anonymity of those photographed. Appearing under a bright light against an orange wall, a bearded young man stands in raised arms. The lens captures his shadowy armpits blending into the darkness of a train tunnel. Standing at the end of a platform, with contrasting marble tiles, the young man's eyes look blurry. Only the shine of dark hair makes distinguishable the contours of a round face with glasses. Stark's careful touch eroticizes the underground infrastructure, that is, playful acts of cruising remake and replace flows of pleasure. Another photograph shows two male couples kissing. Leaning against a well-lit corner, a first couple tightly embraces. A tiled wall offers support to a pair of men wrapped up. While this couple kisses in the background, a second pair of men stands sideways in the middle of the frame. Their eyes are closed. One young man wraps his arms around another's shoulder, while their lips touch. A double kiss scene indexes other queer locales, such as bath houses, porn cabins, or queer bars, expanding the playfulness of queer desire into an underground subway station.

Tracking the intensities of touching underground, Stark's snapshot of a young male couple embracing each other inside a train car exposes a coming together between the erotic, the material, and the affective. This interrelation underscores a queer politics of space, or rather, prompts me to consider how queer nightscapes are directed by space-making practices of play. Queer space-making allows us to question whose desires, affects, and bodies are sustained and allowed to travel across public life. Interconnecting their bodies, in the warmth of an underground subway system, a strong arm pressing against a chest evokes feelings of comfort, safety, and care. Such a warm embrace leaves an indelible mark that travels across time and space, "remind[ing] us that knowledge cannot be separated from the bodily world of feeling and sensation; knowledge is bound up with what makes us sweat, shudder, tremble, all those feelings that are crucially felt on the bodily surface, the skin surface where we touch and are touched by the world" (Ahmed 2014, 171).

As material and affective traces of a short-lived experience, public sex reminds us of how the world is felt, and how such feeling ties into a sensorial knowledge required for queer and trans resistance, survival, and endurance. Although imbued in complex and contradictory structures of feeling, sex maintains a critical relation to shame and violence—perhaps the most defining affects shaping queer and trans worldmaking (Warner 1999, 11). A young guy's hand touching a guy's chest emerges as an experiment of playful sensation.[21] As such, queer touch is always playful as it makes you feel the material infrastructures that sustain acts of cruising.

In a distinct black and white color scheme, another untitled picture depicts a couple wrapped in arms seated inside a subway car as if suspended in time. A bearded guy throws his arm around his companion's neck, tying in each other closely. The rawness of their bodies is only divided by the layers of clothing covering their torsos. Metal rods, handrails, window panels, and a pitch-dark tunnel remind the viewer of the materials framing the shot. Slightly lifting their heads up, they smile in a gesture of joy. With their eyes wide shut, they both look gleefully resting from the judging gaze of the outside world. Their hands touch their bodies, as one guy's back rests against the other's chest. This portrayal stands as a record of queer relajo, evoking what Susanna Paasonen considers the aimless goal of queer playfulness, "[t]here need not be any functional aim, goal or pursuit beyond the enchantment of the activity itself that may give rise to long-standing attachments between individuals, communities, and fields of practice" (2018, 9). Adding to Paasonen's consideration of queer play, Stark's capture not only highlights attachments between people and spaces, but also emphasizes the material entanglements binding queer nightscapes.

Touching recalibrates our capacity to sense the multiplicity of worlds around us, pushing against the capturing logics of rationality that frame event as causation and correlation, and rather bask in flukes of serendipity, of glittery specks of doubt and uncertainty, as a "folding-with that catches the event in the making." A young guy's hand touching a guy's chest directs our attention to another of Eriko Stark's photographs. The shine of a long metallic seat bench gives the illusion of a corrugated texture; the bench reflects the dark silhouettes of other passengers. Seated at the center of such elongated silver-like seat, an older man appears to be looking toward the end of a train car with hands fiddling with a cellphone. The train appears in suspension, resting at an iconic subway station along the blue line—stops away from where Lia García's performance *Próxima Estación* is being staged.

Afterall, David Graham's portrayal of Mexico City's nightlife scene offers a snapshot into the vitality usually extracted to exoticize a queer underground; a vision produced to highlight a progressive queer liberalism for global consumption. It is the encounter with the weary and unwanted that brings into focus a different vision in the work of Eriko Stark, who also gives in to the vulnerability of being exposed and seen by the camera in one of his pictures. Standing in front of a mirror, Stark holds a camera with one hand; the other embraces a guy whose eyes let through a sense of wonder. The young photographer leans into the guy's back to take the shot. The picture registers what happens after the choreographed moves of underground cruising lead all parties involved to another stage of intimacy, in this case, of a bedroom.

While queer touch is present in Graham's photograph, Stark presents visual records that instead get down and dirty with those who hold no value in the economic circuits of queer neoliberalism. Unlike Graham's turning of the queer underground's filthy richness into a global commodity, Stark interrupts foreign visual extraction by becoming impressed with touch, and through a series of gestures, lets the unfolding of something exhilaratingly new seize up the photographic moment, reminding us that any engagement with queer undergrounds requires a letting go of sexual capital and gender identity. Graham's interruption of whiteness shows up in his photograph by framing his own absence against the nakedness of evanescing male bodies left untouched, while Stark is present by posing naked in front of a mirror alongside his photographed lover. This interplay between Stark's presence and Graham's absence, of changing frames inspired by queer relajo, blocks a process of commodification, assisting in the making of another time and place that exists alongside and underneath the public sites of heteronormativity.

Through this messy interweaving, queer nightscapes emerge as fields of playful action exposing how underground sexual practices connect with material spaces and economies. By sticking to material surroundings, queer nightscapes produce queer undergrounds, where the messiness of queer worldmaking debunks neoliberal notions of sexuality, as well as discourses of autonomy, empowerment, self-improvement, and self-determination. Like Eriko Stark's careful photojournalism, a queer underground is visible to those wishing to take risks, as you become impressed by a queer Brownness in motion. Let's then walk down into a queer underground, where queer relajo awaits you.

The Queer Underground

After partying and dancing the night before, I wake up in a motel's bed near the Metro Revolución. My playmate and I rush out to catch a southbound subway train in the early hours of a Sunday morning. We exchange no words, as we are greeted by a swarm of busy commuters scrambling to get inside the station. Once onboard, we hold each other's hand, silently realizing that we won't stay in contact, or see each other again. As if saying goodbye, our touch blends with the rubbing of other bodies making their way across the train. After splitting ways, I am left surrounded by the warmth of strangers rushing through their daily commute, thinking about a distant lover I made out with in a similar train the day before amid street vending and panhandling. All I feel is a breeze trailing a subway train, as if my one-night stand were looking for a tender connection. This memory invoking how to be situated in the queer underground, how to be immersed in its affective economies, moves us to reconsider our own encounters with the ordinary, like the gestures of joy in a quinceañera dance, or a construction worker's urge to cruise during times of labor. It thus presents us with a way of undoing the paralyzing shocks of everyday violence through gentle touching.

Underground encounters describe a queer way of sensing that emerges from dirty subway passageways, as the juggling of street bootleg commerce interact with queer touch. Following this code of movement, I go down into a queer underground, which names an affective undercurrent flowing through cum-stained subway cars, dirty labyrinth-like passageways, echoes of salsa and cumbia, uncomfortable jostling, vending, begging, and careful touching. The queer underground entertains ways of becoming and knowing the world that depart from neoliberal understandings of sexuality, kindling sentient capacities of those wanting to move beyond commodification and extraction; and instead, gravitate toward messy and dirty spaces from below that disrupt whitened sexual frequencies.

In an urban Mexican context, the queer underground places a different understanding to the notion of "queer people of color," a denominator commonly used in US contexts, not because racialization does not happen, but because the ethno-racial formations inherited from a postcolonial caste system become real through a different grammar. In such a context, "to be of color" not only suggests a complex process of racialization through which dark skin color, often associated with other-than-white-mestizo populations, are othered, but also marks a poor or precarious socioeconomic position defining dissident genders and sexualities.[22] The prickly situatedness of "la jota" spells a queerness from below (Monroy 2018) that maintains a distance from neoliberal paradigms of sexuality,[23] and in contention with the precarious spaces of racial techno-capitalism located across Mexico, like in case of the sweatshop, and the hair salon.[24] Embodying a sort of dirtiness, la jota thus situates a rural genealogy in which glamour and filth give texture to an underground sense of queerness.

The multidirectionality of queer displacement, extraction, and relocation (north-south/urban-rural/center-periphery/inside-out) points to the insufficiency of deploying categories of the national, in this case, of enclosed affective structures of Mexicanidad, to grapple with complex hemispheric flows of labor, biopower, and capital. As such, the queer underground extends a space for a "jota rurality," to ground a critical positionality around queerness that does away with visibility, inclusion, and identity in neoliberal terms. By establishing contact with other coordinates of "the *suciedad* of queer sexuality" (Vargas 2014, 717), as well as "the mundane, banal, and ordinariness of queer experience" (Manalansan 2014, 97–98), a dirty messiness of the queer underground requires an attunement into the densely racialized socioeconomic structures cutting through regions and nation-state bordering.

The queer underground recenters a sexual and racial dirtiness to funk up heterosexual scripts of the national without distancing from it altogether, while tracing the emergence of hemispheric queer and sexual practices in the face of economic violence. While expanding notions of Mexicanidad through the worldmaking capacities of queer performance (Gutiérrez 2010), my dealings with the queer underground, in this sense, allows me to situate, collaborate, and resist within an affective tectonic that cuts through regions, spaces, and borders, be them national, social, or otherwise. The queer underground serves me as a hemispheric queer analytic to recalibrate the importance of embracing the poor, popular and working-class as co-constitutive to queerness. By doing so, I can imagine queer interventions against ecological disasters, forced displacement, exploitation, and marginalization in the context of global capitalism across the Americas.

The queer underground magnifies the affective capacities of queer and trans folk situated along the popular and working-class axes of sociality to respond, impact, and transform neoliberal dynamics shaping sexual identity politics at a hemispheric level. The queer underground propels subterranean exchange networks of affectivity, relationality, and value that "allows for questioning the production dynamics of consumption," not only associated with neoliberal "time and money," but also with neo-imperialist expansion (Gago 2017, 17). Appealing to the dynamism of the popular, the queer underground dwells in "the lack of access to material resources" to find in disregarded sites a queer analytic within the porosity of poorness (Brim 2020, 410). As such, the queer underground comes together through a sense of queer relajo, a racialized queer affect that insists on letting go. Queer relajo flows through the underground infrastructures of the subway system as it enacts a dispersed choreography of bodies, objects, and feelings within a queer nightscape that, looked through the rational lens of neoliberalism, appears as chaotic, underdeveloped, wasteful, filthy, and unorganized.

My engagement recognizes how stages of "social movement" rely on a "collective labor that operates both for and against capital gains" (Wilbur 2020, 362). In this sense, the queer underground becomes known only to those who also follow hidden codes of movement and are willing to let go of rationality, identity, and security, while embracing risk, danger, and wonder. As such, "it is a wild place that continuously produces its own unregulated wildness" (Halberstam in Harney and Moten 2013, 7). A disruptive force from the queer underground comes from the unstructured movement of bodies, and materials, that make up interrelations through cruising, dancing, and touching. Although materially bound, it traces the convergence of other worlds enabled by affective co-existence, blurring the distinctive lines separating bodies, and feelings, but that are contingently situated along the socioeconomic crises in Mexico occurring since the 1980s like the devaluation of the Mexican peso vis-à-vis the US dollar, the signing of NAFTA in 1994, and its ratification as USMCA under Trump in 2020, and the recent occupation of Mexico City by digital nomads from the global north.

The queer underground moves as a seismic force that brings into close contact distantly dispersed Brown, poor, working-class queer and trans folk in ambiguous, evanescent, and frugal ways. Such points of touch resist apprehension and containment, as their becoming boosts a relational intermingling with filth, dirt, and excess through touch. The queer underground thus trains our sensorial capacities to become alert in the face of ongoing violence and dispossession, to be overtaken by flows and overflows from below, and literally into subterranean passageways, moving subway cars, unilluminated platforms, tunnels, and overpasses, and physically, through queer and trans movement.

FOUR

Reflections of a City's Nightscapes

"T-E-R-E-S-A," reads an enormous vertical sign attached to one of Mexico City's most iconic cinemas. First opened in 1924, the Cine Teresa featured silent film and musical accompaniments. By 1939, the building closed and reopened in 1942 as a luxury movie theater appealing to a sophisticated metropolitan crowd (Alemán Saavedra 2019). Its art deco architecture and interior design, with sumptuous lounges, crystal handrails, marble neo-classical sculptures, and a large mural, represented structural manifestations of a rampant modernity often historicized as the "Mexican Miracle." By 1972, the decline of such rapid expansion not only led to an economic crisis a decade later but also rearranged urban space, gradually transforming Mexico City's downtown center into a hybrid dwelling for poor, marginal, and working-class people (Davis 1994, 259; Gordon 1993, 351; Ramírez 1986, 39). In line with the urban rearrangements brought about by the 1985 earthquake, the Cine Teresa closed in 1992 for the construction of a new subway line along Eje Central and was transformed into a porn theater two years later (Espinosa 2013). The building turned into a darkroom for queer sexual encounters. A site where sexual fantasies came true in the dark, and anonymity fired up carnal desire. Movie watchers would glimpse dim bodily shapes across seat rows, while bodies off screen would look for an excuse to touch a stranger's bulge. Resounding across dark hallways, moaning was a playlist of queer desire. Knowing how to make contact in the shadows was a grammar of gestures learned by poor, working-class curious men looking to come undone (Zadik 2003).

For more than a decade (1994–2010), the Cine Teresa was popularly regarded as a site for queer encounters, where young gay men would find a refuge for homoerotic desire (intelectual 2012). "Like any utopia, the Cine Teresa existed outside of time," Anne Rubenstein notes, adding that "[s]ex in the movie house usually included acts [mostly between men] of voyeurism, exhibitionism, frottage, masturbation (either solo or with a partner or partners), and fellatio. Anal sex was less common and took place in the second-floor balcony" (2020, 239). But its abrupt closure in 2010 would bring this sexual utopia to an end. No longer a queer playground, the Cine Teresa now provides a space for activities geared toward commercial transaction and consumption. In 2013, the state-sponsored film guardian, Cineteca Nacional, purchased the building and brought it back as a commercial movie theater. While discussing its history, Rubenstein indicates that "the Cine Teresa was reborn once more, participating in the historical transformations that had led to its closure: the rise of digital communications and the neoliberalization of Mexico City's historic center" (241).

I open this chapter with a reflection on the material transformations of a once-exhilarating queer grindhouse in Mexico City, to draw attention to the teleological narrative of liberal progress evident in the nation-state's economic policy ending in the 1982 financial collapse. The case of the Cine Teresa serves as a standpoint from which to trace the racial, sexual, and economic erasure of an underground geography of queer affects and desires that, nonetheless, continues to define nightlife amid spatial gentrification in Mexico City. Akin to the gentrification of public infrastructure, Mexico's neoliberal conversion has also activated a series of media strategies to cleanse poverty from sight. This chapter traces how Mexico City's queer nightscapes produce an afterglow—a residual force that lingers after dark—challenging the neoliberal futures imagined in mainstream Mexican media. I begin by showing how a Televisa's *Solidaridad* (1990) video transmits a vision of an ostensibly unified future that reproduces white mestizaje neoliberal nationalism, positions the poor and working-class as national enemies, and racializes these enemies as non-white. Equally importantly, I trace how queer neoliberalism and homonationalism fit into and support this vision. I then turn to three narrative and documentary films that center Mexico City's poor and working-class queer nightlife and show how they trace an afterglow that unsettles, refuses, and exceeds the white neoliberal nationalist trajectory espoused in the *Solidaridad* video. First, *Mil nubes de paz* (2003) reveals how the afterglow of Brown working-class queer nighttime encounters make white queer neoliberalism sweat with anxiety by locating belonging not in certain futures fixed through property relations but in the continual presence and repeated impossibility of longing, waiting, and cruising. I then show how in *Quebranto (2013)*, the protagonist Coral's refusal to dispose of (and indeed her cherishing of) objects from her travesti becoming challenges the temporality of neoliberal nationalism: her inventory of objects embodies a travesti praxis of survival that brings back what seems to be lost and insists on a politics of presence amid urban displacement and gentrification. Finally, I trace how *Plaza de la Soledad* (2016) centers Mexico City's shadow economies to show how the people within them merge with urban infrastructures to refuse gentrification and queer commodification and to make queer worlds from below. Together, these films insist on a queer presence that exists out of touch with logics of hetero- and homonormativity—one that challenges extractivist practices of neoliberal capitalism while unsettling the commodification of a white-mestizo ideology channeled through the espousal of a national agenda for progress and a neoliberal way of life in Mexico.

Racial Intensities: The White Affect of Neoliberalism in Mexican Media

In 1990, Mexican media conglomerate *Televisa* launched a musical video in support of then-president Carlos Salinas de Gortari's short-lived poverty relief program, Programa Nacional de Solidaridad (Pronasol, 1989–1994). The video, televised across the country through the TV station "Channel of the Stars" (Canal de las Estrellas), features prominent and world-renowned singers, actors, and celebrities from Mexican show business such as Lola Beltrán, Vicente Fernández, Aida Cuevas, Denisse de Kalafe, Rigo Tovar, Lucía Méndez, Angélica María, Manuel Mijares, Verónica Castro, Marco Antonio Múñiz, Paulina Rubio, Pandora, Timbiriche, among others. Fashioning a style akin to supergroup music videos, such as the 1985 USA for Africa single "We Are the World," or the 1988 *No* TV campaign jingle "Chile, la alegría ya viene" (Chile, joy is on its way) for the Chilean national plebiscite, Televisa's *Solidaridad* supergroup video serves as a point of departure from which to trace a national affect of belonging and its compounding intensities of race, class, and gender in Mexico today.

The video begins with a portrayal of two construction workers, followed by a cinematic collage intermixing footage of sunrises and flying doves. Suddenly merging from the middle of the screen, a tri-colored banner reading "Solidaridad" makes a direct reference to the federal state's poverty-relief program. While tacitly gesturing toward a new economic future with images of a bright sunrise, the video appeals to a national sense of belonging. In this interplay, it juxtaposes various frames, combining aerial shots of rural landscapes, historical monuments, churches, and modern city districts, with snapshots of swaying celebrities chanting in unison.[1] Some of the first singers to appear on screen will be Lucía Méndez and Angélica María, the latter an American-born singer-songwriter and actor considered "Mexico's sweetheart."

In tandem with the staging of a charming femininity, these visual registers engage in a sort of gendering of the homeland when "sons of the same mother" (i.e., *hijos de una misma madre*), as the song chants, come together. Here, a performance of femininity refers to dominant gender norms that both commodify and structure the role of mothering as a gendered form of affective labor performed to service the nation. Shuffling footage between a waving Mexican flag and the women's performance, the video embeds a symbol of nationalism into the representation of charming femininity. By alluding to the figure of the kind mother, the moving images transmit a feminized symbol of mestizaje, bringing into mind the *Virgen de Guadalupe*, a founding icon of Mexican independence. Moreover, the visual reference to a tri-color palette further codes a political message akin to Mexico's historically dominant political party, PRI, which by 2000 had remained in power for 71 years and regained control of the presidency from 2012 to 2018. Exemplifying a distinct form of political propaganda, the televised performance calls on a sense of unity, to "form a great nation" (i.e., *formando así una gran nación*), to combat and eradicate poverty. In an emotional appeal to *el pueblo*, the singing celebrities on screen not only embody whiteness through a series of physical traits, evident in their skin color, posture, gesture, or attire, but also in their binding performance of mestizaje.

By focusing on mestizaje's entanglements with economic privilege and discrimination practices, Mónica Moreno Figueroa examines the process of racialization through which "whiteness is a core-structuring motif obscured by the homogenizing racial logic of mestizaje" in Mexico (2010, 388). By comparing the testimonies of Mexican women from rural and urban settings, Moreno Figueroa reveals the underlying "racial logic" of mestizaje "as a complex form of whiteness, that is, as a normative privileged location of identity that is normalized and ambiguous," through which race and nation "consolidated a shift towards racelessness" (399).

Drawing from Moreno Figueroa's "distributed intensity" (392) of racism, I refer to the white affect of neoliberalism in this context as a slippery and ambiguous field of emotion embedded across the intermedial interfaces of race, gender, sexuality, class, citizenship, and labor, as they become entangled with neoliberal agendas not only in Mexico but across its diasporas. In this case, neoliberal capitalism functions as a set of economic policies characterized by the privatization of public infrastructures and the presence of global markets defining social policy, as well as its effects on modes of sociality that emerge from the expansion of neoliberal agendas, something Roderick A. Ferguson calls, "the redistribution of resources to the elite" (2019, 140). If a new economic order is only attainable by activating the country's vast diversity—racial, environmental, cultural, or otherwise—eradicating poverty would lead to implementing a multidimensional strategy to empower the most vulnerable populations in socioeconomical terms. But the video performance frames such diversity as part of a political appeal to national unity, suggesting that economic transformation will only occur if a strong sense of unity upholds an uncontested ideology of white mestizaje. The video thus offers a powerful example through which a networked affect frames poverty as a national enemy (Ahmed 2014, 4; Hillis et al. 2015, 2). For instance, TV star Verónica Castro sings acapella, "Our enemy, poverty/ Let's end it very skillfully" (i.e., *Nuestro enemigo la pobreza/Hay que acabarla con destreza*), followed by Vicente Fernández's and Lola Beltrán's distinctly ranchera pitch, alluding to the country's flag: "green will be hope/white, a pristine trust/red, a rising blood" (i.e., *el verde será la esperanza/el blanco la limpia confianza/el rojo la sangre que alza*). Combining distinct visual and sonic registers, the video equates poverty with an obstacle to economic progress, but rather than explicitly calling to eliminate poverty all together as Salinas de Gortari's program would have it, the performance of national unity orchestrates a series of moves to translate poverty into a sign of rural underdevelopment, as well as a barrier to achieving a strong sense of national unity. Simply put, the video suggests that those unwilling to embrace solidarity as a gesture toward economic progress, whatever its cost might be, stand in opposition to a new era of prosperity, a new futurity via white mestizo unity.

More than reinterpreting Mexican nationalism, the video intensifies its appeals to mestizaje by televising a choreography that celebrates economic progress and transformation, as well as a racial inclination toward whiteness. Celebrities' seemingly improvised movements and powerful singing echo the popular soundscapes of street celebrations commemorating September 16, Mexican Independence Day. As such, a sense of *fiesta*, or working-class festiveness, appears as constitutive of economic development. Furthermore, the televised performance of Mexican nationalism festively re-channels whiteness as a longing for economic privilege. In its transmission of racial intensities, the video functions as a "levered mechanism," a "trapdoor" (Coleman 2009, 180), or "an impasse" (Yépez 2010, 208), that legitimizes the desire to embody a white-mestizo subjectivity. As such, it serves as a networked tool for the development of a neoliberal rationality centered on a specific embodiment of Mexicanidad, or Mexican belonging, one that leaves unchallenged the racial ideologies of a one-party rule. This sociopolitical impasse, or paradox, lies at the core of Mexico's neoliberal conversion and unfulfilled desire to enter globalization as an industrialized nation, whose Indigenous and Black presence must be erased in the present and contained in a romanticized past that, notwithstanding its racist undertones, re-emerges as a eugenic rationality, or "a cosmic race" (Vasconcelos 1997, 3).[2]

I contend that the video's visual intensities, traces, and residues generate an affective attachment to unity, not only stimulating a racial opposition to poverty as a condition for neoliberal transformation, but also signaling to a larger programmatic pattern of structural adjustment policies that include trade agreements, privatization of state-owned industries, free-market reforms, currency devaluation, foreign investment, and state budget reductions, etc. Embracing a national ideology of white mestizaje would also mean fighting against poverty as an embodiment of backwardness. As such, a strong national sense of unity, as transmitted in the video, would combat, and reject the poor and backward.

The neoliberal conversion of Mexico has not only incorporated an economic transformation but also a rearrangement of social space, including the diffused spheres of private/public life. The case of Televisa's *Solidaridad* video exemplifies a long-standing alliance between mediatic and political powers. In particular, the racial intensities transmitted and enmeshed in both the material and affective infrastructures of media attest to the particularities of neoliberal capitalism in Mexico. The affective economies (Ahmed 2004, 121) sustaining a sense of national unity fathom poverty as an enemy constraining economic transformation. This mediatic strategy, however, not only attempts to portray the already economically disadvantaged, including the houseless, the urban working and lower classes, peasants and farmers, and Indigenous, Asian and Afro descendent groups, as national threats, but also racializes their economic marginality as a distinct form of Brownness (i.e., *los prietos*), as outsiders to the desired capital of whiteness and neoliberal economies.

The shocks of neoliberal capitalism have also been felt across the bodies of gender and sexual minorities in Mexico. In discussing queer studies' response to the emergence of queer liberalism, David L. Eng, Jack Halberstam, and José Esteban Muñoz argue that "the problems of political economy cannot be abstracted away from the racial, gendered, and sexual hierarchies of the nation-state but must in fact be understood as operating in and through them" (2005, 11). While they provide a poignant critique of how queer studies has become complicit with the logics of empire in the US, queer liberalism, in this sense, also responds to the flows of neoliberal capitalism and rampant globalization. In the case of Mexico, and in resonance with their critique of queer liberalism, it remains urgent to further untangle a liberal paradigm of sexual diversity from the uneven flows of capital and labor beyond the US, as they consolidate local attacks on the poor, as the case of Mexico City's government pinkwashing strategies, like the gay tourism guide *Capital LGBTTTI* (2019), or even the poverty relief program *Solidaridad*, illustrate.

Along conventional forms of heterosexual belonging, queer neoliberalism brings out a sexual capital that facilitates social mobility within racialized, gendered, sexualized, and classed infrastructures, aligning a sense of queer Mexicanidad with the neoliberal vision evoked in the *Solidaridad* video. Through homonationalism, that is, the perverse alignment between a love for the man-made nation, and the queer love of gay folk, this form of sexual capital is recognized as it measures the degree with which queer practices embrace neoliberal paradigms of sexual identity, seen as visions of progress and development.

I am not suggesting that neoliberal notions of gender and sexuality have completely redefined queer worldmaking, nor that the legal frameworks generated from such sociopolitical assemblages have not offered protections against discrimination and stigma. Rather, I am highlighting and warning against the redemptive quality of neoliberal notions of gender and sexuality when engaging with different articulations of queerness and transness in hemispheric and transregional contexts. In the American hemisphere, histories of colonization, modernization, development, and resource extraction, are not only intimately related to the different trajectories of US imperialism—including cultural and academic knowledge production—but are also very well alive and have evolved into mutant-like machines. In the case of Mexico, neoliberal notions of gender and sexuality advance the marginalization of Brown lives. As such, forms of social mobility attached to a sense of Mexicanidad are inevitably tinged by a racial whiteness, a sociohistorical formation that seeks to aspire, transcend, and erase a history of underdevelopment associated with Indig-enous and Brown people. But, as the films I discuss below show, the past reverberates across time and space, materializing into acts, objects, and affects that perform a queer refusal in the present.

Queer Residues, Affective Re-Mappings

How do pockets of poor Brown queer desire find other affective grammars that disrupt, challenge, and rework the neoliberal logics of a corrupt tech-nocracy? What forms of touch, feeling, and sensing emerge from queer undergrounds within marginal sectors? How can we trace and locate a queer underground embedded in an affective amalgam of concrete, flesh, metal, and soil? Or instead, how do we listen to the working-class Brown-ness, and poorness, in a queer slang that makes (white) queer neoliberal-ism sweat in anxiety? And not less important, how do queer iterations from poor Brown locales inform and shape hemispheric manifestations of sexual and gender dissidence, running from and parallel to (white) queer and trans neoliberalism?

Focusing on the urban geographies of queer affect, Julián Hernández's *Mil nubes de paz* (2003) decenters a particular set of queer metropolitan infrastructures advancing the racial gentrification of queer nighttime space across Mexico City. By mapping out ordinary sites where longing, waiting, and cruising shape a queer sense of belonging beyond neolib-eral logics of consumption and re/production, *Mil nubes de paz* follows a complex meshwork of queer care amid seemingly precarious urban infrastructures. In a black and white style, the film tracks the affective entanglements that sustain and enliven poor Brown forms of queerness amid their mainstream marginalization and erasure. More than just visu-ally representing queer desire, *Mil nubes de paz* deploys a series of haptic and affective registers that makes us feel the sadness and disappointment of Gerardo, a protagonist whose constant heartbreaks point to the impos-sibility of queer love, as well as to a queer remapping of the city through yearning in grief and loss. It is through Gerardo's repeated failures of find-ing everlasting love that the film locates forms of queer belonging not anchored in a future fixed through property relations but in the repeated impossibility and afterglow of longing, waiting, and cruising. The camera thus registers different city textures modulating Gerardo's lustful longing, delineating a queer nightscape that, in this case, tracks an affective sensorium within cinematic shades of gray. *Mil nubes de paz* composes an ode to longing, a traveling melody that unexpectedly queers ordinary urban spaces, reminding its viewership that queer affects imbue, dwell and can even overflow from the underground.

The film is set in Ciudad Azteca, one of the busiest public transit ports of entry connecting Mexico City and Ecatepec. Situated in the neighboring State of Mexico's northeast, Ecatepec is one of Mexico's most populous municipalities, with more than 1.5 million inhabitants. A critical understanding of Ecatepec's overpopulation and limited public infrastructure must consider the complex dynamics of government corruption, drug trade, and crime, as symptoms of uneven neoliberal transformation. Concentrating an underpaid labor force of Brown working-class people, Ecatepec serves as an energy cell providing vital resources to the well-functioning of Mexico City's service, commerce, and manufacturing industries, as overworked commuters travel through a rundown transit system to perform jobs as maids, busboys, coffee baristas, or servers, in the capital city. From a (queer) neoliberal lens, this overcrowded setting of "underdevelopment" poses a threat to the (white) vision of Mexico's future. Painting an urban landscape in a gray color scale with unfinished building blocks, and rows of cracked streets, the film portrays Ecatepec as an underground overshadowed by the capital city's blinding neoliberal logics, exposing the layers of inequality that nonetheless advance and disrupt the circuits of labor sustaining Mexico City. Entangled in Ecatepec's urban landscape, the film reveals queer intimacies that leave an afterglow challenging Mexico's neoliberal vision.

A scene: an urban buzz of traffic sounds, jostling commuters, and street echoes hit the tall concrete walls of a large bridge overpass. Leaning against a concrete contention wall, Gerardo finds himself wiping off his cum-dripping mouth after a blowjob inside a car. The film opens with an expansive shot portraying a pile of brick houses and grayscales of buildings, blending in sighs of pleasure. The underpass of elevated car bridges is a shelter for public sex between men. Driving away from a sex hideout, Gerardo and his lover look at each other multiple times, but their eyes never meet, as José José's "Gente" swallows their silence in the background.

Silence makes us recognize an unspoken yet mutual understanding: both guys are looking to find something neither of them can give back in return. More than a simple question, Gerardo utters a desire to meet again. A so-what's-next, "¿y entonces?," sets a yearning intention to know whether to give oneself away to uncontrollable passion, or to cope with outright rejection after a one-night stand. For his lover, meeting again is not a pressing matter, so when asked about a next date, he says he will eventually reach out but will never contact Gerardo again. Their fleeting encounter ends as Gerardo unwillingly grabs a peso bill, leaving the car with a feeling of emptiness, running fast into urban shades of gray. While looking for more than a quickie, Gerardo starts to realize that his romantic future might be full of uncertain pauses and unfulfilled answers, yet this brief encounter with a stranger will leave an afterglow, manifesting a yearning desire to meet again amid impossibility.

An afterglow condenses queer residues that affect our way of sensing the world. Queer residuality can be found and felt as an echo, a whisper, a gesture, a moment, or can possess a material texture that appears in things, objects, sounds, impressions, or acts. The queer residuality of an afterglow does not rest in inactivity even though its resonance cannot be physically or visually evident. Queer residuality upends a logocentric rationality that insists on finding proof of an existing reality. Queer worldmaking, at times, exists as an ideality, as José Esteban Muñoz would describe it in *Cruising Utopia*; other times, queer worlds take the shape of small figments awaiting possibilities of contact, of minute and imperceivable glitter dust that sustain our striving for survival, and yet afterglows spark our queer ways of thriving.

More one-night encounters would lead to more disillusion, as Gerardo seeks an impossible romantic affair with men in billiards, train tracks, and bridges. Nighttime cruising is eventually interrupted by the presence of Bruno, a client that shows up one night at the billiard room where Gerardo works as a busboy, who quickly notices the latter's svelte physique. Looking for sex, Bruno's set gaze moves as a touching feeling that cuts through the room until the camera frames Gerardo, who quickly responds to Bruno's touching gaze. The film carefully traces the gestures, signs, and movements that orchestrate a random encounter, as it indexes the threading of a queer sensibility of the night. In its working-class and hypermasculine dimensions, the billiard hall, as a space for male socialization, is composed of playful practices of bantering, whereby masculine prowess measures dexterity and coordination through competition. The coordinated arrangement of masculine bodies across space rehearses a homosocial choreography that, far from setting a strict space for hypermasculinity, propels the queer eroticization of same-sex cruising. The film mimics a queer sensibility of cruising by interlayering close camera shots of billiard playing with Bruno's sex cruising gestures. Swift moves, still poses, coy smiles, and furtive gazes, fuse together into a visual amalgam of sensation. The final touch between Bruno and Gerardo happens away from the main hall, while the camera hones into a gesture leading Gerardo to touch Bruno's back.

The film blends in soundwaves of breathing, sighing, corrugated touching, and frottage, replacing an all word-laden story with the urban musicality of queer affect. We feel their embrace as their bodies touch on screen, not only prompting our very need for contact, but also leaving the mark of their bodies on urban infrastructures, such as subway stations, bridge overpasses, cafeterias, tall buildings, street bazaars, etc. By focusing on how queer contact makes its mark on urban spaces, the film engages an affective economy that banks on feeling the city's ordinary worn-down-ness, complicating cleansed images of its neoliberal transformation. While waiting outside a subway station, Gerardo stands amid an urban ecology of rocks, metal beams, light posts, and cables, adding texture to the film's grayscales. We hear the rampant speed of traffic cars in the background, as the camera pieces an image of Gerardo through short scenes portray-ing his feet, hand, face, and back, to later frame an expansive shot. Once Bruno walks in from afar, they take off to a downtown cafeteria where Sara Montiel's song "Nena" plays alongside a voice-off conversation.

While the bright halo of streetlights breaks the monotony of urban passages, the couple moves to a more private setting after their coffee date. Once inside Gerardo's modest one-bedroom apartment, the cam-era follows their undressing, as queer touch engenders a cinematic form of intimacy that envelops viewers within sheets of moaning. Emerging from dark backgrounds, Gerardo's queer cruising is interrupted by naked scenes under dim lights. Sequences fluctuate between dark and gray tones, orchestrating a distinct all-black-and-white aesthetic that rein-scribes Mexican Golden Age cinema. In this sense, the reference to old films invokes a failure of romantic love within working-class and poor spheres, where unrequited love, suffering, and longing mark a sense of queer backwardness.

After having sex, Gerardo is left, again, with a similar feeling to the one evoked in the film's opening sequence: a feeling of emptiness and disil-lusion that prompts his yearning to touch and search for queer love in unexpected places. The film thus offers a critique of heteronormative love and courtship by showing how the concept of property fails to grasp on the choreographies of queer cruising. It is the residue of that failure, of understanding that queer love cannot be held as a property of capitalist possession, that marks a form of queer longing throughout sensuous gray shadows. Gerardo thus gestures toward a queer love present in the longing and movement between lovers rather than as something that can be fixed or captured. This queer presence felt through movement and longing exceeds, in some way, the logics of capital that would otherwise contain them. Upon Bruno's departure in the morning, Gerardo poses the same question pointing to the end of their encounter, "¿entonces?" The uncertainty of a what's-next reveals Gerardo already knows Bruno is not coming back. In other words, the question condenses a refusal to be possessed as a commodity value of desire, exceeding the logics of capital by affectively detaching from heterosexuality. Gerardo can't exactly pin down their sexual encounter to a place and time, yet his insistence on not letting go fires up a desire to meet again under different terms beyond capture.

The potentiality of queer residues will send Gerardo out to look for Bruno, scouting an alternative urban topography usually unseen in mainstream queer media. Gerardo's venturing into Ciudad Azteca, into the dark underpasses to meet new lovers, or even into the labyrinthic tramps of homophobia, draw alternative routes to queer longing. The maps traced by a search for queer love make explicit the material networks that sustain a queer underground of affects like longing, cruising, and waiting. Looking for a trace of their sexual encounter, Gerardo finds Sara Montiel's soundtrack of the 1957 jukebox musical film, *El último cuplé*, in a second-hand street bazaar. One of Montiel's magnificent songs, "Nena" is a chant to the flaming evanescence of kissing. Following the chords of *cuplé*, a popular risqué Spanish cabaret genre usually interpreted by solo female singers, or drag performers, the song opens with delicate chimes and harp notes as if welcoming to a land of queer fairies. Sara Montiel's unique pose, mesmerizing gaze, and deep voice continues to be immortalized through drag performance and queer nighttime melodramas, such as the one portrayed in Gerardo's romantic search.

Mil nubes de paz thus pays tribute to queer camp icon Sara Montiel by turning her melodies into a distinct queer mixtape of longing, cruising, and waiting amid the gray scales of the night. Instead of finding Bruno, Gerardo finds *El último cuplé*'s soundtrack at a street bazaar. More than just an old record, the vinyl disc affectively gels Gerardo and Bruno's coffee date with the subsequent replays of the song "Nena," shaping a residual attachment to fleeting queer sex. It is not a coincidence that Gerardo gives a quick synopsis of the Spanish musical and chants some of the song lyrics while at the second-hand stand,

Juró amarme un hombre sin miedo a la muerte
Sus negros ojazos en mi alma clavó

. . .

Y vi que la vida fugaz escapaba

Sara Montiel's "Nena" replays the sounds of an afterglow. The harp notes evoke a warm welcome into the arms of Bruno, whose physical touch recalls a sense of comfort. Gerardo's memory of their conversation at a downtown cafeteria is tied to the song "Nena," as Bruno's ravishing black eyes, just as those described in the lyrics, are fixed on Gerardo. An ode to fleeting queer passions, "Nena" insists on a form of touching that transcends any tangible words. The scenes filming Gerardo and Bruno's erotic encounter capture conversations more as voice-off echoes than as synchronous speech acts, rehearsing a different affect. Beyond pain and pleasure, the music affectively transmits illusion, passion, and promise as impulses felt on eyes, lips, and mouths. Kissing emerges not only as a way of feeling each other, but also as a mode of measuring the passing of time. The imprint of Bruno's lips onto Gerardo's affective tissue resonates across time and space. Their memory travels as a yearning sensation that flames up a pair of lips ready to touch, or "the divine flame of a kiss," as Sara Montiel poignantly carols.

The night descends upon the screen, and darker tones of gray tinge the large infrastructures of a subway station. Structural metal beams stand perpendicular to a subway train in motion. As the sound of running car engines cut through the road, concrete stairs and sidewalks appear bright under city lamp posts. A voice that breaks in laughter la-la-las "Nena." As a blurry silhouette out of focus, Gerardo walks impatiently around the overpass holding a vinyl disc. After a long wait in the dark, Bruno finally shows up but declines Gerardo's invitation to spend the night. Bridges, subway cars, stairways, billiard halls, and streets offer solace to a broken heart. The city's material fissures remind us of the affective cracks that queer worldmaking endures to give renewed forms of connection. As he wanders the night in disillusion, subsequent hookups with other men complicate Gerardo's ideal of romantic love in a way that finding prince charming seems distantly impossible, yet his longing for Bruno carries on. Mixing wavelengths of sound and emotion, Gerardo's heartbreak resonates with Montiel's song in that "Nena" spells out a queer mode of waiting, longing, and cruising for an unfulfillable promise.

Once back alone, Gerardo gets Bruno's letter that reads, "Words seem

to me, as always, the most cowardly gesture and yet they are still necessary. I am afraid. I am afraid of hurting you." ("Las palabras me parecen
como siempre lo más cobarde y sin embargo no dejan de ser necesarias.
Tengo miedo, tengo miedo de lastimarte.") The letter's contents are gradually released in the film as if dosing the intensity of queer longing. In this
instance, words acquire meaning in the distant echo of their articulation,
as the note's words will resonate as scattered, lost pieces throughout the
film. Bruno's letter alongside Sara Montiel's "Nena" resonate as an afterglow, a hypnotic residue that propels an exhausting search for his kiss and
touch.

Gerardo's disappointment with his male lovers leads him to find solace
with the women in the film who have also been cheated by the promise of
heteronormative love. Waiting for that romance to become real, knowing
perfectly well that it will not be realized, performs a queer refusal to cishet
feeling, while exposing a misogynistic apprehension characterizing male-
to-male sex relations. "Nothing hurts me more than love" ("Nada me
duele más que el amor"), echoes Bruno's voice-off. And his fear of hurting
a lover highlights a masculinist paradigm informing a lack of affective
commitment based on caring for others, as well as a male privilege within
social structures. The film thus shows how masculinist engagements can
perpetuate queer neoliberalism's exploitative logics, in this case, participating in the sexualization of femme embodiments like Gerardo's. When
his body is sexually objectified as a form of sexual capital or emotional
labor, Gerardo's longing, in a sense, is captured by capital, yet an afterglow
shines through the material residues of a letter and the echoes of a song,
activating a queer feminist praxis that overflows neoliberal capture with
its insistence on presence and present-ness despite the exploitation facing queer life. As a feminist formation, afterglow overpowers masculinist
"atmospheres of violence" (Stanley 2021), sparking off affective relations
that eschew hierarchical, vertical, and exploitative terms of engagement.
Helping queers to endure an ever-changing violence, an afterglow lives
through as a repeated impossibility that, despite its virtual, conditional
form, resists being shattered and shines on otherwise.

While its dream-like black-and-white aesthetics might, and does, draw
engaged viewers into a fleeting queer world of shadows, the film portrays
the complexities of queer life in Mexico City, especially for poor and
working-class folk, who might not hold the same economic resources as
their (white) mestizo economically advantaged counterparts. Bruno's letter holds the powerful radiance of an afterglow in that it launches Gerardo

into an endless search for queer love. In a frenzied chase, Gerardo visits old sites, looking to feel the same way he did when walking the same old spots in the company of Bruno. The multiple shots and angles portraying city infrastructures evoke a feeling of queer touch, as each cruising site also reminds us of multiple sex encounters, not only with Bruno, but also with others. Through an afterglow, waiting and longing launch a queer remapping of the city. That is, the feeling of Bruno's absence attunes Gerardo into sensing the urban otherwise, not through the coordinated signals and planned streets of urban development, but through a queer intimacy established with worn-down cityscapes. Park fences, electric power towers, cars, busses, and buildings along with the sounds of bustling urban life enclose queer encounters.

While paying an unexpected visit to an old lover, Gerardo reconnects with the old textures of an underdeveloped urban past, establishing a parallel between his failed love search and the failed promises of neoliberal transformation. By searching for Bruno through old cityscapes, Gerardo rewires a queer sense of loss that undermines ideologies of urban transformation. In a gesture that reconciles a failed search for promising neoliberal futures, like in not finding a happy-ever-after, or enduring the violence of urban redevelopment, an old date mate found by accident hugs Gerardo. As if a sense of queer loss also enacted ways of accepting failed promises, Gerardo's interaction with the past allows mourning in the now, expanding other ways of feeling beyond capture. As they bask in their embrace, the name "Ciudad Azteca," Bruno's neighborhood, is heard as a travelling sound.

The scattered echoes of a love letter come back again, "Empezar a escribir me ha costado superar muchos días de sopor, sobre todo de miedo. Pensar en ti me hace sanar de todo mal, de toda desconfianza en el futuro. No puedo intentarlo ahora. Es así de estúpido." (To begin writing has forced me to overcome many days of torpor, especially of fear. Thinking about you makes me rest from all unease, from all the distrust in the future. I can't try it now. It's that stupid.) Holding onto their words intensifies the need to find ease and comfort in someone amid fear and uncertainty. Gerardo's quest links the affective charges of Bruno's afterglow, carried in a love letter, or a Spanish song, with their actual encounter, blurring the urban lines that separate them.

Afterglows lead Gerardo to come to terms with the past, as looking for his lover leads him to visit an old friend at a basketball court. Scenes of ordinary life show how commuting, playing, or working, converge with the flowering of queer affects like waiting, longing, and cruising. After-glow names a queer sensibility that surfaces, imbues, moves, and brews through material infrastructures. In this sense, afterglow provides insight into the affective matter sustaining queer nightlife, participating in a spa-tial remaking beyond cishet neoliberal nationalism. The mobilization of queer affects, in this case, is only possible within and through a set of public infrastructures that, despite their deteriorated condition, hold space for queer worldmaking. But such space and place do not exist as a set of monolithic structures, but are produced, made, and undone by queer contact, friction, and movement. The interphases between space, infrastructures and affect highlight the performative dynamics driving queer worldmaking, as it shows how poor working-class bodies negoti-ate material-crossing and traverse the world affectively to resist neoliberal displacement.

In considering space, Doreen Massey ruminates, "What if, instead, [space] presents us with a heterogeneity of practices and *processes*? Then it will be not an already-interconnected whole but an ongoing product of interconnections and not . . . This is space as the sphere of a dynamic simultaneity, constantly disconnected by new arrivals, constantly waiting to be determined (and therefore always undetermined) by the construc-tion of new relations" (2005, 235). Massey's consideration resonates with Gerardo's remaking of urban space through queer affects. A subway ter-minal is reshaped affectively to host other practices that not only involve ordinary commuting and transportation, but that also house other pro-cesses that undo the spatial boundaries for queer cruising and longing. Subway bridges turn into resting sites for caressing and making out. Objects and infrastructures also extend support in the making of queer space. A metal beam shifts its capacity to hold as queer human bodies touch each other. At a molecular level, afterglow shimmers particles of queer contact that are otherwise overlooked through a cis gaze. Queer nightlife practices thus overflow into everyday spaces and, in this case, transform Ciudad Azteca's material contours to allow the emergence of a queer sensibility that, through every crack and fissure, shines through an afterglow guiding Gerardo's search.

While looking for a long-gone lover, a shining afterglow also reshapes Gerardo's relationship with the urban. In his unending search, he becomes more alert to a world of sensations that would not be as obvious other-wise. Commonly mistaken for private acts, cruising, longing, and wait-ing constitute affects orchestrating a queer sensibility that allows one to

Fig. 13. Gerardo waits outside a subway station for Bruno. Movie still from *Mil nubes de paz* (2003), dir. Julián Hernández.

rearrange public space. Infrastructures thus turn into fluid bottoms that shift according to affective practices. Cruising, for instance, requires a different attunement to how the world is perceived, as it involves a mode of caring enacted through looking attentively, patiently waiting, and meeting discreetly in public, challenging our own individualistic voyeurism. As acts of cruising take place in the quietness of the night, the fast urban rushing suddenly twiddles as a calmness throbbing during the day. Queer spaces can hold the resonating potency of an afterglow, particularly as Gerardo waits for Bruno in the same overpass bridge outside a subway station. Even in a restless search, afterglows add rich textures and dimensions to the material worlds that surround us. Waiting and longing outside a subway station makes Gerardo become intimately familiar with urban space, one that does not exist either in the abstract, or in the gentrified city neighborhoods, but stands as a working-class infrastructure of city life.

After searching Ciudad Azteca, Gerardo resorts back to cruising. In this instance, he is sadly lured into a trap inside an empty building where he is assaulted by a homophobic hunk. Hurt, bruised and crestfallen, Gerardo returns to the passageways of a local mercado, looking to find solace in the company of his mother at her food stand. Gerardo's way of life, his work as a busboy at a downtown billiard, and his precarious housing situation, makes him an odd bird, as youngsters his age typically stay at their parents' or live with family members. But the encounter with his mom reveals a complicated dynamic. Upon seeing him in such condition, his mother offers money after scolding him for disappearing and running away.

But the brief encounter with his mom exposes the undeniable conditions facing queer and trans youth that decide to run away from traditional households in Mexico: lack of resources, poverty, houselessness, unemployment, violence, and death. As a Brown, working-class queer, Gerardo learns a queer sensibility that strives for survival in Mexico City despite all risks and dangers already impinging on his way of life. Afterglows, in this sense, present us with reminders of the actualities of queer care, queer love, and queer longing, manifesting less as idealized projections into an uncertain future, or even a static placeholder of the present, than as physical verifications of a queer here and now that do away with accumulating property and capital. Afterglows trace a residual materiality that make us stick to moments, to other feelings that emerge in the folding of worlds and that hold our drive to question the structures of heteropatriarchy. In returning to the same subway station bridge, Gerardo can now confirm Bruno was only a one-night stand. Amid waiting and longing, the former once again returns to find the solace, not in the warmth of a male lover, but in the company of women sharing their heartbreak.

As a residual force, afterglow is, inevitably, entangled in histories of racialization, gentrification, and commodification. *Mil nubes de paz* offers a different look at the spatial limits of queer Mexicanidad, that is, the film repositions poor, working-class urban infrastructures perceived as liminal and underdeveloped from a neoliberal standpoint. By tracing the grayscales of Mexico City's periphery, the film frames a queer affect that lies in the residues left behind by whitening forms of order and progress implemented through neoliberal policies. Gerardo's queer survival depends on feeling and sensing the city otherwise, on attending to urban rhythms that queerly desynchronize a neoliberal tempo of reproduction and extraction through waiting and longing, as well as through the playful dynamics of cruising. In this sense, another terrain of affects re-emerges from the ephemerality of queer acts, a queer nightscape that lives and thrives alongside ordinary urban infrastructures.

Paying tribute to a strong sentimentality from the Golden Age of Mexican cinema, the film's grayscales compose a contemporary queer melodrama that occurs out in the everyday. Unlike the enclosure of queer affect, contained within the privacy of billboard rooms, hotel beds, or bathroom stalls, queer longing, waiting, and cruising seize public buildings, entire avenues, parks, street markets, bridge overpasses, and subway stations. Gerardo reroutes the flows of queer longing by moving across economically liminal urban zones, tracing an underground queer cartography of the city. *Mil nubes de paz* not only limns a different queer aesthetic to the triumphalist and heroic stories of queer love but repositions heartbreak as a mode of feeling an afterglow's residual resplendence and, through that shine, attunes our senses to feel the invisible sites of queer affect. In Gerardo's search for an ideal, queer longing, waiting, and cruising inform a sensorial queer pedagogy, that is, a queer way of feeling and being in the world. Such mode of queer knowledge gradually accumulates as we become affected by the material residues of an afterglow. In moving across nightscapes, Gerardo's carrying of an afterglow amplifies the queer sensibilities that teach us how to navigate a heteropatriarchal world. These queer clefs of sensing impel us to feel, look, touch, and play beyond the limits of gayborhoods, or zones of queer tolerance, and rehearse queer acts at the bottom of neoliberal night stages. Nightscapes thus reveal a glowing blueprint whose ciphers are only legible to those who, striving for queer survival, chase after the flaming enchantment of a kiss, as Sara Montiel passionately reminds us.

An Inventory of Travesti Loss

In line with *Solidaridad*'s images of progress, gentrification and urban displacement emerge as methods of erasing the "threats" to Mexico's neoliberal futures. This section thus traces the affective immanence of objects that, entangled in stories of travesti loss, remembrance, and becoming, embody a resistance against urban erasure in Roberto Fiesco's *Quebranto* (2013). The film takes viewers through the life of travesti sex worker Coral Bonelli, who lives in a small apartment filled with memories of her heyday as a cabaret performer and child actor. Showcasing an inventory of old objects, Coral reminisces of a long-gone nightlife displaced by the area's economic transformation. Attending to the affective remains of old objects inside her downtown Mexico City apartment, the camera reframes a neoliberal vision by following the protagonist's interactions within and across shabby urban infrastructures.

Quebranto starts by taking viewers into Coral Bonelli's journey of becoming, extending affective bridges that connect her present everyday life with her past. While seated at a cafeteria bar, Coral begins to speak about her losses and gains in life, highlighting how difficult her life has been along the years, "es muy difícil porque uno acaba mal." As a kid, she used to play with her mother's clothing and, when left alone, would dance, lip-sync, and perform in front of an imaginary audience following the sounds of an old phonograph. As a performance virtuoso, Coral makes an incursion into the itinerant world of *carpas y circos* in urban outskirts, popular entertainment tents and improvised stages where mimicry and juggling, meets lip-syncing and impersonation. Performing Raphaelito would grant her great recognition and eventually bring her closer to the world of Mexican film. This first exposure to showbiz marks the start of a long intimacy with Estudios Churubusco, the prime movie production house in the country commonly known as the Mexican Hollywood.

Coral and her mother, Lilia Ortega, remember their first contact with film membership cards provided by Procinemex, Club Amigos del Cine Mexicano. A scene alternates Coral's and Lilia's voice-off to simulate a dialogue, as the former notes, "la primera vez que vine a los Estudios Churubusco fue en 1970 [. . .] Pues pagamos como 60 pesos o 160 pesos [. . .] Eran, me acuerdo que unas blancas y tenía como un logotipo de un triangulito redondo que decía Procinemex. Y entonces yo tenía la 1801." This retrospective look into Coral's early encounter with film not only reveals the affective entanglements with Mexican cinema, especially with one of the precursors of New Mexican Cinema and one of Mexico's most renown filmmakers, Jorge Fons, but also traces how feelings of loss mediate Coral's and Lilia's relation to filmed urban space. As the voice-off continues to interleave their narration, a montage of multiple shots tracks their walking into Estudios Churubusco.

Two contrasting figures, one taller than the other, wear flowy long skirts that sway with a light breeze under a bright sun. We look at their back, while they walk across the film studios complex trying to tell the old from the new. Coral and Lilia point with their finger where old buildings, palm trees, benches and tents used to be; their remembrance enacts a geographic superimposition of affects, that is, in trying to recognize old structures they are surprised at finding something new. While at the film studios, Coral walks through corridors as if looking to run into something or someone familiar, letting her memories out by naming movie stars such as Sylvia Pasquel, Sara García, Julio Aldama, or Katy Jurado. Coral's walking blurs out conventional demarcations of time and space, drifting into nostalgic remembering. An old sense of wonder mediates the emergence of something, or someone, that is unexpectedly found. Her recounting makes explicit the coexistence of loss and urban infrastructures, or the temporal diffusion of the past and present. Blending in shots that frame the protagonists' moving across a working-class urban landscape, the film maps out different spaces of their nostalgia.

Quebranto's visual technique layers an inventory of sounds, images, objects, and spaces, assembling a vintage music box evoking Coral's past. As the film interplays movie clips from Jorge Fons's *Fe, Esperanza y Caridad* (1974), a film about the complexities of religion, violence, and poverty in Mexico,[3] the visual registers extend affective links out to lived experiences. In sharing the details of how a fight was staged in the film, Coral bursts into tears while re-reading the movie script matching her lines. "Ay volverlo a tener," she exclaims as her voice breaks, "es algo padre. Mi primera película, pues me da, perdóname, no . . . Fe y caridad." The movie script is not only an old object but also reveals a temporal path that reorientates us to her past through bodily touch, or what Laura U. Marks refers to as a "recollection-object," material objects that, holding the incommensurability of memory, reverberate across time and space to make their past presence be felt as "products of personal history" and "intercultural displacement" (2000, 77–78).

The sentient capacities of objects, their animacy, maintain a pellicular attachment to Coral's travesti becoming. The term "pellicular" refers to the miniscule and often unseen capacities that objects hold to disrupt any static notion of agency. In the case of Coral, pellicular also refers to an affective attachment to a film inventory. My deployment of the term functions as a gesture to highlight the material residuality of objects shining through travesti becoming. The script's immanent past, felt through the textures and smells of old paper, or the stains marking the passing of time, awakens the interactions of a sensorium connecting bodies. The interconnectivity enacted by Coral's hands fondling a script enlivens the past through tears. Loss, in this sense, stretches into the present as a way of retexturizing the uselessness, or inactivity, of an old object. Loss is generative for travesti becoming as it recalibrates notions of time and space to be felt as states in flux. Coral's experience of loss thus refuses disposability and holds onto the object in the present, and so rejects the idea of travesti worldmaking being erased as part of the city's neoliberal transformation.

Giancarlo Cornejo traces the liquidity of tears as a poetics of travesti remembrance in Claudia Llosa's film *Loxoro*, arguing that travesti tears "are a utopian gesture to a different way of crying" (2021, 54).[4] If tears dilute "clarity and clear borders," I would further argue that travesti tears also hold a potential to a different way of feeling time. In this sense, Coral's teary eyes and blurry speech reshape a cinematic relationship to the past and present. If *Quebranto* offers a revisioning of the past through film, Coral's story of becoming affects our cinematic experience of feeling time by moving away from an extractive visuality of neoliberalism that consumes the travesti body. Instead, the film reorients a purely extractive relation toward feeling a complex sensorium activated through Coral's fondling with old objects.

Entangling movies, nightlife's sounds, and urban landscapes, her insistence on holding onto the past translates cinematically into scenes of lip-syncing to Raphael's and Lucha Villa's songs, of visiting her childhood neighborhoods, or of rehearsing old dance choreographies. Revisiting her memories impels Coral to reconnect with the urban spaces of her past, like cabarets or old neighborhoods, opening new sites where queer nostalgia comes to life through performance. As in the case of her lip-syncing to Raphael's "Mi gran noche" in the film's ending sequence, Coral performs images of her past to stage a refusal to let go amid urban transformation.

In another scene filmed at the iconic cabaret El Bremel in Mexico City, Coral's performance of Lucha Villa's song "Las Ciudades" complicates the afterglow of queer music in connection to travesti worldmaking and urban displacement. Villa's fierce ranchera song is about how cities play into breaking up a love affair, or as the lyrics spell it, "cities destroy habits." With Lucha Villa's song, she further implicates her relationship with Mexico City, particularly as to how this undeveloped, dirty landscape not only holds her feelings but is also a vital part of her travesti embodiment—it is within the city's working-class circuits of cabaret where she embraces being a travesti woman. By keeping music from her past alive, Coral's performances both, play with the glossing potency of the songs' afterglow, and embody a refusal to be removed from Mexico City's downtown, reshuffling the residual vitality of her travesti inventory, while manifesting a yearning desire to remain present amid urban displacement.

Performance, rehearsal, and impersonation not only insist on how embodiments are ever shifting, but also on how embodiments collide with material infrastructures, enriching our understanding of how space and bodies connect in an ongoing process of undoing, remaking, and reshaping. Shifting career paths, from being a kid actor to becoming a young professional dancer and choreographer, Coral worked for the iconic Teatro Blanquita, located along an important downtown avenue named Lázaro Cárdenas. A wide rectangular marquee with bright red lights would ornament star names like La Sonora Santanera, Vicente Fernández, Carmen Salinas, Pérez Prado, or Lucha Villa. Under the name Gran Teatro Circo Orrin, the two-story building first opened in the 1890s featuring a big top, a small tower, and a stable. Circo Orrin would tour Mexico twice a year, but despite the great success of clown shows, juggling acts, and acrobatics, it closed in 1910. The property was later purchased by actor, writer, and businesswoman Margo Su López, who reopened it in 1949 under the name "Carpa Margo Su," where famous artists first debuted, including María Victoria fondly known as "Mexico's Mermaid." By 1958, the original building was demolished and renovated into a permanent structure with a large, illuminated marquee and 2,000 seats. Named in honor of Margo Su's daughter Blanca Eva Cervantes, Teatro Blanquita was inaugurated on August 27, 1960 (Miranda 2016). For more than 50 years, this was Mexico's prime performance stage for both emerging and consolidated artists.

From music concerts to cabaret shows, this theater was an epicenter of nighttime entertainment in Mexico. The Francis Show, a cabaret-style variety show by travesti actor and performer Francis García, ran successfully at El Blanquita for almost 20 years, from 1980 to 1998. By 1999, the theater was renovated again, but by 2015, with multiple urban transformations, as well as the emergence of bigger concert venues located in gentrified parts of the city, this iconic theater venue was closed indefinitely. Today, the theater faces an uncertain future, as rumors have spread regarding the future of the property still owned by Margo Su's daughter, Eva. What holds value is its urban location for some investors, but for others it also represents a decaying texture characterizing that northeast wing of Mexico City's downtown (Prieto 2015). Blocks away from Plaza Garibaldi and closer to rough neighborhoods of La Lagunilla and Tepito, Teatro Blanquita has been surrounded by unhoused people and street wanderers, factors that have been used against further reinvesting in the area.

As such, the theater occupies a liminal space in the configuration of Mexico City's downtown, as it provides shelter for poor and working-class sectors, and yet is left untouched by urban developers and by city officials who strategize on failing to provide affordable housing or address public insecurity. Nonetheless, Teatro Blanquita's trajectory closely follows and intersects Coral's. Not only does she live in close vicinity, but her professional career boomed alongside the theater's heyday. It is in this instance where a story of travesti becoming and urban infrastructural development intersect to reshape our notions of public space in the city, through the glowing liminality of Coral's personal inventory, or afterglow.

Bright pink walls adorn a small dance studio in Mexico City's downtown. As a way of evoking her old stint at the theater venue, Coral and her former crew rehearse a dance choreography used to play for the king of mambo Dámaso Pérez Prado's "Concierto para Bongó." The sequence shows the resplendence of ceiling lights and mirrored walls. Sitting right across from Teatro Blanquita, Coral's dance studio rests surrounded by a series of distinct urban objects: an improvised advertising poster, a closed metallic shutter, and a contrasting black ink scrawling of graffiti art. It is hard to distinguish the images inside the rectangular picture frames hanging across the four mirrored walls. As the lens zooms in and out of frame, three dancers move following Coral's lead. The scene extends a portrayal of travesti joy, which in the case of Coral, intimately follows her heyday as a dancer and choreographer at Mexico City's iconic Teatro Blanquita. Pérez Prado's effusive trumpets and drum rolls are heard as the camera takes an expansive shot that beautifully portrays a nightscape, a shifting territory of affects entangled in material urban infrastructures.

After her shifts as a choreographer at El Blanquita, Coral would take to her sister's place and dress up to perform in drag as Lucha Villa, Celia Cruz, or Lupita D'Alessio, at a close-by cabaret. After one of the shows, when unable to take off her makeup, Coral finally comes to terms with her own transness as a travesti girl, "Ya estaba como en una olla de frijoles que está a punto de explorar, ¿no? O haces eso o te das chicarrón, ¿no? Y ya, pero entonces, este, al hacer esto, este, perdí unas cosas, pero he ganado otras, ¿no?, entonces, este, primero he [sido] yo misma. Sí, entonces, imagínense si no lo hubiera hecho, yo creo que o ya me hubiera matado o no sé qué hubiera pasado, pero, este, yo voy a ser yo, yo."

It was during her tenure at El Blanquita that Coral embraces her travestismo, and although not explicitly shown, her career gains less prominence. A seeming lack of "luck and success" exposes the undercurrents of job discrimination, social prejudice, stigmatization, and precarity steering the economic condition of travesti life. On the ebb of Coral's trajectory, Doña Lilia even states, "Por eso a mí más que otra cosa, no porque se volviera joto o gay o lo que sea, me preocupaba, me preocupaba en donde se fue a meter. Después de ser un ídolo, caer en un charco de agua sucia y no saber nada. ¿Qué ha hecho de ahora que es mujer? Nada, nada, ¿qué hizo cuando fue niño y fue jovencito? Muchas cosas, muchas cosas." Aware of the obstacles facing "gay o jotos," Coral's mom's understanding of travesti becoming reveals a powerful insight into a sense of loss. For one, Doña Lilia conflates travestismo with homosexuality, that is, in trying to recount Coral's career accomplishments, travesti becoming is not only misrecognized as an exclusive form of same sex desire but is also situated in a dark zone of sex work.

Doña Lilia's sad tears mourn the loss of a success attributed to embodying man-ness and virility to gain social mobility. The story suggests that if it hadn't been up for Coral's decision to walk away from a film and dance career as a boy, they wouldn't have lost many things in the way. Accordingly, success requires virility, while travesti embodiments fail into sweet nothing. In Lilia's words, "nada," or nothing, denotes an irresolute absence, or a continual letting go. Despite framing her story as an irreparable letting go, *Quebranto* unbridles a sense of loss that has so insidiously defined Coral's travesti becoming.

Holding on to past objects regarded as unproductive, however, refashions the material terms of engagement with the world through their affective afterglow. Each object encapsulates the meaning of a lived experience, and their fondling brings out a remanent of the past, emerging as a form of intimacy that sheds away negative undertones of loss. An afterglow flows as a temporal synthesizer that connects past unrealized possibilities into present forms of emotional attachment. The accumulation of useless objects, of junk, might also bring about a sense of queer comfort amid the loss and absence set off throughout the film. Accruing past objects might also define a powerful travesti life praxis, of negotiating loss and temporal ambiguity. Coral's insistence on holding onto the past reveals more than a mere failed subject position in the classed, gendered, and racialized scales of socioeconomic mobility. Rather, the immanence of the past moves us into finding forms of intimacy with the excessive surplus of queer materiality, of old pictures, empty perfume bottles, worn-out shoes, and frayed dresses, that have thus sustained Coral's travesti becoming.

Each object adds texture and dimension, perceptually and affectively, as each brings its own histories, trajectories, and complications into an intricate material enmeshment that troubles neoliberal understandings of ownership and possession, and thrust us into a mess of embodiment, gender, and sexuality. The objects' afterglow, in this sense, eschews a neoliberal understanding of value in that what remains holds a prismatic flair beyond possession. Each held object refuses disposal. What remains posable resists the looming necroviolence of being branded worthless. Coral's material returns gear a travesti sensibility against a necropolitics of nothingness. If junk names old, discarded belongings, articles, and objects considered of little value, Coral's holding on to seemingly useless baggage reorientates her attachments to time and space, making room to hold her junk in the present. Of course, this sensibility does not fall under the assumption that old objects are impermanent or eternal, but that junk disavows the forces that reduce travesti lives to minutiae.

Travesti junk thus expands on the rich, vigorous, and luscious textures of the past. Travesti junk—pun intended—marks an abundance of desires, positions, and experiences that emerge from apparently lowly and poor spheres of queer and trans sociality. Coral's junk bonds an affective inventory around loss, displacing the negative associations of nostalgia. The affective wealth of her inventory extends well beyond the walls of her downtown apartment building. Her junk's afterglow enacts a mode of resisting the obliteration bestowed upon by heteropatriarchal time, reshaping her relation to old urban sites, like Teatro Blanquita, deemed invaluable within the neoliberalization of the city in service of the imagined future depicted in the *Solidaridad* video.

Coral's inventory includes the multiple transformations undergoing the city, particularly of living spaces and nightlife sites. Interspersing different shots of old downtown buildings, the film tracks the way in which Coral travesti becoming is also a story about the changes in the downtown landscape. Zooming into a large metal sign that reads "Hotel San Martin" atop a tall downtown building, the lens captures the softness of bed sheets hanging on the clothesline. We listen to Coral detailing how they ended living in an apartment near Plaza Garibaldi, a downtown spot famously known for its mariachi music and unbridled nightlife. The interplay of camera shots serves to contrast how changes of urban structures have also followed Coral's family history, further complicating the relationship between the urban and the affective. Seating against the skyline, Coral shares that her brother tragically died when their apartment collapsed in the 1985 Mexico City earthquake, also shattering the family dream of opening a night bar. After moving back into a newly repaired apartment, they relocated to the place they now live in because the memory of her deceased brother gruelingly haunted Doña Lilia. Travesti becoming is also a story of transformative loss. Tall apartment buildings, rooftops, cable antennas, water tanks, exposed brick walls, metallic awnings, and windows stand as giant observers to her Sunday laundry routine.

In this sense, *Quebranto* takes us into the inner vitality of seemingly dull urban infrastructures, unsettling mainstream portrayals of Mexico City. The film thus traces the skin of the city as if making us witness its texture, dimension, and condition. The camera moves sideways to establish

Fig. 14. Coral and her mother sit at the table for lunch in their downtown apartment. Movie still from *Quebranto* (2013), dir. Roberto Fiesco.

intimacy between buildings and Coral's routine. Through the ripples of an afterglow, loss re-emerges less as a feeling of nothingness than as a call for interconnectivity. Coral's travesti becoming moves alongside the multiple urban transformations occurring after Mexico City's 1985 earthquake (Coral's brother's death), the eventual economic crisis of the late 1980s and the emergence of neoliberalism during the mid-1990s (Teatro Blanquita's closing), leading up to the gentrification of the downtown core. By basking in the afterglow of old memories, she refuses to let her past be thrown away and subsumed within this economic transformation.

Through Coral's journey, the central vision often associated with Mexico City as a seat of nationalist power, collapses, as the film portrays the internal displacements and inner workings that parallel an underground sociality not far away from the gentrified, gendered, and neoliberal spaces of Colonia Roma, Condesa, or Polanco. Coral's inventory thus points to the intimate infrastructural networks shaping travesti becoming, challenging gendered, classed, and racialized demarcations of space. That is, Coral locates travesti vitality less as a fixed category and destination than as an uneven experience of transformation, one that adapts and shifts according to an everchanging urban topography. If gentrification functions as an urban technology for racial and social cleansing against marginally poor populations, dwelling in loss amid the valueless objects insists on a politics of presence amid urban displacement. Refusing to let go enacts an embodied feeling from below. Tellingly, Coral embodies such refusal through various performances that only index a past time, but also deploy a spatial occupation through the moving body. Coral's refusal to detach from her inventory of loss rehearses an active occupation of those downtown spaces holding no value to neoliberal extractivism. Dwelling in loss deepens the affective attachments to the intimate infrastructures that sustain travesti vitality.

Quebranto thus taps into a living inventory composed of old city build-ings, ballet figurines, VHS tapes, childhood pictures, dark interiors, old poster calendars, ointment containers, old movie scripts, and perfume glass cases surrounding Coral's world. The film certainly probes into the messiness of queer archives as "ephemeral evidence" that "embod-ies the fleeting, nomadic, messy, and elusive experience and processes of self-making" (Manalansan 2014, 105). But Coral's own displacement and nomadic experience within Mexico City not only points to the undeter-mined trajectories of travesti becoming, but also reveals the complexi-ties of how travesti life also intertwines political histories of race, class, and socioeconomic mobility within the city. Coral's personal inventory pushes against the boundaries of the personal and private into the publicly remembered, expanding a travesti politics of occupation amid urban gen-trification and marginalization of the poor. Coral's holding of *Fe, Esper-anza y Caridad*'s script performs a similar gesture to the unearthing of her Teatro Blanquita picture album. These gestures untap a sensorial reservoir of emotions that reshuffles neoliberal logics of urban development and identity formation. Travesti becoming creates a time warp, a spatiotem-poral dissonance affecting neoliberal paradigms of gender, sexuality, and subjectivity through the afterglow of an object's longing.

If loss emerges as a pivotal affect to Coral's travesti experience of gen-der un/becoming, the various musical performances throughout *Que-branto* recalibrate how loss is experienced. In each performance, Coral embodies a travesti praxis of survival by bringing back what seems to be lost and forgotten onto the screen. The camera tracks the loss defining travesti life, extending an invitation to consider who can afford to move on, or remain still. More than insisting on a teleological destination of gender, Coral's sense of loss refers to a space of ambiguity, of gender inde-terminacy, that prompts the anxiety of technical taxonomical organiza-tion. "Volver, volver el tiempo atrás," she sighs when evoking her heyday in film. Yet it is the precise embodiment of the past that fosters intimacy through film with an attentive audience. Coral's travesti praxis of survival furthers a convergence between poorness and travesti becoming in complicated ways that put pressure on the neoliberal logics of (white) trans identity and gender affirmation.

However ethereal, her performance of loss brings out a way of feeling and sensing time otherwise. In the final performance bringing closure to the film, Coral lip-syncs Raphael's queer ode to nightlife "Mi gran noche." Framed in a black and white lens emulating an old night stage, the spotlight shines on a gender-ambiguous Raphael, dressed in a similar two-piece suit as the one shown in old childhood pictures. The song can elicit the moving of the audience, while inadvertently tapping into Coral's inventory. The sharpness of each hand gesture emulates the song's deep affect, contained in the singer's histrionics. Coral briefly embodies another version of Pinolito, but this act is not meant as a sort of closure to the past, or a turning away from it. Coral's final performance of Raphael brings out the differing layers of travesti becoming. Loss, in this sense, does not entail forgetting, or indifference, but demands an acute sensibility to the past. Her gaze stares right at the camera, at the audience, at us, defying our very own notions of loss, remembrance, and un/becoming. Coral, as the film shows, amasses rich textures, modulations, and material transformations, evident in her careful touching of old albums, feeling the dents of time. In this closing act, Coral reminds us of her affective inventory, of traversing time and space, so that with the afterglow of precious junk, the queer mysteries of the night remain uncaptured.

Nightscapes: Queer Feelings, Dark Infrastructures

Tracing what takes place in the dark, in economic, emotional, and spatial terms, Maya Goded's documentary *Plaza de la Soledad (2016)* follows the everyday life of six women who engage in sex work in one of Mexico City's downtown working-class areas commonly known as La Merced. When taking into consideration how floating economic networks, or "shadow economies" (Kendall 2020, 146), sustain queer worldmaking, a specific sense of queerness in such contexts emerges from below. Against this backdrop, a transnational approach to the Mexican context must vitally engage with a dark sense of queerness, not as an attempt to clarify what remains unseen, but rather to embrace it as a radical practice of queer knowledge production. As such, poverty appears not as a national enemy, but as constitutive of queer praxis, epistemology, and relationality.

Capturing the soundscapes of Plaza de la Soledad, a small parish square surrounded by a fountain, street vendors, local businesses, popular markets (i.e., *tianguis*), and a bustling bus terminal, the camera moves across day- and nighttime attending to these women's affective crisscrossing, as well as to their personal lives. Intermixing a soundtrack of tropical music, romantic ballads, and campy ranchera songs, the film opens with a traveling scene in which some of the protagonists begin to banter and sing along "Amor de cabaret." Performed by La Sonora Santanera, this song is popularly regarded as a hymn to cabaret love as it speaks of the vicissitudes and transactions of sex work. Although the song's chorus refers to sex work as insincere, lethal yet desired, the women's presence on screen challenges this definition, as they enact other affects emerging alongside sex work, such as mutual care, romance, and solidarity.[5] Layering sounds of timbal drums, trumpets, and piano notes, the song's low energy and somewhat danceable beat fondle with the mnemonic fibers of the women inside a moving van, as some of them react with a tear or a sigh when listening to the music. Carmen, one of the main protagonists, confesses that this song makes her cry and states that it makes her remember many past things as she clears her throat. The popular song, in this sense, *does* something that elicits a particular emotional reaction, participating in an affective economy through which sound, bodies, and memories become entangled as the moving image unfolds, "allowing us to enter a private moment of female friendship" (Rodríguez 2023, 170). Popular music thus travels across the city as a wave affecting thoughts, perceptions, sensations, and bodies, coming into contact within marginal city spaces.

Besides capturing a sensorium around the spaces they claim, the film mediates an embodied experience felt through the connective tissues of the moving image, entangling bodies of inscribed viewers and protagonists with city infrastructures. As Jennifer M. Barker has noted, "[w]hat we do see is *the film seeing*: we see its own (if humanly enabled) process of perception and expression unfolding in space and time [. . .] The point, though, is that all these bodies—characters', actors', viewers', and films'—are entities whose attitudes and intentions are expressed by embodied behavior" (2009, 10–11). As film director and camerawoman, Maya Goded's body is also immersed in a material and temporal geography of affects, emerging from the encounters with other women, and their nighttime transit. As such, the film's body participates in the making of a shadow economy sustaining queer relationality. By carefully following the women's everyday and everynight interactions with each other, their loved ones, and other passersby, across multiple urban environments, such as Carmen's social gathering with fellow women celebrating *La Virgen de Guadalupe*'s day, Raquel's visit to her mother's tomb in the city outskirts, or Lety's life confession to her cancer-battling daughter, the film traces different zones of queer contact.

The film's juxtaposition of day/night, open/close, public/private, pain/pleasure, expose an in-betweenness characterizing a temporal as well as a material dimension of queer relationality in this context. For instance, the parish fountain at the Plaza de la Soledad, where Carmen's get-together takes place at the beginning of the film, turns into a different night set when Carmen and Raquel are looking for trade. The shifts between day and night, for example, attend to the varying textures urban infrastructures acquire, as these are transformed into material sites hosting and giving shelter to floating erotic economies, such as that of women engaging in sex work. From a bustling sound to a night silence, the film portrays a meaningful encounter when Carmen and Raquel are visited by a houseless person who solemnly pays them tribute by caressing their arm. This houseless man's gesture offers a poignant twist to my critique of queer liberalism. If the gentrification of queer space is centered around a politics of visibility (i.e., businesses waving rainbow flags, a wide offer of queer spaces, an annual gay pride parade, etc.) as exemplified by the Mexico City government's gay tourist guide publication, as an effort to commodify local forms of queer capital, this film moves through a dark infrastructure where acts of touching emerge from otherwise dirty, invisible, and shadowy relational practices. In this sense, far from only transmitting images, and dialogues, the film also invites its audience to partake in the affective exchanges of shadow economies.

Entangled in this context, *nightscapes* refer to the affective exchanges within shadow economies and dark infrastructures invisible to a neoliberal logic of cooptation, gentrification, and transformation. Incompatible with a liberal paradigm of sexuality, the various modes of touching taking place within dark infrastructures in the film, connecting people, bodies, and objects, through caressing, embracing, kissing, and holding, reclaim an underground urban spatiality, while facilitating economies of affect that emerge from and alongside sex work. Tellingly, Esther, another protagonist in this documentary, reflects on her economic autonomy and the queer potentiality such spaces hold: "People or *machismo* don't give me money to survive. I make a living with my ass" (i.e., *no vivo de la gente ni del machismo; vivo de mis nalgas.*) Challenging a misogynistic view of women's sex work, these personal testimonies also reveal the affective flows of care within dark infrastructures and local shadow economies amid everyday violence, precarity, and vulnerability.[6] With nightscapes, I am not only referring to those public spaces holding no value for capitalist accumulation, such as dirty plazas, buildings in decay, popular markets, etc., but also to the flows of affect, such as care, embedded in the materiality that sustains marginalized working-class, poor and queer ways of life in Mexico City. As a queer mode of touching, of making a living with one's ass, queer nightscapes also reclaim a floating erotic economy through touch amid the gentrification of space, while enabling queer forms of contact inapprehensible to the grip of neoliberalism.

One of the last scenes shows Carmen, Lety, Raquel, Ángeles, and Esther, four of the film's protagonists, gathered around the Plaza de la Soledad's fountain. They are joining a wake honoring the life of their recently deceased colleague. The fountain is transformed into a site of remembrance, as they mourn the loss of a beloved friend. Their faces express an uncontainable sadness; our watching of their friend's ceremony might also remind us of our own mortal condition and of the memories we leave behind. The vigil in the film attests to the multidimensionality of a public infrastructure, allowing the loss and sadness surrounding their friend's death to prompt connections, sensations, and imaginings. After sweeping the same fountain steps, in the following scene, Carmen reveals the importance the square (i.e, *la plaza*) holds for poor queer worldmaking: "I have been here for more than 38 years, so the day I die I want my ashes to be scattered around here because this is where I am myself, where I don't have to pretend anything or smile at anyone if I don't want to; for me, this is home, and these women are my family. And I feel the need to be with them" (i.e., *Más de 38 años de estar aquí en esta plaza entonces pienso el día que me muera quiero que mis cenizas las tiren aquí, que queden aquí porque aquí es donde soy yo misma, donde no tengo que fingir nada ni tengo que sonreírle a nadie si no quiero, o sea, para mí, esta es mi casa y las mujeres son mi familia. Y siento la necesidad de estar con ellas*). Carmen's realization prompts me to ask how urban infrastructures sustain the non-homonormative needs of queer kinship, that is, what alternative queer modes of sensing that "sideline Western ocularcentrism—in order to focus on broader sensory engagements with technical systems"

Fig. 15. Raquel and Carmen laugh while seated by the fountain of La Plaza de la Soledad. Movie still from *La Plaza de la Soledad* (2016), dir. Maya Goded.

(Schwenkel 2015) emerge from these sites, or what sensory engagements emerge to better articulate an anticapitalist queer of color critique.

By decentering a liberal sense of queer loss, everynight acts and gestures of working-class poor women, as well as other dispossessed queer populations, establish intimate encounters within dark infrastructures, challenging and negotiating urban gentrification, while unsettling a white-mestizo form of (transnational) belonging and its attacks on the poor, the dirty, and the underground in Mexico. *Plaza de la Soledad's* bodily encounters, as well as the Cine Teresa's queer vitality, situates us, as Chandra Mohanty notes, within a "particular marginalized location [that] makes the politics of knowledge and power investments that go along with it visible so that we can then engage in work to transform the use and abuse of power" (2003, 231). Mohanty's transnational framework for an anticapitalist feminist critique outlines a "look[ing] upward" situated in poor women of color's critical reflections on their lived experience, in this case, on their everynight lives. Borrowing from such anticapitalist feminist critique, queer nightscapes provide a transnational queer of color analytic to look, touch, and sense from below, as it encounters and fondles with a queer sensorium in the shadows.

PART III

The Shade and Shadow of Travesti Nightlife

FIVE

The Shadowy Frames of Travesti Nightlife

The emergence of a LGBTQ+ culture across the 20th century has focused attention on the tensions of a homonational subject, eclipsing the pivotal role of travesti folk shaping nightlife in Mexico. Travestis' place on the night stages of queer Mexicanidad exists in the shadows, that is, their representation has reduced them to ornamental characters of night-time economies, making them fade into the background without fully acknowledging their playful agency in sustaining nightlife spaces for queer/trans intimacy and belonging. But a careful examination of their mainstream portrayal reveals that travesti women playfully move through visual frames of hypervisibility and invisibility, navigating shadows of overexposure, misrepresentation, and commodification. If a shadow, by definition, marks the occlusion of someone or something, and by contrast exposes the distance separating that someone or something, then, what openings make a shadow visible? As a trans provocation that complicates the visual commodification of trans and travesti formations, let's start by asking what a shadow looks or feels like: what does its lines, dimensions, or surface, recall and hide? Through its framing, what dwells within it? Or what is casted by it?

By drawing on travesti acts of queer relajo, this chapter attends to the material folds that hold the vibrancy of travestismo by tuning into the lively things sustaining nightscapes of travesti intimacy. Turning to travesti kissing, dancing, touching, and singing allows me to grapple with the materiality of travestismo as a way of framing an elsewhere of travesti vitality located in the nightly space of cabaret. As such, I extend a hemispheric bridge with trans of color critique to disarray the paradigms of homonationalism, both in Mexico and the US, to make evident the interlocking technologies of race, ethnicity, class, socioeconomic status, gender, ability, location, citizenship, etc., that contribute to the necropolitical conversion of travesti life under neoliberal capitalism. As discussed in the next chapter, tracing the shades of travesti nightlife challenges the necropolitical conversion of trans/travesti identity, while embodying a transfeminist praxis of care that tracks travesti women's playful modulations between shades and shadows. Against death, a transfeminist praxis of queer relajo, places travesti joy, fun, and pleasure in direct dialogue with trans of color critique, to reimagine the political potentialities of travesti nightlife's vibrancy beyond the spectacles of trans violence under neoliberal capitalism.

I further argue that the representation of travesti embodiment in queer Mexican culture has been overshadowed by the emergence of a neoliberal homonational subject. Like the necropolitical conversion of trans representation in the US (Snorton and Haritaworn 2013; Aizura 2018; Gill-Peterson 2018), the visual portrayal of travesti folk is overcast by a shadow in key moments, creating a paradoxical exposure defining travesti representation vis-à-vis neoliberal homonationalism. While the visual commodification of travesti identity sets the basis for the emergence of homonationalism in neoliberal times, travesti embodiments are reduced to objects of homoerotic desire instead of playful negotiators whose pleasures shape queer nightlife. Complicating these shadowy zones and frames reveals that night-making practices depend on travestis's tactics of queer relajo. Pondering what a shadow might cover or expose in relation to travesti representation, makes us consider their "figuration," that is, a critical way of dwelling in the shadows obscuring travesti lives in Mexican queer culture.[1]

Through such configuration, I first argue that travesti identity has not disappeared but been framed against a shadowy background by a national cultural establishment, also referred to as "homomestizaje" (López Toledano 2023, 27), turning the complexity of travesti becoming into an elusive object that nonetheless hides in plain sight. Entangled in the production and circulation of sexual capital, I locate an overshadowing that disrupts travesti women's necropolitical conversion and visual commodification. Visually apparent, this shadowing effect can be traced in the film *El lugar sin límites* (1978), the web series *La Casa de las Flores* (2018), and the film *El Baile de los 41* (2020). This visual code reveals a tension between homosexuality and nationalism, positioning national culture as a cult of men, while tracing the emergence of a homonationalist temperament affecting the vectors of gender, ethnicity, race, class, and sexual orientation. At the interplay of visual exposure, social occlusion, and sexual extraction, the shadow of travesti nightlife refers to a critical concept describing the playful movement of travesti women across the deadly economies of homonational nighttime, as travesti forms of queer relajo are rendered palatable for a consumer within a heteronormative neoliberal economy.

My queer engagement with three artifacts foregrounds the cabaret/brothel house as a shadow economy of the night benefiting from and sustaining travesti expressions of joy, play and pleasure, like dancing, singing, kissing, and, touching. In their nightly dances with life and death, travesti women learn to modulate through shades of hypervisibility and invisibility, that is, they learn how to playfully negotiate how to become legible and illegible amid the dangers of the night, veering away from a dichotomy of survival and resistance. In the following chapter, I turn to the docu-film *Casa Roshell* (2017) to delve into the affective modulations of travesti nightlife against Mexico's trans necropolitics.

Moving away from cultural essentialism and historical stasis, my methodological contouring blends disjunction and disfunction with the brushes of queer relajo, to throw shade at these queer artifacts, that is, throwing shade names playful tactics of modulation that travesti folk embody to mediate death and violence in material and symbolic ways. As a Mexican *jotita* in the diaspora, my queer method lets loose historical incongruity and misalignment to spot the place travestismo has occupied within a neoliberal homonormative cultural memory. Feeling the instability of ever revolving xs and axes—as discussed in chapter 1—taints my transnational sense of queer Brownness that, moving away from national cultural formations, plays with these queer artifacts to situate travesti tactics of queer relajo extending off-screen, while making us find mutual pleasure by recognizing transfemme embodiments as politically erotic. Because of their mainstream circulation, these artifacts play an important role in the making of a queer cultural history, even more so since global media has profited from Mexican LGBTQ+ representation in the last two decades, entangling travesti/trans lives with the economies of visual commodification. Thus, maintaining a critically playful outlook that questions the invention of queer histories reveals how neoliberal frames of sexuality might impact the formation of a travesti memory in Mexico.

While reckoning with the particularities of a homonational context further primed by neoliberalism, my approach to understanding practices of travestismo deploys a global and hemispheric lens to unsettle transnational networks of cultural consumption, production, and circulation (Rivera-Servera 2012, 24). Following acts of queer relajo, I perform a sensorial reading that tracks the intersection of nightlife, affect, and travesti becoming less as case studies of visual representation than as a transfeminist praxis of nightly joy, play, and pleasure. Namely, I attend to how spatial flows of affect and performance enact travesti night intimacy amid the rapid neoliberalization of LGBTQ+ life in Mexico City, and largely the global south.

My first contention here is that travesti becoming has constantly faced material and symbolic death. Paradoxically, this necropolitical conversion has aided the formation of a homonormative cultural history in Mexico. As the country advances perverse forms of neoliberalization, marked by drug-related violence, state militarization, ecological collapse, feminicide, and socioeconomic precarity, to name only a few, global Mexican media has turned to commodifying the real-life consequences of ongoing neoliberal policies by producing ahistorical and depoliticized spectacles of violence. Similarly, the recent boom of trans media, including the portrayal of travestismo, paints the image that travesti and trans folk are a new thing, without fully fleshing out their complex histories across the country. Moreover, the recent visibility of travesti and trans folk on screen does not necessarily translate into an improvement of the living conditions of poor and working-class queer/trans people, who are often excluded from mainstream productions.

The increased media attention on a queer history nonetheless has brought a revision of a homonational past. From the wide recognition of a gay cultural canon—centered around figures such as Xavier Villaurrutia, Salvador Novo, Manuel Rodríguez Lozano, Carlos Monsiváis, José Joaquín Blanco, Horacio Franco, Luis Zapata, Juan Jacobo Hernández, Salvador Irys Gómez, Juan Carlos Bautista, Julián Hernández, among others—to a queer media boom at the turn of the 21st century, the recognition of Mexico's queer cultural genealogies, in contrast, has paralleled the trajectory of the country's neoliberalization. Of note is how the importance placed on homosexuality exposes an obsession with masculinity and its perversions, including a misogynistic and male-centric gaze, guiding the formation of official (queer) cultural history. As Robert Irwin notes about the institutionalization of homophobia in the 1920s postrevolutionary era, the underlying logic of Mexican nationalism brands homosexuality as anti-national.[2]

In its anti-national character, Mexican cultural nationalism has, however, underwritten homosexuality by centering on specific forms of male homosociality as the basis for a queer cultural history. However antinational, an obsession with homosexuality reveals the underlying logic guiding the official writings of national belonging, creating the illusion of disdain toward male homosociality and homoeroticism. If antagonistic sentiments highlight the existing tensions between two poles, opposing views also reveal that they work in tandem to complement each other. In viewing male homoeroticism as antagonistic, Mexican homonationalism paradoxically constitutes itself by embracing a love between men that hides behind heroic images of men fighting to protect the nation's "virtue and honor." Under this nationalistic lens, homoeroticism can only be tolerated, justified, and at times accepted, inasmuch as it openly defends men's love of nation.

In a way, homosexuality hides within the visions of the nation, codifying a plane of sight through which the bodies of difference—be it sexual, racial, or otherwise—remain in the shadows, standing against the backgrounds of plain sight. Their silences, invisibilities, and occlusions are only highlighted when they prove to be of value to the histories of homonationalism.[3] In this sense, the shadowy frames of travesti and trans representation expose how the nightly excess of travesti embodiments only serves to reproduce the value of the male-centric nation, complicating not only issues of hyper/in/visibility, but also trajectories of homosexuality, nationalism, and visual commodification in Mexico. Their shadowy visuality has a direct impact in the way trans folk are actually perceived off-screen, echoing what C. Riley Snorton and Jin Haritaworn argue: trans hyper in/visibility is a matter of life and death, "[t]he discursive construction of the transgender body—and in particular the transgender body of color—as unnatural creates . . . a biopolitics of everyday life, where the transgender body of color is the unruly body, which only in death can be transformed or translated into the service of state power" (2013, 68). Following their argument, homonationalism further benefits from the necropolitical conversion of travesti identities.

While travesti lives only matter if annexed to a cultural memory under the homonational agendas of neoliberal reform, a white gay mestizo, or homonational, memory is built at the expense of travesti ways of life. In this sense, the homonational neoliberal subject, that is, a historically contingent white mestizo model of homosexuality, gains visual recognition inasmuch as travesti life visually fades into shadows, and materially into death. Such shadowy framing exposes how the economies of visual commodification extract travesti vitality to fashion homonational memory, pointing out the ethical considerations of approaching travesti embodiments.

On approaching silence and secrecy as part of a transfeminist praxis, Sara Ahmed calls attention to a matter of "feminist ethics" when deciding when and where to hide a secret or reveal its overextending shadow.[4] Following Ahmed's transfeminist ethics of suspension, naming the shadows cast upon travesti representation unsettles the ways in which travesti ways of life are perceived, imagined, and presented, especially if we consider the mediatic space such lives occupy in contrast to their lived experience (Tolentino 2000). As Mexico City trans performer and activist Lia García maintains, trans and travesti people are often reduced to discursive objects of study by corporate, activist, and academic practices (2019). By fetichizing travesti becoming as exceptionally unnatural, and freshly excessive, a trans necropolitics veers away from the radical potential of a transfeminist praxis around play, fun, and pleasure.

Attending to nightlife's convergence of travesti bodies, affects and sensations can bring into question the hetero/homonormative structures that, on the one hand claim the emergence of a queer cultural memory under neoliberalism, while, on the other, gain from the necropolitical conversion of travesti life to sustain a white gay mestizo status quo. A homonational optic has not only framed travesti histories as postscripts, or addenda, of a queer cultural history, but also as visual objects of commodification and consumption for a global (gay) male gaze.[5] Disorienting the shadowy frames deployed by Mexican global media in representing travesti embodiments can be a way of opening alternatives to sensing the vibrancy of travesti nightlife beyond the queer histories of homonationalism.

The commodification of travesti vitality is wired within a materialist network of neoliberal extraction, rendering travesti lifelines open sources of sexual value and capital. Trying to maintain the illusion of a gender system sustaining re/production under neoliberal capitalism, the biopolitical extraction of travesti life value is necessary to paint a colorful collage of sexual inclusion in the name of political progress. This materialist network, I argue, often works in the space of the cabaret, a nighttime economy that nonetheless facilitates travesti pleasure, intimacy, and survival. By relying on necropolitical extraction of sexual capital across the Americas, a queer neoliberal logic supports the sociocultural and theoretical "uses of travesti corpses" (Cornejo 2019), as well as the US-centric grammars of sexuality studies. Although my approach might dangerously touch on some of these modes of analysis, I sensorially engaged with the playful tactics of travestismo as their renditions of queer relajo turn inside out shadowy frames, and instead, envision other ways of approaching travesti intimacy amid precarity, violence, and death.

The Deadly Economies of Travesti Dancing

The film *El lugar sin límites* (The Place Without Limits, 1978), directed by Arturo Ripstein, exemplifies the necropolitical extraction of travesti vitality.[6] In her re/presentation, La Manuela, the film's main character, is misrecognized as a male homosexual. La Manuela's misrecognition becomes central to an overshadowing effect that makes her hypervisible to the point of death—seen in the film's final sequence. Centering on the pivotal role the cabaret plays in shaping the town's political economy, the film's title serves as a metaphor to refer to the night's unbridled desires and unlimited possibilities. A conventional reading of the film's tension centers on the forbidden longing for travesti intimacy, exemplified in the fatal attraction between Pancho and La Manuela, but by tracing the sensuality of kissing and dancing, La Manuela confronts the accumulation of capital and the heterosexual idea of progress by recognizing the nightlife space of cabaret as fraught with travesti intimacy. In this sense, a queer materialist view of *El lugar sin límites* would point toward the convergence of socially contingent forms of sexuality that, nonetheless, shape the material dimensions of capital.[7] Attentive to a materialist deployment of queer theory, my reading of *El lugar sin límites* aims to situate a shadowing effect evident in representing travesti identity and becoming. A shadowy frame not only indexes a way of looking at the in-between-ness of travesti life in Mexico, but also unveils the biopolitics of framing travesti embodiments through the lens of Mexican media.

The film portrays the intolerance of a society that castigates nonconventional forms of intimacy, kinship, and ownership by presenting La Manuela as the lawful owner of the brothel house, which is one remaining town property cacique Don Alejo seeks to own. In fact, the latter is interested in regaining the property rights of the night venue to carry on with his plan for ultimate territorial and infrastructural control of El Olivo. By making explicit Don Alejo's desire to hold exclusive control of the town through the extractive technologies of a monopoly, the film reflects an unbalanced power dynamic underpinning the interactions with the town's working-class inhabitants, like Pancho and La Manuela. In other words, the film calls attention to the complex relations between sexuality and capital, namely heteronormativity and neoliberalism.

The convergence of sexuality, infrastructure, visuality, and capital becomes more evident when considering the following four aspects of the film: 1) Don Alejo's desire to purchase Manuela's cabaret house is part of a larger plan to demolish the entire town for the construction of a private energy consortium; 2) Don Alejo's push to finalize the purchase of El Olivo stems from an anxiety related to kinship and inheritance since he has no children and fears for the end of his bloodline; 3) The presence of La Japonesita, La Manuela's biological daughter, constitutes an impasse to the law of inheritance, as well as to a heteronormative model of re/productive economies, especially considering that La Japonesita is conceived between La Japonesa and La Manuela, out of a bet made between the former and Don Alejo, over the cabaret's property rights; 4) Pancho's masculinity crisis is connected to his socioeconomic status and class position vis-à-vis Don Alejo's material wealth and symbolic masculine superiority, as the former is repaying a big money loan for his red cargo truck, and such debt is not only read as a failed attempt at moving through the socioeconomic ladder, but also as a sign of male weakness and frustrated virility. As Hortense J. Spillers notes, "property seems wholly the business of the male" (1987, 65), and, while the film focuses on the relationship between La Manuela and Pancho, and their non-conventional desire, the performance of gender becomes a marker of class, race, and socioeconomic location, further entangling the town's affective and spatial economies within a grid of capitalist extraction and re/production. The plot thus intertwines stories of travesti intimacy with histories of capitalism in the Americas.

While issues of gender, sexuality, and desire are more evident in the film, an impetus for industrialization and development reveals the intact "neofeudal" socioeconomic systems of *latifundismo* and *caciquismo*, that is, the total control of property by powerful landlords in Latin America sets the basis for neoliberal transformation (de la Mora 1992, 91). Attending to La Manuela's kissing, dancing, and bantering, our senses are redirected to perceive the cabaret's material conditions that interweave sexuality, gender, and desire, with the accumulation of capital. Under the cabaret's dimmed lights, travesti intimacy can flourish, bringing out of the shadowy frames the shining splendor of La Manuela's dance moves that mesmerize even toughest of looks, like Pancho's. It is within the darkness of the cabaret that a queer nightscape floats to suspend the frantic search for economic siege, and social mobility, as La Manuela's swirling transports the attending audience, including Pancho, Don Alejo, and everyone watching the film, into an obscure fantasyland where travesti desire can be touched. Engaging La Manuela's playful dancing exposes what holds value and who is worth living, dying, and being socially mobile, as well as a politics of life and death intersecting sexuality, class, and desire. Bringing La Manuela's death in the final movie sequence is thus a matter of sexual as much as material violence—consider, for instance, an early scene in which Pancho and La Japonesita discuss that Don Alejo had shut down the town's electricity to force out dwellers and forward his desire for privatization.

A great volume of scholarship about *El lugar sin límites* has focused on Ripstein's innovations of genre, technique, and theme,[8] but few studies have critically engaged how protagonist La Manuela's travesti identity moves in flux with the town's economy. For instance, Sergio de la Mora and David William Foster, respectively, situate La Manuela's travestismo beyond a purely dichotomic gender system, and although Foster briefly taps into issues of homoeroticism, cross-dressing, and fetishism within the brothel, they both concur, in their own way, that "La Manuela is an integral part of the town's economy" (Foster 2003, 385). De la Mora, moreover, finds in La Manuela a stereotype of a "queen homosexual," to argue that although "every *fichera* film features a queen homosexual, [t]his inclusion is double-edged. On the one hand, it makes male homosexuality visible. On the other, this visibility is possible only at the cost of stereotyping him with the most misogynist characteristics heterosexual males attribute to 'femininity,' including weakness, frivolity, and narcissism" (385–86).

Foster further notes that "La Manuela, to be sure, considers herself to be a woman and wishes for everyone to maintain her alignment with the feminine [. . .] and her death both affirms [Pancho's] masculinity (in the sense that it is an appropriate revenge for La Manuela's apparent assumption that Pancho would find her to be a desirable sexual partner) and removes permanently from his world someone who might continue to display to his world the possibility that Pancho might find La Manuela to be a desirable sexual partner" (2003, 381–82). If, for de la Mora, male homosexuality becomes visible at the expense of travesti vitality, Foster reiterates that travesti death sustains the hidden homosociality of "a queer desire" (382) in the film. That numerous studies refer to La Manuela as a stereotypical embodiment of male homoeroticism points to a persistent misrecognition of travesti ways of life, contributing to the formation of a dangerous stereotype that reduces travestismo to either a sexual fetish or a queer affirmation of homosexual desire. Following their respective analyses—Foster's grounded on semiotics; de la Mora's on media and sexuality studies—*El lugar sin límites* offers an example of the necropolitical conversion of the travesti in Mexican media, while nonetheless situating the cabaret as a nightlife site where the logics of heterosexual and neoliberal extraction fall into play.

Fig. 16. A passionate kiss between Pancho and La Manuela. Movie still from *El lugar sin límites* (1978), dir. Arturo Ripstein.

Being travesti appears under a shadow, a grim place in between the visible rays of homosexuality and the public screen. A shadow is but a silhouette of a body. Yet, each shadow acquires a different shape through interaction under a different intensity of light, or even in the dark, casting queer matters into a shadowy economy of travesti intimacy with every silhouette of queer relajo. As in the case of La Manuela, to be held in the shadows does not mean to remain invisible, but rather, it means that her body, flesh, and life are made insubstantial, fleeting, or even disposable to a social arrangement that cracks open at the possibility of her playfulness despite her being reduced to a trace of homoeroticism. Even if the film insists on a stereotypical portrayal, La Manuela's kissing, dancing, and bantering are co-constitutive of a complex shadow economy that sustains social and material relations with the laws of heteronormativity. Benefiting from the extraction of travesti vitality by deploying a series of technologies (i.e., law, economy, family, nationalism, etc.), the monopolistic and neoliberal system constricting horizontal channel flows for value exchange—be it sexual, socioeconomic, symbolic, or material—nonetheless become possible through travesti intimacy. Although the closing sequence undoubtedly shows travesti death, previous erotic performances with Pancho not only foretells La Manuela's physical and symbolic annihilation, but also shows other possibilities for the protagonist to establish different terms of affection beyond heteronormativity. Sadly, the death of La Manuela's former business partner, La Japonesa, reaffirms the cabaret's foreclosure of any alternative modes of kinship and economy beyond monopolistic and neoliberal extraction.

Through La Manuela's last dance, in a sequence leading to the film's deadly scene, the necropolitical conversion of travesti vitality is acutely visible. After initially hiding inside a chicken coop, La Manuela decides to face Pancho, who has been harassing La Japonesita with questions about the protagonist's whereabouts. Dressed in a ravishingly red flamenco dress, La Manuela plays with Pancho and begins to seduce him with a hypnotizing performance under the spell of the Spanish song "El beso" interpreted by Los Churumbeles de España. Following a mesmerizing dance, La Manuela retells "la leyenda del beso," a folktale about a sleeping handsome young man who awakes after being kissed by a beautiful woman in the middle of the forest. La Manuela's embodied storytelling offers a subtext to the film's plot, as the act of kissing, according to the legend, is a balm against blindness, which in turn is expressly manifested as a desire to not knowing, or not wanting to know (i.e., "un beso en los ojos para ya no estar ciego").

Undoubtedly, La Manuela is dancing for Pancho's eyes; Pancho, in turn, is consuming La Manuela's dance performance. Within gay bars, the vitality of travesti and drag ecologies can be reduced to service the entertainment of (gay) men and be confined to the stage of gay consumer culture (Namaste 2000, 11–12). Although La Manuela's cabaret dance perversely sustains a patriarchal and heteronormative economy, her passionate kissing is a queer provocation to such a system. The film's framing of such a transgression of travesti kissing and touching is reason for lethal punishment. In other words, La Manuela's kissing unsettles her confinement to the stage of performance while recasting the cabaret alongside its stage as a vital economy for travesti nightlife.

After La Manuela ends with her captivating flamenco-style dance, the couple passionately kisses, suggesting that once Pancho touches La Manuela's lips, he'd embrace his own desire for her. Hinting at the plasticity of masculinity, Pancho even acknowledges that "a man must be willing to try everything," as he kisses La M 188anuela. But the presence of Octavio, Pancho's brother-in-law, witnessing the eye-opening kiss, triggers a violent response to such an intimate gesture. Now that Pancho, the archetype of toxic male homosexuality, finally comes to face La Manuela, the intimate gesture of kissing unsettles the normative ebbs of homosexual desire, as well as the economies of heteronormativity, namely the nuclear family, the male gaze, the patriarchal accumulation of capital, and the conventional performativity of gender and sexuality. Rather than foretelling the playful possibilities of a "happy ever after" beyond neoliberal terms, the kiss points to the necropolitical conversion of travesti intimacy, as a desire to not wanting to know on his own terms the attraction Pancho feels for La Manuela unleashes the deadly force of homosexual desire.

By confronting viewers with the biopolitics of travesti vitality, *El lugar sin límites* offers a poignant critique against machismo and misogyny in a society that finds perverse joys in hiding its double standards. In doing so, the film participates in the necropolitical conversion of travesti life by situating La Manuela in a place of constant misidentification as a "maricón," or "joto," that is, femme embodiments of queerness. This misidentification places travesti nightlife in a shadowy field of vision, one that is technically and symbolically accomplished by playing with light. In this sense, a shadowy frame refers to the blurring effect through which travesti nightlife is eclipsed by male homosexual desire. At times, this shadowing effect exposes the real cost of sustaining travesti intimacy, materializing in constant effacement and brutal death.

The film's interplay of light and shadow helps foreground my argument concerning travesti intimacy, nightlife, and necropolitical value. Through a sort of fading, the exposure of travesti nightlife shifts along a continuum of hyper/in/visibility, a spectrum that defines the complexity of a travesti dance between life and death. Travesti nightlife survival thus responds to a series of playful maneuvers of queer relajo to fend off hypervisibility, invisibility, consumption, and fatal exposure. The shadows of travesti nightlife thus overexposes a historical intolerance to femme and gender nonconforming ambiguous expressions of intimacy, like the one between La Manuela, La Japonesa, and La Japonesita, or even La Manuela and Pancho. Borrowing from the disruption of queer relajo, La Manuela's playful movements of kissing, dancing, bantering, and touching name travesti shades of action that, making explicit relations with gender and sexual ambiguity, exist in the shadows of a field of vision fixed by the illusion of neoliberal homonationalism.

Even if the brothel/cabaret constitutes a critical infrastructure through which affect and space intersect with the logics of heteronormativity, designing a nocturnal economy that privileges male desire, the cabaret nonetheless becomes part of a sensorial and affective nightscape that facilitates trans and travesti ways of life. *El lugar sin límites* exposes a distinct characteristic defining what Gastón A. Alzate calls "la marginalidad," or marginality of the cabaret (2002, 19). For Alzate, cabaret constitutes a form of theatrical performance that draws on techniques from *teatro de carpa* and *teatro frívolo*, such as improvisation, obscenity, scatological humor, profanity, and coarse language, while creating an ambiance for social critique. While Alzate's definition situates cabaret as a marginal site of performance that weaves together certain strands of political and sexual dissident cultures (2002, 20–21), Laura G. Gutiérrez notes that cabaret is not only "a mixture of different early-twentieth-century performance practices that incorporated farce, parody, and satire as strategies of presentation," but also a space that seeks "to interrogate those fixed notions of gender and sexuality that permeate and are continuously and adamantly perpetuated throughout Mexican society and culture" (2010, 102). Mexican cabaret is intrinsic to what Carlos Monsiváis calls "popular nightlife," a space building a sense of belonging by the disturbances of queer relajo across Mexico City's nightscapes.

The embodied, performative, and affective specificities of the cabaret as one of the primary sites of queer nightlife in Mexican cultural scenes and imaginaries denote a spatial politics of fun, pleasure, and leisure that index queer codes of excess, marginality, transgression, and dissidence against urban uptightness and straight sentiments from the late nineteenth, across the twentieth, and to the early twenty-first century. Aside from its underground and popular characteristics, the space and practice of cabaret also "became congealed in the collective imaginary through the classic urban melodrama films of the 1940s and 1950s" (Gutiérrez 2010, 108), pointing to "the golden age of nightlife in Mexico City" (Monsiváis 2018, 9), a social choreography emerging amid the rapid urbanization of the city, and the consolidation of postrevolutionary cultural industries, like film, print, and radio, to create an urban appeal for the social masses to consume mainstream national cultures from 1930 to the 1960s.

In this sense, I fathom the cabaret not only as a site of performance practice, but also as a critical infrastructure located within marginal socioeconomic locations. Here, the cabaret refers to a shifting site for the contested circulation, not only of affect, movement, and sensation, but also of queer relajo, as in travesti acts of kissing, dancing, or touching. Through a queer lens of relajo, the cabaret adapts and changes according to the complexities of the Mexican context under neoliberal reform. Mexican cabaret nonetheless indexes cultural sites, practices, and relations from working- and lower-class travesti positions facing everyday violence, dispossession, and precarity. The practice and method of queer Mexican cabaret maintain a strong hold for travesti nightlife and every-night survival.

While generating anxieties to established systems of intimacy, economy, and belonging, travesti nightlife unsettles conventional embodiments of masculinity and femininity in Mexico. In this sense, the shade of travesti nightlife names a field of action, a vital continuum emerging from nightscapes, through which travesti identities move through the threats of violence and death across nighttime, not only playing with the in-between-ness of sexuality and gender through kissing, dancing, and touching, but also ruffling the conventions of socioeconomic systems that rely on set definitions of man- and womanhood for potential extraction. Against erasure, extraction, and death, shade thus refers to the travesti embodied modulations of queer relajo, sparking the fires of a transfeminist praxis around nightlife. Located in the space of the brothel/cabaret, travesti playful acts and performances open political possibilities for care, joy, and pleasure mediating the biopolitical economies of nighttime intimacy, and belonging.

The cabaret emerges as a queer nightscape, that is, a fluctuating sensorium of feelings and affects that, in the company of others, facilitate sensorial exchanges during the night. As a queer nightscape that can sustain travesti intimacy and vitality, the cabaret enables multiple forms of contact, sparking a shadow economy of travesti feelings. Queer nightscapes thus lend a critical concept to describe the complexity of travesti nightlife, an affective infrastructure whose material tectonics shift according to the flow of multiple and oppositional views, sensations, and feelings amid neoliberal commodification. As intermittent affective economies, nightscapes also recognize the powerful investments that travesti vitality endure to enliven the necessary circuits of queer intimacy.

Embedded in the affective tectonic of queer nightscapes, the queer cabaret nonetheless obscures modes of neoliberal extraction and commodification by detonating disruptive practices of queer relajo that aid repurposing physical structures, such as old buildings, family houses, or public infrastructures. In doing so, the cabaret hosts disruptive forms of queer joy, and travesti playfulness to eclipse neoliberal forms of pleasure, while carving out fleeting spaces for the exchange of travesti kissing, dancing, bantering, and touching in the grittiness of working-class night venues. In the case of *El lugar sin límites*, La Manuela and La Japonesita, that is, a mother and her daughter, skillfully mediate through queer relajo their impending social and material death, as they both manage a local economy that foreshadows a crisis of masculinity.

In the context of Mexico, neoliberal homonationalism pairs up practices of consumption with forms of national belonging, situating economic privilege and whiteness as a desired embodiment for sexual and gender dissidence. Against the commodification of queer/trans relationality, queer nightscapes function as a sensorial concept, a sort of queer undercurrent that takes us into the depths of unknown feelings, to grapple with neoliberal relationality, that is not to say that they exist separate from neoliberal homonationalism, but that they emerge as parallel queer infrastructures of care and support amid affective, economic, and material precarity. Queer nightscapes do not necessarily replace or eliminate neoliberal logics of extraction and capitalist consumption, as neoliberal capitalism also contributes to the formation of queer and travesti nightlife, but it allows the deployment of a critical concept that highlights the affective exchanges that mediate the necropolitical conversion of travesti and queer vitality amid complex neoliberal transformation in twenty-first-century urban Mexico.

With a LGBTQ+ mainstream media boom in the 2010s, the audiovisual and cinematic treatment of cabaret as a contested site for travesti intimacy has also advanced and disrupted the necropolitical conversion of trans becoming. Films such as Roberto Fiesco's *Quebranto* (2013), Rigoberto Pérezcano's *Carmín Tropical* (2014), Flavio Florencio's *Made in Bangkok* (2015), Roberto Fiesco's *Club Amazonas* (2016), or Alejandro Zuno's *Oasis* (2016), have portrayed some of the complex realities surrounding travesti and trans lives in Mexico. Playing with documentary film, travesti and trans women protagonists grapple with memory, violence, identity, migration, and nightlife. The release of these films has contrasted with a stark rise of transphobic murders.[9] According to a 2016 report prepared by the Transgender Law Center at Cornell University, Mexico ranks second highest in violent cases of transphobia in the Americas, after Brazil.[10] The report suggests that the enactment of legal and civil protections to combat violence, crime, and discrimination against LGBTQ+ people has also seen a backlash in the increasing amount of transphobic crimes.

In the following sections about the web series *La Casa de las Flores*, the cabaret/brothel house furnishes material and economic support to heteronormative lifestyles that fall apart once the institution of marriage falls into shambles, while in *El Baile de los 41*, travesti nightlife serves as a refuge against hetero- and homonormativity, whose social institutions severely punish travesti embodiments that challenge homoerotic desire. In all three instances, travesti shades not only refer to a playful tactic mediating the shadowing of travesti subjects on screen, but also highlights the affective relations of nightscapes by exchanging joy, play, and pleasure, alongside fear, and anger. Bringing out of the shadows and under the shining rays of a mirrorball, queer nightscapes tease out the many contradictions of nighttime queer/travesti play, as they interact with a neoliberal strand of homonationalism—defined here as a coalition between a neoliberal logic of capitalist extraction driving the incorporation of sexual and gender dissidence into the nation-state.

While mainstream media production has benefited from the necropolitical extraction of travesti nightlife by turning to their visual commodification, the mediatic overexposure of travesti and trans women shows an alarming increase of transphobic culture. Although I am not suggesting that the increase of trans and travesti death is a direct consequence of their representation, the necropolitical paradox of travesti becoming does point to a heightened disparity between the hypervisibility of travesti representation in culture and the impoverished life conditions of travesti and trans people. However, the recent media explosion has inevitably brought upon the commodification of travesti and trans ways of life. To point to this paradoxical relation, I turn to Manolo Caro's webseries *La Casa de las Flores* (2018–2021) and David Pablos's film *El Baile de los 41* (2020).

A Dead Bed of Flowers

Released in August 2018, Netflix's *La Casa de las Flores* (2018–2021) is a dark comedy-drama that pictures the dysfunctionality of a white, upper-class family in Mexico City. The series starts by showing the crumbling of the heterosexual family after its patriarch Ernesto de la Mora is forced to come clean about his secret love affair in front of his "official" family. On the second episode of season 1, "Chrysanthemum," the lines separating the public family life and private love affair are blurred by the suicide, in the previous episode, of Roberta Sánchez, Ernesto's lover, and manager of their secretly co-owned nightlife cabaret business *Casa de las Flores*. The series title plays a metaphor that not only reveals the co-existence of two affective economies that share the same name, but also the models of intimacy underpinning each business, namely a flower shop run by a traditional family, and the shadowy economy of a cabaret managed by Ernesto's lover.

The first episode sets the tone for a crisis of heteronormativity by showing Roberta's plans of suicide at the flower shop, an adjacent structure to the family's mansion, during the de la Mora family's celebration of Ernesto and

Virginia de la Mora's marriage anniversary. Once Ernesto's extramarital love affair comes out of the box with Roberta's unexpected suicide, *la casa grande* must reckon with economic insecurity and material precarity, as their flower shop, the supposedly main economic force of a white, upper-class Mexican family, is purchased out by a rival family—actually the flower shop is never a profitable business generating the de la Mora's wealth.

Out of the family's three children, Paulina de la Mora, a divorced single mother whose ex-partner is a Spanish trans woman, only knows about the second house of flowers, the affair between her dad and his now late lover Roberta, and their child Micaela Sánchez. Once the other two siblings become aware of the existence of the cabaret, they pay a visit to the night venue in search of evidence that might exonerate their father from fraud charges. Upon walking into the dimmed lights of the cabaret, Elena and Julián de la Mora appear disgusted by its gritty hallway, dark dance floor, and underground feel, demeaning a poor and working-class aesthetic. Later in the episode, Paulina reveals that her family has been living off the revenue generated by the small cabaret economy. Her two younger siblings Elena de la Mora, a student pursuing graduate education in the US, and Julián de la Mora, a bisexual man who struggles with his sexuality by leading two romantic relationships at the same time, one with the family's accountant, Diego Olvera, economically depend on the cabaret labor of travesti women to pay for exclusive club memberships, vacation trips, and university tuition. Roberta's death further complicates the shadow economies of the other house of flowers—the cabaret name that tacitly describes the femininity of its laboring travesti and trans women. By portraying the dysfunctionality of the heterosexual family, the series highlights the economic fractures of conventional kinship, as is the cabaret that serves as the economic motor sustaining the lifestyles of heterosexuality through drag performance, travesti sex work, and male erotic dancing. The plot thus shows that the cabaret has historically paid for maintaining the illusion of the family, as well as the heteronormative model of Mexican belonging.

Like *El lugar sin límites*, the series underlines the importance of nightlife shadow economies that, in the end, provide heteronormative structures, such as the nuclear family, the economic means to thrive, while depending on and extracting material, economic, and affective resources from queer/travesti nightlife. Emphasizing the strong role of women in both businesses, the series seems to erase the economic vitality of travesti workers by focusing instead on the dysfunctionalities of heteronormative kinship, placing travesti characters into a shadowy frame.

A playful queer comparison of both cultural artifacts, *El lugar sin límites* and *La Casa de las Flores*, teases out the "intimate economies of the developing [sexual] capital" (Wilson 2004, 55) at the cabaret. In the former, the sexual labor performed by the women, La Manuela, La Japonesita, and before her death, La Japonesa, collided with their domestic labor, which is somewhat overlooked by the cacique's desire to privatize the town for his political and economic self-interest. But the coalition established by working-class cabaret women allows them to circumvent the patriarchal logics of capitalist possession. For instance, La Manuela and La Japonesa outplay Don Alejo and obtain the property rights of the cabaret house despite their precarious economic conditions. That their sex work provided the means to maintain the everyday operations of the cabaret after dark, like washing, cooking, cleaning, etc., points to the fraught contradictions of travesti intimacy, class, and capital in Mexican nightlife economies.

Whereas *El lugar sin límites* unveils the proximities between travesti intimacy and capital in a mostly working-class environment, where the cabaret also serves as a site for "kinship labor" (Wilson 39), that is, travesti and cis sex workers work, live in, and contribute to maintaining their living/working space, *La Casa de las Flores* not only marks the neoliberalization of the cabaret space, by showing the separation of previously entangled spheres of sociality, kinship, and business in the making of queer nightlife, but also forecloses any possibility at expanding on the socioeconomic agency of cabaret laborers when Roberta, the cabaret manager, dies. The death is not coincidental since, after her suicide, the focus of the series turns to remedying the inevitable collapse of the heterosexual household. By casting into the shadows travesti cabaret labor, the series eclipses the working-class dimensions of cabaret intimacy, particularly as they sustain the gendered and classed economies of the patriarch, and by extension the embodiment of the nation-state.

La Casa de las Flores's portrayal of travesti embodiment reduces them to the cabaret night stage for visual consumption. In this case, the interchangeable categories between travesti becoming and drag performance, further complicate the distinctive role of travesti and trans workers within queer nightlife economies, especially when these spaces are designed to satisfy a mostly gay white mestizo clientele with economic fluency, or what has been known as pink money markets (Fernandes de Oliveira and Machado 2021; Salinas Hernández 2010). Seen as a pink commodity, director Manolo Caro's visual arrangements in the series not only place travesti and drag identities within the constraining space of the stage but pushes them into embodiments of showbiz femininity, as travesti characters only stiltedly impersonate bubblegum music icons like Paulina Rubio, Amanda Miguel, Gloria Trevi, or Yuri.

While Roberta's funeral scene marks the convergence of two seemingly distant *casas* (houses), the cabaret, *la casa chica*, and the family flower shop/home, *la casa grande*, the four travesti characters borrowing the names of Pau, Amanda, Gloria, and Yuri, are framed in the shadows during the wake, as they stand still as inert figures guarding Roberta's casket. But in contrast to La Manuela's prominent character in *El lugar sin límites*, *La Casa de las Flores* extends a shadow on travesti and drag ecologies by placing travesti women as ornamental flower arrangements to a deathbed. This spatial configuration situates travesti identity at par with death, or at least in the same visual frame as a casket. The necropolitical conversion of travesti life in this series might not appear as explicitly clear as in *El lugar sin límites*, in which the violent death of La Manuela reminds viewers of the consequences of transgressing the heteronormative laws of kinship. While Manolo Caro's black comedy-drama does not engage in the explicit portrayal of travesti death, the placement of travesti subjects throughout the series nonetheless dims them out of light into the shadows, reducing them to stage accessories.

By casting a shadow over travesti characters, the series performs an erasure that is visually present in their representation. Such dimming out depicts the extraction of travesti vitality for the sustenance of heteronormal life. As the plot thickens, the series grapples with the contradictions of holding onto heteronormativity while portraying neoliberal forms of queer sexuality in non-English contexts.[11] In a way, *La Casa de las Flores* perpetuates the ways in which Mexican homonational culture has looked at and consumed travesti identities but does so by portraying the cabaret as a devalued site for travesti intimacy, kinship, and belonging. Its working-class, popular, and gritty nature as showcased in Manolo Caro's *La Casa de las Flores* offers a depoliticized, palatable, and marketable version of a shadow travesti economy that is aesthetically eclipsed by the predominance of white-passing characters, as well as the portrayal of a conventional family in crisis. Once the family's tensions move away from the contested space of cabaret in subsequent episodes, shifting its focus to more conventional sites of heteronormative domesticity (i.e., the home, the church, the family, etc.), the series does away with travesti characters outside the cabaret, casting a shadow over the presentation of travesti becoming, while participating in the process of their commodification.

La Casa de las Flores is representative of what Paul Julian Smith calls a "newly diverse audiovisual culture" of LGBTQ+ media in twenty-first-century Mexico.[12] Although noting the "highly disturbing" trend characterizing a continued interest on "violence and poverty" as "topical themes" attracting the attention of global media publics and academics, the critic seems to equate visual representation with the overall improvement of the living conditions facing sexual and gender dissidence in the country. Smith's contextualization of queer Mexican media in the twenty-first century suggests that, despite the country's inequality, "the increase in size and wealth of the middle class" in parts of the country might have contributed to the advent of a "irreducibly hybrid" queer mediascape (2017, 1). While the LGBTQ+ media boom concerning Smith's text-based audiovisual analysis points to an increased presence of Mexican media production in global markets, his critical analysis fails to account for the flows of cultural capital whereby a neoliberal rationality around sexual identity, and citizenship is co-constitutive to hemispheric technologies of extraction, commodification, and intervention.

The boom of LGBTQ+ media in Mexico must thus be framed within a complex network where the affective, socioeconomic, technological, and biopolitical affect the making of a global and hemispheric constellation of colliding spheres, including those touching on matters of gender, and sexuality, as they assemble transnational publics that establish a mediatized connection with everyday life. Undoubtedly, a grassroots activist cultural movement has brought critical attention to the ways in which mainstream media participate in the commodification and extraction of sexual identity practices across the country. While bringing visibility to travesti intimacy, the media boom in trans and travesti representation complicates the rise of transphobic crimes, further entangling the mediatized spheres of LGBTQ+ culture and the homonational script of the past.

A Travesti Dance in the Shadows

Bringing informed viewpoints into a debate about Mexico's cultural queer memory, TV UNAM's recent LGBTQ+ video series, "Los 41 Tropiezos de la heteronorma en México" (*The 41 slips of heteronormativity in Mexico*, 2021), situates the Dance of the 41 as one of Mexico's pivotal events in the country's queer cultural history.[13] The title of the series precisely points to the sociocultural polysemy of the number 41. Once regarded as a sign of opprobrium, the number now reinscribes a sense of LGBTQ+ pride that

Fig. 17. Film poster of *El Baile de los 41* (2020), dir. David Pablos.

honors the infamous 1901 drag ball as a touchstone of homosexuality in twentieth-century Mexico (Franco 2019, 94).[14] In line with a revisionist outlook, David Pablos's *El Baile de los 41* (2020), released globally through the online streaming platform Netflix, recasts the sociocultural imaginaries around the 1901 event.

Instead of focusing on the drag night ball as the film's gist, Pablos draws from a fictional love story between two members of the "secret" society, Evaristo Rivas and Ignacio de la Torre, son-in-law of then Mexican dictator

Porfirio Díaz. About this adaptation, film critic Manuel Betancourt notes that "Monika Revilla's screenplay doesn't begin with the political scandal that gives the film its title. Instead, it uses it as its climax, an impactful punctuation mark on a tender love story played against the backdrop of the patriarchal power structures of Mexico's turn-of-the-century gentry."[15] Betancourt's review tacitly highlights a disconnect between two stories, the one portrayed by the 2020 film and that one retold by 1900s print media. As presented by the official record, including Mexican corridos alongside José Guadalupe Posada's caricaturized illustrations, the Dance of the 41 indexes the dehumanization, objectification, and moral death of those who engage in practices of gender insubordination, cross-dressing, and effeminacy, while the film's focus relies on a fictional love affair between homosexual men. Albeit the temporal differences, an important point can be made about how the significance of this event has impacted the representation of travesti nightlife in Mexico.

In the media archives recounting the 1901 drag ball raid, as in Posada's etchings, corrido lyrics or newspaper notes, the 41 appear dehumanized, ridiculed, and reduced to animals. In one of such accounts, they are called "chickens" ("los pollos") dressed in women's clothing: "These [men] were wearing very elegant women's dresses, wigs, false breasts, embroidered brogues, and on their face, they had painted a flush on their cheeks and big eyebrows" (in Irwin, McCaughan, and Nasser 2003, 92).[16] Newspaper notes focus on body prosthetics to condemn their gender ambiguity, while dehumanizing their femininity by describing them as animals. Words such as, "41 lizards," "faggots," "well-combed wigs," "overpainted faces," "enormous breasts," follow similar descriptions as those found in a corrido's second-last stanza: "they cry, squeal, and even bark" (in Irwin, McCaughan, and Nasser 2003, 95). While the newspapers describe them as embodying a monstrous femininity, the infamous corrido, "Aquí están los maricones muy chulos y coquetones," similarly compare their gestures to that of animals, while mocking their extravagantly feminine way of dressing to justify their violent injury, and hard punishment.

In describing the 41 as chickens or lizards, the portrayals of the press situate gender transgressors and sexual dissidents within the category of the non-human, making a visual spectacle of such "immoral" deeds. The media coverage thus participates in the dehumanization of the 41 as caricatures of femininity, as well as in the hypervisibility of gender transgression.[17] While the sociocultural meaning of the 41 in the formation of a queer memory in modern Mexico has certainly changed throughout the last century, the early portrayal of drag, cross-dressing, and travestismo consolidates a way of looking at travesti embodiments, as well as their representation. As Robert Franco aptly argues when examining the historical relevance of the 1901 drag ball in contemporary LGBTQ+ activism, "these later uses of memory remind us that while the Forty-One were considered homosexuals by the press, gender transgression was a central part of the story. Although it is impossible to know now either how those 'maricones' self-identified or their sexual practices," to use [Susana] Vargas Cervantes's words, "one can at least entertain the possibility of a prototypical transgender subjectivity during the ball" (Franco 2019, 92).[18]

In considering these queer artifacts, namely Arturo Ripstein's *El lugar sin límites*, Manolo Caro's *La Casa de las Flores*, and David Pablos's *El Baile de los 41*, we can trace a visual lens that frames the representation of travesti people in the shadows, participating in the necropolitical conversion of travesti vitality through a visual economy of commodification. Benefiting from a transregional demand for LGBTQ+ media in neoliberal times, these artifacts extract value from travesti nightlife by situating a homosexual erotic desire as the basis for trans and travesti intimacy. These artifacts also expand on a necropolitical way of looking, that is, a visual pedagogy that normalizes the symbolic and real death of travesti identities in Mexican queer culture aligned with a paradigm of understanding sexuality through the racialized optics of queer neoliberalism. In this sense, travesti subject positions are not only reduced to shadowy fields of vision, but often navigate necropolitical paradoxes through playful maneuvers of representation.

Travesti acts of queer relajo, evident in kissing, bantering, touching, and dancing, show ways of playing in the shadows while extending a transfeminist praxis to re-envision travesti representation. Camila José Donoso's *Casa Roshell* (2017) offers a powerful transfeminist example that vividly captures, technically and thematically, the performative maneuvers through which travesti women in Mexico City move through fields of hypervisibility, and invisibility, insisting on the *shades* of travesti pleasure as ways of looking and participating in queer nightlife. In the next chapter, I engage Donoso's filming of Casa Club Roshell to locate travesti practices of queer relajo that recalibrate a field of necropolitical vision through cabaret. A transfeminist visuality therefore repositions playful ways of feeling and sensing at a travesti club to show how travesti women modulate across the dangers of nightlife.

SIX

The Kaleidoscope of Travesti Nightlife in Casa Roshell

A rain of sparkles falls against a dark background. The resplendence of a rhinestone-studded red dress invites us into the walls of a night cabaret where blue laser beams light a projection screen. You can hear the rubbing of clothes in the background, as a blond cabaret hostess sways her shoulders like a seductive dancer. A screen seen from afar plays images of trans sensuality, showing the semi-nakedness of a trans girl. Her face appears blissful, while her presence on screen soothes the ambiance of a dark room patched with colorful speckles of light. The glimmering effects of blue lights give more than just texture to a dark background. They fill the room with what I see as lightful manifestations of hope moving across the room. A type of hope that is vital to trans and travesti survival.

The shiny rays of disco lights reach out to light the surface of an empty table. Their reflection adds to the quietness sensed before a show starts. A luscious red velvet curtain hangs behind the main stage, which is adorned with strings of sequins. The stage stands in the back of the room, with a raised plateau, a projector, and a powerful sound system. Showing the many rooms of Casa Roshell, the camera guides us through its walls and corridors, making us attend to a hefty closed-circuit TV security system guarding the main entrance door. After checking in, clubgoers are lovingly greeted and welcomed into a night venue known for its well-stocked bar, endless partying, and glittery stage. Casa Roshell opens its doors to clients filled with a yearning anticipation; a handful of travesti women rush inside to find intimacy, gestures of care, instances of communion and longing, as well as a chance for becoming. Such is the promise of Casa Roshell.

Camila José Donoso's docufictional film *Casa Roshell* (2017) re-envisions nightlife practices of travesti women in a working-class nightclub and cabaret. Functioning as an important record of trans-travesti her-story, the film casts established personalities of trans activism in Mexico, including performance artivist Lia García, Liliana Alba, and Roshell Ter-ranova, the two latter co-owners and co-founders of this venue exclusive for transformismo and travestismo. The film also takes us through a night journey of travesti worldmaking, moving across different club spaces such as the dressing room, the bar, the stage, the dance floor, or the darkroom, to engage viewers in the nightlife strategies these women deploy through playful movement and contact, as well as to recognize the importance of this urban oasis for trans intimacy in the face of violence. Within its radi-ant halls, couples find their way through gender together; lovers meet for passing touches; folk explore their sexuality freely; sex workers look for a haven in the middle of the night.

In interacting with this movie, I delve in a method of queer relajo, to trace the modulations travesti women embody to escape shadowy frames of misrepresentation, and instead bask in the affective intensities, body choreographies, and material distributions shaping travesti nightlife in Mexico City. As discussed in the previous chapter, the overexposure of travesti life on mainstream media goes hand in hand with an intensifica-tion of violence affecting travesti women, marking a trans necropolitics occurring off camera (Gill-Peterson 2018; Snorton and Haritaworn 2013). This translates into alarmingly high rates at which travesti women get killed in Mexico, as the second most dangerous country for trans people in the Americas. In the face of their necropolitical conversion, travesti women borrow from tones of lighting and darkness, to concoct a practice of queer relajo based on modulating their bodies, desires, and actions inside the club. Attending to their queer moves across frames of vision, I embrace a queer kaleidoscopic lens to track travesti women's tonal agency of modu-lation. That is, I attend to how they negotiate with frames of hypervisibil-ity, and invisibility, a visual interplay I refer to as shades and shadows of travesti nightlife, by modulating queer relajo on- and off-screen.

Mexico City's Casa Roshell serves as a refuge where queer flights of care, joy, and play, or relajo, converge within a building located in a predominantly working-class neighborhood near the city's southside. Located blocks away from the Viaducto station on the subway blueline, Casa Roshell glistens as an oasis for travesti women, including some sex workers along Calzada de Tlalpán. Calzada de Tlalpán is visibly recogniz-able for its 24-station subway blueline, a vital infrastructure facilitating movement in and out of the megapolis. Known as a corridor for sex work, this major thoroughfare is host to many travesti, trans, and cis-gender women looking for trade every night. In fact, I argue that although Casa Roshell does not market itself as a site for sex trade, its shifting walls not only offer limitless possibilities for travesti sex and intimacy, but also serves as a night stage for cabaret performance.

For over twenty years, this nightclub has built a community hub for travestismo beyond its functions as a performance stage in Mexico City, offering a wide range of cultural activities and healthcare resources, ranging from preventative health workshops, grassroot fundraisers and cultural talks, to drag and travesti performance club nights. Because of its proximity to Calzada de Tlalpán, Casa Roshell sits on a predominantly working-class neighborhood, occupying a liminal space within queer neoliberal economies located in Zona Rosa, Centro Histórico, Colonia Condesa, or Polanco. Casa Roshell brings together a constellation of travesti interactions in a working-class sector of Mexico City, forging a queer nightscape, that is, a provisional affective infrastructure that emerges in the presence of travesti play and queer nightlife. In this sense, the night lights up an affective tectonic, a fluctuating ambiance, that invites us to entangle the interlayering networks that sustain travesti intimacy and belonging in Mexico City.[1]

I look at the practices of performance taking place in a Mexico City's travesti cabaret/nightclub, to further consider how Casa Roshell's orchestrated collective grapples with the powerful forces of dance and movement, to embody playful tactics of survival that help undo and cope with the trans necropolitical dimension of urban nightlife. Namely, Donoso's docufiction tracks sounds, whispers, lights, conversations, and changes of nightly interactions, mimicking a galactic feeling, an outer worldliness reflected onto a bar table as if it was floating in the universe, that turns away from the spectacular violence of travesti representation and toward the constellations and stardust of travesti dreams and longings. Casa Roshell thus erupts from "overkill, the calculated practice of gratuitous force [. . .] the proper expression to the riddle of trans/queer *nothingness*" (Stanley 2021, 34), embedded in a chain of commodification under neoliberal economies. Because the film is made by travesti women and for travesti women, it thus resists the necropolitical conversion of trans life. Through its close angles, focus on shades and lights, intimate dialogue, and scenes of playful cabaret, the film not only reenacts a travesti way of looking, but also centers ways of feeling and sensing nightlife. Casa Roshell enchants viewers, as well as club goers, for its unique affective appeal, crafting a magical site, a queer nightscape of sorts, in which travesti pleasure is possible. The affective interrelations of queer nightscapes flee the eye of hetero-cis rationality while shaping a shared space for travesti night-making through my queer rewriting of the film.

Amid rampant neoliberal redesigns of death, joy and pleasure also emerge as vital tactics of resistance at the very core of travesti becoming. A critical consideration of queer joy and pleasure as political affect of resistance also prompts an examination of how the deployment of the "human" serves to block off those considered less than human, or unhuman, from being able to feel joy, to scream out laughter, and bask in pleasure. At the same time, the interplays of travesti joy and queer relajo forgo monolithic and stable understandings of what and who holds value in feeling pleasurable and joyful through the interlocking assemblages of gender, class, ethnicity, race, sexuality, and belonging. More than uniform experiences, travesti joy and queer relajo emerge as attunements, moods, or modulations, as Eve Sedgwick describes it; affective tectonics that provide playful affordances under social marginalization. These playful assemblages not only give texture to travesti nightlife but also to a sort of queer nightscape of intimacy. If short-lived, these nightscapes assembled by nocturnal encounters between bodies and objects weave an affective network where queer humor, seduction, and laughter converge in cabaret, activating underground circuits of trans care. The friction between the bodily, the spatial, and the material sparks a nightly kaleidoscope, an affective mix that reorients our way of feeling in the dark.

In what follows, I'd like to delve into the affective tectonics of the nightscapes that make possible travesti nightlife through forms of queer relajo and feel how the ground shakes and moves when such interrelations spark a radical pedagogy of care through cabaret performance, especially when those waves give us instructions to extend a spirit of queer play beyond nighttime.

Playful Transfeminism

As a praxis of transfeminism, queer relajo, or queer playfulness, brings out ways to navigate the contested politics of violence in Mexico City. As extensions of a transfeminist playfulness of queer relajo, satire, humor, and laughter help resist and circumvent collectively the paralyzing effects of violence, while fostering intimacy at night. Queer playfulness embodies a way of sensing the world, and through that kaleidoscope, travesti space encompasses more than just the physical and material structures of the cabaret, like its walls, floors, ceilings, dark rooms, or dance stages. Rather, it is produced by multiple flows of affect that recontour the boundaries separating buildings, embodiments, and sensations. Travesti intimacy, that is, the coming together of travesti women at the club, build a queer nightscape, a kind of infrastructure for nightly contact, that only refashions the utilitarian uses of specific spaces, such as an urban house, but also recalibrates the very understanding of what spaces can allow us to do.

As spatial formations, queer nightscapes lay out an infrastructure not only sustained by concrete building walls, but also by affective interactions unfathomable to the rational eye. Travesti formations activate a specific mode of sensing space, moving across the shines, shades, and shadows of the night, expressly a queer nightscape blending the structural, material, and affective. The moving kaleidoscope of travesti nightlife creates an ambiance, a way of reorientating bodily practices that help sustain the very edifices of joy. My understanding of travesti nightlife should not be equated as an attempt to restrain travesti becoming in the dark, that is, a lack of agency, or to hold travesti becoming as ornaments to the cabaret stage. Rather, trans and travesti practices rehearse a politics of presence, of staying alive despite multiple threats of violence and of having fun against all odds.

Repositioning queer and trans night practices of queer relajo, such as travesti cabaret performance, as sites that produce transfeminist knowledge challenges conventional territories of feminist epistemology and space often demarcated by white institutions and centers of power. As shown in *Casa Roshell*, travesti nightlife is not only a queer matter of performance, but also of queer and trans knowledge production. Nightlife practices of queer relajo, like cabaret, dance, and performance, foreground alternative modes of knowing and sensing the world through queer playfulness and joy, veering away from practices of extraction—be it academic, epistemic, economic, or social. A kaleidoscope of travesti nightlife reattunes our senses to be able to perceive queer playfulness and joy from popular and working-class locations, while eschewing any gaze that typically commodifies and extracts travesti life and value.

Casa Roshell moreover proposes a transfeminist praxis rooted in gestures of queer relajo, expanding the conventional definitions of where activism can happen and where political organizing can take place. Nightlife is a political territory where trans and travesti women find intimacy, care, and communion, and where cishet normativity is contested. Night-life shapes economies of trans care. Considering the rich dimensions of travesti nightlife practice, I ponder: how does a transfeminist praxis of queer relajo shape travesti becoming? How do travesti women apply that praxis to shape, modulate, and build the spaces they inhabit? How does a feminist ethics of care resist neoliberal, capitalist, and sexual extraction? And equally important, what worlds can we imagine and concoct if guided by such praxis and care of queer relajo?

Catching their breath, Pina and her partner Euge stand in front of the dressing room mirror. Surrounded by closets, feather boas, makeup, and brushes, Pau, an older travesti woman, listens to Pina exclaim that they almost missed the workshop that night. A dim-lighted room makes Pau show their bruises and burns, as they all start talking about their marks on their bodies. A mark on Pau's thigh, or a clear nail for Euge. Looking to soothe Pina's anxiety, Pau states calmly that the worst is gone and that they have finally arrived, adding that travesti cabaret is a form of therapy, a place where all the worked-up stress and anxiety of the week, vanishes away with the smoke curtains at the dance floor. Echoes of city traffic sound in the background, as Pina asks Euge for help putting on her dress. Facing the mirror, they fondle with makeup and clothes, as wrinkles of fabric rub against their waist. For travesti women, being present at night constitutes a form of life and survival against the daily vicissitudes of urban life. As Pina gets her wig and dress on with the help of her partner, they also banter and joke around with other girls at the club.

Pau, a club regular, unbuckles their belt and removes their business attire. Their back appears naked in the mirror, revealing the lines left from wearing a bra. The stitching and seams of undergarments leave visible impressions on Pau's skin. Skin impressions expose a repetitive synchrony between bodies, materials, and garments, as well as a sensorial entanglement. Accordingly, travesti becoming answers to a choreography of coming undone.

The camera follows the careful moves of Pau and Pina: their chiseling of eyebrows, their contouring of lips, or their putting on body padding. Trying on a new dress, or a new eye shadow, reveals a playful disposition to altering their body shape. As series of playful moves, cross-dressing, as intrinsic to travesti becoming, outlines playful modes of relating to the world through the senses. Under the disruptive lens of queer relajo, cross-dressing reattunes the perception of the world to feel it less as a defined space than a site composed of differing materials. Pau notes that coming

into Casa Roshell and becoming travesti is therapeutic, "es que es la tera-
pia" ("It is therapy").

The sounds of wrinkly plastic bags, of shoes clacking, contrast with
the unperceivable whispering of wigs and feather boas under a yellow
light. The camera moves to a different post in the dressing room to portray other club regulars shaving and applying makeup. The playful matters
of travestimo invoke a sensorial mode of interacting with the world. By
recording the frictions of things, or the close intimation between flesh,
fibers, textiles, and compounds, the film taps into what Jeanne Vaccaro
calls "*trans*-corporeography." Expanding and drawing from Vicky Kir-
by's proposition, transcorporeography envisions "the body in composition with itself, engaged in an autonomous process and choreographic
labor, and foreground transformation or transformative processes that
are not the result of intervention." For Vaccaro, trans embodiment, and
I would also add travesti embodiment, emerge as playful formations that
move, expand, exceed, and travel in relation to other textures, mapping
"the material fabric of the body, its surfaces, inscriptions, energies, and
flows." In a provoking proposition, Vaccaro questions, "Can we think sur-
gical and hormonal transition without succumbing to the additive logics, and instead characterize the lengthening, thinning, and deepening of
body parts, skin, hair, and voice as a labor of *distribution*?" (2010, 255).
The dressing room thus makes tangible the differing distributions of a
choreography shaping travesti embodiments. In the dressing room, the
film picks up the sounds of friction, of garments and body girdles rubbing against the skin, of padding being pulled up, of makeup creamed
onto a face; the blush brush sweeping through, leaving dust particles of a
crimson rouge, folding, and unfolding into multiple textures and densities. Compellingly, the film engages gestures of queer relajo to make us
sense the affective distributions of travesti nightlife.

After getting ready and waiting to get their drinks, Roshell, Pina, and
Euge begin to talk about the downfalls and pleasures of dressing up. Pina
starts the conversation by saying how hot it feels to wear a dress and put
on makeup, "Entre que te vistes y te maquillas, no sabes el calorón que
me da. Pero es un premio para mí de todo el esfuerzo de la semana donde
dejas de ser hombre para convertirte en Pina, al menos aquí." (By the
time I get dressed and made up, I'm so hot. But this is my reward, after
working hard all week, when I stop being a man and I become Pina, at
least in here.) Travesti becoming comes in as a prize for Pina after years
of relationship troubles with Euge, who notes, "Nos costó mucho trabajo,

mucho. Si hubiera existido el internet hace veinte años que me enteré, otra cosa hubiera sido. Pero sí, nos costó mucho, nos costó lágrimas, que nos separáramos dos veces" (It took us a lot of work, a lot. If the internet had existed 20 years ago, when I found out, things would have been different. But it wasn't easy, we shed lots of tears and we split up twice.) In a distinctly joking fashion, Roshell adds to their storytelling, "Pero lo mejor, lo mejor es que ahora tienes un marido y una amiga también." (But now you have a husband who is also your girlfriend!)

Pina's experience presents a rich story of travesti becoming, as each partner reveals their difficulties, pleasures, and negotiations establishing a form of intimacy often stigmatized and marginalized, even if there is a previous understanding between them. These forms of intimacy sustain the vitality of queer and travesti nightscapes at Casa Roshell, expressly the various exchanges and negotiations necessary for a travesti relationship to emerge and come alive require a careful and active involvement of a night collective and sensorial assemblage, or trans-corporeography. Roshell's words of encouragement and affirmation mirror a tender, loving care whirling within the dark spatiality of the cabaret. These difficult exchanges of affect not only shape understandings of space as a site of travesti intimacy, but also serve as the charging forces building a nightlife ambiance.

Beyond feeling hot, both as a marker of sexiness and body temperature, Pina finds respite in dress, heels, and makeup. Each encounter with the material world, be in the shape of a wig, a lipstick, or a stiletto heel, forge a deep connection transmitted emotionally as an expression of longing. The gravitational force of longing, in the case of Pina, interweaves the affective experiences of loss and peril, such as those explained by Euge, Pina's partner, about the difficulty in understanding that Pina was a travesti woman, or by Pina's search of a safe place where she can let go of hegemonic masculinity.

The camera thus tracks the making of material intimacies. Sparking up travesti nightscapes requires an engagement with an affective sensorium that challenges gender stability. The transformative power of queer and trans nightscapes flirts with a capacity to reattune our senses in becoming aware of differing textures and surfaces rubbing against locales, bars, and clubs. Nightscapes bring up different modalities of sensing space that move away from the apprehension and containment of identities. What the film brings into focus is precisely how sensorial modes, affective economies, and space-making practices become entangled through travestismo. Rather than positing gender as a static destination, travesti becoming rests on the indeterminant fluctuation of material and carnal folds, challenging established categories of sex and gender. In doing so, travesti becoming folds in the curls of queer relajo to embody a set of moves and modulations to feel nightlife.

In a scene, Roshell Terranova indeed flirts with a seemingly married club goer seeking to flee the convention of cishet intimacy, while Liliana Alba, Terranova's business and romantic partner, lights up a smoke at the bar space. Although important to psychoanalytic critique, the mirror exposes a system of meaning mediated by embodied practice, as well as a relation to the world, that is, the mirror only reflects what has been culturally, medically, and legally constructed as a technical convention. Back in the change room, the mirrors lined up against the wall directly challenge the outside viewer by exposing the un/folding of gender as clubgoers dress up, banter, and put on makeup. In doing so, trans and travesti reflections not only disrupt a rational gendering of things, but also confront a host of bad feelings, like shame, that emerge when a mirrored reflection precisely burst the illusion of gender conventions. The film thus spends considerable amount of time tracing the bodily, material, and affective encounters within Casa Roshell by playfully framing the mirror less as a gender technology that casts travesti women into shadows, than as a reflective material for gender un/making and transformation.

As a move of queer relajo, the looking into multiple mirrors diffracts stable meanings of gender. In this sense, the broken reflection of mirrors playfully pieces together a kaleidoscopic field of sensing that multiplies, unfolds, and expands travesti embodiments and imaginaries. By expanding a limited line of vision, the film moves through different scenes that attest to the richness of travesti intimacy, while enacting a way of feeling through a kaleidoscopic interplay of reflections, textures, and embodiments. Kaleidoscopic feeling as performed in the film posits that gender is not only a mutable reflection, but also a fantasy, a tantalizing suggestion into queer play, flirtation, and joy.

When the reflection of Liliana's face is seen through a mirrored wall in the bar, the camera not only fractures a male cis gaze that typically capitalizes on the sexual commodification of travesti women, but also multiplies the ways of seeing travesti nightlife. The multiplicity of framed angles in one camera shot unbinds a conventional way of looking. As her face is multiplied across the mirrors on screen, the camera performs a series of movements following the different acts of queer playfulness taking place inside Casa Roshell, like people phone calling, cis men cruising, travesti women talking, etc. The camera enacts a kaleidoscopic mode of feeling by swiftly changing the frame of filmed actions, mimicking the gestures that can take place at night to build a fleeting sense of intimacy.

Practices of travestismo thus engage a transfeminist sensorial praxis rooted in queer playfulness to critically reflect on the constructable infrastructures of space and gender. As seen through club goers' fiddling with materials, travesti becoming also manifests the intricate dynamics, flows, and modulations of nightscapes, or rather, the interactions with a sense of joy bringing about nightlife.

Beams of blue light flash against a red wall. Music beats blend in with the laughter of four women seated around a cabaret table. While leaning in closer, Lia García shuts her eyes and lets Pau gently pad her cheeks with makeup. The whistling notes of cumbia sieve into a voice message Lia sends to her lover. Wondering who she might be texting, Pau shows excitement. A bright screen lights up Lia's glittery nails. As the camera zooms into her mermaid picture, the music pounding behind her makes her move like a mermaid through the waves of sound.

The story of Pina connects affectively with Lia García's. Through such interconnection, a travesti nightscape is shaped. The whispers of words, the swiftness of gazes, or the sensuality of walking along with the longing sensation of putting on a dress, or the long waiting for a distant lover become figments of the night's social fabric. Contact takes place within the cabaret's dark infrastructures, but each story participates in the assemblage of a circuit of trans care. Through Lia's story, such affective economy of care is further unveiled. At first, Lia gets to Casa Roshell, hoping to meet her date. As she patiently awaits, she talks to other clubgoers about it and shows them a picture of herself, dressed in a mermaid suit lying by the beach. But the night turns sour when realizing her lover has stood her up. Suddenly the moment of anticipation quickly fades into a dark scene of the bar. The film does not show again Lia's mermaid picture, but it is such a picture that links her to a memory of a distant lover. As Lia walks and dances, other women approach her to share their difficulty with love and heartbreak. Despite the feelings of disappointment brought on by a no-show-up date, Lia holds on to a digital image, as it weaves a memory of romantic possibility. Later in the night, Lia turns to a young, handsome guy for chatting, but it is the afterglow of her mermaid picture that impels her to keep on searching for a romantic pursuit.

Feltness, a quality in feeling texture, dimension, and distribution, further examined in Vaccaro's work, also shapes a nightscape's interplay between embodiment, and spatial configuration. At Casa Roshell, feltness is expressed through music, as a soundwave texturing space. As an infrastructure of feeling, the film's soundtrack reproduces nighttime intimacy through popular music. The interplays of popular music help reconstruct space, remixing the physical structures that sustain travesti intimacy across the night cabaret, while genres like boleros, cumbia, or salsa, index a distinct working-class soundscape. Playing out feelings of love, loss, nostalgia, and forbidden desire, these songs are not particular to nightlife but can be heard sounding through subway terminals, taco stands, bars, restaurants, buses, street markets, or homes.

Blended into the film's scenes of bantering and dancing, Iztapalapa-based cumbia band Los Ángeles Azules's song "Entrega de amor" (1993) opens with an exhilarating mix of accordions, synthesizers, bass, trumpet, bongos, guacharaca, and timbals. The song is a chant to forbidden sexual experimentation, as it starts naming a "lugar prohibido," a forbidden place that hides lovemaking. "Entrega de amor" engages innuendo in its lyrics and title, while intermixing sexual fantasy and physical intimacy. The rhythmic musical bridges precisely accentuate the distance between imagined sex and bodily contact, as travesti women on screen play with the fantasies men at the nightclub have about them. Following Los Ángeles Azules's "Entrega de amor," Casa Roshell appears as a forbidden place for sexual experimentation, a place where playful looking is kaleidoscopic, or multidirectional, multidimensional, and multisensorial:

> Veo que te sueltas el pelo
> Mirándote al espejo, mirándote a los ojos
> Una mirada entregada, un tiempo
> Sin tiempo de un semblante hermoso
> Y me dices "He pensado mucho en ti"
> Te he soñado tanto aquí
> Que no imaginé
> Que iba a ser así la entrega de mi amor hacia ti

> (I see you let your hair down
> Looking in the mirror, looking into your eyes
> A devoted look, a time
> With no time for a beautiful face
> And you tell me "I've thought a lot about you"

I've dreamed of you here so much
that I did not imagine
That the delivery of my love to you was going to be like this)

The film's soundtrack does more than just connect popular musical soundscapes to sites of travesti nightlife. With each song, travesti relationality is also being reinscribed into the emotional accords of club goers and movie viewers. Songs extend an affective bridge, a necessary connection, that allows a form of identification between film characters and engaged viewers; but beyond acts of listening, the songs fold in people consuming the film into a queer nightscape, or an affective infrastructure of travesti intimacy. In other words, the film also brings music out of place, extending a night sensorium beyond the screen and into the everyday life of the attending audience. In doing so, the film impresses travesti affects into the tracks of Mexican popular music, adding music to the kaleidoscope that reaches out of the screen.

In another scene, Roshell and a male companion linger in the shadows of a corner, listening to Chivirico Dávila's "Arráncame la vida," an originally-tango-turned-bolero song about fleeting love playing in the distance. Roshell's flashy red sequin dress contrasts against a dark background spotted with specks of colorful light. Her male companion appears mesmerized by Roshell's luminosity and quickly falls for the radiantly blond hostess. Making sure her companion is at ease, Roshell asks whether he has felt comfortable during his visits to the cabaret. The spatial arrangement of their encounter positions them both at the same level, looking into each other's gaze. Roshell touches her companion, as the scene closes with a passionate kiss between them, followed by close shots of club regulars, while interweaving the musical feeling of "Arráncame la vida," through its enveloping melody and strident lyrics,

Arráncame la vida
Con el último beso de amor
Arráncala
Toma mi corazón
Arráncame la vida
Y si acaso te hiere el dolor
Ha de ser de no verme
Porque al fin tus ojos
Me los llevo yo

(Rip my life out
With the last kiss of love
Rip it off
Take my heart
Rip my life out
And if the pain still hurts
It must be from not seeing me
Because finally your eyes
I'll take them with me)

The music does more than create a soundscape; it mixes with images of pensive, cruising, or defiant travesti women, demanding engaged viewership, inviting us into their space to feel their ethics of care, as gestures of queer relajo, like flirting, kissing, or touching, unfold around us. Roshell looks right into the lens, raising up her shoulder, gesturing an invitation into the club's nightscapes. "Arráncame la vida" hums a visceral tune about the pain caused by fleeting love. According to the song's lyrics, one last kiss can take one's life away. The singer thus begs her lover to kiss her away. The song plays slow bolero rhythms that give homage to the cabaret music of Mexican fichera films, or sex comedies—B-movies with low budgets aiming to entertain mass audiences.

As curious males walk and cruise around the cabaret, travesti women reveal their vulnerabilities and difficulties in establishing long-term relationships. If hypervisibility contributes to the fetishization of travesti women, the film enacts a different way of looking that moves away from the commodification of travesti becoming seen on screen, and into an attunement to the sensorial registers of travesti life. The film flips the conventional frames of looking at travesti intimacy by emphasizing connectivity and relationality, by focusing on travesti women's ability to decide whether to engage with potential suitors. Additionally, travesti women can encounter each other in careful and caring ways. The resonances of travesti joy, play, and banter form circuits of care. The intimate conversations, not only between lovers, but between travesti women in their retelling of love, loss, and heartbreak, foster affective bonds of attachment.

Betty and Mariela, a pair of twins, convenes unknowingly at a bar table; they suddenly recognize each other as travesti women. The club can also function as a place for confession and reconnection. They had never expected to run into each other at the club, as Mariela shares their awe, "Sí sé quién eres. Déjame darte un abrazo. Sí sé quién eres. Qué gusto me da de haberte encontrado" (I know who you are, let me give you a hug. I'm so pleased to see you). By the tone and content of their conversation, it seems as if Betty and Mariela are not only twin siblings but had distanced each other due to family conflicts. After their unexpected encounter at the bar, Mariela asks Betty about her decision to embrace travesti life; the latter responds,

> Bueno, mira, unos años atrás, yo antes esto lo hacía en un hotel. ¿Cómo? Mira, me iba y me compraba ropa que me gustaba y en el hotel me travestía. Me cambiaba, me pintaba, me arreglaba bien. Había ocasiones en que salía a caminar, aunque fuera una cuadra, pero luego ya me empezaba a dar penar, me metía y así me la pasaba el transcurso de la noche. Pero al otro día ya era diferente porque agarraba la ropa y la desechaba porque pues pensaba que estaba mal, que yo estaba mal. Entonces, este, fue ya de más años que empecé a buscar un lugar, algún lugar como estos

> (A few years ago, I used to do this in a hotel. I used to buy clothes that I liked, and I would transform in the hotel. I got changed, put on make-up. Sometimes I'd go out for a walk, even if it was only around the block, but then I'd start to feel embarrassed and go back to the hotel and that's how I'd spend my nights. But the following day things were different. Then I'd take those clothes and throw them away because I thought it was wrong, that something was wrong with me. But then as I grew older, I started to look for a place, somewhere like this place).

After sharing how they found Casa Roshell, the twin sisters make a pact at Betty's request. They both agree on not telling anyone about each other's travesti life but make plans to keep on meeting at the bar. These instances of night intimacy foster affective attachments at the cabaret. A simple bar table is turned into a nightscape for confession and reunion.

The ambiance felt through the coming together of travesti women at Casa Roshell conjures up a magical fairyland, a trans dollhouse that hides in the deep darkness of the night. A trans magical house exists alongside the heteronormative dimensions of time and space, drilling out possibilities of queer and trans existence amid the flagrant violence directed at the bodies of difference. Conjuring magic and travesti becoming mark a stark departure from the rationalizing logics of (queer) neoliberalism. Sex, playfulness, and other loose queer affects of relajo across travesti nightlife

Fig. 18. Film poster of *Casa Roshell* (2017), dir. Camila José Donoso.

activate modes of caring through touch that overpass marketable profit. Undoubtedly, Casa Roshell finds its sustenance from the economies of nightlife, from selling and buying beverages, smokes, and charging a cover fee for the use of dark rooms, but these circuits of consumption and production, prime the affective economies of care over market driven laws of supply and demand.

Yet caring cannot be fully separated from other practices defining and haunting travesti nightlife, as women inside constantly push against heteropatriarchal dominance when, for instance, talking and educating "straight" men at the club. A travesti magical house opens its doors to those willing to step away from the unnerving violence of everyday life, from the cardiac rhythms of waged labor and exploitation, from an everyday weariness that eats away at the disrupting potentialities of queer relajo. A travesti magical house is a place for dancing, where the sounds of popular music acquire a new tone that weaves melodies, lyrics, and beats into the affective fabric of the night. The residual forces of such soundscapes spring back up as an uncontrollable humming, one that travels far and wide beyond the contours of the cabaret. Casa Roshell performs, if momentarily, the transformation of space through bodily choreographies and cabaret performances of modulation, lifting the cover of a queer nightscape that, in this case, flows through as an underground travesti sensorium.

Taken together, these material components of travesti becoming, in all their iterations, facilitates what Roshell Terranova calls a transfeminist praxis of modulation, a way of intimately fashioning nightlife space through practices of queer relajo, as in flirting, dancing, and laughing, while also exposing the cishet logics operating behind the making of space. Aware that space is not a neutral, unintentional, or universal abstraction, that it is not just a name serving as a placeholder to situate a material relationship between bodies and objects, Roshell teaches, drives, and activates practices of queer relajo that materialize into distinct bodily designs, affective infrastructures, and playful ideologies. Under this light, travesti cabaret reveals the un/making of femininity in relation to space, situating playful space-making practices of queer relajo that insist on dismantling a gender dichotomy that structures the world by rehearsing bodily gestures, poses, and images. Modulation as a transfeminist praxis of queer relajo opens embodied ways of feeling and sensing otherwise, that is, the proximities with different bodies, experienced through rubbing, touching, or caressing, awaken a bodily attunement to recognize the affective materiality that sustains nightlife. As a choreography emerging from travesti women's playful strategies of survival, modulation not only enacts ways of moving through space, but also questions the very assumptions guiding spatial constructions.

Travesti cabaret thus responds to space-making performances of queer relajo, playfully improvising choreographies with objects, bodies, and affect. Casa Roshell especially emerges as a dark infrastructure that facilitates easy passage in and out of nighttime spaces. What takes place within these walls also reveals how such a space is made, remade, and readapted to host varied forms of intimacy shaping a nightscape. As such, intimacy does not emerge either as an abstract concept but, through transfeminist modulation, tracks the material/affective/physical intermixing of travesti and queer worldmaking. In what's to come, I will trace three distinct modulations that draw on gestures of queer relajo at Casa Roshell, leading to a discussion on how modulating emerges from a Personality Workshop, how modulating occurs between the interplay between shade, darkness, and incompleteness off- and on-screen, as well as shapes hemispheric reimaginings of travesti activism and politics.

Modulating Femininity: Roshell Terranova's Personality Workshop

In *Casa Roshell*, the club's eponymous owner begins her Personality Workshop, a crash course on how to become a travesti woman, by outlining a choreography vested in modulation,

> Para formar nuestro cuerpo es bueno pensar en las letras. Al principio, nuestra figura, la de hombre es tipo T. Para parecer mujeres, hay que pensar que nuestra figura se parezca más a una X. Recuerden que tenemos la espalda amplia eso nos forma una T por eso para llegar a la X tenemos que acinturarnos. Hay que usar faldas en forma de A, eso nos va a dar la ilusión óptica de que tenemos cadera y nos va a reducir los hombros. Y si ya tienes el vestuario, tenemos que aprender a caminar. Tenemos que lazar las rodillas y nunca pisar el tacón, apoyarlo. Tenemos que caminar como si estuviéramos flotando, eso es, modular.

> (To shape our body, thinking of letters is helpful. At first, our male bodies are shaped like a T. To look like women, we need our bodies to become more like an X. Remember that we have broad shoulders, which gives us a T shape. So, to become more like an X, we need to highlight our waist. Wearing A-shaped skirts will help create an illusion of broader hips and narrower shoulders. Once we have the outfit, we need to learn how to walk. Lift your knees, and never lean on your heels. Just rest it and walk as if you were floating. That's modulating.)

Roshell then provides a series of instructions on how to walk, how to stride in high heels, how to adapt one's voice, and how to use garments and girdles to create an optical illusion of femininity, shifting from a T shape to a feminine X body form. Roshell's understanding establishes the body as a playful axis of movement, as her notion of "modulating" refers to a series of complex adaptations embodying gender performance. Centering on a playful repertoire of bodily modulation, Roshell explains the importance of wearing a wig proportionate to one's height, or of selecting a pair of comfortable heels. The careful attention to size, length, and girth points to how modulating highlights a deep knowledge about one's body, of identifying textures, and dimensions, that expand the body's capacities for queer play. It is through prolonging, shortening, or lengthening the proportions of the body that gender is technically assembled. Like Vaccaro's "labor of distribution," Roshell Terranova's concept of modulation reshapes travestismo not only as a practice of gender, but also as a playful movement of affect. Knowing how the body interacts with ornaments, materials, or garments, as well as how the body moves across space further highlights the role of queer relajo, or queer playfulness, in the un/making of travestismo.

Roshell's Personality Workshop fathoms travesti becoming as a choreography, a set of moves that signal sensorial reorientation to the world. While workshop attendees breathe in and out, Roshell notes, "del diafragma para arriba tenemos que estar elevadas, estiradas para adelgazar, para sacar la bubi, para estirar el cuello, pero de la parte de abajo, tenemos que flexionar porque somos felinas, panteras, cachondas" (We need to keep upright from the diaphragm up, standing straight to look thinner, to project our breasts, to stretch our necks. But down below, our knees must be flexed because we are feline, like panthers . . . we are sexy). The choreographies of travesti becoming breakdown the gestures and positions involved in the making of gender, joining in on the effort to un/learn gendered positions and destinations. Playfully learning how one's body moves across space is intrinsic to how gender operates in public, while highlighting the malleable materiality of bodies.

According to Roshell Terranova, playful movement is crucial to travestismo, as are the gigs, dresses, and heels, that compound a sense of femme, "Y tienen que traer también a quién me quiero parecer o cómo me quiero proyectar, ¿no? ¿Qué tipo de chica soy? Soy intelectual, soy ingenua, soy agresiva, soy sirenita o soy Marilyn Monroe" (You also need to bring the character that you want to convey, the image that you wish to project.

What kind of girl am I? Am I an intellectual, am I naïve, am I aggressive, am I a mermaid? Or am I Marilyn Monroe?) Through her choreographic directions, Roshell highlights the role of queer playfulness in establishing a connection between femininity and cabaret performance. When asking in particular, "what kind of girl I am?" the cabaret hostess blurs the distinction between being feminine and playing feminine, that is, in her way of understanding movement, femininity emerges less as an essentialist ontology than as a playful performance. A queer sense of relajo drills through bricked categories of gender, while workshop attendees learn the importance of bodily modulation. Indeed, Roshell's tone, cadence, and rhythm precisely reflect how travesti becoming is enacted as a playful disposition to disarray the feminine, as her question about what kind of girl one can imagine is less concerned with defining what femininity is than with what femininity can further produce, enact, and transform.

My critical reading of Roshell's Personality Workshop focuses on the degree in which participants can have fun as the hostess frames femininity as a situated performance of queer relajo, and as a choreographed assemblage that is contextual, contingent, affective, and convinced of its own viability in the face of violence against travesti women. Roshell Terranova's concept of modulating thus renders the body within a larger network of spatial interactions. As such, the body does not only respond to its own rhythms but comes in sync with spaces surrounding it. Spatially, the stage of cabaret claims and holds the line for specific transfemme embodiments. How to walk across the hall, or where to step in, are signals in a flow of playful movement. As a nightscape infrastructure, the cabaret becomes a field of action that rearranges itself in tandem with other bodies in motion. In this moving sense, Casa Roshell turns into a malleable space for travesti intimacy as if it were a folding affect interacting with travesti playful action. While attending the workshop, all travesti women on stage rehearse the hostess's instructions. They elegantly practice swaying across the catwalk. Roshell further insists on teasing out the femme within the sparkliness of dresses, on breathing while holding one's breasts up. Although Roshell's instructions on travesti embodiment might appear as a structured choreography, their teaching reveals the playful improvisation of gestures and movements guiding transfemininity. The Personality Workshop thus presents a queer way of playing with gender, as well as of unveiling the radical possibilities of travestismo.

As a modulation of queer relajo, travestismo unmakes femininity by exposing its performative logics, as well as its embodied textures. By focusing on improvising movements, Roshell highlights the political dimensions of queer playfulness, situating an embodied praxis of travestismo as a queer will to play. My goal is to bring a discussion on the dance of life and death into conversation with the workshop because that lethal dance is also very movement-based and transfeminine-specific. Roshell's workshop reimagines possibilities of travesti becoming by interacting with joy, activating a vital politics of survival through dance.

Roshell's workshop, and conceptualization of transfemininity, also responds to the acts of transphobia and police harassment in Calzada de Tlalpan, where Casa Roshell sits ready to disrupt the cishet spaces of urban life. Although no federal or state law explicitly regulates nor prohibits sex work in the country, some states have implemented policies to protect sex workers from falling into underground rings of sex trafficking and exploitation. Most recently, in 2019, Mexico City lawmakers voted in favor of decriminalizing sex work.[2] Despite the legal efforts at protecting and fighting for the recognition of trans rights and sex labor laws, including a 2008 law allowing change name requests on legal documents in Mexico City, discrimination, violence, and death continues to define trans and travesti vitality in a seemingly "gay-friendly" city.

The complex relationship between travesti life and sex work should nonetheless be considered intrinsic to trans intimacy and belonging given that the imminent danger of performing sex work poignantly defines such urban relations. Sex work, here, is fathomed as a mode of sustenance for those willing to engage with it, and not as an exclusive occupation caging travesti women's choices. Reframing sex work as a site for travesti intimacy would also mean to shift attention to critically understand the material conditions, spatial politics, and public infrastructures sustaining sex labor, as well as advocate for its decriminalization and protection. Thus, the violence impacting travesti sex work must be framed as a larger phenomenon of misogyny resulting in alarming rates of trans/feminicide, as well as a form of gender and sexual gentrification not only taking place in Mexico but also across the Americas.[3]

As an erotic rehearsal, the night poses a series of risks, especially for travesti intimacy and belonging. While the night can facilitate zones of contact, it also presents "a radical violence and unavoidable menace to all travesti sex workers. Indeed, part of becoming travesti [is] to learn the 'power to dance with death'" (Cornejo 2019, 464). This lethal dance not only marks travesti becoming, intimacy and survival, but also informs the embodied knowledge travesti women must generate to survive night after night, and beyond mere survival, find ways to flourish. Roshell gifts this knowledge to workshop participants, while also highlighting those sites that, alongside the dangers of the night, allow and facilitate the circulation of queer pleasure, joy, and play, as complex affective entanglements mediating travesti life. Discussing the violence and precarity affecting the intersectionality of travesti life sheds light upon a travesti "dance with death" that recognizes some of the embodied ways of confronting lethal violence through the tactical maneuvers of survival rooted in queer play, cabaret performance, and travesti modulation. In this case, these embodied and fleshed strategies expand on the disruption of queer relajo to sustain travesti worldmaking. As Joshua Chambers-Letson reminds us of the liberating praxis of queer and trans performance, dance, play, and party, "minoritarian subjects [. . .] keep each other alive [by] mobilizing performance to open up possibility for new worlds and new ways of being in the world together" (2018, 36). As a big travesti party, Casa Roshell extends lifelines of survival, but most importantly fosters intimate ways of political resistance through joy and pleasure.

Queer and trans nightlife venues like Casa Roshell, thus expose the spatial negotiations that occur to maintain sites for travesti and trans intimacy. Standing as a unique, if not stand-alone, night club for travesti intimacy in Mexico City, Casa Roshell began in 2004 as a beauty salon providing makeup classes and organizing events for travesti women. As its popularity grew, it moved into a house sitting on a busy street in one of Mexico City's working-class neighborhoods. Grappling with neoliberal practices of commodification, gentrification, and extraction, Casa Roshell relies on a set of popular economic practices, like charity fêtes, fundraisers, and night parties to maintain its operations. Their profits are placed back into the same nighttime economies of playful consumption Casa Roshell promotes, like cabaret shows, drag and travesti personality workshops, dark rooms, or bar drinking.

Casa Roshell offers an example of an affective infrastructure, a queer nightscape, that is, a local network of consumption affecting nightlife to shelter queer and trans intimacy. Under its roof, Casa Roshell's Personality Workshop reclaims the power of the erotic to rework the operating logics of a gender binary. By insisting on femininity and womanness as contingent assemblages, Casa Roshell's Personality Workshop opens the floor to reconsider how gender and sexuality are made in relation to space. Accordingly, travesti becoming only makes sense in the company of others who are willing to play with queer forms of satire, humor, and laughter. Casa Roshell, ultimately, reshapes the limits of a transfeminist praxis taking place at night, while challenging the violence of the cishet, white-mestizo gaze of sexual imagination through acts of queer relajo.

Modulating Darkness: Shades and Shadows of Intimacy, Longing, and Worldmaking

Behind a hefty security system and vault-like entrance door, the Casa Roshell of both real life and docufiction cracks up the normative straight passages of urban architecture by twirling a night paradise where travesti women and their fans and suitors can interact, touch, flirt, kiss, banter, and dance intimately and safely. A kitchen is reshaped into a bar, while the living room turns into a cabaret stage. Bedrooms host the shadows of fleeting lovers, while the moans of travesti pleasure blend into the soundwaves of cumbia to make the walls of heteronormative architectures tremble. In one scene, two men, a lawyer, and a physician, strike a conversation while having a drink. Their gaze never intersects with each other, as they attentively watch travesti ladies dancing. While one discloses his bisexuality, the second man reveals his heterosexuality, surprising the former. Their conversation brings to the front the contradiction of sexual and gender identity, as the heterosexual man insists that there is compatibility between what he is looking for and the women he sees at the cabaret, stating "Bueno yo aquí lo que veo son mujeres . . . Fuera no lo son, pero estamos dentro y yo lo que veo son damas" (What I see here are women . . . Maybe outside they're not but what I see in here are ladies). While waiting for a potential suitor, travesti women, from different walks of life, gather around a light-sparkled bar table. Intimacy abounds as the gurls talk to each other, sharing their stories of heartbreak and unrequited love. In one conversation, Lia García patiently realizes that her date is not coming. Other travesti and trans women gather around her and begin sharing their complications in establishing relationships. The slow tempo of boleros and romantic ballads frames the interaction between travesti women and male club goers, setting the tone for queer flirting, bantering, and innuendo.

These darkened scenes, and others like them, depict the inside spaces of the cabaret not only as safe for travesti intimacy, but also inaugurate embodied and affective modes of sensing and feeling otherwise. Flirting, for instance, is crafted into a "multisensorial engagement," through which the voyeuristic male gaze is snapped off by being unable to track the multiple orientations bodies take to "come together in the dark" (Gamboa 2021, 92–93). More than centering on the visual registers of flirting, the camera lens approaches scenes of intimacy as if touching and playing with the lovers. The dominant frame of looking cracks into multiple reflections and sensations, a technical move that gestures toward travesti visual empowerment, as well as a tactic mediating travesti visibility. The film thus centers on the sensorial strategies that travesti people embody and enact as ways of consenting, engaging, and welcoming sexual advances.

Conversely, we hear from the cabaret goers that "outside" is notably unsafe. The combination of popular music, dark spaces, and the interplay between light and shadow, orchestrate a choreography of travesti vitality, fending off a dance with death. On a different sequence, a couple begins flirting. The male companion shares why Casa Roshell is a place for joy, while she explains that men usually disrespect them outside this cabaret, "¿Sabes? Aquí los hombres cuando están allá afuera son bien culeros con nosotras. Y cuando están aquí en la oscuridad, quieren que les demos" (You know something? Outside the club men treat us like dirt. But in here, in the dark, they want us to fuck them).

Darkness: It plays with shades and shadows, coding travesti intimacy as unreadable, and protecting travesti intimacy from the outside. The dimming of enlightened rationality blocks the visual apprehension of travestismo and transness, as the conventional basis for understanding the world and for producing knowledge about the world, ceases to exist. Amid this indetermination, travesti women interact with incompleteness and darkness counteracting the lethal consequences they face every night.

The film portrays the beautiful darkness of travesti nightscapes, as it shows the stretching and fetching of affects and their impact on the transformation of heteronormative spaces, challenging cishet economies of sexual capital. The various scenes of cruising and flirting expose playful modes of intimacy between travesti women and men in the cabaret. Travesti women take control over who gets to play and ask for sexual favors. In one instance, a travesti woman turns down the offer of going back into a dark room, stating that she prefers chatting over having sex. Like the men cruising the subway for sex in chapter 3, seemingly "straight" men cruising the cabaret exposes the value of looking for a sort of femininity in the dark. Rather than giving into the forces of straight capture, travesti women in the film rehearse affective choreographies of queer playfulness, as bantering, cruising, and flirting halt the fetishization, sexualization, and commodification of travesti vitality.

In the dark, other modes of sensing the world emerge like touching, playing, and feeling. Travesti nightscapes reshape darkness into a site of knowledge, the modulations taking place within the cabaret providing practical instructions on how to playfully move and navigate through unknown space. Another conversation between men at the cabaret reveals that darkness offers ample opportunities to queerly play with gender and sexual expression. Away from the intrusive light of social expectations, religious beliefs, or toxic masculinity, the darkness of queer nightscapes not only enacts ways of relating otherwise, but even if momentarily, participates in travesti worldmaking. Inside the cabaret, the trans-corporeography of queer relajo marks the distribution of feeling, gesture, and bodies across space, reshaping the contours of the night through the travesti body. Easily misperceived as a straight family house from the outside, Casa Roshell emerges as a dark site for trans kin and care.

Although full of political potential, darkness is not a queer utopia where everything is possible. In fact, a recurrent topic in nighttime gurl talk is the impossibility of finding everlasting love, as many of them express their feelings of rejection. They share their frustrations about how men defined them with the label of "incomplete," referring to travesti women's "lacking" body parts, voice tones, or other feminine traits. Not perceived as being enough, or rather as not embodying an enough-ness of femininity, points to the sociocultural contradictions and expectations shaping travesti intimacy. From their interactions with cis men, darkness seems to define travesti intimacy, particularly as these men play and hide around the "completeness" of heterosexual desire. Tellingly, travesti darkness describes a form of transfeminist fugitivity in that the elusive completeness of femininity is never attainable, but that ways of fleeing the technologies of gender are possible and materially attainable through practices of queer relajo. When exposing the double-faced attitude of flirty men cruising the cabaret, travesti women describe them as, "bien culeros," which literally translates into English as "they are assholes." Her description is quite literal as "straight" men cruising also enjoy being anally penetrated when having sex with travesti women in the dark.

In other words, a sense of being incomplete might mark travesti formations, but it is within such incompleteness that lies a radical transfeminist praxis of queer relajo against the teleologies of (neoliberal) progress shaping gender and sexuality paradigms in a transnational, postcolonial context. That same sense of incompleteness, of being shady, backward and lacking, for instance, has also characterized the geopolitics of knowledge in postcolonial regions across the Americas, including Mexico. Although at two different scales, a sense of incompleteness can also describe the place travesti formations occupy within white gender and sexual epistemologies. Even if some strands of trans and queer studies can articulate a critique against the neo/colonial routes traced by US interventionism, as well as recognize the geopolitical implications of US-centric traveling theory, gender and sexuality studies in the global north have largely failed to recognize queer, travesti, and trans formations in Mexico as generative and agential sources of knowledge in their own terms.

A being and feeling incomplete thus marks a political position that not only rehearses a refusal to be apprehended and contained by imperial technologies of capture and translation, but also that highlights a way of resisting otherwise beyond poles of inclusion/exclusion. A dark incompleteness echoes what one of the travesti women in the film notes as being intimate in the shadows, that is, of playing with sexual positions and gender markers. Darkness and incompleteness are categories that define travesti becoming, as they tease out an in-between of a gender binary, manifesting a spectrum of shades and shadows, or of differing tones of lived practices of resistance that playfully modulate between planes of hypervisibility, and invisibility defining travesti intimacy. Whereas shade refers to comparative tones of travesti exposure, situating a slight degree of difference between visibility and hypervisibility, shadow marks the partial or complete erasure produced by the necropolitical extraction of travesti life across sociocultural spheres. As playfully queer tactics, shade and shadow do not name polarities of queer contestation, but rather consider a travesti praxis of queer relajo fraught with complications, contradictions, betrayals, and hopes, blending in together like layers of makeup. Across these shades and shadows, a dark incompleteness thus points to a politics of survival, of what remains even after everything we come to know, learn, see, and love is decimated by forces of dispossession and indenture in the 21st century.

The film, and Casa Roshell in its reality, thus exposes the difficulties travesti women are forced to navigate, as men at the cabaret approach them. Often mischaracterized as deceitful, untruthful, or unauthentic, travesti women mediate between the shades and shadows of incompleteness and darkness to improvise a choreography of survival. Both states of being, incompleteness and darkness, as embodied and experienced by travesti women in the film, propose a poignant transfeminist praxis, one that seeks to undo a trans necropolitics by turning to a celebration of travesti life. To embody a sense of incompleteness requires a political position situated in the queer disposition of letting loose, that is, of letting go of the idea that gender and sexuality are fully constituted by discourse or practice. A dark incompleteness basks in the fragments, tidbits, and residues that carry with them a shiny energy for transformation, as it also tracks the multiple trajectories of violence that have rendered something or someone incomplete like those instances found across the chapters in Part I. In a similar way, a sense of being incomplete resonates with the practices of queer playfulness. Expressly, queer relajo marks a disposition of not taking things at face value, and of veering away from extractive accumulation of gender and sexuality. To remain incomplete also names a festive disposition of queer refusal, of not conforming to a wholeness awarded to those who remain static within gender and sexual technologies of capture.

Their comments about the cabaret's darkness, and what it allows, disallows, and produces in-between those binaries, leads me to expand on a modulatory concept that Casa Roshell makes possible: shade. Emerging as a space that facilitates queer and trans contact, shade names a quality of nightscapes but also extends a way of protecting travesti becoming from being commodified by the cis gaze. Shades extend their protection amid the vulnerabilities of becoming too visible, too clearly defined as to be further apprehended, seized, and commodified. Travesti shades act as a blinding force of refusal; the queer refusal to conform and be legible. The layering of materials, affects, and bodies reshape the very infrastructures of space, as walls, dark rooms, stages, and bar tables attune our senses to feel the night through travesti relationality. Casa Roshell forms a gravitational force, an immanent aura, surrounding its physical structures. Amid the dangers of the night, the emergence of queer nightscapes, such as Casa Roshell's shade and shadow, also stretch out their contours to extend forms of trans care and expand queer sociality beyond nightlife.

Shade also draws from a long history in Mexican popular visual culture, where the cabaret is recognized as a space where the bourgeois moral values are flippantly suspended, and unbridled fantasies, sexual or otherwise, untethered to cishet white-mestizo sexuality become real—even if only for a night. The cabaret thus makes possible practices of queer relajo that foster a different type of intimacy otherwise forbidden morally, or physically punished by the conventions of heterosexuality. It overshadows forms of heterosexual intimacy, while casting a shade that protects non-conventional practices of intimacy and belonging.

The liminal space of shade also points to a spatially embodied trans-feminist praxis situated in travesti women's tactical moves between hyper-visibility and invisibility. Against the current backdrop defining trans and travesti death and their strategies of hypervisibility and invisibility, or the obstruction of certain forms of trans and travesti life vis-à-vis the ahistori-cal and apolitical celebration of trans and travesti representation, shade and shadow name the dangerous interplay between travesti hypervisibility and invisibility. The camera lens fluctuates between these modes of feel-ing the visual, but beyond mere watching, the film also tracks the dis-tinct sounds, textures, and other sensorial forms shaping nightly contact. Although the camera lens physically focuses on something or someone, shades also populate the screen, melting in a darkness in which bodies and characters are difficult to apprehend. For instance, the scenes of travesti women flirting, a practice preceding a couple going into the darkroom, are visually framed within a shady shine. Characters on screen acquire various degrees of visibility depending on their proximity to a disco light, or a pitch-dark background, for instance. The film thus tests our ability to see, teasing out other ways of sensing that do not solely rely on the visual consumption of travesti women on screen.

In outlining different bodily techniques of modulation, Roshell Ter-ranova also orchestrates a praxis of trans care within shady spaces. Modu-lating points to a set of body maneuvers to feel space through queer relajo; it demands a critical attunement to how space facilitates travesti becom-ing, extending a flirtatious invitation to reconceptualize space. The cam-era locates an interplay between shade—travesti visibility—and shadow—travesti invisibility—to track a queer nightscape centered around travesti women's modulating moves to challenge cishet desire. By learning how and when to move across space, travesti women enact playful forms of embodied knowledge that dislocate the heterosexual logics of space, bringing out a critical sense of vitality at the club.

When all lights are out, shade sparks queer possibilities of escape, play, and refusal to modulate hypervisibility and invisibility through the body. In the darkness of the cabaret, Roshell throws shade at us to open our eyes to how space moves, and through that movement, space is un/made. Like Roshell and her workshop participants, reflecting on the power of shade allows us to throw glitter bombs on neoliberalism, cishet ways of being, or geopolitical imbalances and violences. We can move through shade as a liminal space full of possibility or can relax in the shade of queer relajo.

Modulating Activism: Liberatory Travesti Ethics and Politics in
Hemispheric Context

Casa Roshell's Personality Workshop outlines a transfeminist praxis of modulation through queer relajo, unbinding set definitions of gender and sexuality; swishing through shades and shadows creates a shady choreography that takes travesti women and their suitors away from the constrains of heteronormativity. And both of those modulations occur within Roshell's deep awareness of the history of sexual politics. In fact, in her cabaret show she reflects on travesti activism in Mexico, "Cuando yo comencé en esto. Casi no podíamos existir, había redadas, era un crimen. Éramos la generación X, pero éramos revolucionarias," (When I got started, we had nothing! We were hardly allowed to exist, there were raids, it was a crime. We were generation X, but we were revolutionaries).

Emphasizing the persistence of travesti becoming, Roshell poses an uncomfortable question, "¿En qué ha cambiado?" (So what's changed?); an animated crowd answers back, "En nada!" (Nothing!). In a mocking gesture toward existing trans laws, that allow legal name changes, or discrimination suit filings, Roshell keeps on roasting Mexico City's policies of inclusivity and diversity, "Ahora podemos poner demandas cada vez que nos discriminen, pero ¿tienen tiempo de eso? Porque nos los podemos chingar. Imagínense si cada trans pusiera una demanda cada vez que la discriminen, pasaría toda una vida. Y mañana, te mueres" (Now we can sue anyone for discrimination, but who has time for that? We could screw them! Just imagine if every trans person were to sue every time they suffered discrimination, they'd spend their lives suing. And life is too short.) With jokes, Roshell touches on how state bureaucracy complicates the precarity of travesti and trans life. Although designed to protect travesti and trans people from discrimination, violence, and harassment, Roshell queers humor to argue that such legal protocols sustain trans misogyny.

Dressed as an Adelita, an oufit that indexes Mexican female revolution fighters, Roshell deploys the instruments of drag cabaret performance, like jokes, satire, and costume, to critique the shortcomings of a political establishment that continues to kill travesti vitality. Wearing a traditional female revolutionary outfit indexes the historical absences and archival ghostlings haunting the histories of gender and sexuality in the Mexican context, which outside of Amelio Robles, who has been harnessed to national scripts, has failed to give critical attention to gender nonconformance. The embodiments of Mexican identity portrayed in the film point to the deadly absences of travesti and trans folk in the scripts of homonationalism, as travesti and trans lives continue to occupy a marginal position within the grand cishet myth of the national. It is not that travesti inclusion would positively change the inherently flawed project of Mexican nationalism, but that travesti survival emphasizes the importance of modulating through cishet "atmospheres of violence" (Stanley 2021).

By impersonating a female revolutionary, Roshell not only highlights the failures of sexual inclusivity policies, but also lambasts the neoliberal turn shaping national laws allowing the extraction of value from marginal sexual positions. While unsettling heteronormative attachments to national culture, Roshell's embodiment of Mexicanidad recognizes that the flows of global capital affect practices of consumption in local queer and trans nightlife. In other words, her dressing of a female revolutionary makes her legible to a global audience that recognizes the value of performing national belonging. By dragging Mexicanidad, Roshell's gesture of queer relajo unveils a game of recognition, while also critiquing nationalism.

Her performance of the national further situates the importance of a playful praxis of travesti modulation in recognizing that sexual politics across certain regions of the Americas, including Mexico, are in ever-changing contact with transnational flows of pop culture. In other words, a politics of sexual dissidence is no longer a matter of street activism, but also of transnational networks of queer cultural production, distribution, and consumption, particularly in connection to US-based queer diasporic cultures. In this sense, queer diasporic cultures can help identify a neoliberal impetus that transforms sexual minoritarian practices into hot products of global market consumption. Alongside the gentrification of working-class space, branding LGBTQ+ consumption only reinscribes postcolonial hierarchies of capital; those with a strong acquisitive power are usually members of a socioeconomic and racial elite in Mexico, but such an elite continues to move transnationally across metropolitan sites in search of liberatory queer contact.

But the seemingly different positions between local and globally diasporic forms of queer culture should not stand in opposition, or be framed in contending polarity; rather, I argue that the transnational flows of local forms of queerness advance and disrupt a neoliberal relationality that relies on the production of subjective identity as the basis for any politics. Local and diasporic underground queer and trans sites should question neoliberal paradigms of sexual identity, as well as market capitalist logics that restrict mobile actors from interacting across transnational networks of sexual dissident culture. We must recognize that localizing or situating queer and trans underground practices alone—without really questioning how they become complicit in both, sustaining, and dismantling transregional manifestations of sexual commodification—is not a gesture of hemispheric solidarity, but rather a practice of extraction available to transregional and socioeconomically elevated queer folks, participating in the acritical commodification of queer and trans life, especially for those who already experience an acute precarity given their social location. Furthermore, issues of gender and sexuality in the Mexican context should not be constrained to the dysfunctions of the national but placed against/ in dialogue with multiple postcolonial entanglements of race and ethnicity influencing forms of popular agency at a hemispheric level. As a travesti praxis of playful modulation shows, the embodiments of Mexicanidad exceed imaginary boundaries of the nation, pointing to a complex set of practices shaping what *lo mexicano* might produce at home and abroad, as well as to the marketable appeal such cultural practices hold within networks of global commodity and capital.

Under this critical kaleidoscope, my call for this kind of hemispheric conversation comes directly out of Casa Roshell's transfeminist praxis of modulation, which demands an ethical and political positioning in creating knowledge collaboratively and playfully with queer, travesti, and trans folk located away from global epicenters of knowledge and power in the Americas. Gender and sexual formations in the Mexican context respond to complex histories of how the body has been instrumentalized as a site for capture, vigilance, and profit. Understanding how travesti women move their bodies across nightly cabarets not only points to a set of embodied maneuvers for survival, but also to a politics of knowledge production through queer relajo.

Situating a transfeminist praxis of queer relajo requires joining a strong transfeminist undercurrent of queer playfulness in the Americas. According to Argentinian travesti activist Lohana Berkins, travesti embodiments would open playful possibilities for ways of becoming political. Playfully twisting the pejorative connation of the word *trava*, a term used to demean travesti and trans folk in the Southern Cone, Berkins extends the playful gesture of "travar el saber," or "jamming-as-intervention," redirecting its meaning to cast queer/travesti tactics of survival and political leverage.[4] "Travar el saber" thus names some of the ways through which travesti knowledges are produced, situated, and embodied as playful experiences of becoming, as well as a force of creativity.

Queer playfulness, joy, and pleasure manifest vital possibilities for travesti worldmaking like queer relajo in the case of Mexico. More than abstractions and elusive concepts, Marlene Wayar and Susy Shock underscore a queer sense of play mediating travesti relations with the corporeal, the carnal and the material as necessary textures affecting a pulsion for dreaming otherwise, for materializing the unthinkable and playing with the impossible—a similar pulsion that is found in Casa Roshell's cabaret erotics.[5] The rich textures, modulations, and elongations of travesti experience can often be flattened by the over-encompassing umbrella of "trans." Nonetheless, as in the case of critical trans of color studies, travesti experience and becoming also point to a wild card to disrupt, in the echoes of queer relajo, static epistemologies, ontologies, and knowledges.

Against a flattening of hemispheric transness, I expand on a hemispheric trans epistemology by situating a cabaret erotics that, as playful and joyful modes of travesti relationality, surpasses the boundaries of US-based trans knowledge. As micha cárdenas posits when laying out a set of tools for resistance amid necrocapitalism, "the concept of human has historically been used to delineate who is less than human, who is disposable, who is killable. Black people, women, trans people, queers, witches, and Indigenous people have all been defined as less than human at different times by different regimes of knowledge" (2019, 25).[6] Attentive to the possibilities of playful touch, a hemispheric take on a travesti transfeminist praxis of queer relajo, I argue, also fathoms other spaces not usually associated with systems of knowledge production, but that very well, contain an affective potency to move trans experience out of bounds.

Travesti becoming thus combines a queer sense of playfulness with a political stance against the shortsighted visions of heteropatriarchy, heterorationality and its gender and sexual dichotomies—something that reminds me of what Miguel Sicart describes as political play.[7] The importance of travesti playful ontology resides not only in disrupting but also in changing those processes of knowledge production that materialize infrastructural designs administrating life and death—this latter often imposed on those defined as non-human or less than human. The category of human has also been instrumentalized to partition play, pleasure, and joy. Travesti nightlife poses an unavoidable question about who has and can have access to joy and pleasure, what bodies and subject formations are defined and perceived as pleasurable and pleasure-seeking, or even unpleasurable. By the same token, what bodies and subject formations are reduced to perverse forms of pleasure and thus turned into commodifiable objects of desire by different regimes of power, knowledge, and consumption.

A consideration of who can occupy certain spaces, especially when those are not designed for minoritarian thriving, must remain central to gender and sexuality methods of cultural analysis. Critical approaches to understanding queer and trans nightlife transregionally are gaining more traction as academic settings begin to account for uneven geopolitics of knowledge production. To feel and think through hemispheric queer and trans nightlife thus demands the activation of a playful process of queer critical inquiry, one that is attentive to dangers and contradictions, particularly so when for travesti women, learning how to move across space is a matter of life or death. Understanding that queer and trans night practices of queer relajo emerge from a complex negotiation of loss, sorrow, or shame, alongside joy, laughter, and pleasure, also bring attention to forms of embodied experience as foundational to knowledge production. The affect flowing through queer and trans nightscapes escape any conventional attempt to seize, or explain them, by conventional means of objectivity, rationality, and rigor.

Roshell's transfeminist practice of modulation not only informs my own diasporic queer politics, but also shapes my playful process of queer critical inquiry. Crafting a method of queer relajo stems from a deep commitment to go beyond matters of queer/trans identity politics, which are essential to the functioning of a neoliberal pink market, as well as from a desire to get messed up and unbridle matters in the dark. Namely, to reposition play and joy are central to queer transnational conversations, inside and out academia. Queer play rehearses a vital disposition to stay alive against all odds. Most importantly, to flirt, dance, banter, laugh, cruise, and feel the night alongside these women requires a disposition to let go of conventional modes of queer analysis, letting the intertwining of travesti becoming, space, and stuff, speak up and take up space in their own playful terms and modulations. Transfeminist modulations as shown in Casa Roshell demand careful approaches and sensorial modes that enact a queer and trans solidarity.

By choosing to engage with a glowing materiality, I also reflect on my own displacements as a queer Mexican in the diaspora in navigating the death traps of interlocking systems of oppression, including academia. The transfeminist modulations toward queer relajo also guide my own drag transformation as Piña Colada, who has performed on the stages of Casa Roshell as discussed in Part I. Along with my travesti conspirators,

I position myself to feel, co-inhabit, and carefully write about the complicated contours of travesti nightlife. In this sense, a hemispheric queer politics recognizes on-the-ground tactics of queer play and banter as forms of trans care, defending the existence of travesti nightlife intimacy.

Sabroso! Toward a Nightlife Travesti-festo

Learning from travesti praxis in the Americas would allow me to locate other embodiments of queer relajo, like "travar el placer," as a way of highlighting how Casa Roshell deploys cabaret performance as a political strategy of jamming heterosexual joy and pleasure. Travesti cabaret is a pivotal practice of queer relajo shaping travesti nightlife and, thus, worldmaking. In Liliana's playful proposition, "sabroso" not only functions as a qualifier that describes a degree of delight, indexing a declaration of travesti joy, but also as a gesturing toward reclaiming the erotic. "Sabroso" affirms travesti modes of joy and pleasure, assisting in modulating a position within the political economies of desire. Liliana Alba's cabaret performance outlines a nightscape's "travesti-festo," that is, an affirmation and celebration of travesti vitality despite and alongside the political administration of death. As an evocation of queer relajo, sabroso delineates an attunement toward disruptive queer forms of pleasure and joy, like flirting, cruising, bantering, and chatting, as practices that do not bank on the sexual possession of something or someone but that follow closely sensorial attunements between bodies, textures, objects, and places. Within the confines of Casa Roshell's affective infrastructures, a nightscape's travesti-festo undoes the paralyzing effects of death and violence. In this sense, travesti cabaret performance emerges as an affirmation of travesti intimacy, moving the affective tectonics toward embracing nonheterosexual forms of play, joy, and pleasure. With each playful instantiation like dressing in sequin dresses, wearing high heels, or hiding a sister's wig, Liliana foregrounds cabaret performance as a transfeminist praxis of queer relajo.

Through her monologue, Liliana claims the power of the erotic, as it resonates with Audre Lorde's "erotic knowledge."[8] The sensual, for Lorde, is what bridges the psychic and the political. "The erotic's electrical charge" (2007, 59) shapes an orientation toward feeling and sensing that is potentially awakened through travesti cabaret performance. Liliana Alba's powerful invocation of the erotic enlists ways of sharing joy, informing a radical basis for the flourishing of travesti intimacy by laughing.

Liliana's deployment of queer humor also insists on recognizing the economies sustaining travesti nightscapes. As such, nightscapes emerge as a political economy of affects contingently shaped by material assemblages, connecting bodies, objects, and infrastructures. Nightscapes mark a coming together that extends beyond mere subjective agencies, but revolt in the cusps and lows of emotion and sensation, of discarded objects, and traveling smells. As complexly situated, material and affective assemblages, nightscapes demand an attunement of the senses, as well as a fostering of affects and feelings that are vital to the sustenance and immanence of travesti and queer worldmaking. In line with Lorde's politics of the erotic, Alba's "nightlife commandments" outline an affective code to sense out the night, redirecting our attention to those things that matter the most to travesti women. Through her tantalizing code, Alba queerly appropriates androcentric humor, that is, a form of banter that reaffirms hetero-patriarchal dominance, to extend lifelines through queer relajo, while propelling a *travesti-festo*, a delightful expression of trans and travesti joy emerging from nightlife.

A sparkle-studded dark curtain adorns the stage, the show is about to start. A clacking pair of heels sound in the dark, as Liliana Alba grabs the mic and extends the warmest of welcomes,

> ¡Comadres, buenas noches! ¿Cómo están? ¡Bienvenidas! ¡Qué barbaras, qué guangas! Ya se parecen a mi abuelita y donde que mi abuelita está guanguísima. Ella fue medio puta. Imagínense tuvo 15 hijos, 27 sobrinos, pero qué importa la vida de mi abuela.

> (Good night, sisters! How are you? Welcome! I see some loose women tonight. You look as loose as my grandma, and that's saying a lot! She was a bit of a whore, and she had 15 kids. Fifteen! 27 nephews! But we're not here to talk about my grandma.)

Liliana Alba's monologue engages the audience through queer banter, humor, and satire, and performs what is commonly known in American settings as a roast, that is, a custom of insulting a person as a sign of favor. Liliana thus opens the final show by roasting the establishment of compulsory heterosexuality and reproduction.

Liliana then quickly begins to lay out a list of ten commandments, or terms of engagement, for travesti belonging. Incorporating a distinct Mexico City queer slang, which includes dirty metaphors, popular registers, and codes of innuendo, while following performance strategies akin to political cabaret, such as satire, parody, popular parlance, and improvisation, Liliana Alba outlines a queer code to let loose for trans and travesti night intimacy to happen at the club,

> Primer mandamiento de esta noche, no robarás la ropa interior de tu esposa ni de tu amiga y mucho menos de tu amante, mana. ¡Qué feo! Le dejas la mancha, te excitas por ponerte la lencería y entonces ella va a trabajar al otro día a la oficina. Trae una macha y parece que se nos orinó, manas. No inventen, eso no se hace. Segundo mandamiento: adorarás la lentejuela y las zapatillas sobre todas las cosas. ¿A qué me refiero con eso? Puedes estar enferma, puedes estar deprimida, pero si te pones un vestido de lentejuela, unas zapatillas de quince centímetros, vas a ser feliz, mana.

> (Here's tonight's first commandment: you shall not steal your wife's or your friend's underwear. And especially not your lover's! What if you stain it! You get excited wearing her lingerie, and when she goes to work, the following day, her underwear is stained as if she'd peed in her pants! That's not hot, sisters! Second commandment: you shall adore sequins and pumps above all things. What does that mean? You may feel sick, or depressed, but as soon as you put on a dress or a 6-inch heel, you'll be happy, sister!)

The first travesti commandment establishes not to steal a sister's pair of underwear because accidents can happen. The adoration for glitter, sequins, and high heels comes as a second commandment for nighttime relationality. According to Alba's instructions, a sequin dress, and a pair of 6-inch stiletto heels are the perfect recipe to deal with morning blues. The material radiancy of glitter can make you happy. Interspersed with each commandment, Liliana threads in doses of queer humor by denoting absurd, but potentially real, scenarios, like not returning a pair of stolen underwear, or not having oral sex with your best friend. In her deployment of cabaret satire and humor, Liliana mobilizes queer relajo as a way of laughing at set identities, and particularly travesti identity, as she calls the audience "men dressed in drag." An uninformed response to this type of queer humor might label Alba's piercing jokes as "politically incorrect," or even "transphobic." Travesti humor precisely reveals the complex entanglements between identity, politics, and performance.

With every joke, Alba brings into question the everyday violence trans and travesti women and men face when confronting normalized discourses and practices perpetuating gender misrecognition, discrimination, oppression, and transphobia. In other words, travesti deployments of humor questions the very logics that sustain conventional, binary systems of gender and sexuality. Liliana acknowledges the detrimental effects of gender misrecognition and dysphoria as forms of violence. Rather than channeling a sense of rage, Liliana turns to humor as a queer practice of contestation. Yes, humor is not going to bring back to life all those killed by transphobia, machismo, and gender/sexual violence, but laughing at such horrors, brings into the light, and out of the shadows, not only the rationalizing logic of a patriarchal system that allows violence against women and transwomen, but also names and unhides such fatal forces, insisting on a reparative care binding travesti women at night.

Liliana is certainly tapping into a long genealogy of Mexican queer *relajo*. In the Mexican context, one of the greatest exponents of queer and travesti roasting, also known as *perreo*,[9] was travesti vedette and performer Francis García. For over fifteen years, Francis, known as "The Fantasy Made Woman," dominated Mexico City's night scene with a renowned Vegas-styled show, "El Show de Francis," a variety show featuring Francis as a standup comedian alongside vedette dancers and cabaret choreographers. Francis's show played at the infamous Teatro Blanquita, located close to Plaza Garibaldi, in the downtown-neighboring *colonia* of La Lagunilla. For almost twenty years, the Francis's Show occupied the iconic theater and toured Mexico, and the US. Despite her successful streak in mainstream theater and performance, Francis remains a somewhat contradictory and eclipsed personality of travesti cabaret and politics in Mexico, as many accused the vedette of being homophobic and transphobic at best.[10]

Although explicit or not, consciously, or unconsciously, Liliana Alba and Roshell Terranova invoke the picaresque humor of Francis, as well as her radiant affectivity. Following Francis's pungent queer humor, Liliana moves onto expand the third commandment about travesti intimacy,

Tercer mandamiento: adorarás a tu compadre y a tu comadre. Eso quiere decir, no que le vayas a hacer el sexo oral ni un 69, no, no, no. Eso quiere decir que la vas a apoyar, que la vas a querer, que esta noche van a disfrutar juntas, se van a abrazar y van a cantar.

(Third commandment: you shall adore your brother and your sister. That means that it's not that you should blow them or do a 69! It means that you support them, love them, that tonight you'll have fun together, you'll embrace them and sing together.)

Playing with innuendo, Liliana not only unpacks ways of having fun at night but also lays out modes of caring connected to love and adoration beyond sexual gain. Travesti nightlife conceives care as an extension of queer relajo. At Casa Roshell, travesti women are invited to bask in queer acts of enjoyment, through embrace, touch, and flirt. Dancing, and chanting are not banal vices, but forms of protection and support. Liliana invites the audience to take care of each other through queer joy and laughter, "It means that you support them, love them, that tonight you'll have fun together, you'll embrace them and sing together." Queer humor thus functions as an affective bridge binding together multiple forms of intimacy during nighttime. Although Casa Roshell is frequented mostly by travesti women, the club policies of antidiscrimination allow anyone to be present and have a good time. Liliana's humorous message situates a transfeminist praxis of modulation linked to queer joy, fun, and pleasure.

Before carrying on her monologue to give out more instructions, Liliana briefly pauses to a toast with the audience, "¡Ay qué sabroso! Qué sabroso es el tequila, el tequila de aquí del jardincito de Roshell, del agave que plantamos hace como un mes, que ya dio sus frutos, algo muy delicioso este tequila. ¡Salud, comadres!" ("Mmm, delicious! Tequila is so good. Tequila made from Roshell's little garden, from the agave we planted about a month ago, which is already bearing fruit with this delicious tequila. Cheers, sisters!"). Liliana echoes a sense of delight by shouting "sabroso" after chugging a tequila shot. The tequila she is drinking was made, according to her joke, from an agave plant in Casa Roshell's small garden. "Qué sabroso," which can be loosely translated into English, as "so delicious," denotes a sensorial orientation toward what is sensed as pleasurable, or what can be pleasing. In other words, "sabroso" enacts a nighttime disposition to sensing erotic knowledge.

Through her joke, Liliana tacitly taps into the erotic to tease out a queer mode of playful interaction. The joke makes fun of the individual illusion of preservation and sustenance, stressing that existence, sustenance, and care are impossible without a collective. "Sabroso" animates an erotic sensibility linked to a capacity for sensing otherwise. It awakens an attunement geared toward recognizing and feeling the vitality of a queer nightscape binding things, bodies, and sentient beings during the night. Liliana's joke about the making of tequila appeals to travesti magic, expressly a queer form of playful knowledge running as an intuitive force against hetero-rational thinking. A sense of belonging awakens in a simple joke.

Travesti cabaret performance thus conceives a transfeminist praxis set on embodied modulations, claiming the erotic as a powerful source of political resistance and worldmaking. As an embodiment of queer relajo, modulating thus serves as an affective attachment to forms of erotic knowledge, waiting to be awakened and enlivened through communion. Notice that each nightlife commandment appeals to the sensorial, the affective, and the spatial, as each instruction not only relates to the steps of travesti becoming, referencing wigs, undergarments, glitter, sequin dresses, and heels, but also invites the audience to join in queer cabaret performance every weeknight.

Appealing specifically to the sense of taste, the popular slang use of "qué sabroso" kindles sensorial connections. In this case, the tasting of tequila is only enjoyable in the company of other cabaret goers. The sensorial attunement to taste marks a pleasure-filled, erotic declaration of travesti worldmaking. Queer relajo, pleasure and playfulness infuse and shake up a transfeminist praxis of modulation. "Qué sabroso" is a declaration of travesti vitality, as the women seating in the audience celebrate the joys of being alive, of being able to find a confidant and share their stories of heartbreak, of finding a fleeting lover for the night and holding on to that phone number, or to that aroma that reminds us of a body rubbing against our skin. It manifests a right to queer play and an equal access to queer pleasure, claiming what has been stripped away by a necropolitical economy.

Nightlife is mined with many pleasures, but each of them also demands a positioning, as the right to claim pleasure becomes more commodified and privatized under queer neoliberalism. The transfeminist praxis of modulation is not only a political position based in the power of the erotic, but also outlines a queer way of life, an affective and sensorial attunement to make kin with whatever and whoever brings out pleasure. Travesti intimacy allows an erotic reorganization of the senses, expanding our understanding of what pleasure can do, and more importantly, how pleasure can connect us to the world around us. As Audre Lorde reminds us, "[o]ur erotic knowledge empowers us, becomes a lens through which we can scrutinize all aspects of our existence, forcing us to evaluate those aspects honestly in terms of their relative meaning without our lives" (57).

Travesti intimacy taps into queer playfulness to tease out connections with erotic knowledge. As jokes keep on coming, Liliana makes fun of stealing a sister's wig,

> Séptimo mandamiento: adorarás, pero nunca codiciarás la peluca de tu compañera de al lado. ¿A qué me refiero con esto? No importa que ella esté rubia, no importa que ella sea rojiza, no importa que tenga el cabello negro, largo como cola de yegua pechugona. Sí, la yegua pechugona, esa que no conoce nadie; es como un unicornio, mana, es un ser de la mitología, de la mitología mexicana porque es una yegua pechugona. No codiciarás la peluca, mana, o sea, cómprate la tuya no seas carbona. Además no se la puedes arrancar, mana, porque está calva.

> (Seventh commandment: you shall adore but never covet your neighbor's wig. What does that mean? It doesn't matter whether she's blond, a redhead, it doesn't matter whether she has jet black hair as long as a breasted mare's tail. That's right: a breasted mare. No one's ever seen it, like a unicorn. The breasted mare is a creature of Mexican mythology. Thou shalt not covet the wig, sister. Buy your own, don't be a bitch! And don't pull it off because she's bald! She's bald and she'd look terrible.)

Casting a spell of queer relajo, her reference to the word "commandment" points to an inversion of Judeo-Christian rules, twisting out a sense of seriousness found in religious conservatism. But in her reinterpretation of the divine, Liliana shines out a practice of travesti communion. The seventh commandment proposes to not steal a sister's wig regardless of its color, length, or texture. Alluding to a breasted mare, Liliana taps into improvisation by joking about this mythical creature, a sort of unicorn from a queer Mexican fantasyland. No one is to see your sister looking bald without a wig, she exclaims. The audience bursts into laughter after Liliana outlines the rest of her commandments. The remaining ones will outline other nightclub rules like not screaming inside, not feigning a feminine voice, inviting guests into drinking all night, inciting tipsiness, and beverage consumption, and finally raving over attending Casa Club Roshell every weeknight. Although the monologue has been likely prepared in advance for the final film sequence, expert hostess Liliana Alba makes a couple of adjustments to the script. For instance, the seventh commandment is mixed up and repeated twice under a different instruction. It is precisely those moments of improvisation that expose the erotic power of queer relajo, inspiring a transfeminist praxis of modulation.

Inspired by Liliana's playful commandments, I and Piña Colada propose the following Nightlife Travesti-festo, so you can also act out in the spirit of queer relajo:

- Awaken your senses to attune yourself to the rhythms of nightlife
- Claim the erotic as political resistance and worldmaking possibility
- Shape community and find kinship with whoever and whatever brings you pleasure
- Refashion the divine to tease out the queerness of being in the world
- Fuck up the normal functioning of state institutions that enact abuse
- Embody knowledges that eschew universalizing in favor of sharp specifics
- Expand your queer horizons by embracing other hemispheric sexual formations
- Ruffle the canons of queer studies to make space for diasporic gender nonconformity
- Throw shade, pave away, and never give up the glamour of spark

Travesti nightlife thus emerges from a need to outgrow the necropolitics embedded in the economies of the night. As a place of queer/trans leisure, Casa Roshell extends lifelines to the women and men seeking refuge from the paralyzing effects of heteronormative violence. That is not to say that everyone at the cabaret is exempt from reproducing asymmetrical power dynamics, but that they are made visibly recognizable through their parody. In here lies the transformative potency of queer play, pleasure, and joy, embodied through a multiplicity of travesti and queer nightlife practices of queer relajo, like dancing, touching, kissing, performing, modulating, flirting, laughing, drinking, and caressing. They insist on dwelling and holding on to the ephemerality of the night, looking for the glimmering affects that unbolt dark infrastructures. Travesti embodiments of queer relajo point to a transfeminist praxis of modulation, fluctuating between what becomes loose and what remains, between hypervisibility and invisibility, between shade and shadow. These tactical maneuvers are deeply connected to the queer nightscapes flowing through and beyond the space of cabaret.

As they clear through a hefty security system guarding the main entrance and delve into the deep nightscapes of Casa Roshell, all clubgoers hold certain that the night will never last forever. Sooner or later, the dark contours of the club will become lit by morning light; the magic of the travesti and queer nightscapes carries on, elongating, extending, and holding dearly onto the queer joys, pleasures, and funs felt in the darkness of nightlife.

Coda
Glows of Jotería

On a typical day, the metal fence standing along the US-Mexico border on the outskirts of Ciudad Juárez, right at the meeting point with Anapra, New Mexico, looks like a giant barcode ready to be scanned from afar. From feminicides to border crossings, passing through political diatribes, militarization, and cishet scripts of nationalism, the US-Mexico Borderlands constitutes a particular space for the sensorial making of affects, that is, a space in which feeling moves us into action and thrusts our senses to recognize that the multiple worlds we inhabit are as much familiar as strange places. It is at this meeting point where the Teeter-Totter Wall Project, a binational art installation designed by architects Ronald Rael and Virginia San Fratello, grapples with the irreparable and dehumanizing contradictions shaping the US-Mexico border's geopolitics.

In tandem with Juárez-based architecture group Colectivo Chopeke, the team installed three large bright pink seesaws at the border between Ciudad Juárez and New Mexico on July 28, 2019. As a way of reimagining the carceral aesthetics of the border wall, the bright pink beams extend an improvised playground at a crossing point, replacing its barren sounds with fun and laughter for a few hours. The echoes of joy resonate across metal fences as if its lingering soundwaves were to build an affective bridge of fun, a different ambiance felt within the necropolitical economies of border crossing.

The Borderlands make visible the contradictions of national discourses of liberty and justice, holding categories of citizenship—or a fashionable substitute to name the category of human—, as some people can and indeed claim the right to move freely and crisscross without perjury or injury. Holding contradictory meanings, this zone of contact marks an impasse of transit, as well as a vanishing point through which flow might be restricted but not completely diminished. It marks a juncture where friction and jostling collide, converge, and fall apart in movement. "Movement at the border," argues Jade Power-Sotomayor, "produces space and place," (2020, 101), situating a strategy for spatial remaking through play and performance, as embodied in the Teeter-Totter Wall Project.

Although intended to "demonstrate the delicate balances between the two nations" (San Fratello, 2021), Max Pearl from *Art in America* magazine decried the installation as "tragedy porn masquerading as protest art," adding that "it elicits an immediate, hot-blooded response from the viewer, yet invites no further reflection [. . .] With its spectacle of sentimentality, *Teeter-Totter Wall* fails to provide any insight about who might be responsible for this tragedy, who benefits from it, and how we got here as a country" (2021). While Pearl's critique of the installation's excessive feeling questions the ethical implications of producing and commodifying a sort of voyeuristic gaze, Rael and San Fratello's pink seesaws also reveal how art fails to fulfill the expectation of some US progressive audiences, like Pearl's stance aiming to "decry the cruelty and unnaturalness of the scenario depicted here."

From these opposing viewpoints, the Borderlands seems to hold sociocultural value inasmuch as its meaning banks on the re/production of tropes linked to violence and negative affect. By framing the wall under an optic of pain, fear, loss, or even death, Pearl's critique serves as a case in point to expose how the US-Mexico border appears in the US imagination as a place where no fun is allowed. This kind of liberal expectation paradoxically contributes to the making of affective circuits that position the border as a transnational infrastructure holding cishet scripts of national belonging in contention with each other, producing an economy of violence (Power-Sotomayor 2020). While calling out the immoral nature of such playful intervention, for "these kids are too young to understand the significance of the border fence," Pearl's views inadvertently participate in the production of violence as a commodifiable surplus sustaining the neoliberal rationality they intend to critique. By decrying any possibility of having fun, this tension suggests that the Borderlands could only emerge as a tragic stage of dehumanization, as cruel as that might sound, curtailing the agency migrants and border crossers exert on the violence "often manifest[ed] in tedious bureaucratic experiences" (Pearl 2021). I am not, by any means, denying the material and real consequences of dehumanizing immigration practices, such as caged immigrant children, forced immigrant detention, and inhumane maltreatment, to name only a few of the war-like tactics deployed to defend US imperial sovereignty, but the polemics surrounding the Teeter-Totter Wall Project precisely point to how the infrastructures making space also rely on transregional flows of affect.

Beyond its political and ethical implications, I fathom this installation less as a revolutionary artistic design than as an affective intervention that opens a terrain for play, fun, and pleasure. By associating fun and laughter to the Borderlands, the Teeter-Totter Wall Project disrupts the affective economies usually associated with border crossing. Its bright pink metallic beams seesawing across symbolic, but lethally material boundaries resemble a similar bright pink bridge connecting shared cultural understandings around playfulness and queerness on both sides of the border; a bridge queer Latinx playwright Carlos-Manuel calls "the jotería community [. . .] a community [. . .] part of the Chicano/Latino community, as well as part of the immigrant community." To ponder about the possibilities of joy and pleasure in spaces from the global south designed to become wastelands of neoliberal death and violence, like the Borderlands, not only refuses the imposition of necropolitical imaginings about such places, but also demands an imagining otherwise where queer wonder takes us by surprise.

That is why I situate myself in this coda at the wall along the US-Mexico border to engage with queer playful ways to jump over and circumvent neoliberal logics of containment—be it geographical, socioeconomic, political, affective, or academic. Simply put, I am interested in teasing out the hemispheric tensions between queer Mexicanidad and Latinx jotería to cast away the existing inefficiencies in our categories of cultural analysis in Latin American and Mexican studies as if the violence experienced by queer and trans collectives, as well as by Afrodiasporic people, women, Indigenous or other racialized and displaced populations, were of exclusive concern to national paradigms constituting area studies. This tension allows me to imagine new ways of embracing the indeterminacy of US Latinidad, and as a queer Mexican in the diaspora working in academia, help advance queer modes of knowledge production that are inherently hemispherical. Pointing to the ongoing interconnectedness of capital, technology, sexuality, gender, race, and ethnicity, as socio-technological locations imbuing nationalist scripts of belonging, I consider queer relajo an expansive tool of analysis to confront the many forms of violence impacting those in the global south and across its diasporas.

Queer Relajo is my small contribution to write against an optic reducing Mexican and US-Mexican diasporic cultural formations to matters of death and violence, as signs of neoliberal underdevelopment and modern failure serving to excuse damaging tactics of intervention and containment, like those gestured at in the *Art in America* review. Rather, my engagement in this book resonates with an urgency of thinking fun in the global south to reclaim pleasure and joy not only as political work but also as a methodological tool "to generate new alliances, new modes of being in the world, and to dismantle the elitism that underlies the distance between critics and the people we study" (Anjaria and Anjaria 2020, 240). With queer relajo, I have offered a playful method to describe and become part of the joy, fun, and pleasure shaping, in contradictory ways, queer/trans nightlife and beyond.

The sounds and feelings of fun as well as other surprising pleasures have been central to writing this book. By dwelling in and sitting with affects of queer/trans nightlife that transpire from cultural artifacts, like the ones examined throughout, I have contested an epistemic violence of reading to unveil the "secret" meaning hiding behind cultural texts. Instead, I have channeled bodily rhythms, queer incantations, trans moves, drag textures, travesti ambiances, and other nightscapes that tease out our sensorial complicity. Seen through a performance studies lens, I stand on a doing-and-undoing defying rational apprehension. In many ways, I have veered away from a well-trodden path of academic practice that takes away the queer pleasure of letting loose analytical boundaries. Instead, I have been overcome by the tantalizing messiness of cultural forms.

Throughout this book, I have also insisted that racialized, popular, and working-class sexual expressions are not solely a matter of private space, but rather emerge as affective embodiments that play out in the mappings of public life. If nightscapes refer to the shifting affective tectonics of queer/trans nightlife, in their rich, complex contradiction, where a fine dance between pleasure and danger, between life and death, takes place; from these moving scenes, afterglow emerges as a residual force that pushes against neoliberal logics of spatial consumption. As discussed in chapter 4, afterglow names a sensorial knowledge, an imprint that is carried across the skin, but also contained within the materiality of sequin dresses, of boa feathers, of smeared napkins and used condoms. In this sense, material remnants hold a dirty affect, or what Deborah R. Vargas calls "the dirty and obscene of surplus" in neoliberal capitalism, a "queer surplus [that] tastes and smells *sucio* and cultivates a presence and lingering perseverance of queer sex and joy within neoliberal hetero- and homonormative violences" (2014, 715). Such a "sucio" excess also defines queer Mexicans in the diaspora, extending a glowing resistance to remain well and alive in broad daylight and across geopolitical limits.

The increasingly globalized presence of technologies of surveillance and patrolling, from neoliberal economics to digital communications and global immigration, not only shatter paradigms of the national, but also respond to an increasing racialization and marginalization of vulnerable populations in the global south that, nonetheless, sustain the vital flows of the global north.[1] Capital knows no boundaries and travels across regions beyond national borders, to make manifest a logic of neoliberal extraction and commodification defining rainbow capitalism and to complicate displacement, especially within zones that hold a valuable queer surplus. Dwelling on what it means to occupy public space, the coming together of Mexican queer/trans diasporic fugitives, that is, queer jotas, nonetheless, brings discomfort to a queer strand of neoliberalism resulting in the increasing commodification and policing of queer space in ways that limit access to those who, enduring multiple forms of economic violence, become paralyzed by public policies of austerity. In here, I am speaking about how waves of racial gentrification erase dirty undergrounds of queer fugitivity by increasing the cost of living in cities like San Francisco, Mexico City, LA, or Chicago, driving out shadow and informal economies, and replacing queer street kinship with established forms of cishet trade, etc. In other words, we can attend to how neoliberal and masculinist violence transcends national boundaries through exclusionary economic practices.

To resist this erasure, queer Mexicans enact queer relajo, as discussed in previous chapters, to rehearse a mode of escape to whitened hetero- and homonormative consumption, displacement, and reproduction. In some instances, such hemispheric queer formations, have worked to expose how the consolidation of a narco-state in Mexico follows circuits of global capital.[2] Thus the moves enacted by queers of color in the US resonate with those embodied by working-class, popular, and racialized queer/travesti undergrounds in Mexico. The glows of jotería thus expose how seemingly different experiences of neoliberal violence are similar in effect for queer and trans folk across the US-Mexico border, pushing against nation-state technologies that have succeeded in parceling out forms of queer dispossession as distinctly national.

The cultural practice of queer Chicanx and Latinx artists, whose connection with Mexican pop culture deeply informs their own dis/identification, not only questions the very US imperial logics guiding the nationalist project of Latinidad, but also challenges how queer Mexicanidad is represented, examined, and experienced. Jotería thus extends queer hemispheric "structures of feeling," to borrow cultural critic Raymond Williams's supposition, a glow extending its nightly chiffons over poor, working-class, and racialized queer and trans folk from both sides of the US-Mexico border. I am referring to affect emerging from common queer nightlife practices that revitalize cultural codes and that tease out cishet nationalist cultures. Yes, there might be political differences in the way sociopolitical apparatuses end shaping up histories, but to fathom such differences as obstacles to formulating queer hemispheric approaches and perspectives would only give in to a US imperial project of expansionism that chops up the world according to disciplines, and whose geopolitical layering has served to hide a long-produced interconnectedness.

As a method emerging from the intimate entanglements of queer Mexicanidad and Latinx jotería, queer relajo helps reshape the neoliberal and homonormative spaces of production even when underground nightscapes are privatized to produce sexual capital. By following some of the everynight acts and gestures played by working-class poor queer and trans Latinxs, to grapple with queer neoliberalism, I seek to establish intimate encounters with the affective infrastructures they build through their cultural practice. By naming the attacks on the poor, the dirty, and the underground across regions, these queers of color unsettle and contest a whitened form of (transregional) belonging. Wu Tsang's cinematic incantations in *Wildness*, for instance, reveal how queer and travesti diasporas resist displacement, while Xandra Ibarra's *The Hook Up/Displacement/Barhopping/Drama Tour* reminds us of the afterglows of queer nightlife, affecting the possibilities of resistance even when nightclubs disappear. Considering what remains after dark, in the ephemerality of queer, trans, and travesti nightlife, the glows of jotería reminds us of the radical forms of pleasure that we continue to carry even when the night becomes too expensive to party at.

As a flashing pink neon light whose reflections flicker in the air, this coda points to my argument that queer Mexicanidad and Latinx jotería insist on a spatial politics of queer knowledge production, that is, queer/trans modes of being in the world can and indeed happen outside the walls of the ivory tower. They take place within the dirty contours of the night, when cruising bathroom stalls, when performing at cabaret stages, when dancing at clubs, and when tumbling across streets filled with familiar smells of hot-steaming tacos and fried quesadillas served as late-night snacks for queer nightcrawlers. We learn to take care of each other in improvised tearooms, inside subway cars, or under a traffic-jammed overpass, where a lingering afterglow becomes materially present in cum stains, love letters, or neck hickeys, finding kinship with liminal subject locations deemed the lumpen of neoliberalism. With this, I am not proposing a new theory, but rather I am extending an invitation to fondle with other queer and trans sexual formations that have long existed regardless of their intersection with US sexual epistemologies. Carrying a trace of queer Mexicanidad and vice versa, Latinx jotería thus overflows the geopolitical boundaries of queer of color critique and its intersections with queer Latinidad by highlighting the complicities and contradictions with hemispheric translocalities.[3]

Jotería thus names a translocal queer/trans collective constantly moving across and negotiating forms of lethal violence exerted by masculinist national projects on both sides of the border, as Carlos-Manuel points, "Indeed we have always been there, quietly doing our thing and waiting for the moment to come out and shout: 'We're here; we're queer; get used to it'—or as many jot@s chant while marching in the Marcha del Orgullo in Mexico City, 'De noche o de día, somos parte de la jotería!'" (2014, 207). Carlos-Manuel's evocation of queer chants, both in Mexico and the US, gestures toward a bright pink bridge I have called *queer Mexicanidad*, existing alongside economies of violent surveillance—not made of metal beams, but of icons, gestures, movements, sounds, places, aromas, and feelings. It is through humor and irony, that Carlos-Manuel too writes to understand a queer messy underground shaping,

> what it means to be a Mexican immigrant campesino joto. What it means to have Brown skin, Indian features, an accent, and Catholic beliefs. What it means to be a non-English-speaker and not the six-foot-tall, blond, blue-eyed, all-sports guy next door. What it means to be a Mexican woman, an undocumented immigrant, a "border jumper, a wetback, an illegal." What it means to be a Latino drag queen, or an immigrant with the HIV virus or AIDS. What it means to be a Mexican and/or Latin@ immigrant who dislikes her/his own people—and much more. (2014, 209)

What Carlos-Manuel calls "jotería" indexes a specific sexual formation related to queer popular culture in the Americas, particularly in Mexico,

Central America, and the US, in places like Texas, Florida, Virginia, Maryland, New York, Illinois, or California. Across diasporas, queer jotería presents us with issues of untranslatability, particularly in contexts where poor, working-class, and popular social dynamics are co-constitutive of other shades of sexuality beyond Anglocentric and Eurocentric paradigms. The challenge, in what Héctor Domínguez-Ruvalcaba has referred to as "translating the queer," lies in situating a critical hemispheric praxis that considers the ethical implications of such untranslatability, that is, of who speaks, who is allowed to speak, and who, what and why is recognized as a legitimate speaker in transnational circuits of queer knowledge production (2016).

Situated within global networks of consumption, queer Mexicanidad and Latinx jotería balance out a hemispheric tension visually present in Teeter-Totter Wall's video of a swinging bright pink seesaw. I see in those bright pink beams a tension referencing how displaced queer/trans collectives move and mediate translocally the immanent cishet risk and neoliberal violence marking everynight life, embodying a queer contraband against masculinist logics of national entrapment through border crossing (Power-Sotomayor 2020, 101). Not only does this tension negotiate violence, stigma, and discrimination, but does so unavoidably through the racialization, commodification, and exploitation of popular forms of queer/trans joy, pleasure, and fun. For this coda, I want to dwell in this tension, as it makes evident some of the affective strategies vested in a sense of queer/trans joy and pleasure, in other words, *puro queer relajo*, against the neoliberal shocks seeking the privatization of cherry-picked queer streets and neighborhoods, and against the spatial designs of economic violence. Queer Mexicanidad and Latinx jotería emerge as affective assemblages made of queer contact and trans relation, insisting that sexuality is not only embodied in a relational and intersectional way, but is also spatially reconfigured.

My intention in this coda is to locate a playful fugitivity, a sort of queer relajo, enacted by queer cultural practices that exceed national boundaries but that expose the interconnectedness of queer hemispheric political possibilities against neoliberal violence. I fathom a displaced sense of queer Mexicanidad in the visual work of Julio Salgado, the performances of Xandra Ibarra, or in the cinematic production of Wu Tsang, not in opposition to local expressions of, but rather as lively traces of queer playfulness, as a glow shimmering across queer Brown diasporic imaginings. The glows of queer Mexicanidad stand for erased and absent modes of relationality tethered to pleasure, playfulness, and joy, embodied through practices that hinge on the working-class, popular, and racially Brown contours of the night. By tracing how queer relajo manifests as a refusal for spatial containment, I read in the work of Salgado, Ibarra, and Tsang, a queer Brown playfulness contesting neoliberal immigration, criminalization, and displacement. I argue that this sense of playfulness not only intertwines a queer Brown excess, but that such excess binds together queer Mexicanidad and Latinx jotería in distinct fashions, discourses, and practices, resisting the re/production of capital and, instead, turn into fugitive modes of queerness manifested in plays, joys, and pleasures, like those discussed across *Queer Relajo*.

Impressions of Jotería

Adopted as an avatar for the DREAM Act movement,[4] undocumented multimedia artist Julio Salgado questions US immigration violence. In specific, his self-referential digital art challenges a racial logic that turns migrant children into perverse forms of "illegal" subjectivity, elevating complex issues of queer belonging and Brownness otherwise unspoken and unheard of in mainstream media. Co-founder of the YouTube channel Dreamers Adrift and Migrant Storytelling Manager at The Center for Cultural Power in Oakland, California, Julio channels the glow of jotería by refusing to erase the feelings of undocumented queer migration, making them appear as "bigger than any border" like in the digital image "International Migrants Day 2015."

Fusing a colorful palate to draw images of protection for undocuqueer children crossing infrastructures of surveillance, such as immigration courts, border walls, or ICE raids, each digital composition undoes the public erasure of undocuqueer lives by stripping away the negative connotations of "illegality," while celebrating the joys of queer and undocumented existence. In "I am a butterfly," for instance, a combination of colors resembling the rainbow flag paint Salgado's migrant body. Each wing stands as a slogan for a "migrant queerness" based on "love, family, unity, and peace," feelings that contrast with border insecurity. If having undocumented status means living a life on hold, as many are unable to obtain job security, travel freely domestically or abroad, or be even eligible to receive federal aid, Salgado's digital art pushes against privatized, internalized, and individualized feelings of insufficiency, inviting us into collective action against the systemic marginalization, racialization, and dehumanization produced by US immigration policy.

Echoing Sara Ahmed's description of fear as a spatial relation,[5] these images draw queer forms of proximity to unframe the depiction of migrants as threats to national security by reclaiming their humanity, as in "I Read, I Create, I Mess up, I Fall," suggesting how the everyday actions of undocumented migrants are no different from anyone else's despite their immigration or citizenship status. Against a bright green background, Salgado stands to affirm his right to create, love, and mess up. By reworking fear into rageful political action against draconian immigration practices, the image exposes the hypocrisy of liberal democratic values, which only seem to work for those that don't pose a risk to white nationalism. Instead, Salgado's digital art shows the limits of citizenship and nation-state technologies of containment, advocating for a right to be present, or as another image frames it, "No Sir, I Will Not Show You My Papers," crafting a playful fugitivity dodging the criminalization of queer migrants.

As presented in his art, the magnitude of undocuqueer lives outsizes border walls and national politics, looking instead insignificant and meaningless. The large fonts, wide-opened eyes of queer characters, and unapologetically bright colors assemble a visual celebration of a life that transcends any geopolitical boundaries. By visualizing an undocumented queerness that troubles a neoliberal (white) homonormative paradigm of "coming out," Salgado's digital art deals with a double "coming out," as queer and undocumented, featuring queer Brown affirmations as antiimperialist mantras like "I exist," "Homoland Security," or "undocumented, unafraid, and unapologetic." As queer of color artivism, Salgado's glows of jotería denounces the atrocious treatment of Brown, Indigenous, and Black migrants in the US by making obvious the limits of the American dream, largely defined here as a personal will to (white) happiness and freedom. But for QTBIPOC, the American dream might only appear as a far-reaching illusion evanescing from long-hour shifts and precarious work conditions, finding refuge, for instance, in a queer Brown playfulness that escapes US logics of capture.

Queer Brown joy thus exudes from colorful images, demanding recognition amid a pale sea of whiteness. As such, Salgado's art portrays different scenes of ordinary life against immigration surveillance like in *Quiero Mis Queerce*, in which the image plays with a rite of passage for Latina women like Lia Garcia's performance discussed in chapter 3. In Salgado's quinceañera rendition, a gender nonconforming body standing proud refuses the disposability of feminized labor by celebrating the coming of age of undocumented queer youth despite criminalization. If being undocumented puts life on hold, *Quiero Mis Queerce* basks in queer joy, while embodying a femme Brownness against any fixed categorization.

Playing with the queer chiffons of transnational pop icons like Juan Gabriel, or Selena, the queer visuality of Salgado, reimagines jotería as an ordinary political position found in everyday existence, as shown in "Selena Inspired." In this digital illustration, a queer Brown kid wears a shirt that reads "Because Frida told me so," invoking the disruptive spirit of Frida Kahlo, as posters of Selena and a pink triangle hang in the background alongside other signs reading "Illegal faggots against borders." Reflecting on "the full impact that [Juan] Gabriel has had on Mexican and Mexican Americans" across borders, *LA Times* writer Fidel Martinez further adds, "[h]e gave us a shared language that affords us the opportunity to rejoice or grieve as a community" (2021). That "shared language" moves beyond the grammars of national belonging and language identity but evokes a diasporic queer kinship to find solace transnationally.

By incorporating figures like Selena, Juan Gabriel, or Frida Kahlo, Salgado's art extends a bridge connecting pop culture on both sides of the border, drawing a direct link between Latinx jotería and queer Mexicanidad, that is, between racialized experiences of queerness like undocuqueer Latinx migrants in the US, and poor working-class queers in Mexico, respectively. Crossing this bridge impels us to dance to the rhythms of Selena, and Juan Gabriel, as jota icons whose chants offer protection against border violence, while resisting through queer joy, or as Salgado puts it, "illegally fagging since 1995" in "Gimme All Your Colors: Blue."

I locate in Julio Salgado's digital art a playful engagement with Juan Gabriel's and Selena's music, evoking a queer imagination in the diaspora. By associating these music icons with the feelings of undocumented queer migration, Salgado draws a sonic connection, illustrating the translocal significance of queer Latinx and Mexican music, as Fidel Martinez also writes, "these aren't just songs. They're memories. They're feelings we can't express, and even if we could, why should we when Juanga's already done it better?" (2021). In other words, these illustrations make visible the fugitivity of queer Latinx music, recasting these celebrities not only as jota icons, but also as queer border crossers, dislocating bodies, sounds, and territories.

Depicting Juan Gabriel and Selena as queer Latinx icons of protection exposes the visual artist's own intimacy with them, gesturing toward a sonic memory—like the one evoked in chapter 2—that connects queer

Fig. 19. "Tú Estás Siempre En Mi Mente"

popular cultures in Mexico and the US, while highlighting that what remains absent in undocuqueer lives is, among other things, a pressing immigration reform. That their music performances dwell in queer Brown diasporic imaginings, like in Julio Salgado's undocuqueer experience, situates a strand of queer Mexicanidad that is felt beyond the confines of national territory, but that is sonically present across cultural borders. Juan Gabriel's song, "Tú estás siempre en mi mente," precisely gestures toward a remaining queer presence portrayed in one of Salgado's posters. Named after the song's title, the poster shows a mom teaching her son to clean while listening to a soft tune.

In the digital image, music notes float in the air, as an intimate connection between mom and son stand against a green background. By suspending music notes in the air, Salgado not only traces how pop music travels across space, but through those music waves, spots a queer feeling of intimacy attached to Juan Gabriel's songs. After the singers' deaths in the US—Juan Gabriel's in California in 2016; Selena's in Texas in 1995—, their aura still glows in the remixes of jota music, replaying a queer feeling of loss across bars, night clubs, and queer cantinas throughout the Americas. Selena's songs, for instance, can be heard across nightlife spaces in Tijuana, Chicago, Sacramento, or Mexico City, where drag queens, and nightclub dancers, sway to an ode of queer resilience, "me marcho hoy, yo sé perder, pero ay, ay, ay, cómo me duele." Julio Salgado's undocuqueer illustrations provide a powerful example of how we experience the glows of jotería, a feeling that streams from listening to Latinx pop music, like the gasping of air running through our bodies every time Selena's "Como La Flor" plays.

The visual inscriptions of Juan Gabriel expose a queer twist to Mexicanidad, expressly by incorporating the singer into his digital art, Salgado reworks a feeling of belonging and inserts a queer Latinx diaspora in the US into the structures of Mexican identity. In doing so, his art both challenges the very notion of nation and citizenship, and imagines a queer time and place where fun, joy, and laughter are possible across borders, finding an echo in Juan Gabriel's "El Noa Noa." A song that pays homage to a queer place where everything is different, where people are welcome and can be happy dancing all night long, or as the song lyrics spell it "un lugar de ambiente donde todo es diferente, donde siempre, alegremente, bailarás toda la noche ahí." Played as the soundtrack of a 1981 movie by the same name, the song ties in a tale of an emerging singer, starring Juan Gabriel, who makes kin with sex workers, reminding us of the complicit intimacies among minoritarian queer subjects in the face of austerity and marginalization. Juan Gabriel's presence in Salgado's art thus makes explicit the translocal alliances of queer cultural production, as well as the political solidarities necessary to resist and dodge immigration tactics of capture.

Juan Gabriel's "El Noa Noa" thus becomes a translocal chant of queer Brown joy whose glow has, for instance, inspired Mexican queer artists Liz Misterio, Tadeo Cervantes, and Benjamín Martínez, to form an art collective for "all those fierce beasts who have been expelled from the realm of rationality." Named Instituto de Investigaciones Noa Noa, the collective organizes exhibits showcasing the work of independent queer artists, while providing an alternative forum to the whitened spaces of queer neoliberalism in Mexico City. Interestingly, Juan Gabriel's song forms an anagram for anus in Spanish, "el no*ano*a." By engaging with Juan Gabriel's song titles, both Salgado and other queer artists gesture to revindicate the anus as a site of joy, pleasure, and friendship, despite the word's relation to waste, and expulsion.

To feel and fathom the anus as a backdoor of joy, playfulness, and pleasure, unsettles the heteronormative logics of reproduction. A similar association can be made about the border wall as a point of expulsion or penetration, where queer Brown excess, as Julio's poster art shows, stains the whitened cishet scripts of citizenship, nation, and by extension, immigration. Embodying an unproductive messiness, the backdoors of US immigration hold close resemblance to the anus in that both sites are punished for involving fun, play, and pleasure. In this sense, the sonic waves of Juan Gabriel and Selena takes us to the nightscapes where queer feelings

Fig. 20. Digital logo of "Noa Noa Instituto de Investigaciones."

abound, extending a politics of being present with things, folks, and places that might suddenly disappear. Beyond what is lacking, Julio Salgado's art reminds us of political possibilities, moving bodies into action to radically change the existing order of things. In doing so, the glow of undocumented jotería makes us wonder about what remains once the music ends, enticing us into feeling a Brown space of queer belonging through a diasporic imagination.

The "Wildness" of Jota Nightlife

Wu Tsang's documentary *Wildness* (2012) channels the powerful testimonies and lived experiences of trans Latina migrants searching for intimacy at the Silver Platter, a no-frills queer nightclub in Los Angeles. Borrowing its name from a weekly party organized by the filmmaker and their queer crew, *Wildness* playfully experiments with a night geography in flux, intermixing a magical-realist style to trace the nightly encounters between clubgoers, and a queer performance entourage. From the beginning, this intimate connection is made explicit when director Tsang shares a memory of never wanting to leave the nightclub, "I'll never forget the first time I walked in. I never wanted to leave." Featuring Mariana Marroquin as the voice of the Silver Platter, a trans Latina who migrated from Guatemala to the US in 1998 and at the time of filming worked at the Trans Wellness Center in Los Angeles, the film takes viewers inside the magic grounds of a bar that has existed for over fifty years in a migrant neighborhood quickly gentrifying. While letting the night venue speak for herself as a main protagonist, we follow a cinematic lens that moves across textured walls, traveling sounds, and iridescent lights seen in the glitz of stage curtains, or in the revolving brightness of disco balls, that blend in with urban portraits of buildings, stores, and parking lots found around the MacArthur Park neighborhood.

Tracing a distinct working-class Latinx queer nightscape, Wu Tsang's documentary invites viewers to make kin with trans Latinas by listening to how the Silver Platter lives on as a home for them. Nicol, the welcoming hostess, describes the bar as a bastion for intimacy among trans immigrants from Mexico and Central America. By invoking the Spanish word, "la sala de la casa," or a house living room, she references a comfy space situated inside a bff's home where anyone can relax, rest, and play safely. At this site of comfort, we come into close contact with Karen, Jessica Rodriguez, Jenny, Maricela, Vicki, Monica Love, Nicol, Jackie, and Erika, and through their life stories, we also learn about their journeys of migration to the US, as well as the contradictions producing the nightclub's political economies. Erika, a trans girl that becomes a close friend to the film director, speaks about running away from family turmoil and violence in Central America. After a month and a half of harsh travels, she arrived in Los Angeles, and there a friend took her to the Silver Platter for the first time to have fun, "Cuando llegué al Silver Platter por primera vez, me llevó otra amiga y me dijo 'aquí puedes divertirte, entra.'"

In Erika's story, I find a wild sense of playful fugitivity, not only evident in a pulsating desire to escape and cross the border for a trans life, but also in her looking for a trans migrant space where queer Brownness finds fun, complicity and a home away from home in tune with what José Esteban Muñoz calls "a necessary project of dis-enclosure" in making kin with "the brownness of the world despite the impediments that manifest themselves as enclosure" (2020, 140).[6] In a different scene, Karen feels proud to be there, while her other friend basks in the joy of feeling like

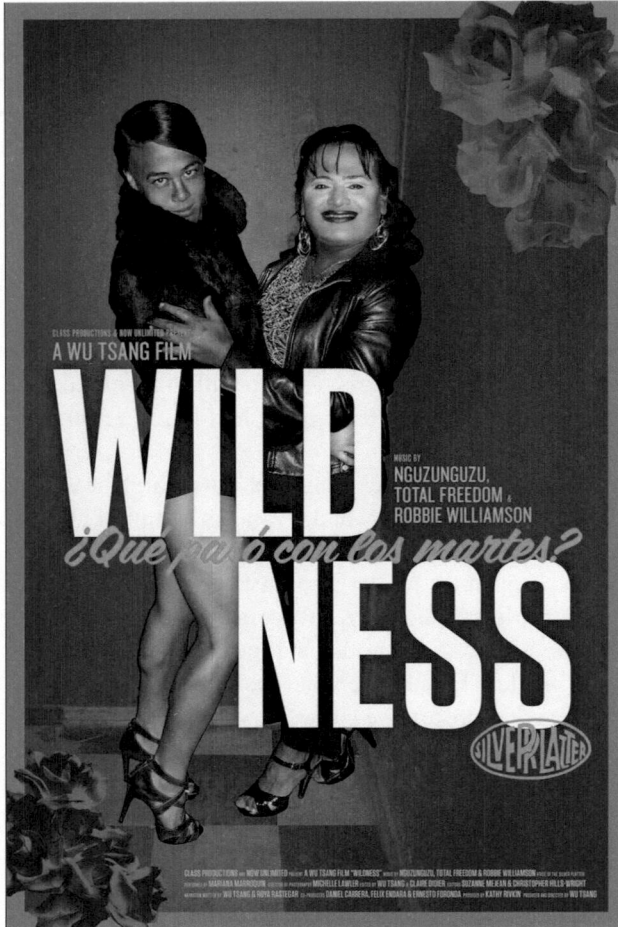

Fig. 21. Film poster of *Wildness* (2012), dir. Wu Tsang.

being in Mexico at the bar. I would like to dwell for a moment in Karen's friend's feeling of being elsewhere, as her comment reveals that the longing for something familiar finds place at the Silver Platter, prompting me to suggest that a lingering afterglow of queer Mexicanidad travels across borders to interact with cinematic sensation and confabulate a nightscape of Latinx jotería through queer relajo. It is not that trans Latinas miss the way they were treated at their places of origin, but that what they seem to long for is found in a nightclub that fosters a sense of belonging embedded in play. Within this nightly ambiance, they feel safe to embrace forms of queer and trans pleasure otherwise punished and forbidden, or as Erika puts it, "Ya estando ya aquí, me siento ya más mejor."

The film portrays scenes of everynight performance like the exhilarating rhythms of salsa, tex-mex, rap, cumbia, and bachata clubgoers dance to, tracking the emergence of a queer Brown sensorium, or as a trans girl phrases it, "pasarla rica." As such, *Wildness* gifts us with scenes of trans Latina joy, not only by portraying them dancing, posing, cheering, and having a good time, but also by framing the nightly designs that turn the inside of a no-frills bar into an invitingly familiar ambiance made of music, sound, warmth, and light. These scenes contain queer Brown diasporic feelings traced, for instance, in the travesti show, "El Show de Morales y sus Geishas," that fills up the stage with drag performances lip-syncing to music of divas like Marisela, Rocío Dúrcal, or Tina Turner. Artistic director Morales describes this type of drag performance that serves a double function of entertaining and educating as uniquely Mexican. As the lens follows the bright pink tulle forming the shoulder frills of a dress worn by a travesti performer singing to Rocío Dúrcal's "Desaires," we might be tempted to find a similar scene at Casa Roshell during a travesti cabaret party in Mexico City like the ones seen in chapter 6, or in the film *Quebranto*, discussed in chapter 4, when Coral lip-syncs to Lucha Villa's "Las Ciudades."

At the risk of overexposure, Tsang lends light to the playful experiences of a trans Latina clientele frequenting the bar, while listening attentively to how they make space at night. Through their playful interactions, trans Latinas learn to navigate the risks the night might hold, as many talk about the safeness of being inside, while enjoying a pair of drinks at the bar. Or, as Nicol frames it, "Not everything is rosy . . . It's like a game of chess. We are all at play here because we are all a part of it, right, with different jobs, but we all complement the Silver Platter." Her comment alludes to the family drama that ensues once co-owner Gonzalo Ramírez dies, leaving his co-owning sister Nora Ramírez in a legal battle over the ownership of the locale with Javier and Koky, Gonzalo's ex-boyfriend. From the vantage point of a working hostess, Nicol's story reveals a deep understanding of the inner dramas playing out in the material economies of the night, as these become inevitably entangled with trans stories of immigration and playfulness. By listening to their stories, the Silver Platter emerges as a refuge for trans Latinas looking to have fun. But beyond having a good time, the film about the Silver Platter has also been immersed in its own polemics. In this fashion, the critical debate around *Wildness* not only exposes an ethics of documentary production, but also points to a politics of consumption, hinting at the ineffable questions of who benefits from making visible trans Latinx underground spaces of play and intimacy, as well as how such spaces might turn unsafe by their overexposure. In this sense, I ponder how and whether queer play can help unmake the necropolitical realities of queer and trans Latinxs in the diaspora.

Eve Oishi remarks that, although negotiating an inherently exploitative medium,[7] Wu Tsang's documentary exposes the tensions between representation and sensationalism around sex work, drug use, and immigration status at this nightclub (2015, 264). A similar critique is voiced by Finn Jackson Ballard's review of the film.[8] According to these critical views, what lies at the core of *Wildness* is precisely an apparent unconscious attempt to partake in an "ongoing process of queer gentrification," that is, of overlooking the risks neoliberal consumption pose to a queer politics of cultural production, like in the film itself. Here lies an example of how the political possibilities of fun, play, and pleasure must undoubtedly navigate the contested territories of queer neoliberalism even when those possibilities might pose dangers. The seeming contradiction of depicting a disenfranchised space while exposing those already at-risk, reminds us of a politics of queer play, of a fine dance between danger and ecstasy, as bell hooks puts it, of who can play at the expenses of others, or in other words, whose queer pleasures are being at stake when we claim our right to play. Although these reviews are important to generating a critical debate around the politics of queer documentary, what remains pivotal to my discussion is to reconsider how the role of play, fun, and pleasure advances or disrupts the very possibilities of survival for marginalized queer and trans folk sitting at the back door of US immigration policy.

Beyond debates on the documentary genre, the film nonetheless renders a productive contradiction by depicting the complicated staging of a queer punk party in a predominantly trans Latina nightclub, rehearsing coalitional, intersectional, and translocal gestures of queer care and solidarity beyond neoliberal gain. By seeking to establish intimacy with the Silver Platter and its night dwellers, like trans Latinas with mixed immigration status, *Wildness* makes possible a desire to inhabit danger and disappointment alongside exposing the scales at which such dangers affect the locations that allows us to play—see for instance the moment in which the queer performance crew's brief running of an immigration clinic fades away. As contested and complicated as it might be, the portrayal of trans fun, joy, and pleasure enacts a wild playful fugitivity that disorders the mechanisms of neoliberal extraction and national containment. Such a space realizes a search for queer Mexicanidad, a feeling that is absorbed by queer Brown diasporic imaginings taking over a night locale like the Silver Platter.

In *Wildness*, a glow of Latinx jotería presents us with an invitation to relax, to grant queer relajo to travesti and trans Latinas experiencing an overexposure to death and violence. As an attempt to outplay a trans necropolitics, I sense in these gestures the reparative and restorative power of fun, joy, and pleasure guiding trans Latinas's desire to remain present at night even when such a possibility is rendered ineffective by other stakes at play. In its portrayal of trans Brown joy, I nonetheless situate in this film a sort of queer relajo channeled through its experimental and kaleidoscopic lens, carrying the residues of queer Mexicanidad. As such, *Wildness* makes visible an affective bridge connecting jota nightlife across borders.

Nightly Occupations of Jotería

At the intersection of 16th and Hoff streets in San Francisco's Mission District, a compilation of vintage clips projected onto the walls of a building show a Latinx drag performer dancing on stage to Nightcrawler's 1995 single "Push the Feeling On." As part of Xandra Ibarra's *The Hook Up/Displacement/Barhopping/Drama Tour* (2017) performance, which received the 2018 Queer/Art/Prize for Recent Work, the footage takes us back to queer Latinx nightclubs that once existed in the Mission where, according to a voice off in Spanish, sex happened inside restrooms in a pre-AIDS time.[9] Showing static lines, visually marking a passing of time, from VHS tapes to digital video, the clip ends with a sequence of lyrics on-repeat from Grace Jones's 1989 "Love me forever," tracking the phrase "Love These Filthy Walls Forever." Recalling a queer fantasyland where Latinx gay migrants, travesti beauties, butch lesbians, and queer women prance in a Brown, emerald city, Ibarra's video brings back to life a Juan Gabriel impersonator that drags sweaty dancers onto the stage. As the video keeps on playing across a busy intersection, another drag queen on screen wearing a distinct "china poblana" dress, a regional attire signaling Mexican cultural identity, lip-syncs to Linda Ronstadt's "Por un amor." Devising a sort of media archaeology of the night, Ibarra's mixtape tracks the flows of feeling as a way of archiving, indexing, and recording the intensities of queer nightlife.

Playfully resisting the racial cleansing undergoing the city since the late 1990s (Rodríguez 2021), Xandra Ibarra describes her performance as "an effort to resurface the 'messy' and 'sucio' spirits of queer Latino and lesbian ghosts from gentrified sites in San Francisco" (2017). I situate in Ibarra's nightly occupation a remapping of jotería, that is, that queer and trans Brown joy dwells not only in the dirty walls of queer bars and night-clubs, but because of their material absence, also moves through and lives on imprinted in the bodies of queer minorities and migrants. Ibarra situates ritualistic bar steps to revive a night ambiance that carries on indefinitely in the bodily memories of attendees. Invoking a queer past through moves and sensations, the queer mob spends time improvising other walls that sustain queer pleasure through their physical bodies, rebuilding absent infrastructures through queer relajo. The collective performance, I argue, not only opens space for queerness, but in doing so, also rehearses forms of playful fugitivity that exceed the spatial boundaries of hetero- and homonormative consumption, as well as of national containment.

Like Wu Tsang's *Wildness*, Ibarra's performance awakens what Juana María Rodríguez calls "a shared sensorium, a collective recognition of belonging that might endure in the afterlife of gentrification" (2021, 211). The clip evokes the warmth of people walking around, the loudness of a drag queen's laughter, or the smell of bodies in motion. While the camera tracks a bright-lit yellow sign hanging outside that reads "Esta Noche," the music beats across images mixing with a moving mob of Latinx queers and lesbians grouping up under streetlights, doing what they would usually do inside a now-nonexistent club. Xandra's performance shows a queer crowd playing out in the streets, posting counterfeit city notices. They are out to summon the queer spirits of flirting, kissing, dancing, and sweating, all contained within a yearning desire to have fun, *echar relajo*, amid queer displacement by performing outside five permanently shut down queer bars in San Francisco, in specific La India Bonita (1970s–1996), Amelia's (1978–91), the Lexington Club (1997–2015), Osento's Bathhouse (1979–2008), and Esta Noche (1979–2014).

Across walls, the sounds of Juan Gabriel's "Yo no sé qué me pasó" captured in Xandra's video, might have inspired travesti women, gay men, or Latina lesbians to come out at night as a way of facing oppression. This Juan Gabriel's song speaks of letting go as the lyrics tell the story of a lover's breakup. The singer's distinct voice announces a sudden end, "Es verdad que te amé" (It is true that I loved you), inviting an ex-lover to find love again, "tarde o temprano/volverás a ver la luz." In this instance, Juan Gabriel sings about ending things with someone hoping to find a better place for queer love. Similarly, many queer and trans migrants, like myself, feel a deep connection to this song as it alludes to a search for a better life in their experiences of migration. At times, they might only find disappointment and heartbreak, as in the way US immigration policies treats Brown, undocumented queer/trans migrants. But the song also emerges as a hymn of resilience and care in the face of adversity and precarity. By singing Mexican songs in harsh places, queer and trans Brown migrants find a sense of queer joy in Spanish music, like in Juan Gabriel's, across the Latinx diaspora. Within the confines of queer bars, like *Esta Noche*, an excess of queer Brown joy is not only found in song, dance, and fun, but also assembles nightscapes of collective emotion, as in feeling loss alongside dancing bodies drenched in sweat. As Iván Ramos reminds us about this queer underground,

> Esta Noche was an explicitly *working class* Latino gay bar that catered to a queer Latino microcosm of culture, adoration, and desires. It carved an autonomous space that wasn't subjected to gay white male nightlife. Sure, it had its own politics, problems, and dramas, but it was a hideaway to the whiteness imposed otherwise in the gay mecca. (2015, 135)

Gentrification in San Francisco has pushed poor, working-class, and racialized communities, out of historically migrant neighborhoods, making us ponder about how the access to queer nightlife might be a luxury not many are able to afford even in a place that prides itself on being the home of LGBTQ+ rights. During the performance, the posting on the wall of a counterfeit city notice, "Public Notice of Application of Jotx Pleasure," seeks to undo the neoliberal violence of queer displacement, as well as inspire modes of spatial resistance through play. As a translocal manifestation of queer Mexicanidad and Latinx jotería, jota pleasures move across and against borders. In the fake notice signed by "Los Jodios/The Fucked Peepo," the artist positions marginalized queers and trans migrants as agents reclaiming an underground space from racial gentrification. This gesture of taking back a dirty queerness, alluded to in "los jodidos," echoes a sense of queer relajo or, as Ibarra spells it, "Puras Mamadas" (Pure Blow

Jobs, Pure Bullshit), of not taking things seriously, and of embracing a queer looseness to relax the neoliberal grip holding onto the sites of queer Brown diasporic imagination. As such, this street occupation teases out a spatial politics of queer play, as living costs and rent prices continue to rise in the Mission District.

When looking at other images of the performance, we find Xandra Ibarra leaning against and kissing a black wall. As her lips pout provocatively, her kiss reminds us of a different time and place, retracing a queer past that, somehow, remains imprinted in the memories our bodies hold of a long-gone *Esta Noche*. The images of the performance show heart drawings, and the writings on the sidewalk spells "Puta Live 4ever," in reference to Ethnic Studies scholar Juana María Rodríguez's *Puta Life: Seeing Latinas, Working Sex* (2023). In a different picture, the artist lies on the street as if making out with pavement cracks, holding a cigarette in her lips. By reenacting scenes of kissing and flirting, the performance plays with what might have taken place inside nightclubs. Like a kiss imprinted into a wall, the circuits of touch between bodies and places enacted in Ibarra's performance, make visible the ways in which queer Latinxs carry the residues of the night—a cigarette butt, a tune, a phone number, a dance move, or a kiss—into the habits and structures of everyday life. Queer touch thus places fun, play, and pleasure as a critical affect to sense out the un/making of space, reaching into a playful fugitivity that, as a residual force, disarrays cishet understandings of time and place. Emerging as bodily traces of the past, the hauntings of queer Brown joy spark modes of spatial resistance, establishing intergenerational coalitions to reimagine the possibilities of queer remembrance in the here and now.

Resisting the spatial displacement of queer undergrounds, the performance makes us consider the interconnections between the erasure of queer Brown joy and the flows of neoliberal capital. In the absence of physical space, *The Hook Up Tour* occupies public streets and structures to bring out the affective potency of joy, playfulness, and pleasure imprinted in the material remnants of buildings, as well as in queer/trans bodies. By displaying kissing, dancing, and touching in the open, Ibarra invokes residual memories to reactivate queer Brown sensations in the now, while rearranging affectively the gentrified landscape of the Mission. The *Hook Up Tour* thus performs a nightly occupation by channeling the filth of Brownness into the heightened whiteness of San Francisco, reminding its hipster economies that jota pleasure carries on.

Sociologist Héctor Carrillo notes that nightlife not only inscribes a moment for play, but also a space for socialization, collective partici-pation, and belonging distinct from everyday life for queer Mexicans at home and abroad (2002, x). While considering the importance of queer nightlife translocally, across borders, it remains vital to critically ques-tion who might benefit from such play, who can and has access to it, at what cost, and whether such subversive acts of joy reinforce or disrupt the mechanisms that have contributed to queer displacement. As I have traced a lingering afterglow of queer Mexicanidad in Julio Salgado, Wu Tsang, and Xandra Ibarra, these examples of queer/trans Latinx perfor-mance and media enact modes of playful resistance to fugitively circum-vent neoliberal extraction and national containment.

In today's Mission District, a scene of gentrification picturing fancy sex shops, coffee shops, restaurants, and boutiques, evokes a similar picture of spatial rearrangement occurring in Mexico City, signaling that the Brown queer/trans experiences of economic violence in the US and Mexico hold similarities despite geopolitical configurations. Seen as wasteful and excessive through a neoliberal lens, queer Mexican nightlife, as the cul-tural artifacts and performances in this book have hopefully unbound, is made of feelings and sensations flowing across places and spaces to grap-ple with unproductivity. As I've felt these nightscapes, queer/trans/travesti Mexicans, and Latinxs alike, employ complex and wild tactics to mediate and negotiate with flows of capital, while weaving fugitive infrastructures through play to fend off transregional violence. The scale at which these mediations happen might minimize a level of extraction, highlighting communal modes of caring. In these very scenes, queer/trans Brown feel-ings of playfulness reshape relationships with space. Tellingly, the queer undergrounds respond to a queer hemispheric formation emerging amid the affective economies of neoliberal relationality. Along their counter-parts across the US-Mexico border, these queer undergrounds provide queer/travesti/trans Brown folk with sustenance filled with playfulness, joy, and pleasure.

Queer Mexicanidad appears and disappears as a flickering disco ball illuminating the dance floor, bringing queer relajo as a possibility to carve spaces of connection, and complicity. Manifesting a glowing jotería into our practices of cultural analysis inspires a revitalization of critique as a playful and disruptive act. As the musical notes of Juan Gabriel and Selena might remind us, a queer hemispheric critique is not about interpreta-tion, or reiteration, but rather about a vital choreography of critique that accounts for what has already taken place but remains unseen, untouched,

and untamed, and must remain so as such. In these final words, I channel the fierceness of my co-conspirator Piña Colada, to bestow you with
a rhinestone-studded wand of queer hemispheric analysis that, emerging from the queer nightscapes of Mexicanidad and its diaspora, casts a
playful spell into the wild geographies of the night, for you to become
overwhelmed by the unknown, to feel what's around us, and still find a
renewed sense of dirtiness lingering after dark.

Notes

Introduction

1. According to data compiled by the state Secretary of Security and Citizenship Protection, a total of 827 femicides were reported in 2023, while the number of trans-feminicides in the period 2008–2023 amounts to 701 as per Transgender Europe. See https://drive.google.com/file/d/1wAeP-Woy4z2jVrA5X49nWLNMbKTUvtnQ/view, and https://transrespect.org/en/map/trans-murder-monitoring/, respectively. In 2020, Reuters called out a deadly surge of extreme violence toward LGBTQ+ people unlike anything else seen in half a decade, https://www.reuters.com/article/idUSKBN22R37X/

2. At the time of the city elections in 2012, Mancera became the nominee of the left-winged political alliance between the PRD, the Labor Party, and the Citizens' Movement Party. The alliance later dissolved shortly after winning the election, and morphed into MORENA, the National Regeneration Movement, the party that has occupied the seat of the Mexican presidency under the aegis of Andrés Manuel López Obrador (AMLO) in 2018. After AMLO's six-year term, the MORENA candidate Claudia Sheinbaum Pardo became the first woman to hold that office after winning the 2024 presidential election. Sheinbaum's impressive qualifications as a politician, scientist, and academic made her stand as a top contender for the Mexican presidency despite her continued commitment to AMLO's Fourth Transformation policies, for which Sheinbaum has received criticism from feminist groups.

3. See the LGBTTTI-Friendly City Declaration, https://www.cipdh.gob.ar/catalogo-politicas-publicas/en/politica-publica/acuerdo-por-el-que-se-declara-a-la-ciudad-de-mexico-ciudad-amigable-con-la-poblacion-lesbico-gay-bisexual-transexual-travesti-transgenero-e-intersexual-lgbttti-declaratoria-cdmx-ciudad-a/

4. In 2019, La Cañita caught the attention of the *L.A. Times* after the venue was targeted for arson. Although the newspaper op-ed piece recounted the constant friction between the lesbian couple who managed the site, and their neighbors, the queer dive subsequently closed due to a conflict of interests between Diana J. Torres and partner Ali Gardoki. In its place, Travesura, another queer femme speakeasy, opened in June 2023.

5. While the scholarly debate revealed the homoerotic tensions in the construction of a masculine subject as an embodiment of the modern nation, the single issue of masculine homosexuality cast into shadows other possibilities of queer and trans intimacy.

6. In this sense, Mexican nationalism has crafted, and continues to craft "attractive"

commodities out of popular cultural practices, such as festivities, dances, or rituals, to create circuits of value that extract from working-class, popular, and minoritarian socio-economic locations.

7. Portilla directs our attention to how relajo holds situational value, which is then, commodified to make things happen. That is, any value possesses an embodied quality that moves people into action, "we can say that *relajo* is possible only when value appears embodied in a repository or agent that can be a person, an institution, or a situation, and at the same [39] time, the value calls on my support in order for it to acquire full reality" (Sánchez 2012, 146–47).

8. Under the influence of Spanish-exile José Gaos, the Grupo Hiperión, or the Hyperion group, is formed by a clique of young intellectuals in 1948, including Leopoldo Zea, Emilio Uranga, Jorge Portilla, Ricardo Guerra, Joaquín Sánchez Macgrégor, Salvador Reyes Nevares, Fausto Vega, and Luis Villoro. Mostly drawing from Martin Heidegger, Maurice Merleau-Ponty, and Jean-Paul Sartre, the group proposed diverging, and contradictory takes on a Mexican ethos, as their first task concerned finding the essence of *mexicanidad*, or Mexicanness, in lived experience, history, and culture to reflect on the universality of a human condition (Hurtado 1994, 274). Based on psychoanalysis, hermeneutics, phenomenology, and existentialism, the group conceives a philosophy oriented toward action and agency (Sánchez 2012, 26). From this group, Jorge Portilla stands for an analysis of relajo, a defining character of Mexicanidad that names one's ability to detach and veer away from a system of values.

9. For the English equivalent, I quote Carlos Alberto Sánchez's translation of Portilla's *Fenomenología del relajo*, which appears fully translated from Spanish into English in the appendix of the former's *The Suspension of Seriousness* (SUNY, 2012).

10. In this sense, Jorge Portilla's phenomenology of relajo locates an antisocial affect of playfulness that echoes a queer praxis of disorientation present in Sara Ahmed's *Queer Phenomenology* (2006), when the latter argues that, "The queer subject within straight culture hence deviates and is made socially present as deviant" (20–21).

11. Grappling with the magnitude of queer Brown femme media influencer Mark Aguhar, Roy Pérez names "critical flippancy" the very gesture of laughing back at power as a form of reinverting the hierarchies of racism, fatphobia, and transphobia. In the Mexican context, a form of critical flippancy is present in the drag cabaret of Las Hermanas Vampiro who use "perreo" to invert structures of homophobia, misogyny, and transphobia in Mexico. Antonio Marquet examines Las Hermanas Vampiro's deployment of perreo.

12. Borrowing from Shane Vogel's "model of situational 'tightness' and 'looseness'" (79), I fathom queer relajo as an embodied gesture through which Mexico City's night scenes expand, stick, and retract based on the spatial, material, and affective structures around them. In short, I call those nighttime expansions, retractions, and attachments, *queer nightscapes*.

13. https://www.proceso.com.mx/opinion/2016/9/27/el-fa-bu-lo-so-imperio-gay-17 1260.html

14. A case in point leads to queer feminist scholar Elizabeth Freeman's proposal of "sense-methods" that "consist of bodywork, of inarticulated or unspoken, carnal forms of knowledge, intervention, and affiliation inhabited and performed either in groups or on behalf of them" (2019, 11).

15. Guided by "the spirit of *doing* queerness," a method of queer relajo builds on what José Esteban Muñoz describes "as a modality of inquiry [that] can surpass the play of interpretation and the limits of epistemology and open new ground by focusing on what acts and objects do in a social matrix," extending a political commitment to "anti-rigor and anti-evidence," in "*making* queer worlds" (1996, 12).

16. Borrowing from Arjun Appadurai's "suffix -scape," queer nightscapes points to the wavering flows of global capital moving through the cracks of "economy, history, and politics" to emphasize the "political situatedness of different sorts of actors" (1996, 33) shaping the manifestations of queer worldmaking in the global arena of late capitalism.

17. See, for instance, Cristina Pacheco's *Los dueños de la noche* (1990), and María José Cuevas's *Bellas de noche* (2016).

18. Tracing the central position capitalism occupies within the decolonial feminism of María Lugones, Sylvia Wynter, and Sayak Valencia, Ashley J. Bohrer expands on a decolonial anticapitalist feminism that is "irreducibly polycentric" in accounting for "the multiple relays among capitalism, colonization, and heterosexism" (537) in the global south.

19. Unlike trajectories of labor and racial formations in the US, the Mexican context offers a complicated history of the making of ethnoraciality, as the erasure of Blackness and Brownness has been molecularly intertwined with narratives of mestizaje, which have served as the main narrative anchor for the emergence of neoliberal rationality. To be white in Mexico does not simply mean having fair skin, but it also means to occupy a socioeconomic location that allows for the projection of white mestizaje to engage with other forms of (white) value elsewhere. In other words, to be white-xican, or the name people commonly use to name white Mexicans in popular jargon, means to embody an alliance to genealogies of miscegenation as a way of "improving one's race," or what people commonly say in Spanish, *mejorar la raza*, a popular saying that reveals the embedded racism in notions of Mexicanidad.

20. Examining the transnational and global manifestations of Asian queerness in Singaporean performance, Eng-Beng Lim calls this framework "glocalqueering" to complicate the progressive politics linked to the "global propagation of Western gay culture" (383).

Chapter 1

1. They write, "The relation between inclusion, money, and peripheral neighborhoods promotes a rhetoric that is the opposite of that of austerity and manages to unify inclusion and exploitation under financial apparatuses. What becomes clear is that these popular, precarious, and feminized economies, which were previously visualized as insignificant and merely subsidiary, have turned into territories that are dynamic and attractive for capital, expanding the frontiers of its valorization and creating new consumers, beyond the guarantee of the wage. Debt thus becomes an apparatus that is increasingly tied to new labor forms, which are largely not waged in the traditional sense (which does not mean that the wage does not still operate in a complementary and intermittent way)." (2021, 9)

Chapter 2

1. In Latin America, the figure of the transvestite was originally used to refer to the deviant practice of cross-dressing. One of the most commemorated cases is the incident of *Los 41*, a police raid that irrupted a private party in the social elite of Mexico City in 1901. The novel under the name, *Los 41*, was published by Eduardo Castrejón and served as one of an early representation of drag culture in Latin/x America. In literature, the representation of drag queens, travesti, and transgender people is often intermixed as those gender and performative categories were not even in use to name political subjectivities until the last decade of the twentieth century. Such categories, however, denote a gender transgression and delineate a politics of sexual dissidence. For instance, José Donoso's *El lugar sin límites* (1966) marks a strong protagonist associated with the transgressive image of the travesti. An adaptation of that movie under the direction of Mexican filmmaker Arturo Ripstein in 1978 popularizes the image of "la vestida." Carlos Montenegro's *Hombres sin mujer* (1928), and Manuel Puig's *El beso de la mujer araña* (1976) situate the travesti in the prison system as a problematic space of virility, violence, and disaffection. Severo Sarduy's essay *La simulación* (1982) elaborates a complex aesthetic treaty on drag queens, that appeared as protagonist of his previous novels, *De donde son los cantantes* (1967), and *Cobra* (1972). Sarduy's essays could mark the start of a literary account of drag culture that merges performativity, materiality, and gender transgression to craft a nightly queer icon in Latin America and its diasporas. At the end of the twentieth century, Pedro Lemebel's *Loco afán: crónicas de sidario* (1996) and Mario Bellatín's *Salón de belleza* (1999) have depicted the struggle of travestis during the AIDS pandemic. In Cuba, Leonardo Padura's *El cazador* (1991) describes a melancholic protagonist in search of love. Both drag culture and transgendered categories, albeit their differences, have been intertwined in the realm of cultural representation. Nonetheless, a more complex and sophisticated characterization of this strand of sexual dissidence emerged in twenty-first-century Latin/x American cultural production. In television, the night show *Desde Gayola* (2002–2013) hosted by Horacio Villalobos became a media sensation in which drag queens and transgender artists made use of parody and satire to ridicule conservative institutions of Mexico, and other Spanish-speaking countries, including the US.

2. Resonating with Verta Taylor and Leila J. Rupp's argument, these genealogies fathom "that transgenderism, same-sex sexuality, and theatrical performance are central to the personal identities of [. . .] drag queens, who use drag to forge personal and collective identities that are [. . .] their own complex genders" (2004, 114).

3. In tracing the representation of drag queens in queer Latin/x American narratives, Ben. Sifuentes-Jáuregui notes that "[r]ather, as [Pedro] Lemebel points out, it's a matter of engaging with a Baroque allegory, the act of extending the name of the metaphor *ad infinitum*, to twist and turn the name so that it gets baptized continuously. In other words, the drag queen's (or the drag queer's) name never stops signifying (or resignifying itself) until exhaustion" (2014, 122). Drag can be read as a representation of *horror vacui* through which "drag queers," to borrow Sifuentes-Jáuregui's presence of drag in queer cultures, makes sense of time and space through fragmentation and excess.

4. Antonio Marquet's *El Coloquio de las Perras* (2010) serves as the first photo-ethnography on Las Hermanas Vampiro, the first drag performance troupe who staged

weekly roasts in Mexico City's Zona Rosa bars in the early 2000s. The queer scholar draws from queer slang in Mexico, namely "joteo" and "perreo," to expand on and situate a drag taxonomy beyond English term equivalents like "draga."

5. In *Neoliberalism from Below: Popular Pragmatics & Baroque Economies* (2017), Gago explains the hybrid nature of Latin American popular economies and the complex microeconomies systems that are propelled as a response to the extractive logics of neoliberal accumulation *from above*. Baroque economies are, according to this author, "a set of interlaced modes of doing, thinking, perceiving, fighting, and working, which supposes the superimposition of nonreconciled term in permanent re-recreation" (14).

6. Here, I am drawing from José Esteban Muñoz's concept of dissing identity: "These identities-in-difference emerge from a failed interpellation within the dominant sphere. Their emergence is predicated on their ability to disidentify with the mass public and instead, through this disidentification, contribute to the function of a counterpublic sphere." (1999, 7)

7. Blanco further explains that the abundance of queer life shatters hierarchies of domination, "[y] el hecho concreto de que alguien viva de otro modo—mucho más si ese alguien se multiplica en cientos, miles o millones—rompe la unanimidad imprescindible para establecer una dominación vertical en la sociedad" (1981, 184).

8. According to queer theory in the US, Elizabeth Freeman's *Time Binds* and Jack Halberstam's *In a Queer Time & Place*, articulate a critique of temporal linearity, or straight time, within the neoliberal dynamics of post capitalism and their impact on the development of a queer culture of resistance. José Joaquín Blanco's essays precede a similar argumentation regarding the neoliberal and capitalist logics being set in place in the 1980s in Mexico, while warning against depoliticized acts of sexual transgression.

9. At the intersection of materiality, history, and glamour, Wayne Koestenbaum passionately reflects on a series of codes that constitute what he calls an "opera queen:" "Diva gowns tell stories. Narratives arise from the seams and the turbans and the fine threads of many colors. Each part of the gown of the coiffure carries with it a period reference, a vanished code . . . The secret that the diva gown conceals is a lack of taste, or too much taste, taste grown grotesquely independent of its context" (122). This capacity of objects to narrate and transmit knowledge is an element of what I refer to as *broken record*.

10. By shedding new light on the ways African diasporic visual and music practices, like hip-hop, engage "surface aesthetics," Krista A. Thompson exposes the commodification of Black bodies in the economies of capitalism, highlighting "how prevailing scopic regimes configured notions of race, both the supposed transparency of whiteness and the glare of blackness" (2015, 233).

11. In the context of the Americas, situating queer epistemologies that consider the contradictions between cultural practices of consumption and queer desire in a neoliberal era, requires activists, writers, and scholars to question the sites from which the very concept of queerness and its several manifestations are articulated. Although the term *queer* per se corresponds to a slur in English, its localization, translation, mediation, and politicization have reignited a debate on the cultural contingencies of sexual dissidence across the Americas. In the context of Latin America, the term finds its equivalent in words such as *joto, marica, pájaro, maricón, tortillera, bollera, cuir*, among others. The term *travesti* not only highlights the contradictions of sexual identity, but also insists

on a performative practice of gender insubordination. Adopting an intersectional approach, the work of Jaime Manrique, *Eminent Maricones* (1999), intertwines homosexuality, diaspora, queer writing, and autobiography to unveil a kind of engaged writing that "defies the definition of what a maricón is supposed to be" (113). Manrique's contribution also points to a necessary geopolitical positioning and an ethical commitment to the cultural criticism around sexually dissident cultures. As in the case of several authors situated in the US, including José Esteban Muñoz, Laura G. Gutiérrez, Juana María Rodríguez, Marcia Ochoa, Deborah Vargas, Larry La Fountain-Stokes, Salvador Vidal-Ortiz, Diana Taylor, and Héctor Domínguez-Ruvalcaba, along with a host of emerging queer and trans scholars of color, cultural criticism, ethics, and politics intersect to inform a theoretical and methodological framework. A queer analytic in the Americas has benefited from hemispheric and multidirectional dialogues with critics, such as Diego Falconí Travéz, Sayak Valencia, Julieta Paredes, Yolanda Arroyo Pizarro, Verónica Gago, Ochy Curiel, Sandra Álvarez, Norge Espinosa, Alberto Abreu, Leticia Sabsay, Giuseppe Campuzano, Antonio Marquet, Norma Mogrovejo, Richard Miskolci, Rodrigo Parrini, to name but a few academics, as well as with countercultural and underground artistic collectives and activist enclaves. In resonance with David William Foster's invitation to move beyond the tyranny of patriarchal textual criticism, queer genealogies, epistemologies, and ontologies from Latinx America can establish generative engagements with popular, digital, visual, and mass media subcultures, from urban, rural, and transregional spaces. In the case of Mexico and drag cabaret performance, or travestismo, the work of Carlos Monsiváis, Antonio Marquet, Benjamín Martínez, Tadeo Cervantes, Alex Xavier Aceves Bernal, Mirna Roldán, Mipanocha Rurru, Liz Misterio, Paul Julian Smith, Miguel Capistrán, Oswaldo Calderón, Michael K. Schuessler, or Antonio Bertrán, and Rodrigo Laguarda, have been pivotal in tracing and mapping out a queer subculture in Mexico.

12. In the afterlives of the COVID pandemic, I was lucky to find this short-lived community hub and drag performance stage run by Pittsburgh-based drag queen and visual artist Jenna Sais Quoi. Greeted by the generosity of this fierce queen, I attended a couple of drag workshops before the shop permanently closed, and like a shiny butterfly, it transformed into the now-running Harold's Haunt queer bar in Millvale, around the greater Pittsburgh area.

13. Roberto Cabral's comment comes up in an interview done for the magazine *TimeOut Mexico* in June 2017. See, https://www.timeoutmexico.mx/ciudad-de-mexico /gay-y-lesbico/roberto-cabral-la-drag-cabaretera-de-la-cdmx

14. Of note in Cabral's performance is the direct reference to Pedro Almodóvar's *Pepi, Luci, Bom y otras chicas del montón* (1980). In particular, the performance title signals the countercultural ideology and aesthetics commonly associated with *la movida madrileña*. Even if Cabral's performance does not include an Almodovarian plot, its title foretells a transgressive theme.

15. Denis de Rougemont, in *Love in the Western World* (1939), traces the historical basis for the social construction of the myth of romantic love. The author argues that the practices of courtship, the marital ceremony of ring exchanging, and monogamy, were misappropriations of secret religious customs of the Cathars, who were accused, chased, and persecuted in the Cathar heresy during the thirteenth century. Despite the original purposes of such religious practices, de Rougemont's account serves to historically trace

the association between intimacy, progress, and development, especially when considering that courtship practices are understood under a teleology of transcendence. In this sense, the social bonding that leads to finding love is framed within a structure of temporal ascension and would be irrupted and flawed if such structure is jettisoned.

16. On September 10, 2016, various conservative groups of a catholic-based ideology marched out in the streets in 19 Mexican states, including Aguascalientes, Jalisco, and Chiapas, to express their opposition against Enrique Peña Nieto's proposed bill for equal marriage, and adoption rights for same-sex marriages across the country. The so-called *Marcha de la Familia* served as a precedent for the official spokesperson of the archdiocese of Mexico, to claim that a homosexual dictatorship was on the rise. The incendiary claim, "Imperio gay en México," took a different turn when it became a social media phenomenon.

17. In the original Spanish version of *Gore Capitalism*, which was published in English by MIT Press in 2018, Valencia argues, "Por ello, pensemos el dolor como un recurso político que no debe confinarnos a la inacción sino a la elaboración de un proceso reflexivo que nos lleve a una identificación con el sufrimiento mismo y a tejer redes intersubjetivas que sean capaces de exigir un redireccionamiento en la forma que entendemos la economía y de enfrentarnos a sus consecuencias distópicas que tienen como blanco nuestros cuerpos." (2010, 197)

18. One of the most obvious differences between drag cabaret performance at small box theaters and nightclubs is that at the latter the entrance fee is cheaper. As such, the cabaret performance of Las Hermanas Vampiro at Papi Fun Bar, or Carlos Bieletto, and even Roberto Cabral, at El Almacén, have a wider reception within the queer circuits of consumption than those offered at performance stages, such as the work of Tito Vasconcelos at Cabaretito, or Las Reinas Chulas during the International Cabaret Festival at El Vicio.

19. These quotes from the original newspaper article in Spanish are found in "El amor; único bastión del teatro La Capilla: Jesusa Rodríguez." *Periódico La Jornada*, 25 de enero de 2013. http://www.jornada.unam.mx/2013/01/25/cultura/a03n1cul

20. During the month of August, this performance venue houses, annually, The International Festival of Cabaret, as one of the few cultural spaces to promote the popular genre of cabaret in Mexico. *Las Reinas Chulas*, an all-female cabaret troupe formed in 1998 by Marisol Gasé, Cecilia Sotres, Ana Francis Mor and Nora Huerta, regularly perform at *Teatro-bar El Vicio*. Their cabaret performances also play with political satire and incorporate drag into their performances. For more information about this cabaret troupe, visit: https://lasreinaschulas.com/webreinas/nosotras/

21. The International Festival of Cabaret has also chosen *El Foro A Poco No, Teatro Cabaret*, as part of its performance venues during the annual festival in Mexico City. All of these venues are located along the street *República de Cuba*, in downtown Mexico City. In August 2017, an envoy of local government authorities closed a series of downtown bars, including *El Oasis* and *Bar Viena*, on the premise that such venues lacked the proper official documentation that certified their functioning. The LGBT collectives in Mexico City read this closure as a radical measure to dismantle a gay corridor in the downtown core, deploying the principles of social cleansing to minimize queer night life in the city: https://www.excelsior.com.mx/comunidad/2017/08/18/1182469

22. Soy honesta con él y contigo

A él lo quiero y a ti te he olvidado
Si tú quieres seremos amigos
Yo te ayudo a olvidar el pasado
No te aferres
Ya no te aferres, a un imposible
Ya no te hagas ni me hagas más daño
Tú bien sabes que no fue mi culpa
Tú te fuiste sin decirme nada
Y a pesar que lloré como nunca
Yo seguía de ti enamorada
Pero te fuiste
Y que regresabas, no me dijiste
Y sin más nada, ¿por qué? No sé
Pero fue así, así fue
Te brindé la mejor de las suertes
Me propuse no hablarte ni verte
Y hoy que has vuelto ya ves, solo hay nada
Ya no puedo ni debo quererte
Ya no te amo
Me he enamorado, de un ser divino
De un buen amor
Que me enseñó a olvidar
Y a perdonar.

23. Carlos Monsiváis argues that Juan Gabriel acquired a mythical presence that forged a very unique market in Mexican popular culture: "Un ídolo es un convenio multigeneracional, la respuesta emocional a la falta de preguntas sentimentales, una versión difícilmente perfeccionable de la alegría, el espíritu romántico, la suave o agresiva ruptura de la norma" (266).

24. *Desde Andalucía* released in 1988 was a success on Latin Music charts, such as the 1988–1989 US *Billboard* for Latin Pop Albums. And, in 1989 was awarded the "Lo Nuestro" Award by Univisión. "Así Fue" was the best-preforming Latin single of 1998 in the US, and won the American Society of Composers, Authors, and Publishers' Latin Award for "Super Song of the Year" in 1999.

Chapter 3

1. Here I draw from Eva Hayward's notion of emplacement to bring "attention to texture, animation, galvanizing drives, such that emplacing is defined by the quality of invigoration and its transfiguration of future emerging, of sense and species that may yet emerge" (2010, 592).

2. I first met Lia in 2015 when I returned to live in Mexico City for a summer while doing research with a young group of queer and trans artists, activists, and intellectuals whose work I have been in dialogue with since the start of my academic career as an assistant professor. After meeting some of Lia's contemporaries like Tadeo Cervantes,

Jessica Marjane, Liz Misterio, and Mipanochia Rurru at a party hosted by Mirna Roldán in the neighborhood Santa María la Ribera, I was asked to contact the absent performer via Facebook. As with any first encounter with a stranger, Lia remained skeptical but invited me out to join her performance inside the Metro Pino Suárez. Since that first encounter, Lia and I have been conspiring together to reach a wider audience with her performances abroad in the US, specifically at the University of Pittsburgh in Pennsylvania, where her work has been featured in 2019, 2021, and 2022.

3. *El metro Pino Suárez*, as it's known in Mexican Spanish, is a vital transfer station located blocks away from Mexico City's Zócalo square. At the intersection of two major subway lines, the pink (Line 1: Observatorio-Pantitlán) and blue (Line 2: Cuatro Caminos-Taxqueña), the Pino Suárez station sits on the remains of what was once a large ceremonial center for Nahua culture. Along its underground structures, the station features the ruins of a pyramid and a circular altar dedicated to the Aztec god of wind, Ehecatl, forming a square of connecting tunnels. The station opened in 1969 as the first transfer point, and since has housed a commercial corridor filled with shops, temporary art exhibits and cultural displays providing a pit stop for busy commuters, as they make their way in and out of the downtown core.

4. *Próxima Estación* stems from a decolonial workshop conducted by the performer in 2012. Since then, the performance has been restaged transnationally under different names across Europe, Mexico, and the US, in cities like Madrid, Mexico City, and Boston, to name but a few. In 2016, García began another encuentro afectivo, *Proyecto 10Bis*, in which the performer would engage artistically with a group of male-bodied inmates at one of Mexico City's prisons.

5. Tiempo de vals es el tiempo hacia atrás
Donde hacerlo de siempre es volver a empezar
Cuando el mundo se para y te observa girar
Es tiempo para amar
Tiempo de vals, tiempo para sentir
Y decir sin hablar y escuchar sin oír
Un silencio que rompe en el aire un violín
Es tiempo de vivir
Bésame en tiempo de vals
Un, dos, tres; un, dos, tres,
Sin parar de bailar
Haz que este tiempo de vals
Un, dos, tres; un, dos, tres,
No termine jamás
(Waltz time is traveling back in time
Where the usual makes you restart
Where the world halts to see you spin around
It's time for loving
Waltz time is time for feeling
And to speak with no words
And to hear with no sounds
The silence in the air brakes a violin
It's time for living

Kiss me in waltz time
One, two, three; one, two, three
Without ceasing to dance
Make this waltz time
One, two, three; one, two, three
A never-ending time)

6. Lia García's transfeminist pedagogy repositions bodily touch as an intimate gesture to undo the necropolitics of trans life in Mexico. García defines her aesthetics of "tactility" in the following video, https://www.youtube.com/watch?v=2lpe5Meif5s

7. https://transrespect.org/en/map/trans-murder-monitoring/

8. I am referring to the Dance of the 41, a drag ball in the Mexican elites that was raided by police in Mexico City. The event marks the public exposure of homosexuality in modern Mexico. Although a social panic around homosexuality is evident in the media coverage of the event at the time, the Dance of the 41 also marks the early criminalization of queer nightlife.

9. Désert, Jean-Ulrick. "Queer Space," in *Queers in Space: Communities, Publics Spaces, Sites of Resistance*, edited by Gordon Brent, Anne-Marie Bouthillette, and Yolanda Retter (Seattle: Bay Press, 1997), p. 20.

10. In *Subtle Strangeness*, a 2019 public performance set on a fountain-reflecting pool outside a university museum in Mexico City, MUAC, Lia García similarly deploys a collective embrace with the audience to assemble a short-lived space for trans remembrance. Although different from staging a quinceañera party in the subway, *Subtle Strangeness* borrows from the affective capacities of trans touch to alter public space, while indexing queer nightlife through her performance props and music. A shiny pink sequin dress, two male escorts, and songs by Mexican rock band Cáifanes's *Viento* and bolero ensemble Trío Los Panchos's *Piel canela*, serve as sounds connecting nightlife. Shouting the name of those trans women lost to transphobia and feminicide, Lía confronts people with her tender touch to build spaces of trans memory in a context that exerts violence upon women and the feminine. A video recording of *Subtle Strangeness* can be found in the digital repository of NYU's Hemispheric Institute of Performance and Politics: https://hemisphericinstitute.org/en/encuentro-2019-performances/item /3102-subtle-strangeness.html

11. https://x.com/Monitoreo103/status/1091460706531192836?s=20

12. https://www.eluniversal.com.mx/autopistas/que-pasa-si-te-atrapan-teniendo-rel aciones-sexuales-en-tu-auto

13. https://www.metro.cdmx.gob.mx/comunicacion/nota/activa-el-stc-centros-de -monitoreo-para-vigilancia-y-seguridad-de-los-usuarios-del-metro-cdmx

14. The subway system has implemented and designed women-only subway spaces, like subway carts only for women during rush hours, to reduce forms of gender-based harassment and violence.

15. Founded in 2007, the Paris-based website is now registered to the Czech multinational WGCZ Holding, which also owns the Miami-based porn studio Bang Bros, the DDF Network, *Penthouse* magazine, Private Media Group, and Erogames. As of 2022, XVideos was the most visited online porn repository, holding the tenth place as the most

visited website in the world. Through its global outreach, XVideos also functions as a search engine forming a transnational gay porn distribution circuit.

16. While Xiomara Cervantes-Gómez's provocative and generative "*pasivo* ethics" grapples with the place of "the radical passivity of the unbecoming of the subject from the positionality of the bottom" (2020, 339), these underground m4m sexual exchanges move beyond a binary of bottom/top, further complicating how the sexual unsettles urban masculinities, as well as disrupts the very tenets through which cultural performance has been usually conceptualized in academic circles.

17. Muñoz further asserts, "this aura, this circuit of luminous halos that surround the work . . . as having a primary relation to emotion, queer memories, and structures of feeling that haunt gay men on both sides of a generational divide that is formed by and through the catastrophe of AIDS" (1996b, 363).

18. The website is banned in ten countries including Russia, Venezuela, Bangladesh, China, India, Lebanon, Malaysia, Philippines, Vietnam, and Algeria, but can be accessed in certain places through IP address spoofing.

19. See Diana Taylor's *The Archive and the Repertoire: Performing Cultural Memory in the Americas* (2003), Rebecca Schneider's *Performing Remains: Art and War in Times of Theatrical Reenactment* (2011), Ann Cvetkovich's *An Archive of Feelings: Trauma, Sexuality, and Lesbian Public Cultures* (2003), or Heather Love's *Feeling Backward: Loss and the Politics of Queer History* (2007).

20. I am referring to "El 8° pasajero. El hombre de las manos arrugadas," and "El 8° pasajero. Chacal ac-tivo." Stark's two blog entries addressing each encounter in the subway can be found in the following links, respectively, https://erikostark001.wordpress .com/2016/08/27/el-8-pasajero-el-hombre-de-las-manos-arrugadas/; https://erikostark 001.wordpress.com/2016/08/30/el-8-pasajero-chacal-ac-tivo/

21. Drawing from Erin Manning's "events of perception," I seek to unpack a "magnitude" of events indexing queer life: "Life is as complex as the actual events that compose it. These actual events are multiple, each of them composed of prehensions culled from the magnitude of pastness non-sensuously felt as the present passing. Non-sensuous perception is the activity of perceiving the tonality of pastness in the present. Non-sensuous perceptions shade the currency of futurity. Perception as the infolding of the potential for activation of the future-past is the relational nexus for life-in-the-making. Perception is not the taking-in of an object or a scene. It is the folding-with that catches the event in the making." (2009, 77)

22. These tensions between sexuality, socioeconomic location, space, and queerness are beautifully unpacked, for instance, in Liz Misterio's online fanzine Hysteria, or in the queer performance collective Invasorix.

23. Soy "jota" rural, marginal; porque crecí pastoreando borregas y me obligaban a tragarme la leche entera que olía a establo, leche que ahora disfruto en la cara. Soy jota campesina, pastora, calabacera, nopalera, porque vengo de una gran dinastía cultural de vestidas que un día decidieron ordeñar de "putifalda", aunque se les llenara el tacón de caca de vaca. "Jotitas" que aguantan el acoso de los campesinos y albañiles de la comunidad y se friegan el lomo en la estética y la maquiladora para mantener a su familia. Porque de chiquito hacía mis muñecas con mazorcas y jugaba a hacer pastelitos de lodo en las zanjas de las parcelas. (2018, 6) [I am a rural, marginal *jota*; because I grew up

herding sheep and they forced me to swallow whole milk that smelled like a barn, milk that I now enjoy on my face. I am a jota peasant, shepherdess, squashy, prickly, because I come from a great cultural dynasty of crossdressers that one day decided to milk wearing "putifalda," (whorish squirt), even if their high heels were filled with cow poop. "Jotitas" who endure the harassment of the peasants and masons of the community and break their backs at the hair salon and the maquiladora to support their family. Because when I was a kid, I made my dolls out of corncobs and used to make mud cakes in the plots' ditches.] Translation is my own.

24. Mario Bellatin's novel *Salón de belleza* (1994) precisely recounts this marginalization through the story of displacement of a HIV-positive travesti that migrates from northern Mexico into Mexico City, where her beauty salon eventually turns into an improvised hospice for queers living with AIDS. The hair salon and her attendant provide an underground infrastructure where travesti folk can have access to a dignified death in the face of public expulsion.

Chapter 4

1. https://youtu.be/hCbnnewabpE
2. In fact, Mexico's neoliberal conversion deepens the country's de-industrialization.
3. According to Paul Julian Smith's reading of Fons's *Fe, Esperanza y Caridad* in Fiesco's *Quebranto:* "Fiesco even has Coral recreate the desperate walk through the city street of [her] fictional mother in the film, cutting back and forward between original and remake. Obligingly, here he offers the former child star the much bigger role of his mother (played in the original by the well-known star Katy Jurado)" (2017, 75). More than paying homage to an old film, Coral's reenactment of a scene from *Fe, Esperanza y Caridad* offers an instance into the peculiar relationship between film and loss I refer to as "pellicular."
4. Cornejo further states, "Makuti's tears trouble vision. Tears trouble any will for indelible clarity and clear borders. Teary and blurry eyes, instead of being an obstacle to moving in the world, become an instance of how to accept the opacity and mobility of gender itself" (2021, 54).
5. The song touches on the fatality of sex work described as insincere, lethal yet desired: "amor de cabaret que no es sincero/ amor de cabaret que se paga con dinero/ amor de cabaret que poco a poco me mata/ sin embargo yo quiero amor de cabaret" (i.e., cabaret love that is not sincere/ cabaret love that is paid for with money/ cabaret love that little by little kills me/ nevertheless I want cabaret love).
6. According to a United Nations University Policy Brief, Mexico shows a Gini coefficient of 0.5, placing the country within the high inequality rank. Between 1989–94, inequality increased followed by a decline in inequality from 1994–2006. Inequality was on the rise, however, between 2006–14: https://www.wider.unu.edu/publication/inequality-mexico-0. Although Mexico has experienced various economic crises leading to the signing of NAFTA in 1994, this trade agreement marked the emergence of global neoliberal policies that would lead to the country's deindustrialization. Among some of NATFA's violent effects include the dismantling of the countryside and of Mexico's capacity to supply itself with food, the development of *maquiladoras*, or the sweatshop

industrial complex, the increase of feminicides and deaths of Juárez related to the war against drugs, the increase in economic inequalities, etc.

Chapter 5

1. Francisco J. Galarte, *Brown Trans Figurations*, 2021, 14–15.

2. Irwin notes, "But the Porfiriato's homophobia nonetheless is intertwined with the era's relentless attraction for the theme [of sexual perversion], whereas after the Revolution homophobia becomes institutional, incorporated implicitly into the construction of a nationalism founded upon coarse machismo. In this sense, the Mexican Revolution transforms male homosexuality from a mere social or moral problem into an antinational category." (2011, n.p.)

3. The most celebrated case of FTM transgender national identity can be found in the figure of Amelio Robles, a soldier that fought during the Revolution, who received an honorary medal for his military service by the National Ministry of Defense in 1973. Robles's case reveals the discursive, material, and affective entanglements between nationalism and gender roles in Mexico. To index a set of practices that fall outside the homonational scripts of belonging, I resort to the concept of "transmarilencha," proposed by the Mexican collective Instituto de Investigaciones Noa Noa, conformed by artists and intellectuals Benjamín Martínez, Tadeo Cervantes, and Liz Misterio, to contextually respond to the cultural practices of trans communities, queers, and lesbians, assembling a politics of sexual and gender dissidence in the 21st century. The Noa Noa Research Institute forum can be accessed through the following link: https://www.facebook.com /Noa-Noa-Instituto-de-Investigaciones-3029654780381891/

4. Ahmed notes, "The point of this 'sometimes' is that we learn that silence and speech have different even contradictory effects given their timing, which is a question not simply of their time, but also of the place in which we reside at a given moment in time, the worlds we find ourselves in. To recognize this contingency as a feminist ethics is to live and work in a state of suspension: we will not always know in advance (though sometimes we might) when it makes sense to be silent when it does not" (2010, xviii).

5. As Giancarlo Cornejo has noted, travestismo "in most cases takes femininity [as] a particular gendered destination" (2019, 457). Like the Peruvian context, the trajectory of a presupposed gendered destination in Mexico also means that travesti identities experience more acutely precarity, violence, and death.

6. Adapted from the 1966 homonym novel by Chilean José Donoso, Ripstein's film portrays the social entanglements of a cabaret/brothel house located in a small town in rural Mexico.

7. Echoing what Kevin Floyd notes about the interconnection between queer and Marxian epistemologies, this film might bring into frame "a rich consideration of the ways in which [these relations are] mediated by a range of normalizing regimes and forms of social hierarchy, including those that operate along axes of gender, race, and nation" (2009, 3). Floyd however cautions that "any representation of sexuality as always already localized, particularized, or privatized, is a misrepresentation of the social as well as the sexual" (2009, 8).

8. In other supposedly critical studies, La Manuela is read as a figure that upholds a

conventional gender binary, and as an allegory of femininity that sustains patriarchy and machismo. See, for instance, Pércio B. de Castro, Jr. *La última sevillana de El Lugar sin límites de José Donoso y de Arturo Ripstein—entre penes y peinetas—el travestismo como representación múltiple*, 2004.

9. International Gay and Lesbian Human Rights Commission, *A Shadow Report*, 2010.

10. Cornell University Transgender Law Center, Report on Human Rights Conditions of Transgender Women in Mexico, 2016.

11. See Arondekar, Anjali; Patel, Geeta, eds. "Area Impossible: The Geopolitics of Queer Studies." Special issue, *GLQ* 22, no. 2 (2016); Eng, David L.; Puar, Jasbir K., eds. "Left of Queer." *Social Text* 38, no. 4 (2020); and Aizura, Aren Z.; Cotton, Trystan; Balzer, Carsten / LaGata, Carla; Ochoa, Marcia; Vidal-Ortiz, Salvador, eds. "Decolonizing the Transgender Imaginary." Special issue, *TSQ* 1, no. 3 (2014).

12. Smith maintains, "a new [country that] exists for queer people that belies macho or conservative Catholic stereotypes [and where] public visibility is matched by marriage equality, a reality in Mexico City again (but not elsewhere), since 2010. And in 2013 the Mexican Supreme Court ruled that the use of homophobic slurs was a violation of fundamental human rights" (2017, 3–6).

13. In a blog post published in 2019 by Mexico's Secretary of Culture, the "raid of the 41" marks the cultural representation of homosexuality in the country, marking a historical bridge between the first LGBTQ+ protest on July 26, 1971, a date that coincides with the anniversary of the Cuban revolution according to the post, and the 1901 Dance of the 41: https://www.gob.mx/cultura/es/articulos/breve-historia-de-la-primera-marcha-lgbttti-de-mexico?idiom=es

14. The transcendence of the drag ball of the 41 have been pivotal for honoring the work of LGBTQ+ Latinx stories. As a multimedia platform founded in 2013, Honor41 elevates and celebrates the voices of LGBTQ+ Latinx communities in the US, https://honor41.org

15. See Manuel Betancourt's film review, "'Dance of the 41' Review: Mexican Netflix Drama Spotlights a 19th-Century Queer Scandal" for *Variety*: https://variety.com/2021/film/news/dance-of-the-forty-one-review-el-baile-de-los-41–1234983809/

16. "Estos vestían elegantísimos trajes de señoras, llevaban pelucas, pechos postizos, aretes, choclos bordados y en las caras tenían pintadas grandes orejas y chapas de color."

17. "41 lagartijos," "jotitos," "pelucas bien peinadas," "caras muy repintadas," "pechos bien abultados." In the second to last stanza, "Lloran, chillan, y hasta ladran," (95).

18. Following the work of Annick Prieur, Susana Vargas Cervantes, Rafael de la Dehesa, and Susan Stryker, Robert Franco succinctly defines *"travesti/vestida"* as a political category that gains traction in the 1990s with LGBT activism. According to Franco, "Before the widespread use of the word "transgender," *travesti* and *vestida* were the preferred terms to refer to a gender-variant identity, and they remain so in many lower-class communities. While many *travestis* also identify as homosexual in their sexual object choice, their identity is derived from the transformation of their bodies through either dress or surgical/hormonal modification to create a feminine appearance. For *travestis*, their identity means going beyond dressing in clothes as-

signed to the opposite gender/sex for temporary periods and instead signals refuting a gender binary" (2019, 85).

Chapter 6

1. See Annick Prieur's *Mema's House, Mexico City: On Transvestites, Queens, and Machos* (1998).
2. https://www.vice.com/es/article/wd3pnb/las-leyes-sobre-prostitucion-en-mexico-protegen-al-cliente-y-marginalizan-a-las-trabajadoras-sexuales
3. See Rita Segato's *La guerra contra las mujeres* (2016), Sayak Valencia's *Gore Capitalism* (2010), and Sergio González Rodríguez's *The Femicide Machine* (2012).
4. In their collaboration with a high school designed for travesti and trans students known as Bachillerato Popular Travesti y Trans Mocha Celis in Buenos Aires, Argentina, Juliana Martínez and Salvador Vidal-Ortiz expand on a reconceptualization of education and knowledge production through a radical pedagogy centering on travesti embodied experiences. Drawing from the activist work of Lohana Berkins, the category travesti denotes a non-binary position, as well as an intersectional political position striving for collective action. Juliana Martínez and Salvador Vidal-Ortiz, further unpack the politics and epistemologies of Lohana's "travar el saber," as it critically recenters travesti and trans experiences, while "*travar's* untranslatable phonic ambivalence in Spanish signals how the concept operates: *travar* is both an interruption and a transformation. *Travar* is an obstruction. *Travar*, in general, interferes with the normal functioning of state institutions that abuse travesti and trans people, neglecting them and denying them their rights" (2021, 669).
5. Travesti activists, artists, and theorists Marlene Wayar and Susy Shock coincide in the search of play as a force of transformation and renewal, one that is associated with a child-like curiosity. As Marlene Wayar puts it,

"la palabra, "niña" me aglutina, sintetiza muchas cosas: el deseo, el ir por tus sueños, el poder tener presente, presentes un montón de posibilidades que están ahí [. . .] Y también en lo niño la posibilidad de proyectar: de estar todo el tiempo proyectando sueños y buscándoles las posibilidades. Hay un mundo que dice que no es posible, que no se hace, que no se puede y la potencia de la creatividad pensando que de todas maneras una posibilidad va a haber de llevar a cabo . . . y también la posibilidad de que esto se teja en el juego, en lo lúdico, que se pueda disfrutar, y en lo oral." (2018, 57)

(The word "girl" brings me together, it synthesizes many things: desire, going for your dreams, the possibility of keeping present a lot of possibilities that are there [. . .] And also in that child, the possibility of projecting dreams all the time and looking for them other possibilities. There is a world that says that it is impossible, that it cannot be done, that it cannot happen and the power of creativity, thinking that in any case a possibility is going to have to be carried out . . . and the possibility that this is woven into the game, in what is playful, that which can be enjoyed, and in the oral tradition.)

6. Bridging the work of Sylvia Wynter, micha finds in the sci-fi image of the android goddess, "a figure of rebellion, deemed less than human but striving to be more than human" (26). Tacitly, micha also gestures toward a playful disposition when devising tools for resistance, as well, as DIY practices emerging from the Poetic Operations Collective lab.

7. Sicart notes, "Play as political action is always ambiguous [. . .] Political play is expression of political ideas in the seams opened by appropriation; it is a critical expression through the playful interpretation of a context. Because it is play, it can thrive in situations of oppression; because it is play, it can allow personal and collective expression, giving voices and actions when no one can be heard" (2014, 81).

8. According to Lorde, "the erotic functions for me in several ways, and the first is in providing the power which comes from sharing deeply any pursuit with another person. The sharing of joy, whether physical, emotional, psychic, or intellectual, forms a bridge between the sharers which can be the basis for understanding much of what is not shared between them, and lessens the threat of their difference" (2007, 56).

9. Based on the nightlife performances of the trans/queer cabaret troupe, *Las Hermanas Vampiro*, Antonio Marquet locates in *perreo*, a loose equivalent to "throwing shade" in trans/queer Anglo-American contexts. *Perrear*, the act of *perreo*, refers to gestures of humor and irony deployed within the trans/queer collective to face the ongoing violent attacks of heterosexual culture. It is a discursive as well as embodied strategy to channel the libels directed at trans/queer people and rework those wounds into instances of perverse laughter.

10. The aura of Francis continues to dwell in the travesti nightscapes of Mexico. In the early 2000s, Francis appeared in the ground-breaking queer and travesti show *Desde Gayola* (2002–2006; 2008–2013), a televised variety show composed of small sketches featuring queer, trans, and travesti actors and comedians playing a queer satire of Mexican moral codes. Combining a type of humor currently characterized as "politically incorrect," Francis fused acerbic social critique with poignant jokes about transsexuality, homosexuality, heterosexuality, and political corruption in Mexico. Her distinct 80s blond hairdo, rhinestone-studded dress, glitzy personality, and contagious laughter positioned her as the queen of the night. Her flames of humor would roast at anyone, anywhere, unleashing unstoppable waves of laughter in her audience.

Coda

1. I am referring to north/south relations less in terms of their geographical location, but rather as embodiments that carry modes of being across geographical boundaries.

2. See O. Hugo Benavides's *Drugs, Thugs, and Divas: Telenovelas and Narco-Dramas in Latin America* (2008), Sayak Valencia's *Gore Capitalism* (2018) and Jason Ruiz's *Narcomedia: Latinidad, Popular Culture, and America's War on Drugs* (2023).

3. In *Translocalities/Translocalidades: Feminist Politics of Translation in the Latin/a Américas*, Sonia Alvarez refers to translocalities as a way of recognizing hemispheric movements, "[r]ather than immigrating or 'assimilating' moreover, many people in the

Latin/a Américas increasingly move back and forth between localities, between histori-cally situated and culturally specific (though increasingly porous) places, across mul-tiple borders, and not just between nations" (2014, 2 in Cowan 2016, 59).

4. Born in Ensenada, Mexico on September 1, 1983, Julio, and his family moved to the US in 1995, looking for a medical treatment for his sister's terminal illness. After overstaying their visas, the Salgado Family became undocumented migrants, and Julio managed to pay his way through college as his undocumented migrant status impeded him from receiving federal financial aid. In 2010, Julio joined the Dream Act movement after coming across a photograph in the Washington Post of Diana Yael Martinez, an undocumented student who was being arrested for refusing to abandon the sit-in at the US senate building. His illustrations have been featured in many news outlets, as well as in the collection of the Smithsonian National Museum of American Art in Washington D.C. Julio's poster art celebrates undocumented Brown experiences, voices, and bodies, bringing visibility to a reality that affects close to 1.2 million undocumented migrants who entered the US as accompanying minors under the age of 16. Under the first Trump administration, DACA faced multiple legal challenges, and once the Biden administra-tion reinstated the program in 2020, a federal circuit judge blocked the executive order, bringing to a halt new registration into the program. According to US Citizenship and Immigration Services, the active count of DACA recipients is close to 600 thousand, with a total of 578,680 as of March 31, 2023, but its expansion could easily double the size of program beneficiaries. In October 2024, however, the Fifth Circuit Court of Ap-peals, arguably the most conservative appeals court in the country, held oral arguments in the case that challenged the legality of the DACA policy. Under a new Trump term, the future of the program remains uncertain given the current administration's hardline views on immigration, as well as Trump's previous deployment of protectionist laws that restrict legal immigration into the US, as in the case of the Reforming American Im-migration for a Strong Economy (RAISE) Act implemented in August 2017.

5. "[F]ear [. . .] re-establishes distance between bodies whose difference is read off the surface, as a reading which produces the surface (shivering, recolouring). Fear involves relationships of proximity, which are crucial to establishing the 'apartness' of white bodies" (2014, 63).

6. In *The Sense of Brown* (2020), Muñoz commits to "a new methetic turn" to move beyond "mainstream sexuality politics" (134), while arguing for "a brownness as a copresence with other modes of difference, a choreography of singularities that touch and contact but do not meld" (138); or a constellation "of objects, human and otherwise, that are browned by the world" (130).

7. "The tensions in Wildness illustrate the fact that the contradictions in early 1990s queer community formation and cinema are still with us today. The film encapsulates paradoxical impulses: on the one hand the desire to close the gap of difference that un-derwrites liberal notions of queer community and a self-reflexive suspicion of identity politics" (2015, 266).

8. "The film highlights a topic more pertinent for young queer artists than ever: our quest for empowerment, often motivated by feelings of disenfranchisement, must be balanced by a recognition of the tensions already inherent within the space we make our own. And our efforts not to disenfranchise others at the same time must be doubled

when we come to occupy a space inhabited by people who have already experienced disenfranchisement. This involves shaking ourselves from complacency and contending with the unwelcome realization that we must examine our own part in the ongoing process of queer gentrification" (2014, 464).

9. Edited by the artist herself, and compiled by Valentin Aguirre and Augie Robles, the 4-min video is available through Xandra Ibarra's Vimeo account, https://vimeo.com /218888629

Works Cited

Adeyemi, Kemi, Kareem Khubchandani, and Ramón Rivera-Servera. 2021. *Queer Nightlife*. University of Michigan Press.

Ahmed, Sara. 2004. "Affective Economies." *Social Text* 22, no. 2 (Summer): 117–39.

Ahmed, Sara. 2006. *Queer Phenomenology: Orientations, Objects, Others*. Duke University Press.

Ahmed, Sara. 2010. Foreword to *Secrecy and Silence in the Research Process: Feminist Reflections, edited* by Rosalind Gill and Roisin Ryan-Flood, xvi–xxi. Routledge. https://doi.org/10.4324/9780203927045

Ahmed, Sara. 2014. *The Cultural Politics of Emotion*. Second edition. Edinburgh University Press.

Aizura, Aren Z. 2018. *Mobile Subjects: Transnational Imaginaries of Gender Reassignment*. Duke University Press. https://doi.org/10.1515/9781478002642

Alemán Saavedra, Tania. 2019. "Antiguo Cine Teresa en la CDMX: mucho más que porno." *México Desconocido,* February 7, 2019. https://www.mexicodesconocido.com.mx/antiguo-cine-teresa-en-la-cdmx-mucho-mas-que-porno.html#galeria

Alvarez, Sonia E. 2014. "Introduction to the Project and the Volume: Enacting a Translocal Feminist Politics of Translation." In *Translocalities/Translocalidades: Feminist Politics of Translation in the Latin/a Américas*, edited by Sonia E. Alvarez, Claudia de Lima Costa, Veronica Feliu, Rebecca Hester, Norma Klahn, and Millie Thayer, 2–18. Duke University Press.

Alzate, Gastón A. 2002. *Teatro de cabaret: Imaginarios disidentes*. Gestos.

Anjaria, Jonathan Shapiro, and Ulka Anjaria. 2020. "*Mazaa*: Rethinking Fun, Pleasure and Play in South Asia." *South Asia: Journal of South Asian Studies* 43 (2): 232–42. https://doi.org/10.1080/00856401.2020.1725718

Appadurai, Arjun. 1996. *Modernity At Large: Cultural Dimensions of Globalization*. University of Minnesota Press.

Arondekar, Anjali, and Geeta Patel. 2016. "Area Impossible: Notes toward an Introduction." *GLQ: A Journal of Lesbian and Gay Studies* 22, no. 2: 151–71. https://doi.org/10.1215/10642684-3428687

Arruzza, Cinzia, Tithi Bhattacharya, and Nancy Fraser. 2019. *Feminism for the 99%: A Manifesto*. Verso Books.

Ballard, Finn Jackson. 2014. "Wu Tsang's *Wildness* and the Quest for Queer Utopia." *TSQ: Transgender Studies Quarterly* 1 (3): 461–65. https://doi.org/10.1215/23289252 -2687555

Bañales, Xamuel. 2014. "Jotería: A Decolonizing Political Project." *Aztlán* 39 (1): 155–66.

Barker, Jennifer M. 2009. *The Tactile Eye: Touch and the Cinematic Experience*. University of California Press.

Bellatin, Mario. 1994. *Salón de belleza*. 1st ed. J. Campodónico.

Berman, Sabina. 2016. "El (fa-bu-lo-so) Imperio Gay." *Proceso*. Septiembre 27, 2016. https://www.proceso.com.mx/opinion/2016/9/27/el-fa-bu-lo-so-imperio-gay-1712 60.html

Betancourt, Manuel. 2021. "'Dance of the 41' Review: Mexican Netflix Drama Spotlights a 19th-Century Queer Scandal." *Variety*, May 27, 2021. https://variety.com/2021/film /news/dance-of-the-forty-one-review-el-baile-de-los-41-1234983809/

Betsky, Aaron. 1997. *Queer Space: Architecture and Same-Sex Desire*. William Morrow.

Bey, Marquis. 2022. *Black Trans Feminism*. Duke University Press. https://doi.org/10.15 15/9781478022428

Blanco, José Joaquín. 1981. *Función de medianoche. Ensayos de literatura cotidiana*. Ediciones Era.

Bohrer, Ashley J. 2020. "Toward a Decolonial Feminist Anticapitalism: María Lugones, Sylvia Wynter, and Sayak Valencia." *Hypatia* 35 (3): 524–41. https://doi.org/10.1017 /hyp.2020.20

Brim, Matt. 2020. "Poor Queer Studies: Class, Race, and the Field." *Journal of Homosexuality* 67 (3): 398–416. https://doi.org/10.1080/00918369.2018.1534410

Brown, Wendy. 2017. *Undoing the Demos: Neoliberalism's Stealth Revolution*. Zone Books.

Brown, Wendy. 2019. *In the Ruins of Neoliberalism: The Rise of Antidemocratic Politics in the West*. Columbia University Press. https://doi.org/10.7312/brow19384

Bruce, Caitlin Frances. 2024. *Voices in Aerosol: Youth Culture, Institutional Attunement, and Graffiti in Urban Mexico*. University of Texas Press.

Campos-Vázquez, Raymundo M., Nora Lustig, and John Scott. 2018. "Inequality in Mexico: On the Rise Again." *WIDER Policy Brief* 5:1–2. https://www.wider.unu.edu /publication/inequality-mexico-0

Cantú, Norma Elia. 1999. *La Quinceañera: Towards an Ethnographic Analysis of a Life Cycle Ritual. Southern Folklore* 56 (1): 73–101.

cárdenas, micha. 2019. "The Android Goddess Declaration: After Man(ifestos)." In *Bodies of Information*, edited by Elizabeth Losh and Jacqueline Wernimont, 25–38. University of Minnesota Press. https://doi.org/10.5749/j.ctv9hj9r9.5

Carlos-Manuel. 2014. "A Funny Joto and an Immigrant." *Aztlán* 39 (1): 207–14.

Caro, Manolo, dir. *La Casa de las Flores*. 2018–2023; Netflix.

Carrillo, Héctor. 2002. *The Night is Young: Sexuality in Mexico in the Time of AIDS*. University of Chicago Press.

Cavallero, Lucí, and Verónica Gago. 2021. *A Feminist Reading of Debt*. Pluto Press.

Cervantes, Tadeo. 2020. "Making space weird [1], some notes on a cuir [2] territoriality." *Stakes and Mistakes* 5, no. 14 (February 20, 2020). https://yalepaprika.com/folds/stak es-and-mistakes/making-space-weird1-some-notes-on-a-cuir2-territoriality

Cervantes-Gómez, Xiomara V. 2020. "Paz's *Pasivo*: Thinking Mexicanness from the Bottom." *Journal of Latin American Cultural Studies* 29 (3): 333–47. https://doi.org/10.10 80/13569325.2019.1675146

Chambers-Letson, Joshua Takano. 2018. *After the Party: A Manifesto for Queer of Color Life*. New York University Press. https://doi.org/10.18574/9781479882632

Chayanne, vocalist. 1990. "Tiempo de vals." Spotify, track 5 on Chayanne, *Tiempo de vals*. Sony Music Latin.

Clough, Patricia T. 2008. "The Affective Turn: Political Economy, Biomedia and Bodies." *Theory, Culture & Society* 25 (1): 1–22. https://doi.org/10.1177/0263276407085156

Coleman, Beth. 2009. "Race as Technology." *Camera Obscura* 24 (1): 177–207.

Cornejo, Giancarlo. 2019. "*Travesti* Dreams Outside in the Ethnographic Machine." *GLQ: A Journal of Lesbian and Gay Studies* 25 (3): 457–82. https://doi.org/10.1215/10642684-7551140

Cornejo, Giancarlo. 2021. "Thinking *Travesti* Tears: Reading *Loxoro*." *Camera Obscura* 36 (3): 33–59. https://doi.org/10.1215/02705346-9349329

Cowan, T. L. 2016. "A Hybrid Present Embodified: Dialectical Mimesis on the Translocal Cabaret Stage. César Enríquez's *Disertaciones de la Chingada* and Alexandra Tigchelaar's *Les Demimondes*." In *Queer Dramaturgies: International Perspectives on Where Performance Leads Queer*, edited by Alyson Campbell and Stephen Farrier, 157–77. Palgrave Macmillan.

Cuellar, Manuel R. 2022. *Choreographing Mexico: Festive Performances and Dancing Histories of a Nation*. University of Texas Press. https://doi.org/10.7560/325162

Dávila, Chivirico. 1972. "Arráncame La Vida." Spotify, track 4 on Chivirico Dávila, *De Nuevo*. Fania.

Davis, Diane E. 1994. *Urban Leviathan: Mexico City in the Twentieth Century*. Temple University Press.

DeFrantz, Thomas F. 2017. "Queer Dance in Three Acts." In *Queer Dance: Meanings & Makings*, edited by Clare Croft, 169–79. Oxford University Press.

de la Mora, Sergio. 1992. "Fascinating Machismo: Toward an Unmasking of Heterosexual Masculinity in Arturo Ripstein's *El Lugar Sin Límites*." *Journal of Film and Video* 44 (3/4): 83–104.

Delany, Samuel R. 1999. *Times Square Red, Times Square Blue*. New York University Press.

Delgado Huitrón, Cynthia Citlallin. 2019. "Haptic Tactic: Hypertenderness for the [Mexican] State and the Performances of Lia García." *Transgender Studies Quarterly* 6 (2): 164–79. https://doi.org/10.1215/23289252-7348454

Désert, Jean-Ulrick. 1997. "Queer Space." In *Queers in Space: Communities, Public Spaces, Sites of Resistance*, edited by Gordon Brent Ingram, Anne-Marie Bouthillette, and Yolanda Retter, 17–26. Bay Press.

Domínguez Ruvalcaba, Héctor. 2016. *Translating the Queer: Body Politics and Transnational Conversations*. Zed Books.

Donoso, Camila José, dir. *Casa Roshell*. 2017; Mexico: Tonalá Lab.

Dussel Peters, Enrique. 2004. "México en la globalización: ¿modernización y/o polarización?" In *Las modernidades de México. Espacios, procesos, trayectorias*, edited by Günther Maihold, 55–80. Miguel Ángel Porrúa.

Edelman, Lee. 2004. *No Future: Queer Theory and the Death Drive*. Duke University Press.

Egert, Gerko. 2020. *Moving Relation: Touch in Contemporary Dance*. Translated by Rett Rossi. Routledge.

Emmelhainz, Irmgard. 2021. *The Tyranny of Common Sense: Mexico's Post-Neoliberal Conversion*. State University of New York Press.

Eng, David L., Jack Halberstam, and José Esteban Muñoz. 2005. "Introduction: What's Queer about Queer Studies Now?" *Social Text* 23, no. 3–4 (Fall–Winter): 1–17.

Espinosa, Luz. 2013. "La seducción del Cine Teresa." *Cultura Colectiva*, October 1, 2013. https://culturacolectiva.com/letras/la-seduccion-del-cine-teresa

Ferguson, Roderick A. 2019. *One-Dimensional Queer*. Polity.

Fiesco, Roberto, dir. *Quebranto*. 2013; México: Mundo en DVD, 2014. DVD.

Flores, Juan, and George Yúdice. 1990. "Living Borders/Buscando America: Languages of Latino Self-formation." *Social Text*, no. 24: 57–84.

Flores, Marcos. 1990. "Solidaridad," *Televisa*, November 7, 1990. Video, 8:43. https://you tu.be/hCbnnewabpE

Floyd, Kevin. 2009. *The Reification of Desire: Toward a Queer Marxism*. University of Minnesota Press.

Foster, David William. 2000. *Producción cultural e identidades homoeróticas: teoría y aplicaciones*. Editorial de la Universidad de Costa Rica.

Foster, David William. 2003. *Queer Issues in Contemporary Latin American Cinema*. University of Texas Press.

Franco, Robert. 2019. "'Todos/as somos 41': The Dance of the Forty-One from Homosexual Reappropriation to Transgender Representation in Mexico, 1945–2001." *Journal of the History of Sexuality* 28 (1): 66–95. https://muse.jhu.edu/article/716126

Fraser, Nancy. 2013. *Fortunes of Feminism: From State-Managed Capitalism to Neoliberal Crisis*. Verso.

Freeman, Elizabeth. 2010. *Time Binds: Queer Temporalities, Queer Histories*. Duke University Press.

Freeman, Elizabeth. 2019. *Beside You in Time: Sense Methods & Queer Sociabilities in the American 19th Century*. Duke University Press.

Gabriel, Juan, vocalist. 1998. "Así fue." Spotify, track 5 on Juan Gabriel, *Celebrando 25 años de Juan Gabriel En Concierto en El Palacio De Bellas Artes*, Ariola.

Gago, Verónica. 2017. *Neoliberalism from Below: Popular Pragmatics and Baroque Economies*. Duke University Press.

Gago, Verónica. 2020. *Feminist International: How to Change Everything*. Translated by Liz Mason-Deese. Verso.

Galarte, Francisco J. 2021. *Brown Trans Figurations: Rethinking Race, Gender, and Sexuality in Chicanx/Latinx Studies*. University of Texas Press. https://doi.org/10.7560 /322123

Galindo, Jorge Lionel, and César Torres. 2018. "Diálogo de miradas. Un acercamiento al "metreo" como orden interactivo." *Sociológica* 33 (93): 319–53. https://www.redalyc .org/comocitar.oa?id=305054868010

Galindo, María. 2021. *Feminismo bastardo*. 2da edición. Mujeres Creando.

Gamboa, Eddie. 2021. "Pedagogies of the Dark: Making Sense of Queer Nightlife." In *Queer Nightlife*, edited by Kemi Adeyemi, Kareem Khubchandani, and Ramón Rivera-Servera, 91–100. University of Michigan Press.

García, Ana Karen. 2018. "7 de cada 10 indígenas en México son pobres." El Economista, September 16, 2018. https://www.eleconomista.com.mx/economia/7-de-cada-10-in digenas-en-Mexico-son-pobres-20180916-0007.html

García Canclini, Néstor. 2005. *Hybrid Cultures: Strategies for Entering and Leaving Modernity*. University of Minnesota Press.

García, Lia (La Novia Sirena), and Tadeo Cervantes. 2019. "Towards a Radical Pedagogy of Proxemics and the Inhabitable." *Terremoto*, January 14, 2019. https://terremoto .mx/en/revista/hacia-otra-pedagogia-radical-de-la-proxemica-y-de-lo-habitable/

Garcia Torres, Juan. 2023. "Jorge Portilla on Philosophy and Agential Liberation." *The Southern Journal of Philosophy*. https://doi.org/10.1111/sjp.12548

Gill-Peterson, Jules. 2018. *Histories of the Transgender Child*. University of Minnesota Press.

Goded, Maya, dir. *Plaza de la soledad*. 2016; Mexico: Zima Entertainment. DVD.

González, Rachel Valentina. 2019. *Quinceañera Style: Social Belonging and Latinx Consumer Identities*. University of Texas Press.

González Rodríguez, Sergio. 2012. *The Femicide Machine*. MIT Press.

Goodman, Elyssa Maxx. 2023. *Glitter and Concrete: A Cultural History of Drag in New York City*. Hanover Square Press.

Gordon R., Sara. 1993. "La política y el Programa Nacional de Solidaridad." *Revista Mexicana de Sociología* 55 (2): 351–66.

Graham, David. 2017. *The Last Car: Cruising in Mexico City*. Kehrer.

Gutiérrez, Laura G. 2010. *Performing Mexicanidad: Vendidas y Cabareteras on the Transnational Stage*. University of Texas Press. https://doi.org/10.7560/722088

Halberstam, J. Jack. 2005. *In a Queer Time & Place: Transgender Bodies, Subcultural Lives*. New York University Press.

Halberstam, J. Jack. 2011. *The Queer Art of Failure*. Duke University Press.

Halberstam, J. Jack. 2020. *Wild Things: The Disorder of Desire*. Duke University Press.

Han, Byung-Chul. 2017. *Psychopolitics: Neoliberalism and New Technologies of Power*. Verso.

Harney, Stefano, and Fred Moten. 2013. *The Undercommons: Fugitive Planning & Black Study*. Minor Compositions.

Hartman, Saidiya. 2008. "Venus in Two Acts." *Small Axe: A Caribbean Journal of Criticism* 12 (2): 1–14. https://doi.org/10.1215/-12-2-1

Harvey, David. 2005. *A Brief History of Neoliberalism*. Oxford University Press.

Harvey, Penny, and Hannah Knox. 2012. "The Enchantments of Infrastructure." *Mobilities* 7 (4): 521–36. http://dx.doi.org/10.1080/17450101.2012.718935

Hayward, Eva. 2010. "FINGERYEYES: Impressions of Cup Corals." *Cultural Anthropology* 25, no. 4: 577–99. http://www.jstor.org/stable/40930490

Heller, Meredith. 2020. *Queering Drag: Redefining the Discourse of Gender-Bending*. Indiana University Press.

Hernández, Julián, dir. *Mil nubes de paz cercan el cielo*. 2003; United States: Strand Releasing, 2004. DVD.

Hillis, Ken, Susanna Paasonen, and Michael Petit, eds. 2015. *Networked Affect*. MIT Press.

Holert, Tom, Julieta Aranda, Brian Kuan Wood, and Anton Vidokle. 2015. "Politics of Shine." *e-flux journal* no. 61. http://www.e-flux.com/journal/61/60985/editorial-pol itics-of-shine/

hooks, bell. 1994. *Teaching to Transgress: Education as the Practice of Freedom*. Routledge.

Hurtado, Guillermo. 1994. "Dos mitos de la mexicanidad." *Diánoia* 40 (40), 263–93.

intelectual. 2012. "me inicie en el cine teresa," Mi Diario Gay (blog), May 11, 2012. http://midiariosexygay.blogspot.com/2012/05/me-inicie-en-el-cine-teresa.html

Irwin, Robert McKee. 2003. *Mexican Masculinities*. University of Minnesota Press.

Irwin, Robert McKee, Ed McCaughan, and Michelle Rocío Nasser. 2003. *The Famous 41: Sexuality and Social Control in Mexico, c. 1901*. Palgrave Macmillan.

Irwin, Robert McKee. 2011. "Centenary of Mexican Homophobia." In 1810 ~ 1910 ~ 2010: *Mexico's Unfinished Revolutions*, edited by Charles B. Faulhaber, n.p. University of California Press.

Kaoma. 1989. "Lambada." By Gonzalo Hermosa and Ulises Hermosa. Spotify, track 1 on Kaoma, *Lambada—Les originaux No.1 de l'été*. Melting Pop.

Kaplan, Dana, and Eva Illouz. 2022. *What Is Sexual Capital?* Polity Press.

Keeling, Kara. 2019. *Queer Times, Black Futures*. New York University Press.

Kendall, Mikki. 2020. *Hood Feminism: Notes from the Women That a Movement Forgot*. Viking.

Khubchandani, Kareem. 2020. *Ishtyle: Accenting Gay Indian Nightlife*. University of Michigan Press. https://doi.org/10.3998/mpub.9958984

Koestenbaum, Wayne. 1993. *The Queen's Throat: Opera, Homosexuality, and The Mystery of Desire*. Poseidon Press.

La Sonora Santanera. 1950. "Amor de cabaret." Track 14 on *Sonora Santanera 15 Éxitos Bailables*. Sony Music Entertainment, 2012, compact disc.

Lim, Eng-Beng. 2005. "Glocalqueering in New Asia: The Politics of Performing Gay in Singapore." Theatre *Journal* 57 (3): 383–405. http://www.jstor.org/stable/25069670

Linthicum, Kate. 2019. "A Mexico City queer bar resists attacks with love and cumbia." *Los Angeles Times*. July 2, 2019. https://www.latimes.com/world/mexico-americas/la-fg-col1-mexico-queer-bar-attack-20190702-story.html

López Toledano, Ganda/Max D. 2023. "Rumbo al Homomestizaje." In *Otro Deporte es Posible: Atletas LGBTTTI+ en México*, edited by Rodrigo Castillo Aguilar and Ganda/Max D. López Toledano, 19–32. Rizoma Gestión Cultural.

Lorde, Audre. 2007. *Sister Outsider: Essays and Speeches*. Penguin Publishing Group.

Los Ángeles Azules. 1993. "Entrega de amor." Spotify, track 1 on Los Ángeles Azules, *Entrega de amor*. Universal Music Mexico.

Los 41 Tropiezos de la heteronorma en México. Season 1, episode 1, "El baile de los 41." Aired April 13, 2021, on TV UNAM. https://tv.unam.mx/41-tropiezos-de-la-hetero norma-en-mexico/

Macharia, Keguro. 2019. *Frottage: Frictions of Intimacy Across the Black Diaspora*. New York University Press.

Manalansan, Martin F. 2014. "The 'Stuff' of Archives: Mess, Migration, and Queer Lives." *Radical History Review* 120: 94–107. https://doi-org.pitt.idm.oclc.org/10.1215/01636 545-2703742

Manning, Erin. 2009. *Relationscapes: Movement, Art, Philosophy*. MIT Press.

Manning, Erin. 2020. *For a Pragmatics of the Useless*. Duke University Press.

Manrique, Jaime. 1999. University of Wisconsin Press.

Marks, Laura U. 2000. *The Skin of the Film: Intercultural Cinema, Embodiment, and the Senses*. Duke University Press.

Marquet, Antonio. 2010. *El coloquio de las perras: ensayo de documentación fotográfica y crónica (a ratos ensayística; a ratos perra; ¡siempre Jota!).* Universidad Autónoma Metropolitana.

Martín, Ana, vocalist. 1983. "Dulce Amor." By Bebu Silvetti and Sue Y. Javier. Spotify, track 3 on Ana Martín, *Ana Martín*. Discos America.

Martínez, Benjamín. 2020. *peDRAGogía. Laboratorio de travestismo y producción artística*. House of Inventadas.

Martinez, Fidel. 2021. "Latinx Files: Remembering Juan Gabriel five years after his death." *Los Angeles Times*, August 26, 2021. https://www.latimes.com/world-nation /newsletter/2021-08-26/latinx-files-juan-gabriel-memorial-latinx-files

Martínez, Juliana, and Salvador Vidal-Ortiz. 2021. "*Travar El Saber: Travesti*-Centred Knowledge-Making and Education." *Bulletin of Latin American Research* 40 (5): 665–78. https://doi.org/10.1111/blar.13239

Massey, Doreen. 2005. *For Space*. Sage Publications.

Mbembe, Achille. 2002. "The Power of the Archive and its Limits." In *Refiguring the Archive*, edited by Carolyn Hamilton, Verne Harris, Jane Taylor, Michele Pickover, Graeme Reid, and Razia Saleh, 19–26. Kluwer Academic Publishers.

McGlotten, Shaka. 2019. *Dragging: Or, In the Drag of a Queer Life*. Taylor & Francis.

Milian, Claudia. 2019. *LatinX*. University of Minnesota Press.

Miranda, Perla. 2016. "Teatro Blanquita: de catedral del espectáculo a hogar de indigentes." *El Universal*, July 8, 2016. https://www.eluniversal.com.mx/entrada-de-opi nion/colaboracion/mochilazo-en-el-tiempo/nacion/sociedad/2016/07/9/de-catedr al-del/

Moctezuma Mendoza, Vicente. 2021. *El desvanecimiento de lo popular: gentrificación en el Centro Histórico de la Ciudad de México*. Primera edición digital. El Colegio de México.

Mohanty, Chandra Talpade. 2003. "'Under Western Eyes' Revisited: Feminist Solidarity through Anticapitalist Struggles." *Signs: Journal of Women in Culture and Society* 28 (2): 499–535. https://doi.org/10.1086/342914

Monitoreo De Redes Sociales (@Monitoreo103). 2019. "#SiLoReconocesDenuncialo." X formerly Twitter post, February 1, 2019. https://twitter.com/Monitoreo103/status/10 91460706531192836?s=20

Monroy, Norman. 2018. "La J-Otredad." *Revista Alerta Sociológica*, no. 2: n.p.

Monsiváis, Carlos. 1988. *Escenas de pudor y liviandad*. Grijalbo.

Monsiváis, Carlos. 2018. "Círculos de perdición y salvación, pulquerías, cantinas, cabaret." *Diario de Campo, no.* 89: 4–12.

Monsiváis, Carlos. 2010a. *Que se abra esa puerta. Crónicas y ensayos sobre la diversidad sexual*. Paidós.

Monsiváis, Carlos. 2010b. *Los rituales del caos*. Era.

Montiel, Sara, vocalist. 2020. "Nena." Spotify, track 4 on Sara Montiel, *Grandes Éxitos de Sara Montiel*. Capital Music.

Muñoz, José Esteban. 1996a. "Ephemera as Evidence: Introductory Notes to Queer Acts." *Women & Performance: a journal of feminist theory* 8 (2): 5–16.

Muñoz, José Esteban. 1996b. "Ghosts of Public Sex: Utopian Longings, Queer Memories." In *Policing Public Sex: Queer Politics and the Future of AIDS Activism*, edited by Dangerous Bedfellows, 355–72. South End Press.

Muñoz, José Esteban. 1999. *Disidentifications: Queers of Color and the Performance of Politics*. University of Minnesota Press.

Muñoz, José Esteban. 2009. *Cruising Utopia: The Then and There of Queer Futurity*. New York University Press.

Muñoz, José Esteban. 2020. *The Sense of Brown*. Duke University Press.

Moraga, Cherríe. 2004. "Queer Aztlán: the Re-formation of Chicano Tribe." In *Queer Cultures*, edited by Deborah Carlin and Jennifer DiGrazia, 224–38. Pearson/Prentice Hall.

Moraga, Cherríe. 2011. *A Xicana Codex of Changing Consciousness: Writings, 2000-2010*. Duke University Press.

Moreno Figueroa, Mónica G. 2010. "Distributed Intensities: Whiteness, Mestizaje and the Logics of Mexican Racism." *Ethnicities* 10 (3): 387–401.

Namaste, Viviane K. 2000. *Invisible Lives: The Erasure of Transsexual and Transgendered People*. University of Chicago Press.

Navarrete, Federico. 2017. *Alfabeto del racismo mexicano*. Malpaso Ediciones.

Newton, Esther. 1979. *Mother Camp: Female Impersonators in America*. University of Chicago Press.

Novo, Salvador. 1938. *En defensa de lo usado y otros ensayos*. Editorial Polis.

Ofield, Simon. 2005. "Cruising the Archive." *Journal of Visual Culture* 4 (3): 351–64. https://doi.org/10.1177/1470412905058353

Oishi, Eve. 2015. "Reading Realness." In *A Companion to Contemporary Documentary Film*, edited by Alexandra Juhasz and Alisa Lebow, 252–70. John Wiley & Sons. https://doi.org/10.1002/9781118884584.ch12

Oliveira, Arize Souza Fernandes de, and Mônica Machado. 2021. "Mais Do Que Dinheiro: Pink Money E a circulação De Sentidos Na Comunidade LGBT+." *Signos Do Consumo* 13 (1): 20–31. https://doi.org/10.11606/issn.1984-5057.v13i1p20-31

Ortiz, Tareke, and Nayar Rivera. 2010. "El éxtasis a una identidad de deseo: La música como experiencia de libertad." In *México se escribe con J: Una historia de la cultura gay*, edited by Michael K. Schuessler and Miguel Capistrán, 187–201. Temas de hoy.

Paasonen, Susanna. 2018. *Many Splendored Things: Thinking Sex and Play*. Goldsmiths Press.

Pablos, David, dir. *El baile de los 41*. 2020; Netflix.

Palapa Quijas, Fabiola. 2013. "El amor, único bastión del teatro La Capilla: Jesusa Rodríguez." *La Jornada*, January 25, 2013. http://www.jornada.unam.mx/2013/01/25/cultura/a03n1cul

Paz, Octavio. 1993. *El laberinto de la soledad*. Cátedra.

Pearl, Max. 2021. "The Terrifying Cynicism of Teeter-Totter Wall." *Art in America*, January 21, 2021. https://www.artnews.com/art-in-america/columns/teeter-totter-wall-1234581905/

Pelaez Lopez, Alan. 2018. "The X In Latinx Is A Wound, Not A Trend." *Color Bloq*, Fall 2018. https://www.colorbloq.org/article/the-x-in-latinx-is-a-wound-not-a-trend

Pérez, Roy. 2012. "Mark Aguhar's Critical Flippancy," Bully Bloggers (blog), August 4, 2012. https://bullybloggers.wordpress.com/2012/08/04/mark-aguhars-critical-flippancy/

Prieto, Alain. 2015. "El Blanquita, la historia del teatro que hoy vive . . . ¿el ocaso?" *Obras por Expansión*. November 11, 2015. https://obras.expansion.mx/inmobiliario/2015/11/11/el-blanquita-la-historia-del-teatro-que-hoy-vive-el-ocaso

Portilla, Jorge. 1984. *Fenomenología del relajo y otros ensayos*. Fondo de Cultura Económica.

Power-Sotomayor, Jade. 2020. "Moving Borders and Dancing in Place: Son Jarocho's Speaking Bodies at the Fandango Fronterizo." *TDR* 64 (4): 84–107. https://doi.org/10.1162/dram_a_00966

Prieur, Annick. 1998. *Mema's House, Mexico City: On Transvestites, Queens, and Machos.* University of Chicago Press.

Puar, Jasbir K. 2007. *Terrorist Assemblages: Homonationalism in Queer Times.* Duke University Press.

Pulido Llano, Gabriela. 2018. *El mapa "rojo" del pecado: miedo y vida nocturna en la Ciudad de México, 1940–1950.* Instituto Nacional de Antropología e Historia.

Ramírez, Miguel D. 1986. "Mexico's Development Experience, 1950–85: Lessons and Future Prospects." *Journal of Interamerican Studies and World Affairs* 28 (2): 39–65.

Ramos, Iván A. 2015. "The Dirt That Haunts: *Looking* at Esta Noche." *Studies in Gender and Sexuality* 16 (2): 135–36. https://doi.org/10.1080/15240657.2015.1038195

Rault, Jasmine. 2017. "'Ridiculizing' Power: Relajo and the Affects of Queer Activism in Mexico." *The Scholar & Feminist Online* 14 (2). https://sfonline.barnard.edu/thinking-queer-activism-transnationally/ridiculizing-power-relajo-and-the-affects-of-queer-activism-in-mexico/

Revilla, Anita, and José Santillana. 2014. "Jotería Identity and Consciousness." *Aztlán* 39, no. 1: 167–80.

Reynoso, José Luis. 2023. *Dancing Mestizo Modernisms: Choreographing Postcolonial and Postrevolutionary Mexico.* Oxford University Press. https://doi.org/10.1093/oso/9780197622551.001.0001

Ripstein, Arturo, dir. *El lugar sin límites.* 1977; Mexico: Mexican Film Institute IMCINE.

Rivera-Servera, Ramón. 2012. *Performing Queer Latinidad: Dance, Sexuality, Politics.* University of Michigan Press.

Rivera-Servera, Ramón. 2017. "History in Drag: Latina/o Queer Affective Circuits in Chicago." In *The Latino/a Midwest Reader,* edited by Omar Valerio-Jiménez, Santiago R. Vaquera-Vásquez, and Claire F. Fox, 185–96. University of Illinois Press.

Rodríguez, Evelyn Ibatan. 2013. *Celebrating Debutantes and Quinceañeras: Coming of Age in American Ethnic Communities.* Temple University Press.

Rodríguez, Juana María. 2021. "Public Notice from the Fucked Peepo: Xandra Ibarra's "The Hookup/Displacement/Barhopping/Drama Tour"" In *Queer Nightlife,* edited by Kemi Adeyemi, Kareem Khubchandani, and Ramón Rivera-Servera, 211–21. University of Michigan Press.

Rodríguez, Juana María. 2023. *Puta Life: Seeing Latinas, Working Sex.* Duke University Press.

Rougemont, Denis de. 1956. *Love in the Western World.* Pantheon.

Rubenstein, Anne. 2020. "A Sentimental and Sexual Education: Men, Sex, and Movie Theaters in Mexico City, 1920–2010." *Mexican Studies* 36, no. 1–2 (Winter–Summer): 216–42.

Salinas Hernández, Héctor Miguel. 2010. *Políticas de disidencia sexual en América Latina: sujetos sociales, gobierno y mercado en México, Bogotá y Buenos Aires.* Ediciones y Gráficos Eón.

Sánchez, Carlos Alberto. 2012. *The Suspension of Seriousness: On the Phenomenology of Jorge Portilla.* State University of New York Press.

Sánchez, Montserrat, and César Carrera. 2019. "Drag Queens rompiendo cánones." *Re-*

porte Indigo, June 28, 2019. https://www.reporteindigo.com/piensa/drag-queens-ro mpiendo-canones-hermanas-vampiro-show-cabaret-orgullo-lgbti/

Sarduy, Severo. 1982. *La simulación*. Monte Ávila Editores.

San Fratello, Rael. 2021. "Teeter-totter wall." Accessed August 10, 2023. https://www.rael -sanfratello.com/made/teetertotter-wall

Schwenkel, Christina. 2015. "Sense." Theorizing the Contemporary, Fieldsights, September 24, 2015. https://culanth.org/fieldsights/sense

Secretaría de Turismo. n.d. "Capital LGBTTTI: Guía de la Diversidad en la Ciudad de México." Accessed September 9, 2023. https://www.turismo.cdmx.gob.mx/storage /app/media/guia_2019/CAPITAL%20LGBTTTI.pdf

Sedgwick, Eve Kosofsky. 2003. *Touching Feeling: Affect, Pedagogy, Performativity*. Duke University Press.

Segato, Rita. 2016. *La guerra contra las mujeres*. Traficantes de Sueños.

Segato, Rita. 2022. *The Critique of Coloniality: Eight Essays*. Taylor & Francis.

Sifuentes-Jáuregui, Ben. 2014. *The Avowal of Difference: Queer Latino American Narratives*. State University of New York Press.

Sicart, Miguel. 2014. *Play Matters*. MIT Press.

Simone, AbdouMaliq. 2004. "People as Infrastructure: Intersecting Fragments in Johannesburg." *Public Culture* 16 (3): 407–29. https://doi.org/10.1215/08992363-16-3-407

Smith, Paul Julian. 2017. *Queer Mexico: Cinema and Television Since 2000*. Wayne State University Press.

Snorton, C. Riley, and Jin Haritaworn. 2013. "Trans Necropolitics: A Transnational Reflection on Violence, Death, and the Trans of Color Afterlife." In *The Transgender Studies Reader 2*, edited by Susan Stryker and Aren Z. Aizura, 66–76. Routledge.

Spillers, Hortense. 1987. "Mama's Baby, Papa's Maybe: An American Grammar Book." *Diacritics* 17 (2): 65–81.

Stanley, Eric A. 2021. *Atmospheres of Violence: Structuring Antagonism and the Trans/ Queer Ungovernable*. Duke University Press. https://doi.org/10.1515/978147802 1520

Taylor, Diana. 2003. *The Archive and the Repertoire: Performing Cultural Memory in the Americas*. Duke University Press.

Taylor, Diana. 2016. "We have always been queer." *GLQ: A Journal of Lesbian and Gay Studies* 22 (2): 205–14.

Taylor, Verta, and Leila Rupp. 2004. "Chicks with Dicks, Men in Dresses." *Journal of Homosexuality* 46 (3–4): 113–33. https://doi.org/10.1300/J082v46n03_07

Thompson, Krista A. 2015. *Shine: The Visual Economy of Light in African Diasporic Aesthetic Practice*. Duke University Press. https://doi.org/10.1515/9780822375982

Tolentino, Rolando B. 2000. "Transvestites and Transgressions: Panggagaya in Philippine Gay Cinema." *Journal of Homosexuality* 39 (3–4): 325–37. https://doi.org/10.13 00/J082v39n03_17

Tompkins, Avery. 2014. "Asterisk." *Transgender Studies Quarterly* 1(1–2): 26–27. https:// doi.org/10.1215/23289252-2399497

Tortorici, Zeb. 2020. "Circulating Erotica: Flea Markets, Collections, and Archives in Mexico." *Journal of Popular Culture* 53 (6): 1335–57. https://doi.org/10.1111/jpcu .12976

Transgender Law Center. 2016. *Report on Human Rights Conditions of Transgender Women in Mexico*. Cornell University Law School.

Tyburczy, Jennifer. 2022. "Queer Traffic on NAFTA Time." Paper presented at the Annual Conference of the Dance Studies Association, Vancouver.

Vaccaro, Jeanne. 2010. "Felt matters." *Women & Performance: a journal of feminist theory* 20 (3): 253–66. https://doi.org/10.1080/0740770X.2010.529245

Valencia, Sayak. 2018. *Gore Capitalism*. Translated by John Pluecker. MIT Press.

Valencia, Sayak. 2010. *Capitalismo gore*. Melusina.

Vargas, Deborah R. 2014. "Ruminations on 'Lo Sucio' as a Latino Queer Analytic." *American Quarterly* 66 (3): 715–26. https://doi.org/10.1353/aq.2014.0046

Vasconcelos, José. 1997. *The Cosmic Race: A Bilingual Edition*. Translated by Didier T. Jaén. Johns Hopkins University Press.

Velour, Sasha. 2023. *The Big Reveal: An Illustrated Manifesto of Drag*. HarperCollins.

Villa, Lucha, vocalist. 1998. "Las Ciudades." By José Alfredo Jiménez. Spotify, track 4 on Lucha Villa, *Lucha Villa Interpreta a José Alfredo Jiménez*. Musart-Balboa.

Villaurrutia, Xavier. 1938. *Nostalgia de la muerte*. Sur.

Vogel, Shane. 2009. The *Scene of Harlem Cabaret: Race, Sexuality, Performance*. University of Chicago Press.

Wark, McKenzie. 2019. *Capital Is Dead: Is This Something Worse?* Verso.

Warner, Michael. 1999. *The Trouble with Normal: Sex, Politics, and The Ethics of Queer Life*. Harvard University Press.

Wayar, Marlene. 2018. *Travesti: una teoría lo suficientemente buena*. Editorial Muchas Nueces.

Wilson, Ara. 2004. *The Intimate Economies of Bangkok: Tomboys, Tycoons, and Avon Ladies in the Global City*. University of California Press.

Yépez, Heriberto. 2010. *La increíble hazaña de ser mexicano*. Editorial Planeta.

Zadik. 2003. "En el Cine Teresa," Todo Relatos (blog), August 17, 2003. https://www.todorelatos.com/relato/12462/

Index

"41 Tropiezos de la heteronorma en México, Los," 184
See also El Baile de los 41 (Pablo); heteronormativity

absence, 3, 31, 93, 95, 126, 144, 154, 248, 250, 260–61n2
  historical, 215–16
  See also haunting; loss
abstraction, 9, 14, 71, 136, 146, 203–04, 218
  See also materiality
academia, 18, 27, 110, 184, 219, 231–32, 260–61n2, 263n16
  epistemic limits of, 33–34, 93, 116–18, 170
  institutions of, 136
  white heteronormative logics of, 13–14, 22, 31, 40–41
  See also studies; writing
academics, 56, 253n2, 257–58n11
  See also studies; writing
accumulation, 73, 148, 154, 213
  of property and capital, 12, 20, 71, 75, 147, 161, 171–72, 175, 257n5
  See also capitalism
activism, 33, 56, 106, 184, 189, 192, 204, 215–16, 266–67n18
  practices of, 33
  See also activists; praxis
activists, 10, 80, 100, 170, 217, 257–58n11, 260–61n2, 267nn4–5
  See also activism

actors, 132–33, 152, 159, 268n10
  child, 148, 151
  social, 6, 15, 44, 77, 91, 216, 255n16
  See also agency; icons
aesthetics, 58, 72–73, 85–87, 106, 112, 120, 183, 256n1, 257n10, 258n14, 262n6
  black and white, 124, 137, 140, 143, 158
  drag, 77–78,
  carceral, 229
  pinkwashed, 3
  working-class, 181
  See also baroque; materiality
afterglow, 17, 44, 59, 139, 197, 235, 244, 251
  of objects, 152, 154–58
  resisting neoliberalism, 138, 232, 234
  spatial, 142–48, 151
  See also glow; worldmaking
agency, 10, 12, 68, 106, 150, 182, 192, 217, 230, 254n8
  queer, 24, 73, 75, 104, 110, 116, 164, 189
  See also actors
Ahmed, Sara, 8, 36, 73, 105, 124, 134–35, 170, 238, 254n10, 265n4
  See also encounters; praxis; shadows
AIDS, 4, 113, 235, 247, 256n1, 263n17, 264n24
Alba, Liliana, 64, 189, 196, 220–24, 226–27
  See also activism; bantering; *Casa Roshell* (Donoso); laughter; intimacy; travestis
Aldama, Julio, 149

Alice in Wonderland (film), 81
Alien (Scott), 123
"All Coming Back To Me" (Dion), 92
alternatives, 16, 36, 78, 90, 110, 141, 170,
    175, 241
    knowledge, 33, 192
    practice, 57, 70–71
    space, 19–20
    See also potential
Alzate, Gastón A., 85, 176–77
    See also cabarets; marginalization;
        Teatro de cabaret (Alzate)
ambiances, 42, 46, 177, 188, 190, 229, 241
    nighttime, 5–8, 16, 18, 20, 89, 92, 103,
        192, 195, 201, 245, 248
    See also music; night-making; night-
        scapes; worldmaking
Amelia's, 248
"Amor de cabaret" (Santanera) 18, 159,
    264n5
    See also cabarets; Goded, Maya; *Plaza
        de la Soledad* (Goded)
Los Ángeles Azules, 6, 198
    See also music
Angélica María, 132–33
    See also icons; media; music
anonymity, 60, 110, 116, 118, 120–21, 123,
    130
anuses. *See* asses
appropriation, 44, 69, 221, 258–59n15,
    268n7
architecture, 105, 114–16, 130, 209, 229
    drag, 76–78
    See also infrastructures; urban spaces
archives, 5, 15, 27, 44, 94–95, 186, 215, 248,
    263n19
    queer, 110, 115–18, 157
    See also haunting; indexing
Argentina, 217, 267n4
    See also Latin America
"Arráncame la vida" (Dávila), 199–200
    See also Casa Roshell; music
Art in America (magazine), 230
    See also Teeter-Totter Wall Project
        (Rael and San Fratello)
artifacts, 8, 15–20, 34, 167, 182, 187, 232, 251

artistry, 40–41, 231
artists, 85, 152, 241, 245, 249–50, 265n3
    Chicanx/Latinx, 233–34
    emerging, 122
    multimedia, 237
    performance, 50
    photo, 16, 100–01, 119
    queer/trans, 256n1, 257–58n11, 258n12,
        260–61n2, 261n4, 267n5, 269–70n8
    visual, 239
    See also actors; artistry; beauty; world-
        making
assault, 4, 10, 146
    See also homophobia; transphobia;
        violence
"Así Fue" (Pantoja), 49, 93–95
    See also longing; lover; nostalgia
assemblage, 35, 80, 221, 236
asses, 28, 31, 34–35, 112–13, 161, 241
attachments, 20, 28, 55, 67, 125, 141, 155,
    216, 254n12
    affective, 8, 53, 74, 81, 135, 150, 154, 157,
        200–01, 225
attraction, 69, 171, 176, 265n2
    See also desire; lover
audiences, 1, 27, 42, 64, 149, 158, 172, 199–
    200, 216, 230, 260–61n2
    challenging, 81–82, 85
    engagement with, 35, 49, 63, 76, 87–
        89, 102–03, 107–08, 160, 221–26,
        262n10, 268n10
    See also stages
aunts, 41–46, 49, 52, 58–59, 77
    See also motherhood; mothers
autoethnography, 13–14, 27, 123
    See also writing
autonomy, 126, 160, 194, 249
axis, 42, 56
    theoretical, 7, 13, 29, 31, 35–36, 128, 167,
        265n7

El Baile de los 41 (Pablo), 4, 21, 166, 179–
    80, 185–87, 256n1, 262n8, 266n13
    See also becoming; capture; homosex-
        uality; nationalism; Pablo, David
Ballard, Finn Jackson, 246

bantering, 37–39, 61, 65, 159, 172, 193, 196, 198, 200, 209
  as resistance, 69, 139, 174, 176, 178, 187, 210–11, 219–21
Barker, Jennifer M., 159
baroque, 42, 68–70, 76, 86–87, 256n3, 257n5
  See also aesthetics; drag queens
Barretto, Antonio Morales, 95
  See also Dúrcal, Rocío; Gabriel, Juan; impossibility
bars, 195, 198
  gay, 106, 175
  queer, 80, 90, 92, 95, 118–19, 124, 240, 248–49, 257–58n4
  underground, 3–4, 69, 72, 75, 259n21
  See also cabarets; night-making; nightscapes; underground
BearMex festival, 90
beauty, 39, 49, 61, 208, 264n24
  pageantry, 41–42, 46, 51–53, 57–58
becoming, 12, 24, 66, 69, 71, 73, 84–85, 87, 94, 119, 126, 129, 188, 217, 263n16
  drag, 13, 46, 52, 58, 76, 78
  nationalist, 36, 55
  trans, 21, 101–07, 179
  travesti, 22, 131, 148, 150–58, 180–83, 192–97, 200–08, 212–15, 218–19, 225
  See also drag queens; queer relajo; worldmaking
"Believe" (Cher), 92
belonging, 4, 17–18, 57–58, 66–68, 72–76, 91–92, 165, 221, 225, 242–44, 248, 251, 265n3
  intimacy and, 207, 214
  national, 9–13, 27–29, 53–55, 83, 87–89, 131–37, 162, 169, 177–83, 190–91, 216, 230–41
  See also nationalism; unbelonging
Beltrán, Lola, 132, 134
  See also icons
Berkins, Lohana, 217, 267n4
  See also activism; becoming; playfulness
Berlant, Lauren, 93

"El beso" (Churumbeles de España), 175
Betancourt, Manuel, 186, 266n15
Betsky, Aaron, 120
binaries, 112, 213, 263n16
  gender, 70, 173, 208, 212, 223, 265–66n8
  See also alternatives; dichotomy; heteronormativity; heterosexuality
bisexuality, 181, 209, 253n3
Black people, 23, 33, 36, 77, 135, 218, 238, 255n19, 257n10
Blanco, José Joaquín, 2–3, 72–73, 168, 257n7
  See also commodification; pinkwashing
blowjobs, 112, 131, 138, 224, 249–50
  See also cruising; encounters; metreo
blue, 47, 75, 76, 79, 92, 101–03, 108, 188, 197, 235
  See also pink; subway
Blue Moon, 47–48, 93
bodies, 12–14, 16, 31–32, 34, 50–51, 56, 59, 99, 121–22, 150–51, 239–40
  cruising, 112–14, 124–27, 139–40
  femme, 22, 159
  modulating, 189, 193, 203–05, 266–67n18
  nighttime, 19, 21, 37–38, 109, 129–30, 160, 191, 210–11, 220–21, 225, 249–50
  otherized, 77, 83, 85, 169–70, 201, 218, 248, 257n10, 269nn4–5
  performing drag, 27, 66, 68, 76, 80
  resisting, 10, 29, 73, 78, 88, 104–08, 145, 213–14, 217, 242
  young, 53, 55
  See also embodiments
Bonelli, Coral, 148
bootleg commerce, 46, 77, 99, 127
Borderlands, 50, 229–231
  See also US-Mexico border
borders, 27, 29, 39, 84, 128, 150, 240–41, 244, 247, 249, 251, 264n4, 268–69n3
boundaries, 15, 18, 32, 84, 103, 107, 114, 157, 192, 217–18, 231–33, 235–36, 238
  spatiotemporal, 11, 73, 78, 103, 145, 248
  See also limits

Brazil, 51, 106, 115, 179
  See also Latin America
"Break Free" (Grande), 92
El Bremel (cabaret), 151
bridges, 138–40, 142, 145–48
  metaphorical, 31–35, 105, 107, 165, 198–
    00, 220, 224, 229, 231, 235, 239, 247,
    266n13, 268n6, 268n8
  See also connections
Brownness, 126, 135, 167, 237, 239, 243,
    250, 265n19, 269n6
  See also working class
Bruce, Caitlin Frances, 88
butterflies, 76, 237, 258n12

cabarets, 3–4, 22, 69, 72, 165, 167, 170–78,
    192–93, 195–201, 210–28, 264n5,
    265n6
  in film, 18, 148, 151–53, 159, 180–83,
    188–89
  performances in, 14, 63, 66, 80, 85–91,
    141, 190–91, 203, 206–09, 220–27,
    234, 245, 254, 258–59, 268n9
  See also bars; Casa Roshell; *Casa
    Roshell* (Donoso); night-making;
    nightscapes; queer relajo
Cabral, Roberto, 14, 66, 71, 80–85, 87–91,
    96, 258n13, 259n18
  See also cabarets; drag queens; satire
Calderón, Felipe, 82
California, 76, 236, 240
  Los Angeles, 242–43
  Oakland, 237
  Sacramento, 240
  San Francisco, 3, 233, 247–50
  See also US-Mexico border
Calle Ámberes (thoroughfare), 4, 118
Calzada de Tlalpán (neighborhood),
    189–90
cameras
  in film, 137, 139–40, 148, 153–59, 188–
    89, 193–97, 210, 214, 248
  looking directly into, 101, 120
  video, 109–112, 116–17, 123, 125
  See also capture; Graham, David;
    photography; Stark, Eriko

Canclini, Néstor García, 88
capitalism, 33, 56, 68, 77, 127–28, 172, 218,
    255n16, 257n10, 259n17, 268n2
  neoliberal, 13, 20, 23, 27–28, 57, 72, 75,
    105–06, 132–36, 166, 170, 232–33
  See also commodification; consump-
    tion; pinkwashing
capture, 28, 38, 41, 121, 141–45, 158, 187,
    210, 217
  neoliberal, 16, 20–21, 78, 110
  of public space, 4
  photographic, 122, 124–25, 155
  technologies of, 15, 212–13, 238, 241
  See also cameras; commodification;
    consumption
Cárdenas, Lázaro, 151
cárdenas, micha, 218
the Caribbean, 29, 38, 59
  See also Latin America
Carlos-Manuel, 231, 235
Carmín Tropical (Pérezcano), 179
Caro, Manolo, 180–83, 187
Carpa Margo Su (performance space),
    152
Carr, Vikki, 92
Carrillo, Héctor, 250
La Casa de las Flores, (Caro), 21, 166,
    179–80, 182–84, 187
  See also capture; commodification;
    erasure; travestis; travestismo
Casa Roshell (Donoso), 22, 167, 187, 192,
    202
  See also Alba, Liliana; cabarets; Casa
    Roshell; García, Lia; Terranova,
    Roshell
"Castillos" (Miguel), 92
Castro, Verónica, 132, 134
catalog. *See* indexing
catholic church, 11, 51, 235, 259n16,
    266n12
  See also institutions
Cavallero, Lucí, 21, 24, 57
The Center for Cultural Power, 237
Central America, 236, 243
  See also Latin America
Cervantes-Gómez, Xiomara, 263n16

Cervantes, Blanca Eva, 152
Cervantes, Susana Vargas, 182, 266n18
Cervantes, Tadeo, 50, 241, 257–58n11,
    260–61n2, 265n3
Chambers-Letson, Joshua, 208
Chayanne, 103
Cher, 71, 92
children, 38, 40, 42, 49, 53, 99, 149, 151,
    221, 230, 239, 263–64n23
Chile, 132, 265n6
    See also Latin America
"La Chingada," 81–82, 108
choreography, 7, 29, 33, 56, 109, 129,
    251
    performance of, 49, 110, 151, 153
    social, 5, 58–59, 101, 104–05, 134, 139,
    177
    of touch, 16, 99–100, 112, 117, 123, 126,
    140, 269n6
    travesti, 189, 193–94, 203–06, 210, 212,
    215
    working-class queer underground, 20
    See also ambiances
Los Churumbeles de España, 175
Cine Teresa (theater), 130–31, 162
cinema, 42, 147, 149, 269n7
Cineteca Nacional (theater), 131
citizenship, 14, 29, 32, 78, 83–85, 88, 101,
    133, 165, 229, 238
    queer, 3, 50
    sexual, 70, 89, 91, 120, 184
    shaping national, 53, 55, 241
    See also nationalism; scripts
Ciudad Azteca (station), 138, 141,
    144–46
"Las Ciudades" (Villa), 151, 245
Ciudad Juárez, 95, 229
clothes, 47, 75–78, 114, 117, 125, 149, 186–
    88, 193, 201, 266–67n18
    See also dresses; materiality
Club Amazonas (Fiesco), 179
Colectivo Chopeke, 229
collectives, 6, 22, 31, 67–69, 73, 92, 106,
    190, 231, 235, 257–58n11, 259n21
    See also community
collectivity, 9–10, 23, 49, 89–90, 104–05,

    129, 177, 191, 195, 224, 238, 248–49,
    251, 256n2
    See also assemblage
Colonia Roma (neighborhood), 156
"Come Into My World" (Minogue),
    92
comfort, 37, 63, 79, 103, 121, 142, 144, 154,
    199, 205, 243
commodification, 147, 168, 208, 217, 230,
    233, 236, 254n7, 257n10
    of affect, 15, 31
    heterosexual, 2–3, 58, 133, 184
    pink, 70
    of public space, 4, 18–19
    queer, 89–90, 100, 115–16, 119, 121, 132,
    160
    resistance to, 5–6, 17, 20, 23, 50, 126–27,
    190–92
    thriving amid, 56, 88, 178–79
    of travesti identity, 165–66, 169–70,
    180, 183, 187, 196, 200, 211–13
    See also capitalism; consumption
communion, 8, 32, 46
community, 3, 33, 57, 60, 70, 107, 125
commuting, 99–100, 102–05, 107–08,
    110, 112, 114–15, 118, 123, 126–27, 138,
    144–45, 261
    See also cruising; metreo; subway
"Concierto para Bongó" (Prado), 153
Condesa (neighborhood), 156, 190
connections, 32–37, 51–52, 58, 101, 117–18,
    123, 127, 151, 184, 195, 199–00, 206,
    216, 251
    of feeling and sensing, 1, 44, 104, 161,
    225
    nighttime, 8, 16, 27–28, 68, 142, 243
    to normative value, 12
    sexual, 49
    sonic, 239, 249
    See also encounters; intimacy
constraint, 72, 81, 105–06, 135, 182, 215,
    217
consumerism, 2–3, 68, 74–75, 88–89, 106,
    167, 175, 255
    See also capitalism; commodification;
    consumption

consumption, 10, 64, 74–75, 131, 170, 176,
    179, 202, 219, 232–33, 236
  neoliberal, 69–72, 88, 137, 246–48
  cultural, 167, 257–58n11
  queer spaces of, 5, 78, 90, 106–11, 116,
    120–22, 125, 216, 259n18
  sexual, 2, 67
  sites of, 3
  underground networks of, 19, 57, 80,
    128, 208
  of violence, 85
  visual, 182, 214
  See also capitalism; commodification;
    hypervisibility; materiality; nation-
    alism; pinkwashing
contingency, 34, 88–89, 206, 208
  cultural, 70, 73–74, 83, 169, 171,
    257
  material, 71, 77, 114, 129, 221
  practices of, 20, 265n4
  See also impossibility
contradictions, 9–10, 124, 182, 219, 232,
    235, 146, 254n8, 269n7
  of neoliberal states, 15, 29, 70, 78, 81,
    84, 86, 100, 122, 209, 211–12, 229,
    243, 257–58n11
  theoretical, 31, 35, 38, 56, 115, 265n4
conventions, 58, 103, 149, 181, 210
  heterosexual, 52, 73, 86, 94, 136, 172,
    174, 178, 183, 196, 213, 214, 223, 265–
    66n8
  nationalist, 8
  scholarly, 14–15, 18, 29, 31, 40, 117–18,
    123, 171, 192, 219
  See also alternatives
Cornejo, Giancarlo, 150, 170, 207, 264n4,
    265n5
Cornell University, 179, 266n10
corruption, 5, 18, 46, 52, 106, 137–38,
    268n10
"Cosas del Amor" (Gabriel and Carr),
    92
COVID pandemic, 113, 258
Coyoacán (neighborhood), 90
crime, 36, 138, 179, 184, 215
criminalization, 4, 207, 237–39, 262n8

Cristina La Veneno, 92
cross-dressing, 173, 186–87, 193, 256n1,
    266–67n18
  See also clothes; drag queens; dresses;
    travestismo
crowns, 27, 30, 39, 42–44, 49–52, 56, 58–
    59, 64, 103, 107
  See also drag queens; glitter; glitz;
    materiality
cruising, 32–33, 127, 131, 139–40, 196,
    200
  subway, 20, 100, 108–126, 146, 210
  as relajo, 5, 11, 16–17, 19, 50, 99, 129, 137,
    141–45, 147–48, 211, 219–20, 234
  See also longing; metreo; subway;
    waiting
Cruz, Celia, 153
Cuevas, Aida, 132
Cuevas, Ximena, 80

D'Alessio, Lupita, 153
dancing
  club, 33, 37, 46, 126, 198, 234, 241
  performance of, 56, 247
  relajo, 5, 19–20, 50, 99–100, 103, 106–
    07, 112, 129, 165, 167, 224, 227, 245,
    248–50
  travesti, 171–78, 181, 187, 203, 209
  See also ambiances; bars; cabarets;
    music
danger, 11, 14, 18, 37, 123, 129, 167, 170, 173,
    214, 232, 246
  discourse of, 10, 19, 120
  threatening queer and trans life, 2, 38,
    106, 147, 187, 189, 207–08, 213, 219
  See also risks; violence
darkness, 1, 8, 99, 124, 172, 189, 201, 204,
    209–14, 228
  See also shade; shadow
darkrooms, 32, 63, 130, 189, 214
Dávila, Chivirico, 199
death, 28, 31, 38, 46, 180, 186–87, 214,
    264n24, 264–65n6
  on film, 156, 161, 171–76, 181–83
  life and, 4, 21, 113, 207–08, 218–20
  resistance to, 166–70, 191, 210, 240

and violence, 18, 50, 57, 147, 178, 230–32, 247
See also loss; violence
defrantz, thomas f., 106
dehumanization, 16, 186, 229, 230, 238
Delany, Samuel, 121
"Desaires" (Dúrcal), 245
Desde Andalucía (Pantoja), 93, 260n24
Désert, Jean-Ulrick, 106
desire, 2, 7, 56–57, 78–80, 110–14, 120–124, 130–31
collective, 49
See also attraction; lover
destruction, 9, 38, 40, 92, 151
devaluation, 77, 129, 135, 183
development, 36, 87–91, 95, 105, 122, 172, 258–59n15
national, 10, 50, 55, 69–71, 81–84
under-, 18, 46, 134–38, 232, 264–65n6
urban, 144, 152, 157
See also capitalism; dispossession; progress
dialogues, 9, 28, 149, 160, 166, 190, 217, 257–58n11, 260–61n2
diaspora, 246, 249, 256n1, 257–58n11
queer Mexican, 27–29, 52, 56, 60, 96, 134, 167, 219, 231–41, 252
See also Mexicanidad
Díaz, Porfirio, 186
dichotomy, 15, 35, 167, 173, 203, 218
See also binaries
Dion, Celine, 92
dirtiness, 50, 56, 100, 111–12, 119–23, 126–29, 151, 160–62, 221, 232–34, 248–52
See also filth; grittiness
discomfort, 29, 60, 99, 123, 127, 215, 233
discrimination, 81, 86, 133, 136, 153, 179, 207, 215, 223–24, 236
See also danger; homophobia; risks; transphobia
disillusionment, 64, 92, 95, 139–40, 142
displacement, 6, 44, 79, 127–28
from gentrification, 17, 19–20, 90, 122, 132, 145, 148, 156–57, 233
Indigenous, 81, 87, 89, 231

from migration, 38, 84, 219, 264n24
resisting, 51, 55, 58, 151, 155, 234, 236–37, 248–51
See also diaspora; gentrification
dispossession, 21, 83–89, 121, 129, 162, 177, 212
resistance to, 13, 44, 50, 79, 233
See also capitalism; gentrification
disruption, 41, 69, 76, 88–89, 95, 129, 150, 193, 216–20, 231, 239, 246, 251, 263n16
of cishet systems, 12, 24, 57, 100–02, 196, 207–08
of commodification, 166
in consumption, 80
intimacy as, 18
of Mexicanidad, 44, 176–79
physical, 28–29
possibilities of, 105–08, 203
of whiteness, 46, 127, 137
See also activism; interruption; possibilities; resistance
dissidence, 70–72, 91
gender, 127, 137, 179–80, 184, 265n3
sexual, 2, 18, 40–41, 67, 77–78, 88, 95, 177, 186, 216–17, 256n1, 257–58n11
See also alternatives; heterosexuality
dissonance, 33–35, 41, 95–95, 108, 157
Domínguez-Ruvalcaba, Héctor, 236, 257–58n11
Donoso, Camila José, 22, 187–88, 190, 202, 256n1, 265n6, 267–68n8
See also cabarets; Casa Roshell; *Casa Roshell* (Donoso)
drag queens, 50, 66, 235, 240, 247–48, 256n1, 258n12
accessories, 32, 76, 78–80, 103
culture, 14, 46, 67–71, 74
iconic, 72
performers, 49, 84–96
See also becoming: drag; dressing rooms; glitter; glitz; materiality; Piña Colada; travesties; travestismo
Drag Race (show), 75

dresses, 47, 61, 92, 154, 186, 193–95, 206,
    245, 266–67n18, 268n10
  distinct Mexican, 81, 215, 247
  materiality of, 27, 197, 200, 222
  Piña Colada, 1, 14, 32, 58, 60, 63, 66
  quinceañera, 42, 102–03
  red, 175, 188, 199
  second-hand, 70, 75–79, 93
  sequin, 220, 225, 232, 262n10
  See also drag queens; glitter; glitz;
    heels; makeup; materiality; wigs
dressing rooms, 37, 49, 60–61, 189,
    193–94
Dúrcal, Rocío, 39, 46, 63, 95, 245

earthquake (1985), 130, 155–56
e-flux (journal), 77–78
Ecatepec (neighborhood), 138
echoes, 15, 24, 73, 139, 143–44, 212, 218,
    249
  scholarly, 32, 34, 41, 50, 104, 106, 113,
    120, 169, 238, 254n10, 265n7
  sonic, 6, 59, 92, 95, 127, 134, 138, 142,
    193, 224, 229, 241
  See also music
ecology, 56, 76, 80, 96, 128, 140, 168
  drag, 14, 44, 66, 71, 91, 175, 183
  queer, 6, 32
economy, 68–70, 100, 136, 167, 170–71,
    187, 225
  affective, 121–22, 140, 159, 161, 197, 221
  local, 51, 173
  shadow, 57, 160, 174–83, 255n16
  of violence, 21, 230, 269n4
  See also capitalism; commodification;
    consumption; development
education, 40–41, 53, 55, 100, 181, 203,
    245
Eje Central (thoroughfare), 130
embodiments, 56, 59, 66–67, 101–04, 157,
    179, 182–83, 192, 198, 268n1
  affective, 232
  femme, 58, 143, 176
  gender and sexual, 120
  of male homoeroticism, 173, 253n5
  of Mexicanidad, 28, 135, 215–17

of queer refusal, 8
of queer relajo, 6, 10, 87, 110, 118, 220,
    225
travesti, 21, 151, 154, 166–71, 187, 194–
    96, 206, 227
  See also bodies; night-making; night-
    scapes
emotion, 34, 40, 71, 83, 92, 95, 133, 142–
    43, 154, 157–59, 199, 221, 263n17
  collective, 90, 249
  expressing, 37, 195, 268n8
En defensa de lo usado y otros ensayos
    (Novo), 74
enclosure, 11, 19, 55, 101, 128, 144, 147, 243
  See also capitalism; gentrification
encounters, 127, 147, 159–62, 199–200,
    260–61n2
  affective, 100, 104, 196, 234
  intimate, 22
  material, 13, 32, 195
  nighttime, 19, 191, 242
  sexual, 112–18, 139–44, 263n20
  urban, 17
  See also cruising; intimacy; night-
    scapes
enslavement, 38, 51, 77
  See also dispossession
entanglements, 58, 116, 133, 222, 234,
    265n6
  affective, 118, 137, 149, 208, 265n3
  material, 126
  postcolonial, 69, 217
  of socioeconomic, 57
  See also commodification; infrastruc-
    tures; photography; urban spaces
entertainment, 56, 77, 110, 127, 152, 175,
    187, 245
  mass, 68, 85, 149, 200
"Entrega de amor" (Los Ángles Azules),
    198
ephemera, 34, 103, 117, 157
ephemerality, 6, 28, 33, 50, 59, 69, 72, 78,
    139, 141–43, 157, 174, 178, 197, 199–
    200, 209, 225
  knowledge, 16–19
  of the night, 104, 147, 227, 234

See also ambiances; fugitivity; materiality; night-making; nightscapes

epistemologies, 29, 159, 192, 267n4
global south, 15
trans and queer, 107, 257–58n11, 265n7
violent, 31, 33, 218, 232, 235, 255n15
See also academia; ontologies; studies

erasure, 28, 31, 36, 67, 82, 122, 131, 135–37, 148, 150, 181, 183, 212, 233, 255n19
resistance to, 73, 80–81, 87, 178, 236–37, 250
See also discrimination; silences; violence

escape, 32, 67, 94, 142, 189, 214, 219, 233, 238, 243

ethics, 200, 217, 230–31, 236, 246, 263n16
feminist, 170, 193, 281n4
queer, 115, 119–20
research, 31, 110, 116, 169, 257–58n11

ethnicity, 24, 29, 52, 57, 101, 120, 165–66, 191, 217, 231
See also racialization

excess, 95, 129
in drag culture, 67–68, 70, 74, 77–78, 87, 92, 256n3
misrepresentation of, 14, 28, 50, 56, 170, 230, 251
of the night, 37, 39, 169
queer, 10, 20, 32, 42, 44, 113, 154, 177, 233, 237, 241, 249
See also aesthetics; baroque; drag queens; glitter; glitz; materiality

exchanges, 109, 112, 115, 126, 128, 160, 174, 178–80, 195, 258–59n15, 263n16
economic, 19, 57

exoticization, 24, 38, 58, 120, 125
See also fetishization

exploitation, 4, 23–24, 31, 38, 85, 143, 203, 207, 236, 255–56n1
artistic, 100, 246
resistance to, 16, 57, 128
See also capitalism; commodification

exposure, 149, 166
violence of, 115–16, 119, 121–22, 165, 176, 180, 189, 212, 245–47, 262n8

failure, 8, 58, 73, 84, 92, 95, 154, 172, 184, 212, 215–16, 230, 257n6
national progress, 29, 46, 50, 52, 152, 232
romantic, 81, 137, 140, 144
See also development; progress

fantasy, 12, 15, 73–74, 80–81, 93, 130, 196, 198, 213
larger-than-life, 42, 58, 66, 95–96, 172, 223, 226, 247
nighttime, 18, 32–33
as resistance, 12, 32–33, 66, 73–74, 95–96, 130, 172, 196, 198, 213, 247
social, 56, 86
See also drag queens

Fe, Esperanza y Caridad (Fons), 150, 157, 264n3

fear, 33, 73, 93, 143–44, 172, 180, 230, 238, 268n5
See also danger; risks

Felipe, Liliana, 80

fellatio. *See* blowjobs

feminicide, 21, 28, 106, 168, 207, 229, 253n1, 262n10, 264–65n6
See also crime; death; discrimination; homophobia; transphobia; violence

femininity, 56, 58, 186, 210–11, 265n5
performance of, 44, 104, 107, 133
queer, 27, 36
trans, 76, 181
travesti, 203–08
See also masculinity

Ferguson, Roderick A., 134

Fernández, Vicente, 132, 134, 152

festival, 53–54, 57, 90, 259n18, 259nn20–21

festiveness, 32, 57, 103, 134–35, 213

fetishization, 200, 211
See also exoticization

Fiesco, Roberto, 17, 148, 156, 159, 264n3
See also Club Amazonas (Fiesco); *Quebranto* (Fiesco)

filth, 126–27, 129, 247, 250
See also dirtiness; grittiness

Flans, 71

Florencio, Flavio, 179

Florida, 236

Fons, Jorge, 149–50, 264n3
See also *Fe, Esperanza y Caridad*
(Fons)

food, 32, 57, 72, 100, 146, 198, 235
insecurity, 3, 264–65n6
See also vendors

Foro A Poco No (theater), 89–90, 259n21

Foster, David William, 71, 173, 257–58n11

Fox, Vicente, 82

fragmentation, 27, 44, 66–67, 73–78, 85–
87, 99, 213, 256n3

"The Francis Show" (García), 152, 223
See also cabarets; García, Francis;
travestis

Franco, Horacio, 168

Franco, Robert, 185, 187, 266–67n18

friction, 16, 99, 104, 112–14, 117, 120, 145,
191, 194, 230, 253n4

frottage, 112, 131, 140

fugitivity, 21, 27, 32, 66–67, 84
queer, 14, 19, 233, 236–39, 243, 247–48,
250–51
transfeminist, 211
See also ephemerality

Furias Nocturnas (Stark), 15, 100, 119, 122
See also cameras; cruising; metreo;
Graham, David; photography;
Stark, Eriko; subway

futurity, 10, 13, 36, 91, 263n21
See also imaginaries

Gabriel, Ana, 32, 92

Gabriel, Juan, 12, 64–66, 93–95, 239–41,
247–49, 251, 260n23

Gago, Verónica, 21, 23–24, 57, 69, 128,
257n5, 257–58n11

Galería José María Velasco, 122

García, Lia (La Novia Sirena), 16, 100–
10, 125, 170, 189, 197, 209, 262n6
See also connections; encounters; *Mis
XXy años* (García); quinceañera;
subway

García, Francis, 152, 223, 268n10
See also cabarets; "The Francis Show"
(García)

García, Sara, 149

gaze, 39, 69, 123, 139–41, 158, 197, 199
neoliberal cis, 120–21, 125, 168, 170,
175, 192, 196, 209–10, 213, 230
queer, 100
See also capture; photography

gender nonconformity, 2, 5, 105, 176, 227,
238
See also binaries; heteronormativity

"Gente" (José José), 138

gentrification, 17, 46, 121, 207, 216, 233,
243, 246, 248–51
of Mexico City, 3, 19, 110, 122, 131–32,
137, 146–48, 152, 156, 160–62, 208
queer, 88, 269–70n8
See also capitalism; enclosure

geographies, 35, 70, 84, 149, 231, 242, 252,
268n1
diasporic, 27
queer, 44, 68, 89, 137
underground, 7, 131
See also gentrification; mappings;
working class; territory; underground

gestures, 56, 76, 83, 107, 116, 127, 130, 143–
44, 175, 186, 197, 210–11, 234–35
affective, 150, 157, 188
bold, 35
of drag performance, 1, 7, 64, 86–89,
158
of metreo, 110–15, 117–19, 123, 125–26
of parody, 66, 215–17, 254n11
performing mestizaje, 133–34
poses and, 58, 68–69
of queer sociality, 8–9, 21, 139–41, 160,
194, 200, 204–05, 246, 249, 254n12
theoretical, 38, 49, 84, 102, 232, 240–
41, 268n6
See also connections; embodiments

"Gimme All Your Colors: Blue" (Salgado), 239

Giorgo, John, 113

glitter, 1, 7, 47, 53, 58, 63, 66, 71, 76–79, 87,
95, 188, 222, 225
an affect of, 32, 39, 41, 51, 73, 80, 125,
139, 197, 214

See also drag queens; glitz; shine
glitz, 39, 42, 63, 76, 78, 87, 243, 268n10
   See also drag queens; glitter; shine
global south, 5, 15–16, 22–23, 69, 100,
   116, 121, 128, 168, 217, 231–33, 255n18,
   268n1
   See also postcoloniality
globalization, 10, 14, 69, 83, 85, 87, 136,
   233
Glorieta Insurgentes (neighborhood),
   118
glow, 41, 47, 58, 63–65, 113, 219
   of drag queens, 32, 39
   of jotería, 229–38, 240–42, 247
   See also afterglow; glitter; glitz
Goded, Maya, 17, 15–59, 162
   See also La Merced (neighborhood);
   Plaza de la Soledad (Goded)
Gortari, Salinas de, 132, 134
Graham, David, 16, 100, 118–22, 125–26
   See also cruising; "Last Car, The:
      Cruising in Mexico City" (Gra-
      ham); metreo; photography; Stark,
      Eriko; subway
grammars, 117, 127, 130, 137, 170, 239
Gran Teatro Circo Orrin, 152
Grande, Ariana, 92
grayscale, 138–42, 147
   grittiness, 3, 96, 178, 181, 183
   See also dirtiness; filth
Guatemala, 243
   See also Latin America
Gutiérrez, Laura G., 55, 85, 128, 177

El Hábito (stage), 90
Hadad, Astrid, 80
Haritaworn, Jin, 166, 169, 189
haunting, 52, 74, 88, 113, 155, 202, 215, 248,
   250, 263n17
   See also archives
healing, 3, 19, 23, 64, 93–94, 190, 243
   See also collectivity; danger; illness;
   loss; risks
heartbreak, 46, 95, 137, 142, 147–48, 197,
   200, 209, 225, 249
   See also loss; lover

heels, 6, 47, 49, 72, 195, 204–05, 220–22,
   225, 263–64n23
   red stiletto, 1, 12, 22, 60, 63
   See also drag queens; dresses; makeup;
   materiality; wigs
Hernández, Julián, 17, 137, 146, 168
heteronormativity, 5, 8, 13, 81, 143, 167,
   171–76, 179–84
   Mexican, 7, 11, 106
   refusing, 24, 69, 94–95, 112, 126, 140,
   201, 209–10, 215–16, 227, 241
   See also nationalism
heterosexuality, 55, 57–58, 81, 171, 173,
   180–82, 209, 211
   challenging, 6, 8, 33, 36, 73–75, 92–94,
   128, 141, 220–21
   structural violence of, 2, 52, 87, 105,
   136, 213–14, 268nn9–10
   See also binaries; dichotomy
homelessness, 135, 147, 152, 160
   See also displacement; gentrification
homoeroticism, 21, 130, 166, 169, 173–74,
   179, 253n5
homonormativity, 17, 70, 132, 161, 167–68,
   170, 179, 233–34, 238, 248
homophobia, 5, 106, 141, 146, 168, 223,
   254n11, 265n2, 266n12
   See also discrimination; transphobia;
   violence
Hook Up/Displacement/Barhopping/
   Drama Tour, The (Ibarra), 234,
   247
hope, 17, 35, 78, 92–93, 107, 122, 134, 188,
   212, 251
humor, 81–82, 84, 89, 177, 235
   queer, 91, 191, 208, 215, 221–24,
   268n9
   See also laughter; satire
hybridity, 69, 90, 130, 184, 257n5
hypervisibility, 21, 115–17, 165, 167, 171,
   176, 180, 186–87, 189, 200, 212, 214,
   227
   See also risks; travestis

Ibarra, Xandra, 34, 234, 236–37, 247–51,
   270n9

ICE, 237
  See also immigration; migrants; migration; US-Mexico border
icons, 141, 235, 239, 256n1
  drag, 39, 72
  of Mexican nationalism, 53, 55, 133
  music, 63, 183
  place, 1, 38, 46, 90, 125, 130, 151–53, 223
  See also actors; cinema; music
Illinois
  Chicago, 236
illness, 60, 63, 222, 269n4
  See also AIDS
illusion, 18, 47, 59, 70, 86, 142, 169–70, 176, 181, 196, 238
  optical, 125, 204–05
imaginaries, 67, 177, 185, 196, 217
  See also futurity
immigration, 29, 56, 230, 233, 237–38, 240–41, 245–46, 249, 269n4
  See also diaspora; ICE; migrants; migration; US-Mexico border
imperialism, 15, 36, 83, 128
  so-called gay, 11–12
  US, 136, 231, 234
impossibility, 17, 20, 38, 93–95, 112, 131, 137, 139, 142–43, 211, 218
improvisation, 20, 37, 42, 69, 72, 153, 212, 229, 235, 248
  in performance, 49, 85–86, 95, 102–03, 105, 108, 110, 134, 149, 177, 203, 206–07, 226–27
incompleteness, 107, 204, 210–13
indexing, 36, 44, 94, 115–16, 157, 171, 186, 198, 215, 220
  queer life, 7, 12, 95, 108, 124, 139, 177, 235, 248, 262n10, 263n21, 265n3
La India Bonita, 248
Indigenous people, 23, 33, 52, 81–82, 85, 87, 108, 135, 218, 231, 238
  See also dispossession; displacement; mestizaje; Nahua culture; racialization
infrastructures, 157, 171, 264n24
  affective, 56, 90, 178, 190, 220–21, 234
  critical, 176–77

of belonging, 68
dark, 158–62, 197–99, 203, 206, 208, 213, 227
glittery, 51
market, 3
of neoliberal state, 135–38, 230–31, 237
public urban, 17, 131–32, 140, 144–48, 150–55, 207
subway, 16, 99–100, 105–13, 116–20, 124, 142, 189
of queer relajo, 19–20, 44, 50, 59, 192, 248
of whiteness, 23, 55
  See also cruising; heteronormativity; heterosexuality
institutions, 83, 85–86, 88, 93, 168, 179, 192, 227, 254n7, 256n1, 265n2, 267n4
  See also catholic church; academia
Instituto de Investigaciones Noa Noa, 242, 265n3
  See also fantasy; Gabriel, Juan; playfulness
interruption, 16, 46, 57–58, 71, 108, 112, 126, 139–40, 267n4
  See also disruption
intersectionality, 34, 208, 236, 246, 267n4
intimacy, 20, 61, 89, 91–96 144 149 156–58 180, 239–40
  and belonging, 4, 17–18, 33, 165 242–43
  through modulation, 204–14
  and nationalism, 80–81, 87, 258–59n15
  politics of, 23, 154, 246, 253n5
  in public, 103–06, 110–12, 115–20as resistance, 11, 99–100 168
  and sex, 2, 121, 126, 140
  travesti, 60, 170–79, 182–83, 187–92, 195–201, 220–25
  See also Casa Roshell; modulation
intolerance, 12, 171, 176
  See also discrimination
inventory, 17, 132, 148, 150–52, 155–58
invisibility, 1, 95, 148, 227
  choreographies, 100, 109, 112, 114
  violent, 21, 76, 79, 105, 160, 165, 167, 169, 174, 176, 187, 189, 212, 214
Irwin, Robert, 168, 186, 265n2

jewelry, 1, 14, 66, 78, 92
Jones, Grace, 247
José José, 138
jotería, 24, 29, 231–44, 247–51
  commodification of, 121
  identity, 27, 33, 127–28, 263–64n23
  See also afterglow; glow; Mexicanidad;
    queer relajo
Jurado, Katy, 149, 264n3
Jurado, Rocío, 39, 64, 92
Just, Tony, 113

Kahlo, Frida, 239
Kalafe, Denisse de, 132
kinship, 83, 92, 101, 171–72, 175, 181–83,
    227, 235
  queer, 161, 233, 239
kissing, 11, 37, 112–15, 165–67, 187, 209,
    227, 248
  in film, 141–43, 160, 171–72, 174–78,
    199–200
  in photography, 119–21, 124, 250
  in song lyrics, 49, 148, 2*See also* ban-
    tering; laughter; playfulness
knowledge, 148, 158–59, 236
  academic, 29, 136
  collective transfer of, 89, 118, 192, 208–
    14, 257n9, 267n4
  insurgent, 14–18, 33
  politics of, 162, 214–20, 234
  sensorial, 93–96, 114–15, 120, 123–24,
    205–07, 224–27, 231–32, 254n14
  transfeminist, 61
  working-class, 86
  See also academia; alternatives

labor, 15, 19, 35, 49, 105, 108, 112, 127–29,
    194, 255n19
  affective, 133, 143
  and capital, 29, 53, 84, 136–38, 203
  domestic, 82
  drag, 70
  feminized, 12–13, 20–24, 57, 239
  travesti, 181–82, 205, 207
  See also capitalism; mestizaje; sex
    work

El laberinto de la soledad (Paz), 55, 81
La Chinga (comedy troupe), 80
La Lagunilla, 75, 152, 223
"Last Car, The: Cruising in Mexico City"
    (Graham), 16, 100, 116, 118
LA Times (newspaper), 239
  See also diaspora; Gabriel, Juan; Mar-
    tinez, Fidel; Selena
Latin America, 15, 28–29, 231, 256n1,
    257n5
  See also the Caribbean
Latinidad, 36, 231, 234–35
  See also jotería; Latin America; Mexi-
    canidad
laughter, 162
  as resistance, 11–12, 18, 33, 61, 65, 69,
    83, 89, 91, 191, 203, 208–09, 219–31,
    241, 254n11, 268n9
  sounds of, 6, 142, 197, 248
  See also glow; playfulness; resistance;
    satire
legibility, 22, 148, 167, 213, 216
lesbians, 3, 91, 247–48, 253n4
Lexington Club, 248
LGBTQ+
  activism, 12, 41, 187, 259n21
  commodification of, 70, 122, 136, 167–
    68, 179, 184, 216, 249, 253n1
  community, 2–3, 42, 165, 266n13
  See also bisexuality; lesbians; travestis
liberalism, 37–39, 59
liminality, 21, 50, 56, 69, 111, 147–48, 152,
    190, 214, 235
limits, 34, 41, 50, 68, 110, 190, 196, 233,
    238, 255n15
  of nightlife, 18, 20, 209
  temporal, 8, 103, 147–48
  See also boundaries
linearity, 69, 75–76, 83, 87, 114, 257n8
  See also development; progress
lip-syncing, 1, 7, 46, 48–49, 61, 63–64, 92,
    95–96, 149, 151, 158, 245, 247
  See also bars; cabarets; drag queens;
    Piña Colada
literary representation, 14, 31, 67, 71,
    256n1

longing, 80, 137–48, 157, 195, 197, 209–14
  impossibility of, 131, 171
  in music, 44, 64, 95
  as relajo, 5, 11, 17, 19, 50, 188, 190
  See also cruising; darkness impossibility; *Mil nubes de paz* (Hernández); modulation; traveling: spatiotemporal
looseness, 5, 7–9, 11–12, 15, 18, 24, 110, 167, 201, 213, 221–22, 227, 232, 250, 254
  See also dirtiness; filth; grittiness; messiness
López, Margo Su, 152
Lorde, Audre, 220–21, 225, 268n8
loss, 94, 144, 148–51, 153, 155–58, 162, 195, 198, 200, 219, 230, 240, 249, 264n3
  grief and, 137, 154, 161
  spatial, 19, 73, 121–22
  See also death; heartbreak
"Love me forever" (Jones), 247
lover, 49, 126–27, 138–39, 141, 143–47, 180, 181, 189, 197, 200, 209–10, 222, 225
  ex-, 60, 64, 93–94, 249
  See also attraction; desire; romance
Lozano, Manuel Rodríguez, 168
El Lugar sin límites (Ripstein), 21, 166, 171, 173–74, 176, 178, 181–83, 187, 256n1, 265–66n8
See also travestis; travestismo
Luna, Diego, 80

m4m intimacy, 16, 99–100, 110, 113, 118, 122
  See also encounters
Macharia, Keguro, 112
Made in Bangkok (Florencio), 179
magic, 40, 46–47, 55, 64, 191, 201, 203, 225, 228, 242–43
  See also ambiances; fantasy
mainstream, 44, 84, 110, 137, 165, 223, 237, 269n6
  Mexican media, 17, 131, 155, 167–68, 179–80, 184, 189
makeup, 27, 39, 47, 60–61, 68, 72, 76, 92–93, 153, 193–97, 208, 212

See also dresses; glitter; glitz; heels; materiality; wigs
mappings, 8, 12, 27, 32, 50–52, 76, 89, 104, 108, 115, 137, 141, 144, 150, 194, 248, 257–58n11
  sociocultural, 13, 56, 68, 232
  See also geographies; territory
marginalization, 2–4, 52, 67, 73, 101, 110, 113, 136, 157, 176, 195, 233
  economic, 19, 107, 135
  resistance to, 69, 86, 96, 128, 137, 161–62, 177, 191, 237–38, 241, 246, 249
  See also discrimination; displacement
Marisela, 245
markets, 2, 5, 10, 51, 77, 101, 134–35, 159, 161, 198, 202, 216, 260n23
  flea, 70, 72, 116, 148
  pinkwashed, 3, 75, 88–89, 182–84, 219
  See also capitalism; consumerism; vendors
El Marrakech (club), 3, 90
Martínez, Benjamín, 40, 241, 257–58n11, 265n3
Martinez, Fidel, 239
Maryland, 236
masculinity, 103, 139, 143, 172–73, 175, 195, 233, 235–36, 263n16
  Mexican, 7, 10–11, 37, 55, 67, 81, 168, 178, 253n5
  toxic, 93, 211
  See also femininity
Massey, Doreen, 145
materiality, 66, 78–79, 105, 116, 147, 165, 205, 219, 232, 256n2, 257n9
  second-hand, 71–72, 75–77, 92, 96
  See also baroque; drag queens; ephemerality
Mbembe, Achille, 116
media, 14, 19, 22, 44, 179–80, 184, 186–87, 189, 237, 248, 251, 256n1, 257–58n11, 262n8, 266n14
  influencer, 10, 254n11
  Mexican, 17, 131, 132–37, 141, 168, 170–71, 173
  studies, 15
mediation, 6, 41, 59, 86, 91, 113, 116–17,

120, 149, 208, 210, 212, 236, 251, 265n7
affective, 19–20, 67
embodied, 15, 159, 167, 196, 218
to resist extraction, 77, 100, 178–79
See also necropolitics
Méndez, Lucía, 132
La Merced (neighborhood), 158
messiness, 34, 94, 126–28, 154, 157, 219, 232, 235, 238, 241, 248
See also dirtiness; filth; grittiness; looseness
mestizaje, 52–53, 82, 166
white, 17, 31, 55, 131, 133–35, 255n19
See also Mexicanidad; nationalism
metreo, 112–17, 274
See also cruising; subway
metro. *See* subway
Mexican Revolution, 10, 52–53, 55, 80, 83, 87, 168, 177, 216, 265n3
See also Partido Revolucionario Institucional (PRI)
Mexicanidad, 9, 11, 255n19
embodiment of, 28, 135, 216–17
performing, 55, 59
queer, 7–8, 23, 46, 51, 121, 136, 147, 165, 231, 234–40, 244, 247, 249–54
sense of, 44, 128
See also mestizaje
"Mi gran noche" (Raphael), 158
migrants, 23, 230–31, 237–39, 269n4
queer, 33, 84, 235, 242–43, 247–49
migration, 56, 81, 84, 105, 179, 233, 243, 245, 264n24, 268–69n3
See also diaspora; displacement; US-Mexico border
Miguel, Amanda, 92, 183
Mijares, Manuel, 132
Mil nubes de paz (Hernández), 137–38, 141, 146–48
See also cruising; metreo; subway
Minogue, Kylie, 71, 92
mirrorball, 1–2, 6–7, 13, 18, 22, 62, 71, 93, 180
See also glitter; glitz; shine
mirrors, 47, 49, 93, 119, 125–26, 153, 193, 195–96, 198

misogyny, 5, 85, 143, 161, 168, 173, 176, 207, 215, 254n11
Mission District, 247, 250–51
See also gentrification
Misterio, Liz, 241, 257–58n11, 260–61n2, 263n22, 265n3
Mis XXy años (García), 16, 100–01
See also García, Lia; quinceañera; subway
mobility, 32, 81, 83–84, 136, 154, 157, 172, 216, 264n4
modernity, 9–11, 13, 15–16, 18, 27, 29, 38, 52, 69, 72, 77–78, 83–89, 100, 120–22, 130, 133, 136, 186, 253n5, 262n8
See also capitalism; development
modulation, 6–7, 19–23, 50, 58, 67, 77, 88, 95, 137, 158, 167, 178, 187, 191, 193, 196–97, 220, 224–25
physical, 55, 189, 203–209, 211–19, 227
See also Casa Roshell; travestis; travestismo
Mohanty, Chandra, 23, 162
Monroe, Marilyn, 205–06
Monroy, Norman, 120, 127
Monsiváis, Carlos, 19, 22, 66–69, 91, 168, 177, 257–58n11, 260n23
Montiel, Sara, 140–43, 148
Mor, Ana Francis, 80, 259n20
Mora, Sergio de la, 173
Moreno Figueroa, Mónica, 133
motherhood, 83
mothers, 38–39, 53, 56, 77, 81, 133, 146–47, 149, 153, 156–60, 178, 181, 240, 264n3
drag, 46
See also aunts
movements, 32, 105, 109, 112, 114, 118, 127, 134, 139, 141, 145, 167, 176–77, 189, 205–07, 214, 230, 235
activist, 20, 184, 237, 253n2, 265–66n3–4
diasporic, 13
queer/trans, 8, 72–73, 103, 129, 196
See also activism; disruption
Múñiz, Marco Antonio, 132

Muñoz, José Esteban, 34, 36, 83, 113, 117,
    136, 139, 243, 255n15, 257n6, 257–
    58n11, 263n17, 269n6
music, 34, 67, 69, 72, 91–92, 130, 150–52,
    157, 242, 257n10, 260n24, 262n10
    as ambiance, 15, 51, 89, 140–42, 197–
        200, 245
    background, 6, 32, 99, 155, 159
    on the dance floor, 37, 46
    in diaspora, 239–40, 248–51
    lip sync to, 39, 49, 64, 93–96
    pop, 12, 75, 1023, 183, 203, 210
    video, 42, 132
    See also ambiances; echoes; Gabriel,
        Juan; night-making; nightscapes;
        queer relajo; rhythms; Selena

NAFTA, 84, 129, 264–65n6
Nahua culture, 40, 51, 103, 261n3
    See also Indigenous people; mestizaje;
        Mexicanidad
nationalism, 67–69, 91, 229, 238
    heterosexual, 74
    homonationalism, 165–70
    Mexican, 53–55, 58, 83–85, 216, 253–
        54n6, 265n2
    neoliberal, 17, 22, 131–36, 145, 174–80
    See also development; icons; Mexi-
        canidad; progress
National School for Theater Arts
    (Mexico City), 80
necropolitics, 50, 154, 166–71, 173, 175–76,
    179–80, 183, 187, 212–13, 225, 229,
    231
    queer/trans, 7, 22, 106–07, 189–90,
        246, 262n6
    See also capitalism; capture; death;
        extraction
"Nena" (Montiel), 140–43
neon, 3, 32, 89, 99, 118, 234
    See also glitter; glitz; shine
Netflix, 180, 185, 266n15
networks, 15, 35, 57, 134–35, 156, 158, 190–
    91, 206, 216–17
    affective, 5, 128, 184
    of consumption, 2, 72, 167, 208

material, 14, 66, 141, 170
    See also connections
New Mexico
    Anapra, 229
New York, 121, 236
    New York City, 76, 120
Nieto, Enrique Peña, 80, 82, 259
Nightcrawler, 247
night-making, 4, 24
    digital, 12
    queer/trans, 80, 95
    as resistance, 90–91
    travesti, 166, 191
    See also afterglow; bantering; jotería;
        kissing; laughing; queer relajo
nightscapes, 6–8, 16–24, 129, 160–62,
    197–201, 227–28, 232, 241–44, 249–
    55, 268n10
    in daylight, 100, 103, 110–13, 116–20
    of drag, 66, 69, 71, 89–93
    materiality of, 124–26, 153
    protective, 165, 172, 176–80, 190–92,
        195, 203–14, 219–21
    resisting neoliberalism, 137, 148
    See also afterglow; bars; cabarets;
        darkness; queer relajo; shade;
        shadow
"El Noa Noa" (Gabriel), 64–65, 241
Nocturno de Los Ángeles (Villaurrutia),
    78
nostalgia, 49, 67, 91, 96, 121, 149–50,
    155
    See also longing; waiting
Novo, Salvador, 74–75, 79, 90, 168

Oasis (Zuno), 90, 179, 259n21
El Oasis (club), 90, 179, 259n21
Oishi, Eve, 246
ontologies, 10, 105, 206, 218, 258n11
    See also academia; epistemologies;
        studies
oppression, 24, 72, 105, 219, 223, 248,
    268n7
    See also marginalization
Orozco, Regina, 80
Osento's Bathhouse, 248

Paasonen, Susanna, 125
Pablo, David, 180, 185, 187
pain, 22, 63
  emotional, 35, 59, 88, 91, 94, 142, 160,
    200, 230
  See also loss
Pandora, 132
Pantoja, Isabel, 39, 49, 93–95
paradigms, 88–89, 143, 165, 231, 233, 238
  sexual, 16, 104, 114, 118, 127, 136, 157,
    160, 187, 212, 216
  See also conventions; heteronormativ-
    ity
paradox, 77, 135, 166, 168–69, 180, 187,
    269n7
Partido Revolucionario Institucional
    (PRI), 52, 80, 133–35, 235n2
  See also Mexican Revolution
parties, 12, 32, 51, 58, 75, 92, 101, 103, 106,
    108, 119, 126, 188, 208, 234, 242, 245–
    46, 256n1, 260–61n2, 262n10
  See also bars; cabarets; dancing; night-
    making; nightscapes
partners, 64, 93, 95, 114–15, 131, 173, 175,
    181, 193, 195–96, 253n4
Pasquel, Sylvia, 149
patriarchy, 31, 33, 87, 105, 175, 180, 182,
    186, 223, 257–58n11, 265–66n8
  hetero, 23, 55, 74, 148, 155, 203, 218, 221
  in nationalist development, 10, 50, 58
  See also Mexicanidad
Paz, Octavio, 55, 81
Pearl, Max, 230
pedragogy, 13, 27, 40–41
Pérez Prado, Dámaso, 11, 152–53
Pérezcano, Rigoberto, 179
phenomenology, 9, 34, 73, 254n8
photography, 16, 44, 61, 100, 109–10,
    119–26, 269n4
  See also cameras; Graham, David;
    Stark, Eriko
Piña Colada, 14, 17, 27, 30, 58–60, 66–67,
    71, 96, 219, 252
  accessories, 47, 49–51, 79
  at Casa Roshell, 22, 62–63
  origins of, 38–39

pedragogy, 40–42, 44, 46
performances, 1, 7, 13, 24, *48*, 93
  reflections from, 28, 31–34, 227
  See also becoming: drag; drag queens;
    glitter; glitz
pink, 2, 42, 47, 61, 63–64, 153, 229–31,
    234–36, 239, 245, 262n10
  market, 70, 75, 182, 219
  subway line, 101–02, 261n3
  See also commodification
pinkwashing, 3, 136
  See also commodification
Pino Suárez (station), 100–01, 260–
    61n2
Pittsburgh, 13, 27, 46, 48–49, 76, 79,
    258n12, 260–61n2
playfulness, 7, 10, 32, 55–58, 111, 174, 178,
    231, 241, 245, 250, 254
  queer, 8, 19, 90, 117–18, 120, 124–25,
    191–92, 196–97, 201, 205–07, 210,
    213, 217–18, 225, 236–38, 251
  See also bantering; kissing; laughter;
    satire
Plaza de la Soledad (Goded), 17, 132,
    158–62
  See also Goded, Maya; La Merced
    (neighborhood)
Plaza Garibaldi (neighborhood), 37, 155,
    223
poetics, 56, 78, 150, 268n6
Polanco (neighborhood), 2, 156, 190
PornHub, 116
  See also cruising; pornography
pornography, 100, 116–17, 124, 130, 230,
    262–63n15
  amateur, 5, 16, 110, 115, 122
portrayal, 83, 123, 125, 132, 153, 155, 165–
    66, 174, 182–83, 186–87, 247
Posada, José Guadalupe, 186
possibilities, 3, 21, 59, 71, 78, 88–90, 105–
    07, 120, 154, 171–76, 187, 197, 206–08,
    214, 234, 251, 253n5, 267n5
  of drag performance, 13
  foreclosing, 182, 230
  political, 11, 35–37, 56, 178, 217–18, 227,
    242, 246–47

possibilities (*continued*)
 sexual, 7–8, 28, 31–32, 112, 190
 See also disruption; futurity; impossibility; potential; shade; shadow;
  shine
postcoloniality, 2, 9, 18, 20, 52, 70, 73, 121,
 212, 216–27
 See also global south
potential, 22, 24, 33, 41, 55, 78, 91, 101,
  103, 114, 117, 120, 141, 151, 161, 170,
  178, 200, 203, 209, 220, 222, 263n21
 for refusal, 11
 political, 73, 166, 211
 See also futurity; possibilities
poverty, 131–36, 147, 150, 159, 180, 184
 See also gentrification; marginalization; working class
Power-Sotomayor, Jade, 230, 236
practices,
 of care, 70, 114, 166
 of survival, 19, 177
praxis, 41, 71, 143, 159, 220, 236, 254n10
 modulation, 224–25, 227
 play, 117, 191, 197, 206–09
 survival, 17, 132, 154, 157–58
 transfeminist, 7, 21, 23–24, 89, 104–05,
  168, 170, 178, 187, 192–93, 203
precarity, 2, 20, 137, 146, 153, 161,170, 177,
  208, 215, 217, 238, 249, 255n1, 265n5
 economic, 6, 23, 57, 67, 78, 101, 127, 168,
  179, 181–82
 See also gentrification; marginalization; risks
presence, 20, 29, 81, 87, 126, 134–35, 150,
  159, 175, 184, 188–90, 260n23, 269n6
 of drag performance, 39, 85, 256n3
 politics of, 17, 44, 66, 132, 157, 192
 queer spirit of, 49–51, 141–43, 232–33,
  240–41
 toxic, 93–94, 123
 See also absence; ambiances; shine
privacy, 11, 19, 147
privatization, 2–4, 6, 11–12, 17–20, 70,
  110, 134–35, 173, 182, 225, 234–37,
  265n7
 See also capitalism; enclosure

privilege, 2, 29, 57, 74, 78, 116, 121, 133, 135,
  143, 176, 179
Procinemex, 149
progress, 6, 53, 55, 70–71, 84, 95, 121, 134,
  136, 147–48, 170–71, 230, 255n20,
  258–59n15
 national, 86–88, 131–32
 teleologies of, 10, 12, 77, 211
 See also capitalism; development
property, 12, 24, 71, 131, 137, 140, 147, 152,
  171–72, 182
 See also capitalism
public sphere, 2–6, 50, 61, 71, 84–90, 131,
  160–61, 174, 180, 184, 205–07, 232–33,
  237, 257n6, 262n8, 264n24, 266n12
 infrastructures of, 138, 145–47, 152, 178
 privatization of, 134–35
 queer intimacy within, 11–12, 20–23,
  99–126, 157, 250
 See also cruising; hypervisibility;
  night-making; privatization; subway; underground
Puebla, 5
"Punto de Partida" (Jurado), 64, 92
La Purísima, 3, 90
"Push the Feeling On" (Nightcrawler),
 247
Puta Life: Seeing Latinas, Working Sex
 (Rodríguez), 250

Quebranto (Fiesco), 131, 148, 150–51, 154–
 57, 179, 245, 264n3
 See also Fiesco, Roberto; travestis;
  travestismo
Queer/Art/Prize for Recent Work, 247
queer relajo (definition), 5–20, 66–67,
  87–91, 108, 125–26, 176–78, 187,
  203–04, 219–23, 227, 233–34, 251,
  254nn7–10, 254n12, 255n15
 See also afterglow; bantering; glitter;
  glow; kissing; jotería; laughter;
  intimacy; shine; worldmaking
Quiero Mis Queerce (Salgado), 238–39
quinceañera, 42, 100–02, 104, 108, 127,
  238, 262n10
 See also García, Lia (La Novia Sirena)

racialization, 5–6, 12–13, 18, 23–24, 35, 56, 78, 82, 92, 100, 122, 127–28, 131, 133, 135, 147, 154, 156, 187, 231–34, 236, 238–39, 249
racism, anti-Black, 28–29
Rael, Ronald, 229–30
Ramos, Iván, 249
Raphael, 151, 158
reclaiming, 6–7, 11, 104, 110, 160–61, 208, 220, 232, 238, 249
recycling, 19, 56, 70–72, 75, 78
refuge, 130, 179, 189, 238
refusal, 9, 17, 57, 131–32, 150–51, 154, 156–57, 231, 237–39, 269n4
   queer, 7–8, 11–14, 24, 28, 94–95, 117, 137, 141–43, 212–14
   See also alternatives; resistance
Las Reinas Chulas, 80, 259n18
reproduction, 20, 69, 78, 121, 198, 227, 233
   heteronormative logics of, 17, 23–24, 29, 74, 94–95, 131, 147, 169, 221, 241
República de Cuba (thoroughfare), 3, 89–90, 118, 259n21
resilience, 36, 55, 59, 77, 93, 240, 249
   queer/trans, 35, 124
   See also practices; praxis
resistance, 29, 56, 69, 76, 100, 118, 148, 167, 191, 208, 212, 218, 225–27, 233–34, 249–51, 247n8, 268n6
resonances, 21, 50, 66, 74, 85, 88, 91, 93, 95–96, 139,142–43, 145, 200, 213, 220, 229, 232–33, 257–58n11
   See also echoes
Revilla, Monika, 186
revolutionaries, 10, 55, 215–16, 231
rhythms, 58, 92, 104–05, 108, 123, 147, 203, 206, 227, 232
   of pleasure, 17
   sonic, 19, 32, 37, 49, 59, 64, 71, 96, 99, 103, 198–200, 239, 245
   See also echoes; music; resonances
risks, 11, 35, 106, 112–15, 118–20, 123, 126, 129, 147, 207, 236–38, 245–46
   See also danger; resilience; violence
Roberta y las otras chicas del montón (Mor), 80–83, 88–91, 96

See also cabarets; Cabral, Roberto; Mor, Ana Francis
Rodríguez de Ruíz, Alexandra, 67
Rodríguez, Jesusa, 80, 90, 259n19
Rodríguez, Juana María, 159, 248, 250, 258
romance, 29, 42, 44, 94, 122, 135, 139–43, 181, 196–97
   fantasies of, 80–81, 83, 258–59n15
   in music, 39, 64, 103, 159, 209
   See also lover
Romo, Daniela, 49, 92
Rubenstein, Anne, 130–31
Rubio, Paulina, 132, 183
RuPaul, 75
rural space, 19, 42, 46, 51–52, 58–59, 81, 120, 127–28, 133–34, 257–58n11, 263–64n23

La Sacristía (club), 90
Salgado, Julio, 236, 238–42, 251, 269n4
Salinas, Carmen, 132, 134, 152
San Fratello, Virginia, 229–30
Santanera, La Sonora, 18, 152, 159
Sarduy, Severo, 66–68, 76, 256n1
Sasha Velour, 72
satire, 67–69, 80–89, 177, 191, 208, 215, 221–22, 256n1, 259n20, 268n10
saturation, 20, 66–67, 69–70, 75, 77, 80, 85, 92, 104
   See also aesthetics; excess; materiality
Scott, Ridley, 123
scripts, 17, 41, 59, 71, 80–91, 150, 157, 226, 229–31, 265n3
   national, 9, 55, 126, 184, 215–16
   See also conventions
secrecy, 1, 4, 6, 21, 38, 42, 91, 95, 170, 180, 185, 232, 257n9, 258–59n15
Secretaría de Transporte Colectivo, 109
Sedgwick, Eve, 191
Selena, 39, 46, 93, 239–41, 251
sensing, 5, 15–16, 18, 31, 40, 44, 46, 51, 66, 113, 118, 127, 137, 139, 144, 147–48, 161, 170, 187, 190–92, 195–96, 203, 209, 211, 214, 220, 224
   time, 49, 59, 85, 158
   See also ambiances; worldmaking

sensorium, 34, 150–51, 159, 162, 195, 199, 203, 245, 248

sensuality, 36, 39, 171, 188, 197, 220

sentimentality, 42, 92–93, 147, 260n23
    See also nostalgia

sequins, 14, 17, 47, 63, 66, 71–72, 75–79, 93, 188, 199, 220, 222, 232, 262n10
    See also baroque; drag queens; excess; glitter; glitz; mirrorball

sex work, 18, 23, 60, 148, 182, 189, 207, 241
    See also labor

shade, 32, 166, 176–79, 187, 189–92, 204, 209–15, 263n21
    throwing, 39, 167, 227, 268n9
    See also darkness; shadow

shadow, 24, 47, 78, 118, 124, 130, 141, 143, 162, 166, 170, 172, 174, 176, 182, 184–87, 189, 192, 196, 209–14, 215, 223, 227, 233, 253n5
    economy, 17, 19, 57, 67, 70–72, 75, 88, 90, 132, 158, 160–61, 178, 180
    See also darkness; shade

shame, 115–16, 123–24, 196, 219

Sheinbaum, Claudia, 108, 253n2

shine, 15, 21, 143, 145, 148, 192, 214
    performance of, 63, 66, 71, 75–80, 85, 226
    visual, 1, 42, 61, 101–02, 124–25, 158
    See also glitter; glitz; glow

Shock, Susy, 218, 267n5

Sicart, Miguel, 11, 218, 268n7

silences, 63, 160, 170, 261, 265n4
    historical, 67, 81, 87, 169
    playful, 32, 109–11, 113, 117, 123, 126, 138
    See also archives; erasure

Silver Platter, 242–46

La simulación (Sarduy), 68, 76, 256n1

"Sissy That Walk" (RuPaul), 75

Smith, Paul Julian, 184, 257–58n11, 264n3

Snorton, C. Riley, 166, 169, 189

social media, 11–12, 60, 108, 110, 118, 258–59nn15–16, 260–61n2, 265n3

Solidaridad, 17, 131, 135–36, 148, 155

Somos Voces (cultural center), 90

Southern Cone, 217
    See also Latin America

Spillers, Hortese J., 172

stages, 41–42, 126, 175, 243–47, 256–57n4
    bar, 46, 49
    beauty pageant, 59
    cabaret, 63, 89–90, 206, 209, 234, 259n18
    at Casa Roshell, 22, 188–92, 213, 219–21
    drag on, 1, 6–7, 39, 63–64, 68–71, 80–86, 126, 256–57n4, 258n12
    night, 148–52, 158, 165, 182
    nightclub, 19
    public, 101–06, 111, 125, 261n4
    school, 53–55
    See also cabarets; drag queens; Piña Colada

Stark, Eriko, 16, 82, 100, 109, 119, 122–26, 263n20
    See also cameras; cruising; *Furias Nocturnas* (Stark); Graham, David; metreo; photography; subway

stereotypes, 81, 173–74, 266n12

stickiness, 16, 99–100, 103, 105, 110–14, 126, 147, 254n12

stigmatization, 41, 69, 111, 136, 153, 195, 236

studies, 14–15, 29, 168, 173, 231, 265
    ethnic, 250
    Latinx, 35
    Mexican, 31
    performance, 117, 232
    queer, 136, 212, 227, 266n11
    sexuality, 170, 212
    trans, 107, 212, 218
    See also academia; academics; media; writing

subjectivity, 69, 71, 76, 78, 105, 135, 157, 187, 216, 221, 237

subway, 16–20, 50, 99–130, 140, 142, 145–48, 189, 198, 210, 235, 261n3, 262n10
    See also cruising; García, Lia; Graham, David; metreo; Stark, Eriko

surveillance, 32, 89, 109, 233, 235, 237–38
    See also gaze

survival, 96, 124, 139, 147–48, 167, 170, 176, 188, 193, 203, 207–08, 212, 216–17, 246
    See also resilience; resistance

symbols, 38, 67, 80–81, 102, 133, 167, 172, 174, 176, 187, 231

tactics, 83–84, 86, 105, 231–32, 251
　of survival, 12, 22, 41, 55, 170, 179, 190–91, 208
　queer, 6–7, 23, 59, 166–67, 210, 212, 214, 220, 227
Tahúr, El, 90
Taylor, Diana, 16, 88, 257–58n11, 263n19
tears, 6, 11, 17, 32, 49, 59, 106, 150–51, 154, 159, 186, 195, 264n4
　See also loss; pain
Teatro Blanquita, 151–53, 155–57, 223
Teatro de cabaret (Alzate), 85
Teatro La Capilla, 259n19
Teatro-Bar El Vicio, 90, 259n18
technologies, 31, 70, 78, 156, 165, 211, 231
　of capture, 15, 212–13, 233, 238
　extractive, 171, 174, 184
Teeter-Totter Wall Project (Rael and San Fratello), 229–31, 236
teleology, 10, 74, 77, 105, 131, 157, 211, 258–59n15
　See also development; progress
Televisa, 17, 131–32, 135
temporality, 13, 67, 71, 75, 77, 83, 88, 103, 132
tenderness, 37, 104, 107, 127, 186, 195, 262n10
tension, 21, 29, 50, 165–66, 169, 171, 183, 230–31, 236, 246, 253n5, 263n22, 269–70nn7–8
　productive, 13, 27
Tepito (neighborhood), 77, 152
　See also clothes; consumerism
Terranova, Roshell, 196, 203–05, 223
　See also Casa Roshell; *Casa Roshell* (Donoso); modulation
territoriality, 18, 20, 50, 171
territory, 8, 31–32, 56–57, 153, 192, 239–40, 246, 255n1
Texas, 236, 240
　See also US-Mexico border
theaters, 2, 53, 80, 85, 90, 152–53, 223
　blackbox, 86, 89, 259n18
　movie, 130–31

"Tiempo de vals" (Chayanne), 103, 108
Tijuana, 240
Timbiriche, 132
Times Square Red, Times Square Blue (Delany), 121
tolerance, 2, 7, 148
Tortorici, Zeb, 116
tourism, 2–3, 136, 160
Tovar, Rigo, 132
Transgender Europe, 106
Transgender Law Center, 179
transgression, 21, 41, 58, 80, 87, 106, 175, 177, 183, 186–87, 256n1, 257n8, 258n14
transience, 102, 104, 106, 108
　See also fugitivity
transit, 7, 9, 100–09, 112–13, 138, 160, 230
　See also fugitivity; subway
transitioning, 104–05, 194
transness, 16, 21, 63, 100, 104–05, 107–08, 136, 153, 210, 218
transphobia, 5, 106, 179–80, 184, 207, 222–23, 254n11, 262n10
　See also discrimination; homophobia; violence
Trans Wellness Center, 243
trauma, 83, 85, 87, 91, 263n19
traveling, 6, 60–61, 85, 103, 113, 122, 159, 212, 221, 233, 237
　sounds, 92, 138, 144, 203, 240, 243, 261–62n5
　spatiotemporal, 34, 44, 72, 105, 124, 142, 194, 244
travestis, 68–69, 76, 91, 165–66, 256n1
　See also drag queens; *El lugar sin límites* (Ripstein); travestismo; *Quebranto* (Fiesco)
travestismo, 21, 40, 55, 67, 153, 167–68, 173, 187–90, 195, 197, 205–07, 210, 258n11, 265n5, 265–66n8
　See also drag queens; *El lugar sin límites* (Ripstein); travestis; *Quebranto* (Fiesco)
Trevi, Gloria, 12, 183
troupes, 80, 85, 256–57n4, 259n20, 268n9
Tsang, Wu, 234, 236–37, 242–46, 248, 251

"Tú estás siempre en mi mente"
    (Gabriel), 240
Turner, Tina, 245
Tyburczy, Jennifer, 104

El último cuplé, 141
UNAM, 184
unbelonging, 20, 35, 88
    See also belonging
uncertainty, 6, 13, 27, 38, 125, 139, 141, 144,
    147, 152, 269n4
underground, 6–7, 16, 20, 33, 50, 70,
    137–38, 162, 216–17, 233, 246, 249–51,
    261n3, 263n16, 264n24
    See also afterglow; cruising; fugitivity;
    metreo; subway
United States, 27, 29, 84, 122, 129, 136,
    212, 229–32, 234, 236, 238, 240–41,
    243, 249, 251, 257n8, 257–58n11,
    260–61n2
    See also imperialism; US-Mexico
    border
unmaking, 34, 41, 105, 206, 246
urban spaces, 3, 11, 82, 189, 192, 209,
    257–58n11
    in Mexico, 2, 5, 8, 68, 179
    pinkwashed, 20
    reshaping, 6–7, 86–91
    See also cruising; metreo; night-
    making; nightscapes; privatization
US-Mexico border, 32, 56, 59, 85, 229–31,
    233–39, 243
    See also ICE; immigration
USMCA, 129
utopias, 13, 19, 34, 71, 86, 88, 130–31, 139,
    150
    See also futurity; imaginaries

Vaccaro, Jeanne, 194, 198, 205
Valencia, Sayak, 50, 88, 104, 106, 255n18,
    257–58n11, 267n3, 268n2
Vargas, Deborah R., 128, 232, 257–58n11
Vasconcelos, Tito, 4, 80
vendors, 99, 103, 159
    bootleg, 46, 77, 99, 127
"Veneno Pa' Tu Piel" (La Veneno), 92

Viaducto (station), 189
vibrancy, 36, 44, 95, 165–66, 170
    See also shine
Victoria, María, 152
Villa, Lucha, 151–53, 245
Villaurrutia, Xavier (poet), 78, 168
violence, 1, 44, 110, 113–15, 118, 123–24,
    147, 150, 166–68, 173, 230–39, 243,
    251
    against travestis, 101, 201, 206–09, 223,
    265n5
    death and, 50, 220, 247
    of erasure, 36
    gender- and sexual-based, 2, 106, 178–
    79, 227, 253n1, 262n10, 262n13
    history of, 4–6, 81–87, 91
    neoliberal, 8, 10, 12–13, 16, 18–21, 23–
    24, 28, 107, 122, 128–29, 161, 177, 184,
    203, 249
    racial-based, 29–33, 108
    thriving amid violence, 56–63, 104,
    127, 143, 189–92, 213–16
    See also capitalism; commodification;
    consumption; heteronormativ-
    ity; heterosexuality; homophobia;
    transphobia
Virgin of Guadalupe, 133, 160
    See also catholic church
Virginia, 236
virility, 55, 87, 154, 172, 256n1
voyeurism, 1, 130, 146, 210, 230
    See also gaze
vulnerability, 16, 101, 103, 115, 125, 134,
    161, 200, 213, 233

waiting, 32, 81, 197, 225, 235
    as queer relajo, 17, 19, 111, 123, 131, 137,
    139–41, 143–48, 209
    See also cruising; longing; nostalgia
water, 1, 46, 60, 155, 159–62, 262n10
Wayar, Marlene, 218, 267n5
wealth, 4, 78, 155, 172, 181, 184
"We Are the World" (USA for Africa),
    132
whiteness, 46, 126, 238, 249–50, 257n10
    ideological, 22, 35, 84, 121, 179

and Mexicanidad, 23, 52–53, 55, 59, 133–36
wigs, 14, 17, 47, 64, 66, 72, 76, 78–79, 87, 92–93, 186, 193–95, 205, 220, 225–26
See also drag queens; glitter; glitz; heels; makeup; materiality
Wildness (Tsang), 234, 242, 244–48, 269, 272
Williams, Raymond, 234
working class, 52, 105, 108, 130, 135, 138, 143–45, 162, 168, 171
See also capitalism; dispossession
working-class neighborhoods, 1, 107, 146–47, 150–52, 158, 189–90, 192, 208, 216
See also bars; cabarets; Ecatepec; La Merced; nightscapes
workshops, 41, 74, 89, 190, 193, 204–08, 214–15, 258n12, 261n4
worldmaking
queer/trans 5, 7, 18, 22, 27, 35, 44, 50, 56, 58–59, 63–64, 67, 105–07, 112–13, 124, 126, 128, 132, 136, 139, 142, 145, 158, 161

travesti, 150–51, 189, 204, 208, 211, 218, 220–21, 225–27, 255nn15–16
See also becoming; belonging; nightscapes; queer relajo
writers, 2, 11, 29, 35, 55, 69, 73–74, 76, 152, 235, 239, 257–58n11
writing, 2, 33, 144, 168–69, 250, 269n7
academic, 31, 34, 67, 93, 191, 220, 232, 255n1
music, 94, 133
See also academia; academics; studies

XNXX, 116
See also cruising, pornography
XVideos, 110, 115–16, 262–63n15
See also cruising, pornography

"Yo No Te Pido La Luna" (Romo), 49, 92
YouTube, 237
Yuri, 183

Zapata, Luis, 168
Zona Rosa, 2, 4, 32, 90, 118, 190, 256–57n4
Zuno, Alejandro, 179